Lecture Notes in Computer Scie

T0238388

Commenced Publication in 1973
Founding and Former Series Editors:
Gerhard Goos, Juris Hartmanis, and Jan van Leeuwen

Editorial Board

Jadwiga Indulska   Donald J. Patterson
Tom Rodden   Max Ott (Eds.)

Pervasive Computing

6th International Conference, Pervasive 2008
Sydney, Australia, May 19-22, 2008
Proceedings

 Springer

Volume Editors

Jadwiga Indulska
The University of Queensland
School of Information Technology and Electrical Engineering
Brisbane, Australia
E-mail: jaga@itee.uq.edu.au

Donald J. Patterson
University of California-Irvine
Department of Informatics
Irvine, CA 92697, USA
E-mail: djp3@ics.uci.edu

Tom Rodden
University of Nottingham
Department of Computer Science
Jubilee Campus, Nottingham NG8 1BB, UK
E-mail: tar@cs.nott.ac.uk

Max Ott
NICTA
Australian Technology Park, Eveleigh, NSW 1430, Australia
E-mail: Max.Ott@nicta.com.au

Library of Congress Control Number: 2008925662

CR Subject Classification (1998): C.2.4, C.3, C.5.3, D.4, H.3-5, K.4, K.6.5, J.7

LNCS Sublibrary: SL 3 – Information Systems and Application, incl. Internet/Web
and HCI

ISSN   0302-9743
ISBN-10   3-540-79575-8 Springer Berlin Heidelberg New York
ISBN-13   978-3-540-79575-9 Springer Berlin Heidelberg New York

Springer is a part of Springer Science+Business Media

springer.com

© Springer-Verlag Berlin Heidelberg 2008

Typesetting: Camera-ready by author, data conversion by Scientific Publishing Services, Chennai, India
Printed on acid-free paper   SPIN: 12265114   06/3180   5 4 3 2 1 0

Preface

On behalf of the Organizing Committee for Pervasive 2008, welcome to the proceedings of the 6th International Conference on Pervasive Computing. The year 2008 was the second time in as many years that the Pervasive conference has attempted to "globalize": For the second year in a row the conference was held outside of Europe. The conference is seen as one of the most respected venues for publishing research on pervasive and ubiquitous computing and captures the state of the art in pervasive computing research. In 2008, as in previous years, the proceedings present solutions for challenging research problems and help to identify upcoming research opportunities.

Pervasive 2008 attracted 114 high-quality submissions, from which the Technical Program Committee accepted 18 papers, resulting in a competitive 15.8% acceptance rate. There were over 335 individual authors from 27 countries, coming from a wide range of disciplines and from both academic and industrial organizations. Papers were selected solely on the quality of their peer reviews using a double-blind review process. The review process was carried out by 38 members of the international Technical Program Committee (TPC) who are experts of international standing. The TPC members were aided by 104 external reviewers. It was a rigorous review process, in which each paper had at least four reviews: three reviews provided by by the Committee members and one review written by an external reviewer. The reviews were followed by a substantive deliberation on each paper during an electronic discussion phase before the start of the Committee meeting. As a result, 36 submissions were selected for discussion at the one-day, nine-hour Program Committee meeting. The meeting was the first Committee meeting for the Pervasive conference that was run as a distributed event. The TPC members travelled to their choice among three meeting places: University of California-Irvine, Stuttgart University, and NICTA Queensland Lab in Australia. The meeting was run as a video conference between these three sites and was moderated by the three TPC Co-chairs, one at each site. A strict schedule and many additional paper reading assignments ensured that each candidate paper was thoroughly evaluated during the Committe meeting. Out of the 18 accepted papers, 17 were assigned shepherds to further improve the paper quality.

Pervasive 2008 followed the tradition of the previous conferences in this series in focusing not only on novelty but also applicability and feasibility. As pervasive and ubiquitous computing are gradually coming of age, research papers have to provided rigorous evaluation of their findings. The papers accepted for presentation at Pervasive 2008 addressed a variety of research issues including pervasive applications for small devices, pervasive computing platforms, sensing and activity recognitions, and lessons learned in applying pervasive computing in various domains. As in the previous years, location technology as well as security and privacy continued to attract the attention of the research community.

While the research papers are the core of the Pervasive conference series, the conference has a rich program that includes other activities in addition to the paper sessions. Pervasive 2008 featured a keynote speech by Mark Billinghurst — an internationally recognized expert in human–computer interface technology, particularly in the area of augmented reality. As with all of its predecessors, the 2008 conference also contained a poster and demo reception, as well as a full day of workshops and a doctoral colloquium. As in the previous year the final day of the conference was dedicated to tutorials focusing on the fundamentals of pervasive computing. The tutorials were intended as an introduction for new researchers and practitioners in the field.

Several organizations provided financial and logistical assistance in putting Pervasive 2008 together, and we would like to acknowledge their support. We thank NICTA, National Centre of Excellence in Information and Communication Technology in Australia, for helping to manage the local logistics of the conference organization. We would also like to thank the staff at the University of California-Irvine, University of Stuttgart, and NICTA for hosting the distributed Program Committee meeting. In particular, we would like to thank Daniela Nicklas for organizing the European part of the meeting at the University of Stuttgart. Lastly, we would like to thank the authors who submitted their work to Pervasive, the Program Committee members and external reviewers who reviewed, provided feedback and shepherded papers, and the Publication Chairs for helping with the preparation of the proceedings.

May 2008

Jadwiga Indulska
Donald J. Patterson
Tom Rodden
Max Ott

Organization

Conference Committee

General Chair:	Max Ott, NICTA, Australia
Program Co-chairs:	Jadwiga Indulska, University of Queensland/NICTA, Australia
	Donald J. Patterson, University of California Irvine, USA
	Tom Rodden, Nottingham University, UK
Demonstrations:	Sebastien Ardon, NICTA, Australia
	Enrico Rukzio, Lancaster University, UK
Doctoral Colloquium:	Gregory Abowd, Georgia Tech, USA
	Judy Kay, University of Sydney, Australia
	Koji Suginuma, Sony, Japan
Late-Breaking Results:	Aaron Quigley, University College Dublin, Ireland
	Rene Mayrhofer, Vienna University, Austria
Tutorials:	John Krumm, Microsoft Research, USA
	Tom Pfeifer, Waterford Institute of Technology, Ireland
Videos:	Gerd Kortuem, University of Lancaster, UK
	Andrew Vande Moere, University of Sydney, Australia
Workshops:	Arkady Zaslavsky, Monash University, Australia
	Khai Truong, University of Toronto, Canada
Publications:	Waltenegus Dargie, Technical University of Dresden, Germany
	Marius Portmann, University of Queensland/NICTA, Australia
Publicity:	Alex Varshavsky, University of Toronto, Canada
	Florian Michahelles, ETH Zurich/AutoID-Labs, Switzerland
	Zhiwen Yu, Kyoto University, Japan
Web:	Youmna Borghol, NICTA, Australia

Program Committee

Christian Becker, University of Mannheim, Germany
Gaetano Borriello, University of Washington, USA
Nigel Davies, University of Lancaster, UK
Anind Dey, Carnegie Mellon University, USA
Alois Ferscha, University of Linz, Austria
Geraldine Fitzpatrick, University of Sussex, UK
Morten Fjeld, Chalmers University of Technology, Sweden
Christian Floerkemeier, MIT, USA
Marco Gruteser, Rutgers University, USA
Jonna Hakkila, Nokia Corporation, Finland
Gilian Hayes, UCI, USA
Karen Henricksen, NICTA, Australia
Steve Hodges, Microsoft Research, UK
Pedro Jose Marron, University of Bonn, Germany
Antonio Krüger, University of Münster, Germany
John Krumm, Microsoft Research, USA
Mohan Kumar, University of Texas at Arlington, USA
Anthony LaMarca, Intel Research, USA
Marc Langheinrich, ETH Zurich, Switzerland
Seng Loke, La Trobe University, Australia
Kenji Mase, Nagoya University, Japan
Joe McCarthy, Nokia Research, USA
Daniela Nicklas, University of Stuttgart, Germany
Fabio Paterno, ISTI, CNR, Italy
Trevor Pering, Intel Research, USA
Tom Pfeifer, Waterford Institute of Technology, Ireland
Aaron Quigley, University College Dublin, Ireland
Anand Ranganathan, IBM Research, USA
Jun Rekimoto, Sony/University of Tokyo, Japan
Alexander Schill, University of Dresden, Germany
Chris Schmandt, MIT Media Lab, USA
Albrecht Schmidt, University of Duisburg-Essen, Germany
James Scott, Microsoft Research, UK
Thomas Strang, German Aerospace Center, Germany
Khai Truong, University of Toronto, Canada
Daqing Zhang, National Institute of Telecommunication, France
Kristof van Learhoven, University of Darmstadt, Germany

Steering Committee

Hans Gellersen, Lancaster University, UK
Anthony LaMarca, Intel Research, USA
Marc Langheinrich, ETH Zurich, Switzerland

Aaron Quigley, University College Dublin, Ireland
Bernt Schiele, TU Darmstadt, Germany
Albrecht Schmidt, University of Duisburg-Essen, Germany
Khai Troung, University of Toronto, Canada

Reviewers

Julio Abascal, University of the Basque Country, Spain
Jalal Al Muhtadi, King Saud University, Saudi Arabia
Marcin Anglart, Chalmers University of Technology, Sweden
Aslan Askarov, Chalmers University of Technology, Sweden
Rafael Ballagas, Nokia Research Center, USA
Louise Barkhuus, University of California, San Diego, USA
Martin Bauer, NEC Europe Ltd, Germany
Mike Bennett, University College Dublin, Ireland
Jan Beutel, ETH Zurich, Switzerland
Susanne Boll, University of Oldenburg, Germany
Philipp Bolliger, ETH Zurich, Switzerland
Barry Brown, University of California, San Diego, USA
A.J. Brush, Microsoft Research, USA
Rohit Chaudhri, University of Washington/Motorola, USA
Yingying Chen, Stevens Institute of Technology, USA
Karen Church, University College Dublin, Ireland
Kay Connelly, Indiana University, USA
Sunny Consolvo, Intel Research, Seattle, USA
Lorcan Coyle, University College Dublin, Ireland
Waltenegus Dargie, Technical University of Dresden, Germany
Richard Davies, University of Ulster, UK
Matt Duckham, University of Melbourne, Australia
Nathan Eagle, MIT, USA
Christos Efstratiou, Lancaster University, UK
James Fogarty, University of Washington, USA
Brooke Foucault, Northwestern University, USA
Zlatko Franjcic, Chalmers University of Technology, Sweden
Adrian Friday, Lancaster University, UK
Michael Fry, The University of Sydney, Australia
Eric Gilbert, University of Illinois at Urbana-Champaign, USA
Chris Greenhalgh, University of Nottingham, UK
Jörg Hähner, Leibniz Universität Hannover, Germany
Kari Hamnes, Telenor Research & Innovation, Norway
Marcus Handte, University of Bonn, Germany
Carl Hartung, University of Washington, USA
Hannes Heller, Chalmers University of Technology, Sweden
Steve Hinske, ETH Zurich, Switzerland

Daniel Schuster, TU Dresden, Germany
Tim Schwartz, Saarland University, Germany
Frank Siegemund, European Microsoft Innovation Center, Germany
Timothy Sohn, University of California, San Diego, USA
Thomas Springer, Technische Universität Dresden, Germany
Bruce Sterling, Independent, USA
Graeme Stevenson, UCD Dublin, Ireland
Maja Stikic, Fraunhofer IGD, Germany
Oliver Storz, Lancaster University, UK
Martin Strohbach, NEC Europe Ltd., Germany
Jindong Tan, Michigan Technological University, USA
Alex Varshavsky, University of Toronto, Canada
Sunil Vemuri, MIT, USA
Johan Wannheden, Chalmers University of Technology, Sweden
Torben Weis, Universität Duisburg-Essen, Germany
Andy Wilson, Microsoft Research, USA
Ryan Wishart, NICTA, Australia
Allison Woodruff, Intel Research, Berkeley, USA
Danny Wyatt, University of Washington, USA
Wenwei Xue, National University of Singapore, Singapore
Zhiwen Yu, Kyoto University, Japan
Andreas Zinnen, SAP Research, Germany

Table of Contents

Sensing and Activity Recognition

Applications for Mobile Devices

Location in Pervasive Systems

Platforms for Pervasive Computing

Lessons Learned from Displays, Games and Health Applications

Privacy and Security

Detecting Human Movement by Differential Air Pressure Sensing in HVAC System Ductwork: An Exploration in Infrastructure Mediated Sensing

Shwetak N. Patel[1], Matthew S. Reynolds[2], and Gregory D. Abowd[1]

[1] College of Computing, School of Interactive Computing, & GVU Center
Georgia Institute of Technology
85 5th Street NW, Atlanta GA 30332-0280 USA
{shwetak,abowd}@cc.gatech.edu
[2] Department of Electrical and Computer Engineering
Duke University
Box 90291, Durham, NC 27708 USA
matt.reynolds@duke.edu

Abstract. We have developed an approach for whole-house gross movement and room transition detection through sensing at only one point in the home. We consider this system to be one member of an important new class of human activity monitoring approaches based on what we call infrastructure mediated sensing, or "home bus snooping." Our solution leverages the existing ductwork infrastructure of central heating, ventilation, and air conditioning (HVAC) systems found in many homes. Disruptions in airflow, caused by human inter-room movement, result in static pressure changes in the HVAC air handler unit. This is particularly apparent for room-to-room transitions and door open/close events involving full or partial blockage of doorways and thresholds. We detect and record this pressure variation from sensors mounted on the air filter and classify where certain movement events are occurring in the house, such as an adult walking through a particular doorway or the opening and closing of a particular door. In contrast to more complex distributed sensing approaches for motion detection in the home, our method requires the installation of only a single sensing unit (*i.e.*, an instrumented air filter) connected to an embedded or personal computer that performs the classification function. Preliminary results show we can classify unique transition events with up to 75-80% accuracy.

1 Introduction and Motivation

The development of low-cost and easy-to-deploy sensing systems to support activity detection in the home has been an important trend in the pervasive computing community. Much of this research has centered on the deployment of a network of inexpensive sensors throughout the home, such as motion detectors or simple contact switches [23, 24, 26]. Although these solutions are cost-effective on an individual sensor basis, they are not without some important drawbacks that limit their desirability as research tools as well as their likelihood of eventual commercial success through broad consumer acceptance.

J. Indulska et al. (Eds.): Pervasive 2008, LNCS 5013, pp. 1–18, 2008.

We have developed an approach that provides a whole-house solution for detecting gross movement and room transitions by sensing differential air pressure at a single point in the home. Our solution leverages the central heating, ventilation, and air conditioning (HVAC) systems found in many homes. The home forms a closed circuit for air circulation, where the HVAC system provides a centralized airflow source and therefore a convenient single monitoring point for the whole airflow circuit.

Disruptions in home airflow caused by human movement through the house, especially those caused by the blockage of doorways and thresholds, results in static pressure changes in the HVAC air handler unit when the HVAC is operating. Our system detects and records this pressure variation from differential sensors mounted on the air filter and classifies where exactly certain movement events are occurring in the house, such as an adult walking through a particular doorway or the opening and closing of a door. Preliminary results show we can classify unique transition events with up to 75-80% accuracy. We also show how we detect movement events when the HVAC is not operating.

The principal advantage of this approach, when compared to installing motion sensors throughout an entire house space, is that it requires the installation of only a single sensing unit (*i.e.*, an instrumented air filter) that connects to a computer. By observing the opening and closing of doors and the movement of people transitioning from room to room, the location and activity of people in the space can later be inferred. In addition, detecting a series of room transitions can be used for simple occupancy detection or to estimate a person's path in the house.

Because of the use of a single monitoring point on an existing home infrastructure (the HVAC air handler, in this example) to detect human activity throughout an entire house, we consider our system a member of an important new class of activity monitoring systems that we call *infrastructure mediated sensing*. In the remainder of this paper, we further define this new category of sensing and explain the theory and implementation of the HVAC-facilitated motion detection.

2 Related Work

We distinguish between distributed direct sensing and a newly described category, infrastructure mediated sensing, which we informally call "home bus snooping" by analogy to computer network snooping. Distributed direct sensing involves the installation of a new sensing infrastructure into the home. This sensing infrastructure directly senses the presence, motion or activities of its residents through sensors that are physically located in each space where activity is occurring. Example systems include a new set of sensors and an associated sensor network (wired or wireless) to transfer the sensor data to a centralized monitoring system where sensor fusion and activity inference take place. In contrast, infrastructure mediated sensing leverages existing home infrastructure, such as the plumbing or electrical systems, to mediate the transduction of events. In these systems, infrastructure activity is used as a proxy for a human activity involving the infrastructure (see Figure 1). A primary goal of this second category of systems is to reduce economic, aesthetic, installation, and maintenance barriers to adoption by reducing the cost and complexity of deploying and maintaining the activity sensing infrastructure.

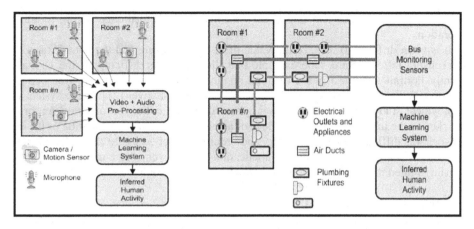

Fig. 1. The distributed direct sensing (DDS) approach for activity detection and classification (left). The infrastructure mediated sensing approach for activity detection and classification (right).

2.1 Prior Work in Distributed Direct Sensing

Most of the existing literature in human activity sensing in the home falls into the distributed direct sensing category. In the pervasive computing research context, commonly used sensors for detecting human activity in the home include high-fidelity sensors such as visible light and IR cameras [25, 28] or microphones [4], as well as low-fidelity sensors such as passive infrared (PIR) motion detectors [27] and floor weight sensors [18]. High-fidelity distributed direct sensing has a long history of use in activity detection and classification research, primarily focused on computer vision or machine learning systems that capture the movement of people in spaces [13]. For example, Chen *et al.* installed microphones in a bathroom to sense activities such as showering, toileting, and hand washing [6]. The use of these high fidelity sensors in certain spaces often raises concerns about the balance between value-added services and acceptable surveillance, particularly in home settings [5, 9, 10]. Low-fidelity, distributed direct sensing work includes the use of a large collection of simple, low-cost sensors, such as motion detectors, pressure mats, break beam sensors, and contact switches, to determine activity and movement [23, 24, 26]. The principal advantages are lower per-sensor cost and reduced privacy concerns.

All distributed direct sensing approaches share the advantages and disadvantages of placing each sensor in close proximity to where human activity occurs. For example, commonly used cameras or PIR sensors require a clear line of sight to the desired room coverage area; the person being sensed will be able to see the camera or PIR sensor. Generally, cameras or PIR sensors are deployed in places that have adverse aesthetics, such as on walls, on ceilings, or above a door [7, 9]. The large number of sensors required for coverage of an entire building presents an inherent complexity hurdle. Installation and maintenance of (typically) tens of sensors in a home, or hundreds to thousands of sensors in a larger building such as a hotel, hospital, or assisted living facility, results in high labor costs during installation, and an ongoing maintenance and sensor network management challenge during routine operation.

It is often difficult to balance the value of in-home sensing and the complexity of the sensing infrastructure. One example that illustrates this difficulty is the Digital Family Portrait system, a peace of mind application for communicating well-being information from an elderly person's home to a remote caregiver [21]. In the system's deployment study, movement data was gathered from a collection of strain sensors attached to the underside of the first floor of an elder's home. The installation of these sensors was difficult, time-consuming, and required direct access to the underside of the floor. Though the value of the application was proven, the complexity of the sensing limited the number of homes in which the system could be easily deployed.

2.2 Infrastructure Mediated Sensing

Some recent innovative work in the infrastructure mediated sensing category leverages the existing infrastructure in a home to collect signals at a single location. A few researchers have recently begun exploring the use of existing home infrastructure to detect human originated events [8, 19, 20]. A few microphones on the plumbing infrastructure in the basement of a home can infer basic activities, such as bathing or washing dishes, through acoustically-transduced signals [8]. A single plug-in sensor can classify events, such as the actuation of a light switch, through the analysis of noise, transduced along the power line, from the switching and operation of electrical devices [19]. These two approaches cover a complementary set of human activities, depending on whether a water- or power-related event precedes that activity.

Both of these approaches require human-initiated events, as identified through signals carried via the infrastructure of their corresponding resources, in order to provide human activity information. They ignore activities that do not include the use of the plumbing or electrical systems, such as movement and transitions between parts of the home. In the case of water event detection, there may be only a few water usage events per person per day, whereas with electrical event detection, there may be limited electrical actuations during the day when incoming sunlight illumination may result in reduced light switch use. This results in a relatively sparse activity dataset compared to a dataset obtained using a dense network of PIR motion sensors located throughout the home. Therefore, we were motivated to find an infrastructure mediated sensing technique that delivers movement information.

We contrast infrastructure mediated sensing with a "piggybacking" approach that simply reuses an existing sensing infrastructure in the home that may be present for other purposes. For example, ADT Security System's QuietCare [1] offers a peace of mind service that gathers activity data from the security system's PIR motion detectors. Although a promising approach, security motion sensors are typically only installed in a few locations in the home, primarily on the ground floors, resulting in a much sparser dataset than is needed for general activity recognition.

3 Our Approach and System Details

We instrumented an HVAC's air filter with five pressure sensor units, each sensing in both directions (see Figure 2). The sensors do not interfere with the operation of the

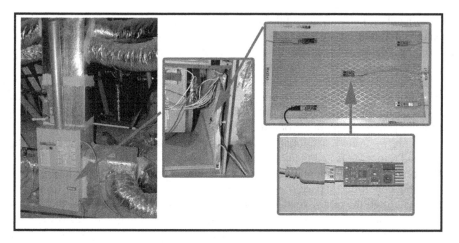

Fig. 2. We instrument a standard HVAC air filter with pressure sensors that are able to detect airflow in both directions. The air filter is then installed in the HVAC's air handler unit.

air filter or HVAC and instrumenting the air filter allows for easy installation in standard HVAC units. The sensors on the air filter capture the pressure differential across the filter in the air handler chamber. The magnitude of the pressure change across all the sensors is used to identify unique disruptions in airflow in the physical space. Machine learning techniques then classify these disruption signatures.

3.1 Theory of Operation

The HVAC system's air handler is a device used to circulate conditioned air throughout a space. Typically, an air handler is a large, sealed metal box containing a blower, heating/cooling coils, filter, and dampers (see Figure 3). An air handler consists of a discharge, or supply, chamber where the conditioned air exits through ductwork, and is drawn back into the return chamber through a separate set of vents and ductwork. During its operation, a pressure differential, ΔP, is built up in the

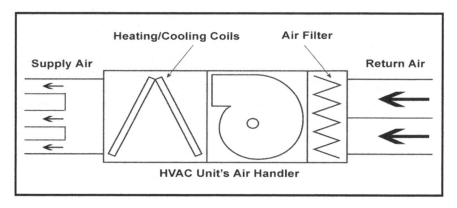

Fig. 3. Cross section of a HVAC air handler unit

blower chamber, know as the total static pressure. The static pressure is a measure of resistance imposed on the HVAC's blower in the air handler. The static pressure is affected by a variety of factors that impede the airflow between the supply and return. These includes the length of ducting, number of fittings used in the ductwork, closed air vents, or dirty air filters. When installing an HVAC unit, a technician usually takes care in properly balancing the static pressure to ensure its proper operation. This includes installing sufficient supply and return ductwork in the right locations. Technicians also install ductwork to various rooms to ensure effective coverage. Figure 4 shows a cross-sectional drawing of a home and example locations of the supply and return vents and the potential airflow paths.

When the HVAC is running, air flows from the supply vents to the return vents through the conditioned space (*i.e.*, a room). There is always some airflow from each supply vent to all the return vents. Depending on the location of the vents, the airflow paths and amount of airflow can vary. When there is disruption to the airflow, there is a change in the static pressure in the air handler as a result of the resistance in the airflow. Depending on the location of return vents, a disruption in airflow can cause a more persistent change in the overall static pressure, such as from a direct blockage of a return vent. In a home, one contributor to this airflow disruption is doorways, where airflow can either be disrupted by the closing or opening of a door or the partial blockage of an adult passing through the threshold. Sometimes, an individual may even feel the "resistance" from the airflow when trying to open a door. Also depending on the location in the house where this disruption is occurring, the "resistance" differs because of the airflow path. Another way to look this phenomenon is using an electrical circuit analogy (see Figure 4).

When the HVAC is not in operation, the ductwork acts as a "wave guide." Significant airflow produced in the space flows through the ductwork. Although small movements cannot generate enough airflow, the movements of large surfaces, such as doors, can produce detectible amounts of airflow through the air handler. Thus, there are opportunities to detect certain movement in the space with the HVAC both in operation and not in operation.

We use the air filter chamber as the sensing point for two important reasons. First, it is between the supply and return chambers and near the blower assembly, making it a good place for recording the static pressure changes. Second, the filtration unit typically has the easiest access to the air handler, potentially making it easy-to-deploy for installers and end-users. The static air pressure is determined by installing pressure sensors facing each direction on the air filter and calculating the differential (ΔP). A single differential pressure sensor would also be appropriate. However, using two pressure sensors makes their placement easier. This is because typical differential pressure sensors have the pressure ports on one side, which requires routing an air tube to the other side. The sensors required for our approach are capable of measuring up to 2 bars of pressure and sensitive enough to measure small pressure changes down to .1 mbar. Figure 5 shows a graph of the change in static pressure as a door it is opened and closed. There is an initial spike in the pressure followed by a flattening. After the door is reopened, the pressure returns to the previous state.

We placed multiple pressure sensors on the air filter to help estimate the location of the resulting pressure change. In standard ductwork, multiple ducts combine to feed larger trunks, which then attach to the supply and return chambers. Because multiple

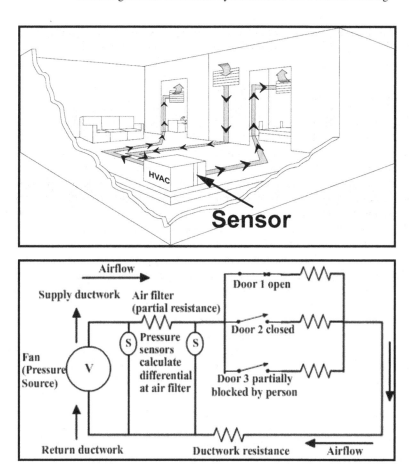

Fig. 4. Diagram of airflow from return and supply ducting in a home (top). Electrical circuit diagram analogy of our sensing approach (bottom).

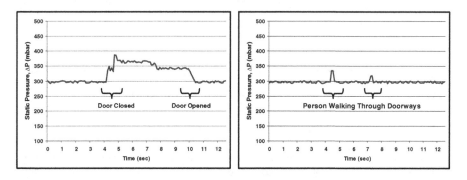

Fig. 5. Examples of the pressure changes in the air handler as a result of an opening and closing of a door (left) and an adult walking through two different doorways (right)

ducts feed into the chambers, pressure sensors closer to the ductwork that is contributing to the airflow disruptions will see greater initial change in pressure compared to the other sensors.

3.2 Data Collection Hardware and Software

We used the Intersema MS5536 piezoresistive pressure sensor module for building our sensor units. The MS5536 modules are high resolution (.1 mbar), provide a stable output of up to 2 bars, and have a maximum rating of up to 5 bars, which is sufficient for many residential HVAC applications. The modules incorporate a temperature sensor for proper pressure compensation, a built-in 15-bit ADC, and also provide easy communication using SPI. To obtain pressure differentials, the MS5536 uses two sensors facing opposite directions. The pressure sensor modules are connected to an ATMEL microcontroller (see Figure 6). The microcontroller samples the pressure and temperature sensors on the MS5536 and calculates a temperature-compensated pressure value every 35 milliseconds. Intersema's temperature compensation formula was used in our calculations [12]. The pressure values are then transferred to a PC via a USB connection. Multiple sensor units are connected to a single PC using a USB hub. We chose to use individual units to give us some flexibility when experimenting with a variety of sensor placements on the air filter. The sensor units are small enough to attach easily to the air filter with zip ties. In a production version, the sensors would be mounted on a framed bracket that would just attach to the air filter. A fully deployable unit would have all the pressure sensors feeding into it a single microcontroller. A unit incorporating five differential pressure sensors costs about $100 USD at low volumes.

The software used in our data collection is written in C++ and records the temperature-compensated pressure data, the raw pressure values, and the temperature from the sensors units. The application continually timestamps and records the pressure-related data from all the sensor units every 50 millisecond.

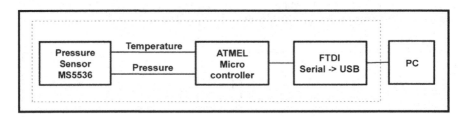

Fig. 6. Block diagram of our pressure sensor unit

3.3 Detecting Door Opening and Closing Events

We observed two important features that were characteristic of door opening and closing events. When a door is closed, there is first an initial abrupt change in static pressure (change in ΔP) followed by persistent change until the door is reopened (see Figure 5). After opening the door, the static pressure gradually drops to the previous state. We detect this phenomenon by first looking for a significant change in the static pressure by at least one of the five sensing units. We do this by comparing the average of the 5 previous pressure differential reading with the current. When there is a pressure change greater than 10 mbar, we record the subsequent pressure values for further processing until there are no more changes for a period of 4000 ms. All other sensors also record at the same time. The 10 mbar threshold is to avoid detecting any slight variations from the senor or noise from the ADC. From the recorded data we next extract the initial pressure value, the initial maximum pressure change, and the resulting final stable pressure. These features are extracted for all 5 sensor units, producing a final feature vector of 15 components.

3.4 Detecting Movement of People through Doorways

A person passing through a doorway is a brief event, and the size of the individual can vary, decreasing the likelihood of detection. However, we still wanted to explore the feasibility of detecting those events. During our experimentation, we observed variations in the static pressure as individuals moved through various doorways. Unlike the door events, the changes in pressure are very short-lived. There is a slight change in the static pressure and then the pressure settles back to its original state. The effect is dependent on the location of the supply and return vents relative to the doorway and the ratio of the size of the person to the size of the doorway. From our observations, a ratio of 1:3 resulted in detectable airflow disruptions (>10 mbar).

We isolated these events by comparing the average of the 5 prior pressure differentials to the current. We recorded the pressure values when there was a change of more than 10 mbar by at least one sensor unit. All other sensor units also triggered to record at the same time. Values were gathered until the pressure stabilized. We use the maximum pressure change from each of the 5 sensor units as the feature vector.

3.5 Detecting Door Transition Events with HVAC Off

When the HVAC is not operating, there is no static pressure build-up in the air handler. Instead, the pressure is equal to the atmospheric pressure of approximately 1 bar. Any significant airflow generated in the conditioned space is guided through either the supply or return ducts and eventually reaches the sensor units on the filters. The sensitivity of the sensor units make it possible to detect airflow reaching the sensors. We can use the pressure values from both sides of the filter to help determine where the airflow originated. Similar to the previous approaches, we also use the multiple sensing points to help localize the origination of the induced airflow. Theoretically, it is also possible to detect airflow caused by people moving near an air vent and by other devices, such as a ceiling or desk fan. However, these events produce very small amounts of airflow and require more expensive, high-resolution and low-noise pressure sensors. In this case, we focus on just the movement of doors when the HVAC is not operating.

When the HVAC is off, we isolate door events by comparing the average of the 5 prior pressure differentials to the current. We then record the pressure values when there are any changes of more than 10 mbar by at least one sensor unit. All other sensor units are recorded at the same time. Values are gathered until the pressure stabilizes, and the feature vector of the maximum pressure change from each of the 5 sensor units is calculated.

3.6 Classifying Events

For our classification scheme, we used support vector machines (SVMs). SVMs perform classification by constructing an N-dimensional hyperplane that optimally separates the data into multiple categories. The separation is chosen to have the largest distance from the hyperplane to the nearest positive and negative examples. Thus, the classification is appropriate for testing data that is near, but not identical, to the training data as is the case for the feature vectors in our approach. In addition, SVMs can automatically determine the appropriate kernel type based on the data build characteristics, so kernels beyond linear functions can be factored in. For our experiments, we created three different SVM models for each of the three scenarios, using their respective feature vectors with each transition event labeled as the class. The open transition and the close transition for each door of interest were used as the classes in the learner. This was the case for both the HVAC in operation and not in operation. In the case of classifying human movement through a doorway, we do not differentiate between the directions of movement, thus the class labels were of the door where the movement occurred.

4 Feasibility Experiments

The goal of the feasibility experiments was to determine if and how often we could detect transition movements (*e.g.,* adults walking through doorways and the opening and closing of doors) and how accurately we could classify unique transition events. In this section, we present the results from experiments in four different homes for the following three conditions: opening and closing of doors while the HVAC is in operation, adults moving through doorways while the HVAC is in operation, and the opening and closing of doors while the HVAC is not in operation.

4.1 Setup of Feasibility Experiments

We conducted experiments and observations in four different homes for a period ranging from 3 to 4 weeks (see Table 1). Home 1 and Home 2 were fairly large homes, with Home 1 having three separate central HVAC units, and Home 2 having two separate central HVAC units. We instrumented all three units in Home 1 and one unit in Home 2. Homes 3 and 4 were smaller apartments with a single, central HVAC system. Thus, we evaluated a total of six different spaces and HVAC units. For each HVAC unit, we installed an instrumented air filter (see Figure 2). The sensors were securely attached to prevent any movement from the airflow. The cables were run around the edge of the filter to prevent them from being drawn in to the fan assembly. Finally, the cables were connected to a laptop placed near the HVAC unit.

We used two techniques for obtaining labeled ground truth data. First, throughout the 3-4 week period we manually labeled numerous door close and open events and a person walking through doorways with the house in a closed and sealed state (windows and exterior doors closed). Second, we captured data for a longer time period using motion sensors placed at various locations in the house. Sensors on both sides of the top of the doorways (facing downwards) detected the direction of movement through

Table 1. Descriptions of the homes in which our system was tested. The deployment lasted approximately 3-4 weeks.

Home	Year Built	No. of HVAC Units Tested	Floors/ Total Size (Sq Ft)/ (Sq M)	Style/ No. of occupants	Bedrooms/ Bathrooms/ Total Rms./ Doorways considered	Deploy Length (weeks)
1	2003	3	3/4000/371	1 Family Home/3	4/4/13/20	4
2	2001	1	1/1600/149	1 Family Home/5	3/2/7/10	3
3	1997	1	1/700/58	1 Bed Apt/2	1/1/5/5	3
4	1986	1	1/500/46	1 Bed Studio/1	1/1/3/4	4

the doorway. Although we were not able to accurately differentiate door movement and people movement, the motion sensors did allow us to determine if any transition events occurred at various times during the day. The large dataset allowed us to partition the data into sufficient training and test sets.

4.2 Manually-Labeled Controlled Experiments

In these experiments, we wanted to test the feasibility of accurately classifying the various kinds of unique door or movement events in a quasi-controlled manner. For all four homes, we manually labeled sensor readings for each event using a remote handheld computer wirelessly connected to the data collection PC. We were able to accurately label the sensor readings for each of the five sensors after triggering the various events. We then used our feature extraction algorithms to construct the appropriate feature vectors to feed our classifier. For these experiments, all interior doors of interest were kept in the open position (90 degrees from the opening), while we were manually opening and closing each door. For the human movement experiments, the same individual triggered those events. We collected 25 instances for each of the doorway events three different times during the 3-4 week period (175 instances).

Table 2 shows the classification accuracies of all the spaces. We have also included an example confusion matrix (Table 3). It is clear that door transition events were more accurate than people transitions. However, the overall accuracy of classifying unique movement events was around 65%, which is still promising. Door events were classified correctly on an average of 75-80% of the time, suggesting that we can combine both of these events to provide good predictions on the location or movement of people through the space. Some of the low classification accuracies, such as from Floor 2 in Home 1, were attributed to the lack of door and doorways. That space was very open with the air vent a significant distance away from the interior doors. The results of the HVAC off experiment also showed some promising results (see Table 4). Although the accuracies are lower than with the HVAC in operation, there is still some predictive power. The higher performance came in smaller spaces where the vents tended to be closer to the doorway and in spaces where there were many vents, such as Homes 1 and 2.

Table 2. Performance results of our manually-labeled experiments with the HVAC in operation. The accuracies are shown using 10-fold cross validation.

Home/ Floor	No. of Doorways Tested	No. of Door Instances/People Instances	Door Majority Classif. (%)	Door Classif. Accuracy (%)	People Majority Classif. (%)	People Classif. Accuracy (%)
1/1	5	375/375	21	84	23	72
1/2	4	300/300	18	61	18	42
1/3	11	825/600	9	77	12	61
2	10	750/400	8	73	10	63
3	5	375/375	20	74	20	70
4	4	300/300	26	81	25	76

Table 3. Confusion matrix of the classification results from the controlled experiments in Home 1/3 (HVAC in operation). D1 - D11 represent each doorway.

	D1	D2	D3	D4	D5	D6	D7	D8	D9	D10	D11
D1	72	0	0	0	1	0	0	1	0	0	1
D2	1	57	0	2	0	2	6	4	0	1	2
D3	0	1	60	1	0	1	3	2	5	2	0
D4	0	0	1	57	2	0	0	4	3	6	2
D5	4	0	1	4	52	5	0	6	2	0	1
D6	5	1	0	0	6	53	4	2	0	1	3
D7	0	2	3	3	0	1	61	0	3	2	0
D8	6	0	0	0	2	1	1	55	5	0	5
D9	1	0	4	0	1	5	2	0	59	2	1
D10	2	2	7	0	3	3	8	0	2	43	5
D11	0	1	0	0	0	2	0	0	0	2	70

Table 4. Performance results of our manually labeled door open/close events for when the HVAC is not in operation

Home/ Floor	No. of Doorways Tested	No. of Door Event Instances	Door Majority Classif. (%)	Door Classif. Accuracy (%)
1/1	5	125	20	66
1/2	4	100	25	47
1/3	11	275	9	64
2	10	250	10	69
3	5	125	20	71
4	4	100	25	68

4.3 Long-Term Deployment

For the long-term deployment, we wanted to gather *in situ* or "more natural" data on the various events occurring in the home and provide some initial long-term *in situ* results for our sensing approach. For labeling, we used motion sensors placed at various doorways to determine any door movement or motion through the doorway and matched those events up with the corresponding sensor values from the HVAC. We conducted two analyses; one was the percentage of time we were able to determine particular events with our system and the second was to determine the classification accuracies of detecting unique events. Table 5 shows the number of events that were detected by our system, either as a door transition event or a human movement through the doorway, for each of the 4 homes. We present the results for two cases. One is with the HVAC in operation and the other is with the HVAC off.

Table 5. The percentage of events that our approach was able to detect. This is determined by comparing the number of detected events to the number of doorway events gathered by the motion sensors. These results include events detected with HVAC both on and off.

Home/ Floor	No. of Doorways Tested	No. of Total Motion Sensor Events	No. of Total Detected Events	HVAC On: Detected Events (%)	HVAC Off: Detected Events (%)
1/1	5	53	48	91	68
1/2	4	94	60	64	35
1/3	11	238	195	82	73
2	10	467	334	72	64
3	5	245	198	81	70
4	4	61	51	84	77

The results show that a larger percentage of events were detected with the HVAC in operation than with it in the off state. The reason for the lower percentage for the HVAC off case was because of the location of the return and supply vents. In some cases, the vents were not close enough to a door for the airflow to reach the sensing units, which we saw in our controlled experiment. The smaller spaces and the spaces with many doorways actually resulted in a higher number of detectable events. This is attributed to the greater number of vents and the likelihood that the doorways were near vents. The results with the HVAC in operation are promising, with almost 80% of the events being detected when compared to the motion sensors. Table 6 shows the results of classifying unique events in the house. We applied our SVM classification scheme to the entire *in situ* dataset for each of the 4 homes (6 spaces). This dataset included events from all three of the possible conditions (door open/close with HVAC on and off and human movement with HVAC on). The triggering of the motion sensor was used to provide the location label to the air pressure data collected by our sensing system. Because we did not know the type of event, we used the signal response to determine the event (*i.e.*, person or door).

We report the accuracy of our approach using 10-fold cross validation across the entire data set. Compared to the first controlled experiments, the overall accuracy on average is 15-20% lower. However, considering that we did not control the various other events occurring during that time, the results are still promising with classification accuracies between 60-70%. From these we can see that the status of other doors did not have a large impact on the classification accuracy of detecting

Table 6. The performance of using our learning approach to the data from the long-term deployment. The motion sensor data was used to label each event, so the dataset consists of *in situ* event instances. The accuracies are show using 10-fold cross validation.

Home/ Floor	No. of Doorways Tested	No. of Doorway Transition Instances	Door Majority Classif. (%)	Door Classif. Accuracy (%)	People Majority Classif. (%)	People Classif. Accuracy (%)
1/1	5	48	26	65	28	61
1/2	4	60	26	53	26	42
1/3	11	195	14	72	17	63
2	10	334	19	62	12	65
3	5	198	28	72	23	71
4	4	51	34	78	38	81

door transitions with the HVAC off. The larger difference while the HVAC is in operation compared to the controlled experiment does indicate the door states have an impact on the pressure differentials, as expected. However, since we trained from a subset of the entire dataset, the learner seemed to incorporate the various door combinations. This is intuitive because people tend to be consistent with how they leave many of their doors throughout the day, while only actually using a few doors.

5 Deployability: Prevalence of Central HVAC Systems

Although central home HVAC systems are not as prevalent in some geographic regions as plumbing or electrical infrastructure, our approach is still useful in the significant number of homes or buildings that do have central HVAC. Because central HVACs are more efficient than using a collection of window units [16], the upward trend in energy cost has driven the use of central HVAC systems to a growing number of homes. In 1997, 66% of the homes in the United States and Canada were reported to have central HVAC, and its prevalence is growing at a fast rate [3, 15, 22]. In addition, nearly all new homes built in the southern part of the U.S. and 80% in the rest of the U.S. and Canada have central HVAC installed during construction [15]. Europe and Australia show a similar trend, with approximately 55% homes using central HVAC [14, 11]. However, in some Asian counties such as Japan and Korea, central HVAC is not as common in homes because of the smaller dwelling sizes prevalent in those regions. If the home is very small, such as a small Japanese or Korean home, the deployment of distributed direct sensors may not be as arduous because of the smaller amount of floor space to cover. Regardless of the regional prevalence of central HVAC, the value of our approach becomes more apparent in larger homes or in assisted living facilities that have many rooms, precisely the settings where installing many distributed sensors is economically unattractive.

HVAC systems will probably increase in prevalence because they can provide more functionality than just heating and cooling. Recent EnergyStar reports have shown that running the HVAC for longer periods of time, but using alternate conditioning features, such an air-to-air exchanger, is more energy efficient [16]. This EnergyStar report also recommends that HVAC units incorporate whole house HEPA filtration. Construction codes, such as for hospitals and assistive care facilities, also have a minimum air movement requirements to ensure proper filtration [2, 17]. All of these factors increase the motivation for having the HVAC in operation, increasing the effectiveness of our sensing approach. If we take a standard 2-ton (24,000 BTU) HVAC unit and run the air handler's fan continuously for an entire month it would cost about $6 US (assuming an electricity price of $0.05 US per 1 kW-h), which would need to be balanced against any value-added capability our sensing provides.

6 Discussion of Limitations and Potential Improvements

Our approach is certainly not without limitation. It does require a training phase and further research is still needed in coming up with a mechanism to ease the training process. Some possible directions are to use events generated from other calibrated systems (water line or power line) to feed the training of this system. Although this might not cover all possible training cases, it can be used to relieve some of the burden. Those systems can also provide continual feedback for verifying the training set. In addition, partial training may also be feasible for certain applications, where only certain doorways are first trained. Then, if there is any interest in observing other events, the training can occur after the fact and the other past events can be reviewed.

We considered only the amplitude of the static pressure change and using multiple pressure sensor units to determine unique movement and door events. Other possible approaches would look at the changes in the laminar airflow. Although we use the temperature values for calculating the temperature-compensated pressure values, we could use the temperature reading as an additional feature. Our current focus was on residential central HVAC systems, but our system can scale reasonably to larger units used in most commercial buildings. Further investigations are needed to explore those systems. Our feasibility experiments did not directly factor in the opening and closing windows and doors. Finally, our current approach does not directly address compound events—multiple simultaneous door and person movements— although these events occurred in the long-term studies. Modeling airflow variations and creating a new learning approach that incorporates that domain knowledge could address this.

7 Conclusion

We have developed an approach for whole-house gross movement and room transition detection through sensing at only one point in the home. We consider this system to be one member of an important new class of human activity monitoring approaches based on infrastructure mediated sensing, or "home bus snooping." Our solution leverages the existing ductwork infrastructure of central heating, ventilation, and air conditioning (HVAC) systems found in many homes. Disruptions in airflow caused by human inter-room movement result in static pressure changes in the HVAC air handler unit. This is particularly apparent for room-to-room transitions and door open/close events involving partial blockage of doorways and thresholds. We detect and record this pressure variation from sensors mounted on the air filter and classify where certain movement events are occurring in the house, such as an adult walking through a particular doorway or the opening and closing of a door. Although less precise, we also show the detection of movement when the HVAC is not operating. In contrast to more complex distributed sensing approaches for motion detection in the home, our method requires the installation of only a single sensing unit.

The combination of different types of infrastructure mediated sensors offers a number of attractive properties for deployment of useful applications in the home. For example, the combination of detecting human-initiated electrical [19] or water events [8] with our work on movement detection through airflow sensing enables a variety of new approaches for integrating energy and environmental conservation with ordinary human activities in the home. A system could alert an individual that he or she should attend to an energy or environmental conservation task, such as turning off an un-needed light or a running faucet, when the system detects that he or she is near that part of the house. The combination of electrical event detection and airflow detected movement information can also provide important correlation data for energy conservation applications by relating a person's usage of the physical space with the usage of electrical devices. One could design an energy-efficient zoned HVAC unit that selectively heats or cools each zone on the basis of activity information passively sensed through the HVAC system itself, which would offer a tremendous installation and maintenance cost benefit over competing distributed sensing approaches.

Acknowledgments

This work was sponsored in part by the National Science Foundation Graduate Fellowship and the Intel Research Council. The authors would also like to thank the members of the Ubicomp Research Group at Georgia Tech, in particular Julie Kientz and Lana Yarosh.

References

1. ADT QuietCare (2008), http://www.adt.com/quietcare/
2. American Institute of Architects. Guidelines for Design and Construction of Hospital and Health Care Facilities. The American Institute of Architects Press, Washington D.C. (2001)
3. Barnes Reports. 2008 U.S. Plumbing & Heating & A/C Contractors Report (October 2007)
4. Bian, X., Abowd, G.D., Rehg, J.M.: Using Sound Source Localization in a Home Environment. In: Proc. of the Pervasive 2005, pp. 19–26 (2005)
5. Beckmann, C., Consolvo, S., LaMarca, A.: Some Assembly Required: Supporting End-User Sensor Installation in Domestic Ubiquitous Computing Environments. In: Davies, N., Mynatt, E.D., Siio, I. (eds.) UbiComp 2004. LNCS, vol. 3205, pp. 383–399. Springer, Heidelberg (2004)
6. Chen, J., Kam, A.H., Zhang, J., Liu, N., Shue, L.: Bathroom Activity Monitoring Based on Sound. In: Gellersen, H.-W., Want, R., Schmidt, A. (eds.) PERVASIVE 2005. LNCS, vol. 3468, pp. 47–61. Springer, Heidelberg (2005)

7. Chetty, M., Sung, J., Grinter, R.E.: How Smart Homes Learn: The Evolution of the Networked Home and Household. In: Krumm, J., Abowd, G.D., Seneviratne, A., Strang, T. (eds.) UbiComp 2007. LNCS, vol. 4717, pp. 127–144. Springer, Heidelberg (2007)
8. Fogarty, J., Au, C., Hudson, S.E.: Sensing from the Basement: A Feasibility Study of Unobtrusive and Low-Cost Home Activity Recognition. In: The Proc. of UIST 2006, pp. 91–100 (2006)
9. Hirsch, T., Forlizzi, J., Hyder, E., Goetz, J., Kurtz, C., Stroback, J.: The ELDer Project: Social, Emotional, and Environmental Factors in the Design of Eldercare Technologies. In: The Proc. of the ACM Conference on Universal Usability, pp. 72–79 (2000)
10. Iachello, G., Abowd, G.D.: Privacy and Proportionality: Adapting Legal Evaluation Techniques to Inform Design in Ubiquitous Computing. In: The Proc. of CHI 2005, pp. 91–100 (2005)
11. IBISWorld. AC and Heating Services in Australia-Industry Market Research Report (August 2007)
12. Intersema (2008), http://www.intersema.com/site/technical/ms5536.php
13. Koile, K., Tollmar, K., Demirdjian, D., Howard, S., Trevor, D.: Activity Zones for Context-Aware Computing. In: Dey, A.K., Schmidt, A., McCarthy, J.F. (eds.) UbiComp 2003. LNCS, vol. 2864, pp. 90–106. Springer, Heidelberg (2003)
14. Market and Bus. Development. UK Domestic Central Heating Market Development (September 2007)
15. Menzer, M.: Heat Pump Status and Trends in North America. In: IEA Heat Pump Conference, May 31 (1999), http://www.ari.org/research/engineering_research/
16. Nadel, S.: Increasing Appliance Energy Savings by Looking Beyond the Current Energy Star. In: ACEEE 2004 Energy Star Appliance Partner Meeting (2004), http://www.energystar.gov/ia/partners/downloads/Plenary_B_Steve_Nadel.pdf
17. Ninomura, P., Bartley, J.: New Ventilation Guidelines For Health Care Facilities. Air Conditioning and Refrigeration Journal, July-September Issue (2002)
18. Orr, R.J., Abowd, G.D.: The Smart Floor: A Mechanism for Natural User Identification and Tracking. In: Proc. of the Extended Abstracts of CHI 2000, pp. 275–276 (2000)
19. Patel, S.N., Robertson, T., Kientz, J.A., Reynolds, M.S., Abowd, G.D.: At the Flick of a Switch: Detecting and Classifying Unique Electrical Events on the Residential Power Line. In: The Proc. of Ubicomp 2007, pp. 271–288 (2007)
20. Patel, S.N., Truong, K.N., Abowd, G.D.: PowerLine Positioning: A Practical Sub-Room-Level Indoor Location System for Domestic Use. In: The Proc. of Ubicomp 2006, pp. 441–458 (2006)
21. Rowan, J., Mynatt, E.D.: Digital Family Portrait Field Trial: Support for Aging in Place. In: Proc. of CHI 2005, pp. 521–530 (2005)
22. Supplier Relations US, LLC. Ventilation, Heating, Air-Conditioning, and Commercial Refrigeration Equipment Manufacturing Industry in the U.S. and its Foreign Trade (August 2007)
23. Tapia, E.M., Intille, S.S., Larson, K.: Activity recognition in the home setting using simple and ubiquitous sensors. In: Ferscha, A., Mattern, F. (eds.) PERVASIVE 2004. LNCS, vol. 3001, pp. 158–175. Springer, Heidelberg (2004)
24. Tapia, E.M., Intille, S.S., Lopez, L., Larson, K.: The design of a portable kit of wireless sensors for naturalistic data collection. In: Fishkin, K.P., Schiele, B., Nixon, P., Quigley, A. (eds.) PERVASIVE 2006. LNCS, vol. 3968, pp. 117–134. Springer, Heidelberg (2006)
25. Vicon MX (2008), http://www.vicon.com/products/systems.html

26. Wilson, D.H., Atkeson, C.G.: Simultaneous Tracking and Activity Recognition (STAR) Using Many Anonymous, Binary Sensors. In: Gellersen, H.-W., Want, R., Schmidt, A. (eds.) PERVASIVE 2005. LNCS, vol. 3468, pp. 62–79. Springer, Heidelberg (2005)
27. Wren, C.R., Munguia-Tapia, E.: Toward Scalable Activity Recognition for Sensor Networks. In: The Proc. of the International Workshop in Location and Context-Awareness (LoCA 2006), pp. 168–185 (2006)
28. Yang, Z., Bobick, A.F.: Visual Integration from Multiple Cameras. In: The Proc. of Application of Computer Vision, WACV/MOTIONS 2005, pp. 488–493 (2005)

Robust Recognition of Reading Activity in Transit Using Wearable Electrooculography

Andreas Bulling[1], Jamie A. Ward[2], Hans Gellersen[2], and Gerhard Tröster[1]

[1] ETH Zurich, Wearable Computing Laboratory
bulling@ife.ee.ethz.ch
[2] Lancaster University, Embedded Interactive Systems Group
j.a.ward@lancaster.ac.uk

Abstract. In this work we analyse the eye movements of people in transit in an everyday environment using a wearable electrooculographic (EOG) system. We compare three approaches for continuous recognition of reading activities: a string matching algorithm which exploits typical characteristics of reading signals, such as saccades and fixations; and two variants of Hidden Markov Models (HMMs) - mixed Gaussian and discrete. The recognition algorithms are evaluated in an experiment performed with eight subjects reading freely chosen text without pictures while sitting at a desk, standing, walking indoors and outdoors, and riding a tram. A total dataset of roughly 6 hours was collected with reading activity accounting for about half of the time. We were able to detect reading activities over all subjects with a top recognition rate of 80.2% (71.0% recall, 11.6% false positives) using string matching. We show that EOG is a potentially robust technique for reading recognition across a number of typical daily situations.

1 Introduction

Activity recognition has recently emerged as a key area of research in building context-aware interfaces for mobile and pervasive computing. The problem of recognising physical activity in mobile situations, for example using body worn sensors, has been investigated by several researchers [17,21]. However, recognition of activities based on more subtle cues, such as user attention and intention - a far more difficult problem - remains relatively unexplored.

A rich source of information on user activity is in the movement of the eyes. The paths that our eyes follow as we carry out specific activities also reveal much about the activities themselves. This is particularly true for activities with very specific eye movements, such as reading. Reading is a pervasive activity, e.g. on computer screens at work, advertisements and signs in public, and books read at home or while travelling. Thus information on a person's reading activities can be a useful indicator of his daily situation as well as a gauge of task engagement and attention. Attentive user interfaces could comprise the current level of user interruptability or provide assistance to people with reading disabilities by automatically magnifying or explaining words or context in the text (for example see [15,10]).

J. Indulska et al. (Eds.): Pervasive 2008, LNCS 5013, pp. 19–37, 2008.

We propose Electrooculography (EOG) as a novel measurement technique for recognition of user activity and attention in wearable settings. EOG, in contrast to well established vision-based eye tracking, is measured with body-worn sensors, and can be implemented as a wearable system. Although requiring facial skin contact, we believe EOG electrodes can be designed to be relatively unobtrusive, such as through integration into spectacles. A compact on-body device can then be used to process the incoming EOG signals.

The primary aim of this research is to assess the feasibility of recognising reading activity in different daily situations using wearable EOG. The wider goal of this is to gain insight into the potential of EOG for activity recognition. The specific contributions of the work are (1) an experiment involving data collection of subjects reading text while travelling to and from work, (2) a new method for saccade detection as a basis for reading recognition, and (3) an analysis of reading classification using string matching and Hidden Markov Models (HMMs).

The aim of our experiment is to capture reading in transit during different mobile situations. Despite the unavoidable fact that subjects wore sensing equipment on their faces, we took particular care to ensure that the chosen scenario - reading while travelling to and from work - was as realistic as possible. This scenario involved a continuous sequence of daily activities such as sitting at a desk, walking along a corridor, walking along a street, waiting at a tram stop and riding a tram. We recorded an 8 subject, ground truth annotated dataset, totalling nearly 6 hours of recordings - half of which involved reading.

Our work makes use of a new algorithm for detecting saccade features in EOG signals using Wavelet decomposition. Inspired by the typical characteristics of EOG signals during reading, we carry out a preliminary investigation into three different classification algorithms: a string matching algorithm on the horizontal saccade features; a discrete HMM also using the horizontal features; and a mixture of Gaussian HMM using the denoised signals from both horizontal and vertical EOGs. Our best result over all datasets was obtained using the string matching algorithm. Our main finding is that reading can be detected regardless of whether the subject is sitting, standing or walking, and in a variety of indoor and outdoor situations.

1.1   Related Work

In a recent work, Logan *et al.* aimed at recognising common activities in a "real world" setting using a large variety and number of common sensors such as wired reed switches, RFID tags and infra-red motion detectors in the environment [9]. They discovered that reading was one of the most difficult activities to detect and concluded that for covering all types of physical activity in daily life, additional sensors and improved algorithms need to be found.

All previous attempts to recognise reading have been based on vision to record eye movements. With the goal of building a more natural computer interface based on user activity, Campbell *et al.* investigated on-screen reading recognition using infra-red cameras to track eye movements [4]. The approach used was subject independent, robust to noise and had a reported accuracy of 100%. However, the system required that each subject's head was kept still using a chin rest.

In a later work, Keat *et al.* proposed an improved algorithm to determine whether a user is engaged in reading activity on a computer monitor [8]. Using an ordinary video camera placed between the subject and monitor, 10 subjects were asked to read an interesting text from a list of preselected articles. The subjects were explicitly asked to undertake other types of common computer-related activities such as playing computer games or watching video clips during the course of the experiment. Using user-dependent training, they achieved an average reading detection accuracy of 85.0% with a false alarm rate of 14.2%. However, to ensure correct detection of gaze direction, subjects were required to face the screen throughout the experiments.

Motivated by the goal of improving reading skills for people with reading disabilities, Sibert *et al.* developed a system for remedial reading instruction [15]. Based on visual scanning patterns, the system used visually controlled auditory prompting to help the user with recognition and pronunciation of words. Following the study, subjects reported that the most obtrusive part of the system was the video camera used to track eye movements.

Eye tracking using vision is a well studied field with a growing number of researchers looking at the movements of the eyes during daily activities in natural environments. Important advances are being made to the understanding of how our brains process tasks, and of the role that our visual system plays in this [7]. To assist with this work, a number of commercial trackers are available, some of which are targeted at mobile use. The most wearable of these - the Mobile Eye from Applied Science Laboratories (ASL) and the iView X HED from SensoMotoric Instruments (SMI) - both require bulky headgear and additional, cumbersome equipment to process the incoming video streams. To-date no solution for portable eye tracking exists that is convenient and unobtrusive enough to allow for unaffected physical activity.

Eye movement characteristics such as saccades, fixations and blinks, as well as deliberate movement patterns detected in EOG signals, have already been used for hands-free operation of static human-computer [13] and human-robot [23] command interfaces. All of these studies show that EOG is a promising measurement technique that can be remarkably accurate, easy to operate, reliable and can also be made cosmetically acceptable. Another interesting application is the use of EOG-based switches in a hospital alarm system which provide immobile patients with a safe and reliable way of signalling an alarm [19].

EOG-based interfaces have also been developed for assistive robots [22] and particularly as a control for an electric wheelchair [2]. These systems are intended to be used by physically disabled people who have extremely limited peripheral mobility but still retain eye motor coordination. Although both applications target mobile settings the peoples' movements are constrained and the situation therefore differs from the one investigated in this work.

For EOG to be truly unobtrusive - particularly for mobile settings - the design of novel electrodes and electrode configurations is a critical topic and still subject to research. Manabe *et al.* propose the idea of an EOG gaze detector using an electrode array mounted on ordinary headphones [11]. While this placement might reduce the problem of obtrusiveness, it raises two other issues - namely, low signal-noise ratio (SNR) and poor separation of horizontal and vertical components. In another work, Vehkaoja *et al.* made electrodes from conducting fibres and sewed them into a head cap [18]. As yet the device is still to be evaluated in operation.

2 Eye Movement Analysis

2.1 Wearable Electrooculography

The eyes are the origin of a steady electric potential field. This can be detected in total darkness and even while the eyes are closed. It can be described as a fixed dipole with its positive pole at the cornea and its negative pole at the retina. The magnitude of this corneoretinal potential (CRP) is in the range of 0.4–1.0 mV. It is not generated by excitable tissue but is rather attributed to a higher metabolic rate in the retina. This potential difference is the basis for a signal measured between two pairs of surface electrodes placed in periorbital positions around one eye, the so-called Electrooculogram.

If the eyes move from the centre position towards one of these electrodes, the retina approaches this electrode while the cornea approaches the opposing one. This results in a change in the potential - the EOG signal - which can be used to track eye movements. The movement is split into horizontal and vertical signal components reflecting the discretisation given by the electrode setup.

2.2 Eye Movement Characteristics

To be able to take advantage of the typical characteristics of eye movements during reading, it is important to understand its two main types, namely saccades and fixations.

Saccades: Humans do not look at a scene in a steady way. Instead, their eyes move around and locate interesting parts of the scene to build up a mental "map" representing it. The main reason for this is that only a very small central part of the retina, the fovea, can sense in high resolution. The fovea has a very narrow field of view and in order to be able to see a wider scene, the eye must move constantly. The simultaneous movement of both eyes in the same direction is called a saccade. This is the fastest movement of any external part of the human body. The peak angular speed of the eyes during a saccade reaches up to 1000 degrees per second while lasting from about 20 to 200ms. The amplitude of a saccade is the angular distance that the eye needs to travel during a movement. For amplitudes of up to about 60 degrees, the duration of a saccade linearly depends on the amplitude. But beyond this, the velocity of the saccade remains constant and the duration of the larger saccades is no longer linearly dependent on the amplitude.

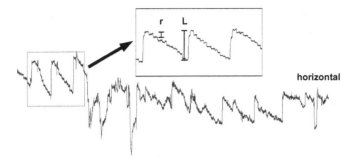

Fig. 1. Example signal from the horizontal EOG component with a reading segment in detail. The reading signal was denoised and baseline drift removed and shows typical large left (L) and small right (r) saccades occurring during reading.

Eye movements during reading are characterised by a typical sequence of small and large saccades: First, sequences of small saccades occur while the eyes move over the words in a line of text. A large saccade is observed when the eyes move back to the beginning of the next line of text. Figure 1 shows how both of these types of saccade look in the horizontal part of an EOG reading signal.

Fixations: Fixation is the static state of the eye during which gaze is held upon a specific location. Humans typically alternate saccadic eye movements and fixations. However, visual fixation is never perfectly steady and fixational eye movements can also occur involuntarily. The term "fixation" can also be referred to as the time between two saccades during which the eyes are relatively stationary. Reading involves fixating on successive locations within a line but also across a page to reach different sections of the text.

2.3   Baseline Drift

Baseline drift is a slow signal change mostly unrelated to the actual eye movements but superposing the EOG signal. Baseline drift has many possible sources as for instance interfering background signals, electrode polarisation [6] or physical influences such as varying contact pressure of the electrodes. In a four electrode setup as used in this study, baseline drift can also be different for the horizontal and vertical EOG signal components.

Baseline drift poses problems on the various types of eye movement: For saccades, the difference between start and end can be assumed to be drift-free, as saccades are performed in a very short period of time. Only signal segments before and after a saccade can become subject to changes caused by baseline drift. During periods of smooth pursuit movements it is difficult to distinguish baseline drift from actual eye movement; similarly for fixations drift alters the EOG signal in a way that can be indistinguishable from that of a slow eye movement.

Several approaches to remove baseline drift from electrocardiogram signals (ECG) have been proposed in recent literature (for example see [16,5]). As ECG shows repetitive characteristics, some of the algorithms perform sufficiently well at removing baseline drift from these signals. However, they perform worse for signals with non-repetitive characteristics such as EOG. Thus the development of robust algorithms for baseline drift removal is still an active topic of research.

3   Data Collection

The experimental setup devised in this work was designed with two main objectives in mind: (1) to record eye movements using EOG in an unobtrusive manner in a real-world setting, and (2) to evaluate how well reading can be recognised using EOG for persons in transit. We defined a scenario of travelling to and from work containing a semi-naturalistic set of reading activities. It involved subjects reading text while engaged in a sequence of activities such as sitting at a desk, walking along a corridor, walking along a street, waiting at a tram stop and riding a tram.

3.1   Experimental Procedure

Subjects were asked to follow two different sequences: A first calibration step involved walking around a circular corridor for approximately 2 minutes while reading continuously. The second sequence involved a walk and tram ride to and

Table 1. Scenario of travelling to and from work. This was repeated 3 times for each subject: Once as a baseline measurement without reading and twice with subjects reading interesting texts. The total time per scenario averaged around 17 minutes: 6 min. indoors, 10 min. outdoors and 4 min. on tram).

Average Time (min:sec)	Activity
00:00	Start synchronisation gesture
00:10	Sit at desk (on 3rd floor, indoors)
01:00	Walk to lift
01:10	Stand and wait for lift
01:40	Take lift to ground floor
02:10	Walk to exit
02:40	Walk to tram stop (outdoors)
04:40	Wait at tram stop
07:00	Ride the tram down a stop
08:00	Wait at tram stop (outdoors)
11:00	Ride the tram up a stop
12:00	Walk to entrance (outdoors)
14:00	Walk to lift (indoors)
14:30	Stand and wait for lift
15:00	Take lift up
15:30	Walk to office
16:00	Sit in comfortable chair
17:00	End synchronisation gesture

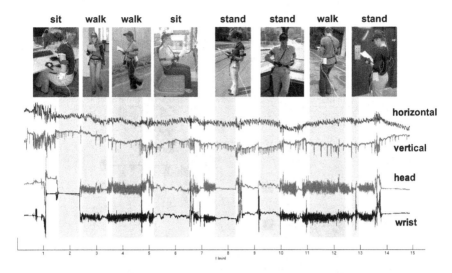

Fig. 2. Experimental procedure involving a sequence of semi-naturalistic reading activities including sitting at a desk, walking along a corridor, walking along a street, waiting at a tram stop and riding a tram. The figure also shows the corresponding horizontal and vertical EOG signals as well as acceleration data from the head and the right wrist of one complete dataset.

from work (see Table 1). This sequence was repeated in three runs: The first run was carried out as a baseline case without any reading task. This was both to accustom the subjects to the route, but also to provide a reasonable amount of *NULL* data - which contributed to the objective of obtaining a realistic dataset. In two subsequent runs the subjects were asked to read a text throughout. Between each run the subjects rested for about 5 minutes. The total experiment time for each subject was about one hour. At the end of each experiment, the subjects were asked on their experiences on the procedure in a questionnaire.

In contrast to a previous study [4] we opted to allow a free choice on reading material. Only two conditions were made: (1) that the material was text-only, i.e. no pictures and (2) that subjects only chose material they found interesting and long enough to provide up to an hour's worth of reading. Thus the type of text, its style as well as page and font size could be chosen to each subject's personal preference. Our objective was to induce a state where readers were engrossed in the task for the relatively long recording time, thus allowing us to gather realistic data without having to coerce subjects. A further benefit was that if subjects were engrossed in the task, they would be less likely to be distracted by other people.

We were able to collect data from 8 subjects - 4 male and 4 female - between the ages of 23 and 35. (Originally there were 10 subjects, but 2 had to be withdrawn due to recording problems resulting in incomplete data.) Most of the experiments were carried out in well lit, fair to cloudy conditions with two exceptions: One of the male subjects was recorded at night where we had to rely on street lights while walking around outdoors. Another male was recorded

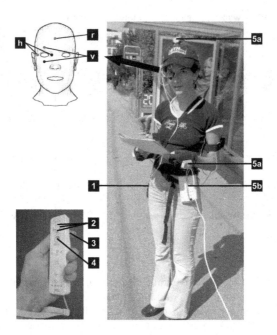

Fig. 3. Experimental setup consisting of five EOG electrodes (h: horizontal, v: vertical, r: reference) and the Mobi (1). The bottom figure shows the wireless Wii controller used for annotating the ground truth with three thumb control buttons (2), the reading trigger button (3) and a button for labelling special events (4). Also shown though not used in the current work are three Xsens motion sensors on the head and on the back of both hands (5a) and the XBus Master (5b).

in rain where an assistant had to hold an umbrella over the subject to protect the sensors and reading material. However, as neither of the datasets showed a decrease in signal quality, both were used for the analysis.

Annotation of Ground Truth. Each subject was tailed by an assistant who annotated both the subject's current activity (sitting, standing, walking) and whether he was reading. For this level of detail (is the subject's eyes on the page or not) the assistant had to monitor the subject from a close proximity - but without being so close as to cause a distraction. For this purpose we used a wireless controller from Nintendo, the Wii Remote (see Figure 3). Using the Wii's thumb control buttons "up", "down" and "right", the assistant could annotate the basic activities of standing, sitting and walking. In parallel, the trigger button was held down whenever the subject appeared to be reading and released when he stopped. A fifth button was used to annotate special events of interest, such as when the subject passed through a door and while entering or leaving the tram. All other buttons were not used and disabled to not interfere with the labelling.

Eye Movements. For EOG data collection we used a commercial system, the Mobi from Twente Medical Systems International (TMSI), which was worn on a belt around each subject's waist (see Figure 3). The device is capable of recording a four-channel EOG with a joint sampling rate of 128Hz and transmitting aggregated data to a laptop carried by an assistant via Bluetooth.

The data was collected using an array of five electrodes positioned around the right eye (see Figure 3). The electrodes used were the 24mm Ag/AgCl wet ARBO type from Tyco Healthcare equipped with an adhesive brim to stick them to the skin. The horizontal signal was collected using one electrode on the nose and another directly across from this on the edge of the eye socket. The vertical signal was collected using one electrode above the eyebrow and another on the lower edge of the eye socket. The fifth electrode, the signal reference, was placed away from the other electrodes in the middle of the forehead.

Physical Activity. One of our objectives for future work is to analyse the correlation of reading activities with physical movement and posture. Though beyond the focus of this current work, for completeness we include a short description of the additional recording setup. Briefly, this included MTx sensor nodes from XSens Technologies containing 3-axis accelerometers, magnetic field sensors and gyroscopes positioned on each subject's head as well as on the back of their hands (see Figure 3).

Unfortunately, the MTx system performed poorly using its bluetooth connection and so we were forced to use a wired connection. This was the only physical connection between the subject and assistant. Care was taken throughout by the assistant to ensure that the trailing wire did not interfere or distract the subject.

Data Recording. All recorded data was sent to a laptop in the backpack worn by the assistant. Data synchronisation was handled using the Context Recognition Network (CRN) Toolbox (see [1] for details). We made two extensions to the toolbox: the first was a reader to process and synchronise labelled data from the Wii Remote controller; the second extension was to implement a "heartbeat" component that provided audio feedback to the assistant on whether the toolbox was running and recording data, thus providing instant notification of device failures. The addition of the "heartbeat" was particularly useful as it allowed the assistant to concentrate on labelling and observing the subjects rather than continually disturbing the procedure by checking the recording status.

4   Continuous Recognition Methods

The methods in this work were all implemented offline using MATLAB. However, with a view to a future online implementation on a wearable device, the algorithms were chosen to keep computation costs low. In this section we first describe the signal processing steps required for removing noise and baseline drift, and for extracting saccade information. We then describe three algorithms we use for classification: string matching (STR), discrete HMM (D-HMM) and mixed Gaussian HMM.

Noise and Baseline Drift Removal. In a parallel work we evaluated algorithms for baseline drift removal and integrated them into a general artefact compensation framework for EOG signals [3]. There, we adapted a wavelet packet approach originally proposed for ECG signals [16]. First, the data is stripped of high frequency noise using a simple median filter. The algorithm then performs an approximated multilevel 1-D wavelet decomposition at level nine using Daubechies wavelets on the horizontal signal component. The reconstructed decomposition coefficients then give a baseline drift estimation. Subtracting this estimation from the original signal finally yields the corrected signal with reduced drift offset.

Saccade Detection and String Encoding. Both the string matching and the D-HMM algorithms rely on the detection of saccades in the horizontal component of the reading signal. For this purpose we developed the so-called *Continuous Wavelet Transform - Saccade Detection* (CWT-SD) algorithm, and applied it to the de-noised, baseline drift removed, horizontal EOG signal [3]. The CWT-SD first computes the continuous 1-D wavelet coefficients from the signal at scale 20 using Haar wavelets. A saccade is detected for all samples where the absolute value of the corresponding coefficient vector exceeds a threshold.

To keep the algorithm simple, the string encoding for this initial work only uses the horizontal component of the signal[1]. The saccade detection is run twice using two different threshold values: T^s_{sac} represents small saccades, such as jumps between words during reading; and T^L_{sac} represents large saccades, such as those observed during an end of line "carriage return". The resulting sequence of large and small saccades together with their direction are then encoded into a string using characters according to the following scheme:

- "**L**": large saccade to the left
- "**R**": large saccade to the right
- "**l**": small saccade to the left
- "**r**": small saccade to the right

An example of an encoded reading segment is shown in Figure 4.

4.1   String Matching

Of all the algorithms presented here, string matching is computationally the most simple. It can be considered a light-weight approach, using only simple arithmetic, and can be easily adapted to a future online implementation, for example on a wearable device.

The matching is performed by moving a prototype string, representing a typical reading segment, over the signal string encoding, character by character. In each of these steps, the Levenshtein distance between the string template and the current signal string is calculated. The Levenshtein distance between two strings is given by the minimum number of operations needed to transform one string into the other, where an operation is an insertion, deletion, or substitution of a single character.

---

[1] Our future work will be based on 2D encoding using both horizontal and vertical information.

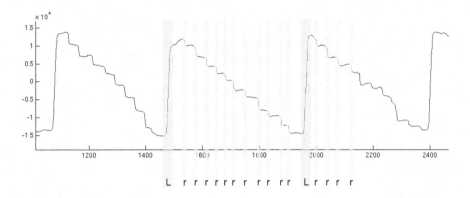

L   r r r r r r r   r r   r r   L r r r   r

Fig. 4. Horizontal EOG reading signal and corresponding string encoding

The algorithm then applies a threshold T_{ed} on the Levenshtein distance vector to separate the two classes "reading" and "not reading". This threshold defines how tolerant the classification is towards relative error in the edit distances. As this method does not yet adapt the string template to the signal while calculating the distances, it is sensitive to fluctuations in the number of small saccades. This results in a high number of false insertions. To counter this we slide a majority vote window W_{str} across the event-based output classification to "smooth" the final result.

4.2   Hidden Markov Models

Hidden Markov Models are probabilistic models used to represent non-deterministic processes in partially observable domains and are defined over a set of states, transitions and observations. In this work we evaluate two different implementations of HMM: discrete and mixture of Gaussian. In each we use a 2-state model. This helps to keep the computation costs low. Intuitively, the two states represent the large left saccades when the eyes move back to the beginning of a line and the saccades during word reading. The parameters - state transition probabilities, observation likelihoods and Gaussian mixture settings - are set in a training step using the Baum-Welch (*forwards-backwards*) algorithm. For classification, we recursively apply the *forward* algorithm on incoming data samples. See [14] for details on these algorithms, and [12] for the Matlab implementation we used.

HMMs with Discrete Observations. For the discrete case, we use the same character features as for string matching. First we segment the incoming data using the large left saccades as boundaries (with each saccade beginning with an "L"). This leaves us with a sub-string of saccades ("r","l" and "R") for each segment, which we then feed into the discrete HMM. Note that in this simplified model, the influence of a large right saccade, "R", which might be encountered during page turns, is not modelled explicitly. For each segment, the *forward* algorithm returns a single log likelihood value. A threshold T_{dhmm} is then applied and if the threshold is passed, the classifier returns reading, if not *NULL* is returned.

HMMs with Gaussian Observations. For the Gaussian case, we use the horizontal and the vertical EOG signal component as the observation feature space (de-noised and baseline drift removed). To avoid singularities with the implementation of the *forward-backward* algorithm, we standardise the signals by setting the variance of the entire dataset to 1. Our model is again 2 state, but with a mixture of two Gaussian probability density functions to model the observations.

At each of its steps, the *forward* algorithm outputs a log likelihood value. We then smooth the sequence of these likelihoods using a sliding mean window W_{hmm}. Finally, a threshold T_{hmm} is applied and if the threshold is passed, the classifier returns reading, if not *NULL* is returned.

5   Results

5.1   Parameter Selection and Training

Saccade Detection and String Matching. To determine the threshold parameters we applied the saccade detection algorithm using a threshold sweep on a manually cut subset of the data. On average for all subjects, this subset of data contained 15 large reading saccades plus noise and artifacts caused by interrupting eye movements. For each threshold, we counted the number of large saccades that were detected and calculated the *relative error* $(\frac{Total-Detected}{Total})$. Based on this sweep we chose the large saccade threshold at $T_{sac}^{L} = 7000$. Due to the difficulties in manually segmenting samples of small saccades, we approximated the small threshold $T_{sac}^{s} = 1500$.

The string matching parameters were evaluated across a sweep of the majority vote window length W_{str}, the distance threshold T_{ed} and a selection of different templates. In the analysis presented below, we chose to fix $W_{str} = 30$ and template "*Lrrrrrrrr*" for all subjects. Figure 5 shows an example output of the basic algorithm compared against the smoothed result and the ground truth labelling. Note the typical errors encountered: "merge" (m) when the output detects a single reading sequence where there should be two; "overfill" (o) when

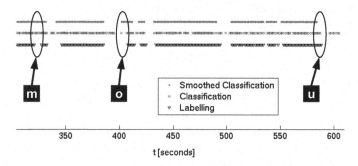

Fig. 5. Example string matching result showing the ground truth labelling, the classification result returned by the algorithm and the result after applying the smoothing filter. Also shown is an example merge (m) and an overfill (o) and underfill (u) error.

the output correctly detects reading just outside the labelling; and "underfill" (u) where the detected reading signal falls short of the labelling. These error types are explored in more detail later in this section.

HMM Training. Both HMM and D-HMM models were trained using data from the recordings of reading while walking around a corridor. Two leave-one-out training schemes were used: subject dependent only using the calibration data from the subject being tested and subject independent using calibration data only from other subjects.

We evaluated the HMMs over a sweep of the main parameters. For the mixed Gaussian HMM, we discovered that sliding window size had limited influence, and so could be fixed at $W_{hmm} = 5$ seconds.

5.2   Continuous Classification

The different methods were compared across a sweep of their main parameters: $T_{ed} = 1...10$ (in 10 steps), $T_{hmm} = T_{dhmm} = -1...-9$ (in 32 steps). The results from all subjects were then summed together. The resulting Receiver Operating Characteristics (ROC) curves are shown on the left of Figure 6. These plot true positive rate (recall) ($\frac{TP}{TP+FN}$) against false positive rate (FPR) ($\frac{FP}{FP+TN}$), where TP, FP, TN and FN represent true positive, false positive, true negative and false positive counts respectively. Best case results approach the top left corner while worst case (which means random) follow the diagonal.

The ROC clearly shows that string matching outperforms the HMMs. At its "best" ($T_{ed} = 5$), string matching returns a recall of 71.0% and FPR of 11.6% (total accuracy 80.2%). The mixed Gaussian returns a lower best-case at recall 62.0%, FPR 24.0% and accuracy 68.9% for $T_{hmm} = -3.5$ and subject independent training. The worst performing algorithm is the discrete HMM. However, both types of HMMs perform similar for the subject-dependent and the subject-independent case.

Further Analysis of String Matching. Based on these results, we chose string matching (with $T_{ed} = 5$) for further analysis. The error division diagram (EDD) of Figure 6 shows a detailed timewise breakdown of the errors. The EDD highlights typical errors that occur in continuous recognition systems - beyond the basic FP and FN categorisation. Specifically there are three classes of error that we consider. Details on how these error classes are derived is outwith the scope of the current work, but can be found in [20]:

1. The "classical" errors, such as insertion (a reading event is detected where there is none in the ground truth) and deletion (failure to detect a reading event).
2. Fragmentation and merge: *Fragmentation* errors describe when a reading event in the ground truth corresponds to several events in the recognition system output. *Merge* is the opposite: several ground truth reading events are combined into one event - see (m) in Figure 5.

3. Timing errors: *Overfill* errors are where an event in the output of the system extends into regions of *NULL*, such as in the event (o) in Figure 5. The opposite of *overfill* is *underfill* (u), in this case the event recognised by the system fails to "cover" some parts of the ground truth event.

In addition, EDDs also show the total true negative (TN) and true positive (TP) times. Using this breakdown, Figure 6 shows that 9.0% of the total time is underfill and overfill "error". These are cases where the fault may be slightly offset labelling, or delays in the recognition system. The errors that might be regarded as more serious - insertion, deletion, merge and fragmenting - account for 10.8% of the total experiment time, this is the so-called serious error level (SEL).

Reading in Different Situations. To analyse the performance of string matching for the different activity situations, we divided the data into three sets, separating sitting, standing or walking activities. Each activity represented roughly equal sized portions of the dataset (88, 98 and 95 minutes respectively). The EDDs in Figure 7 show the results of this evaluation over all subjects.

For standing, the best case result shows 72.8% recall and 9.2% FPR; for sitting the result is 73.9% recall, 13.2% FPR; and for walking it is 64.9% recall and 11.0% FPR. Looking further at the type of errors encountered, we see that both sit and walk contain large periods of underfill timing errors. Also of interest is the fact that 3.3% of the time during sit is classed as a fragmentation error.

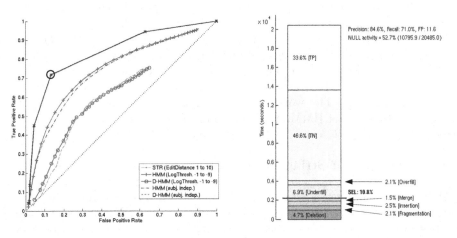

Fig. 6. Left: ROC curves showing a performance comparison between string matching (STR) over a sweep of edit distance T_{ed}, Gaussian HMMs over a sweep of log threshold T_{hmm} and discrete HMM over a sweep of T_{dhmm}. For the HMMs, both the subject-dependent and the subject-independent results are shown. Right: Detailed result for string matching with $T_{ed} = 5$ (corresponding to the point circled on the ROC curve). The EDD shows the proportion of the total dataset comprising true positives (TP), true negatives (TN), overfill, underfill, merge, insertion and fragmentation errors. Note that the proportion of negatives (*NULL*) in the dataset is roughly half (52.7%). Though overall accuracy is 80.2% ($TP + TN = 33.6\% + 46.6\%$), a large part of the errors are actually underfill and overfill timing errors.

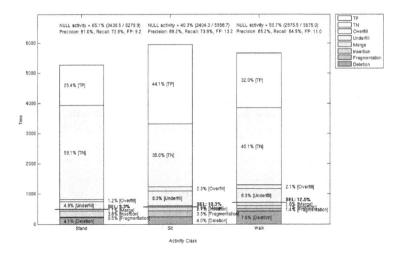

Fig. 7. Performance evaluation for reading recognition during distinct activities - stand, sit and walk - using the string matching algorithm. The EDD shows the proportion of the total dataset comprising true positives (TP), true negatives (TN), overfill, underfill, merge, insertion and fragmentation errors. Note the different distributions of *NULL* in each of these cases: 65.1%, 40.3% and 50.7% for stand, sit and walk respectively. As expected, the results for walking are slightly worse than the others, with 12.5% serious error level (SEL). Interestingly, the sit case is slightly worse than stand. This is due in part to the greater number of fragmentation errors from sit.

Table 2. Recall and FPR for each individual subject, and the median over all, using string matching. The table also shows the subjects' gender (f: female, m: male); the dataset recorded at night is marked with * while the one recorded in heavy rain with **.

	S1 (f)	S2 (m*)	S3 (f)	S4 (m**)	S5 (f)	S6 (m)	S7 (f)	S8 (m)	median
Recall [%]	25.9	65.2	92.9	83.1	47.9	89.5	71.3	85.7	**77.2**
FPR [%]	3.8	12.1	15.6	17.9	4.3	18.3	12.9	8.9	**12.5**

Results for Each Subject. The results for each individual subject show a range of differences in recognition performance using the string matching algorithm (see Table 2). The highest recall result is 92.9% (subject 3) but with a FPR of 15.5%. The worst result was for subject 1, with 25.9% recall and 3.8% FPR. This was to be expected as the raw EOG signal quality for that subject was extremely low. During the experiment recordings, the overall signal level for this subject was known to be weak and reading saccades could hardly be seen. This was also a problem for subject 5 and was most likely caused by poor electrode placement and dry skin.

What can be seen from the table, however, is that the differences do not seem to correlate to the gender of the person. Also the two special datasets recorded at night and in rain do not show marked differences, but have comparable performance to the other sets.

6   Discussion

On the Recognition Performance. Three different approaches of recognising reading based on EOG in a wearable setting have been described and investigated in this work. Among the algorithms evaluated, string matching performs best, with an overall recognition rate of 80.2% (71.0% recall, 11.6% FPR). It is interesting to note that almost half of all errors are overfill and underfill. The most probable causes of these errors are the inaccuracies of the sliding majority filter and the labelling process.

The D-HMM method does not perform well. This is probably due the lack of sufficiently descriptive features. We see in Figure 6 that it is robust to different training configurations. This indicates that the novel method of saccade detection CWT-SD, upon which both string matching and D-HMM methods are based, is fairly robust to variations in EOG signals. This is a particularly useful trait for applications where a "training" step would be inconvenient or impractical. A further advantage of the CWT-SD is that it only requires the horizontal EOG signal component and therefore only 2 electrodes. Although we strongly believe that most of the useful information lies in the horizontal component, the (as yet unused) vertical component might also contain information that in a future study could improve the performance of both methods.

Despite using both horizontal and vertical signal components and the perceived aptitude of HMMs for this type of problem, the Gaussian HMM did not produce the results that have been expected. Part of the reason for this relatively poor performance (compared to the simple string matching) might be due to the specifics of our initial implementation. It is the authors' belief that with careful selection of more descriptive features and perhaps a larger number of states, this method can be improved.

By analysing the different activity situations - reading while standing, sitting and walking - we uncover some interesting results. As expected, walking produces the worst results but only by a small margin - its serious error level is only 2.2% worse than sitting (Figure 7). Surprisingly, recognition is better while subjects stand than when they sit. We would have expected the "sit" class to perform best as this is the one with potentially the least external influences. So far, we have no satisfactory explanation for this behaviour but we plan to investigate this further in detail in future experiments.

On EOG. From this initial study we found that EOG is a robust technique for recording eye movements in wearable settings. The main advantage of the EOG-based measurement technique is the fact that, in contrast to common video-based eye trackers, the subject only has to wear relatively unobtrusive and light-weight equipment. This contributes to the subjects feeling unconstrained during the experiments and therefore allows for natural reading behaviour and unaffected physical activity.

One drawback is that EOG electrodes require good skin contact. Poor placement of electrodes was the reason for many of the problems in our work, particularly with subjects 1 and 5 (see Table 2). This problem was usually solved by removal and reattachment of fresh electrodes. The fact that these electrodes are stuck to the face can also be regarded as inconvenient. In the post-experiment questionnaire, the subjects from our study reported that they did not feel physically constrained by the sensors and wires - not even by the electrodes. However, it is clear that for long-term use a more comfortable and robust solution would be desirable.

Baseline drift is perhaps an unavoidable problem for wearable EOG recording. It is for this reason that accurate gaze tracking, for purposes such as target detection, might be difficult to achieve using mobile EOG. By analysing only the rough patterns created by eye movement, however, we can detect activities (such as reading) without the need for such pinpoint tracking.

On the Experiment. The Wii-remote proved to be a useful and unobtrusive annotation tool - and was certainly preferable to the chore of video-based offline annotation. This method is certainly subject to inaccuracies when, for example, the assistant is distracted, or when buttons are pressed and released too early or too late. However, labelling errors are an intrinsic problem especially in wearable settings and a satisfying solution has not been found yet. One possible approach for a future study could be to introduce redundancy to the labelling process: either a second assistant, or some semi-automatic solution, perhaps using additional sensors (e.g. using body movements or video-based eye tracking).

In the questionnaire, all subjects declared that they did not feel distracted by people on the street and were only partially conscious about the experiment assistant. Half of the subjects did report a feeling of unease while reading and walking. This unease could clearly be seen in the EOG signal by the occasional presence of small vertical saccades during reading - indicating whenever a subject looked up to check the way ahead.

Obviously reading while walking can be a dangerous activity, however this does not detract from the fact that many people actually do it. The other half of our subjects found no problem with reading and walking - they all claimed to have occasionally read long texts (a book, newspaper or scientific paper) while in transit. It is more common for people to read shorter texts while walking, for example advertisements, timetables, etc., and this would be an interesting scenario for future study. Because such reading sequences are usually very short, the recognition methods and also the labelling scheme would probably have to be adapted.

Ideally, the most natural scenario would have involved recordings over a period of weeks or months. This would allow us to better study the general reading behaviour of our subjects - and to open up interesting questions regarding daily reading habits. Unfortunately, the battery life and reliability of our recording equipment limited recordings to a few hours. Therefore, the main improvement concerning the experimental setup is to develop a wearable EOG device which does not impose these restrictions but allows for robust long-term eye movement recordings. This would also include an investigation of how to apply dry electrodes, e.g. by integrating them into spectacle frames, as they are more convenient for everyday use than wet electrodes stuck to the skin. Another interesting question is how dry electrodes would influence the quality of the signals and recognition performance.

7   Conclusion

Our work has shown that wearable EOG is a feasible approach for recognising reading in daily-life scenarios and is robust across an example set of activities for different subjects. This raises the question of whether different reading behaviours and attention levels to written text can be detected automatically. A "reading detector" could enable novel attentive user interfaces which take into account aspects such as user interruptability and level of task engagement.

Given appropriate hardware, EOG offers the potential of long-term eye movement recordings. The movement patterns the eyes follow in daily routine reveal much about what people are doing - as well as what they intend to do. With growing interest in activity recognition as a topic within pervasive computing, this information may prove extremely relevant. In the future, eye movements may be used as a new sensing modality, providing access to the underlying cognitive processes not available with current sensing modalities.

Acknowledgements

This work was part funded by the EU Intermedia project.

References

1. Bannach, D., Kunze, K., Lukowicz, P., Amft, O.: chapter Distributed Modular Toolbox for Multi-modal Context Recognition, pp. 99–113 (2006)
2. Barea, R., Boquete, L., Mazo, M., Lopez, E., Bergasa, L.M.: EOG guidance of a wheelchair using neural networks. In: Proceedings. 15th International Conference on Pattern Recognition, 2000, Barcelona, Spain, vol. 4, pp. 668–671 (2000)
3. Bulling, A., Herter, P., Wirz, M., Tröster, G.: Automatic artefact compensation in EOG signals. In: EuroSSC 2007: Adjunct Proceedings of the 2nd European Conference on Smart Sensing and Context, October 23–25 (2007)
4. Campbell, C.S., Maglio, P.P.: A robust algorithm for reading detection. In: PUI 2001: Proceedings of the 2001 workshop on Perceptive user interfaces, pp. 1–7. ACM Press, New York (2001)
5. Chouhan, V.S., Mehta, S.S.: Total removal of baseline drift from ECG signal. In: International Conference on Computing: Theory and Applications, ICCTA 2007, March 2007, pp. 512–515 (2007)
6. Gu, J.J., Meng, M., Cook, A., Faulkner, M.G.: A study of natural eye movement detection and ocular implant movement control using processed EOG signals. In: Proceedings 2001 ICRA. IEEE International Conference on Robotics and Automation, 2001, vol. 2, pp. 1555–1560 (2001)
7. Hayhoe, M., Ballard, D.: Eye movements in natural behavior. Trends in Cognitive Sciences 9, 188–194 (2005)

8. Keat, F.T., Ranganath, S., Venkatesh, Y.V.: Eye gaze based reading detection. In: TENCON 2003. Conference on Convergent Technologies for Asia-Pacific Region, October 15–17, vol. 2, pp. 825–828 (2003)

9. Logan, B., Healey, J., Philipose, M., Tapia, E., Intille, S.: chapter A Long-Term Evaluation of Sensing Modalities for Activity Recognition, pp. 483–500 (2007)

10. Maglio, P.P., Matlock, T., Campbell, C.S., Zhai, S., Smith, B.A.: Gaze and Speech in Attentive User Interfaces, p. 1 (2000)

11. Manabe, H., Fukumoto, M.: Full-time wearable headphone-type gaze detector. In: CHI 2006: CHI 2006 extended abstracts on Human factors in computing systems, pp. 1073–1078. ACM Press, New York (2006)

12. Murphy, K.P.: The HMM toolbox for MATLAB (1998), http://www.ai.mit.edu/~murphyk/software/hmm/hmm.html

13. Qiuping, D., Kaiyu, T., Guang, L.: Development of an EOG (electro-oculography) based human-computer interface. In: 27th Annual International Conference of the Engineering in Medicine and Biology Society IEEE-EMBS 2005, September 01–04, pp. 6829–6831 (2005)

14. Rabiner, L.R., Juang, B.H.: An introduction to hidden Markov models. IEEE ASSP Magazine, 4–16 (January 1986)

15. Sibert, J.L., Gokturk, M., Lavine, R.A.: The reading assistant: eye gaze triggered auditory prompting for reading remediation. In: UIST 2000: Proceedings of the 13th annual ACM symposium on User interface software and technology, pp. 101–107. ACM Press, New York (2000)

16. Tinati, M.A., Mozaffary, B.: A wavelet packets approach to electrocardiograph baseline drift cancellation. International Journal of Biomedical Imaging Article ID 97157, 9 pages (2006)

17. Van Laerhoven, K., Gellersen, H.-W., Malliaris, Y.G.: Long-term activity monitoring with a wearable sensor node. bsn 0, 171–174 (2006)

18. Vehkaoja, A.T., Verho, J.A., Puurtinen, M.M., Nojd, N.M., Lekkala, J.O., Hyttinen, J.A.: Wireless head cap for EOG and facial EMG measurements. In: 27th Annual International Conference of the Engineering in Medicine and Biology Society IEEE-EMBS 2005, September 01–04, pp. 5865–5868 (2005)

19. Venkataramanan, S., Prabhat, P., Choudhury, S.R., Nemade, H.B., Sahambi, J.S.: Biomedical instrumentation based on electrooculogram (EOG) signal processing and application to a hospital alarm system. In: Proceedings of 2005 International Conference on Intelligent Sensing and Information Processing, January 4–7, pp. 535–540 (2005)

20. Ward, J.A., Lukowicz, P., Tröster, G.: Evaluating performance in continuous context recognition using event-driven error characterisation. Location- and Context-Awareness, 239–255 (2006)

21. Ward, J.A., Lukowicz, P., Tröster, G., Starner, T.E.: Activity recognition of assembly tasks using body-worn microphones and accelerometers. IEEE Transactions on Pattern Analysis and Machine Intelligence 28(10), 1553–1567 (2006)

22. Wijesoma, W.S., Kang, S.W., Ong, C.W., Balasuriya, A.P., Koh, T.S., Kow, K.S.: EOG based control of mobile assistive platforms for the severely disabled. In: IEEE International Conference on Robotics and Biomimetics (ROBIO), pp. 490–494 (2005)

23. Yingxi, C., Newman, W.S.: A human-robot interface based on electrooculography. In: 2004 IEEE International Conference on Robotics and Automation Proceedings ICRA 2004, April 26–May 1, vol. 1, pp. 243–248 (2004)

Pressing the Flesh: Sensing Multiple Touch and Finger Pressure on Arbitrary Surfaces

Joe Marshall, Tony Pridmore, Mike Pound, Steve Benford, and Boriana Koleva

Mixed Reality Lab, University of Nottingham, NG8 1BB, UK
{jqm,tpp,mpp,sdb,bnk}@cs.nott.ac.uk

Abstract. This paper identifies a new physical correlate of finger pressure that can be detected and measured visually in a wide variety of situations. When a human finger is pressed onto a hard object the flesh is compressed between two rigid surfaces: the surface of the target object and the fingernail. This forces blood out of the vessels in the fingertip, changing its colour slightly, but systematically. The effect is visible to the naked eye and can be measured using techniques from computer vision. As measurements are made of properties of the hand, and not the target surface, multiple-touch and pressure sensing can be added to a range of surfaces - including opaque, transparent, smooth, textured and non-planar examples - without modification of the underlying physical object. The proposed approach allows touch sensing to be fitted to surfaces unsuitable for previous technologies, and objects which cannot be altered, without forfeiting the extra range of expression of pressure sensitivity. The methods involved are simple to set up and low cost, requiring only a domestic-quality camera and a typical computer in order to augment a surface. Two systems which exploit this cue to generate a response to pressure are presented, along with a case study of an interactive art installation contructed using the resulting technology. Initial experiments are reported which suggest that visual monitoring of finger colour will support recogntion of push events.

1   Introduction

Touch sensitive surfaces, such as graphics tablets, interactive whiteboards, touch screens etc. have existed for some time. Touch sensitivity, however, typically requires the surface to be enhanced with some kind of embedded electronics, or in the case of capacitive sensing on glass [1], to have electronics below the surface. Computer vision has the potential to create touch interfaces without embedding electronics in the target surface, and also to detect multiple touches. Current systems, however, are typically either unable to detect the difference between touching and moving a hand or object near the surface [2], or can only detect the presence of a finger or object next to the surface (by using cameras at right angles to the surface [3], or multiple cameras and some form of 3d disparity measurement [4,5]).

The main contribution of this paper is to identify a new physical correlate of finger pressure that can be detected and measured visually in a wide variety

J. Indulska et al. (Eds.): Pervasive 2008, LNCS 5013, pp. 38–55, 2008.

of situations. When a human finger is pressed onto a hard object the flesh is compressed between two rigid surfaces: the surface of the target object and the fingernail. This forces blood out of the vessels in the fingertip, changing its colour slightly, but systematically. Increased pressure increases the effect, up to a limit determined by the thickness of flesh on the finger. Colour change may be seen either by examining the pattern of colours in the fingernail or, if the target surface is transparent, by looking at the fingertip through the surface. When viewed through a transparent target surface, increasing pressure increases the amount of flesh from which blood is expelled, creating a larger region of paler skin. When viewed from above the hand, through the nail, increased pressure forces more blood to the base of the nail, concentrating colour there. Both these events are clearly visible to the naked eye.

In what follows we describe computer vision-based sensing methods which exploit this cue. As the approach relies on measurements of the physical properties of the hand, and not the target surface, it has the potential to add multiple-touch and pressure sensing to a range of surfaces - including opaque, transparent, smooth, textured and non-planar examples - without modification of the underlying physical object. This allows for many new items, such as stone carvings or wood, to become touch sensitive interfaces. No technology need be embedded into the target object; all that is required is that a colour camera be positioned to view the effect. The proposed method is therefore potentially highly flexible, easy to install, low cost and portable. It requires only a domestic-quality camera and a typical computer in order to augment a surface.

The proposed approach is expected to be of particular use in environments such as museums, science centres and galleries. Here, visual sensing of finger colour can allow people to interact directly with existing physical objects, or with glass cabinets containing objects of interest, without having to customise the objects or cabinets themselves. The method has benefits for installation designers, allowing museum and science centre staff to construct interactive exhibits and environments based upon their existing catalogue of objects. For example, historic tools in a countryside museum could be touched in order to trigger audiovisual material about their use. The flexibility of the approach means that exhibits could also be reconfigured easily and on a regular basis, maintaining visitor interest.

The paper is organised as follows. Section 2 briefly reviews relevant prior work, before Section 3 describes finger pressure sensing by viewing the tip of the fingernail from above. Section 4 then describes a method which uses the same visual cue, but views the hand from the rear of a transparent glass surface. The fingernail-based method was used to create an interactive art installation, in which the user was able to interact with a pressure and touch sensitive rock. This installation is presented as a case study in Section 5. A key motivation for the development of touch sensitive interfaces is the ability to detect touch events such as contact, pushes, taps, etc. Initial experiments are reported which suggest that visual monitoring of finger colour will support recogntion of push events are described in Section 6. Finally, conclusions are drawn in Section 7.

2   Prior Work

Touch sensitive graphics tablets [6] and touch screens [7] are widely available pressure sensing interfaces. The most common pressure sensitive interface in production is the laptop touch pad. Whilst these are typically used purely for on/off touch pressure, most, such as those made by Synaptics [8] also are able to detect variations in pressure. Some models, for example the Mitsubishi DiamondTouch table [9], even allow the detection of multiple touches, although not pressure.

Following a different approach, Schmidt et al. [10] used load sensors to create a touch sensitive table. In addition to touch events, they detect several contextual events such as objects being put down on a table, which is interesting as it relates to our goal of augmenting existing objects. Schmidt et al, however, cannot support interactions with objects other than moving them around on the table. This does not require additional technology in the sensed object itself, but load cells are required to be fitted at four corners of the surface. It is also limited to single touch interaction on horizontal surfaces.

Exploiting vision and related technology to create a touch detecting screen is not a new idea. Various methods have been used, such as scanning laser rangefinders [11], internal reflection inside a glass plane[12], multiple cameras and planar homographies to detect only pixels that are near the screen [5], and the visual detection of (somewhat exaggerated) finger gestures in order to detect touches on a virtual keypad [13]. These visual methods typically fail to detect pressure differences during touching, although some level of pressure sensing has been demonstrated with the internal reflection method, by using the size of the finger's contact area. The finger surface area is also used in Benko et al's multi touch table[14]. Benko et al suggest it is too innacurate to detect pushing reliably and define a special rocking gesture for clicking which their system is able to detect. The two sided LucidTouch system[15] also uses visual tracking to detect the hand position, however it uses a separate touch sensitive pad in order to to detect touches on the surface (as the vision tracking method used is unable to detect touch).

These technologies are designed for use in interactive whiteboard, wall display or table interfaces. They usually require modification of the sensing surfaces in some way, or place restrictions on the surface being monitored. They are also currently designed for completely flat user interfaces. This may be suitable when used as an interface to standard GUI style applications; however as interface designers move beyond the GUI, this may become a limitation. When augmenting existing objects, it is hard to guarantee complete flatness. Bumpy or angled surfaces may also be useful to allow tactile feedback as to where the hands are, which is commonly seen as a reason why touchscreen interfaces such as virtual keyboards have only had success in niche applications.

3   Fingernail Sensing

When the fingertip is pressed down on a surface, the blood under the nail concentrates at the bottom of the nail, and the tip of the nail becomes whiter (Fig. 1).

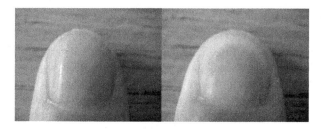

Fig. 1. Nail at different pressures

This effect is very consistent, and only requires a small amount of finger pressure for a difference to be clearly visible to a human observer. This section discusses the automatic visual detection of this cue.

The fingernail sensing system uses a basic background segmentation algorithm, followed by a contour detection operation to find the fingertips. When a finger is detected which has not moved more than a small threshold since the last frame, the image of the fingertip is examined, and the distribution of colour in the nail quantified. This reflects the pressure exerted by that finger.

Initial attempts at sensing pressure used the two parts of the nail, the tip and the bottom, and compared the colours of these to detect a change. However, the exact location of the white areas on the tip of the finger proved to vary significantly between individuals, and is also difficult to sense from any distance. For example, when viewed from 60cm with a 320x240 pixel camera, the nail is approximately 10x12 pixels in size, which means that the tip area in particular is too small. However, while the fingernail is almost uniformly coloured when no pressure is applied, two distinct colours appear on the nail when pressure is exerted. Because of this, rather than use located features on the nail, we simply take the variance of the hue of the pixels in the nail area. In order to calculate a mean hue, the hue is represented as a 2d vector, and an arctangent applied to this. Variance is calculated with an allowance for the circular nature of the hue metric.

$$MeanHue = \text{atan2}\left(\left[\sum_{1}^{n} \cos(Hue)\right], \left[\sum_{1}^{n} \sin(Hue)\right]\right)$$

$$VarHue = \frac{1}{n}\sum_{1}^{n} min((Hue - MeanHue)^2, (360 - (Hue - MeanHue))^2)$$

Initial testing has shown this metric to relate strongly to finger pressure. It is also much more detectable at a distance, and produces similar results on different fingers. Variance of the brightness of the pixels can also produce useful data in some conditions, however it is, as might be expected, extremely sensitive to illumination changes. When the finger is pressed down hue variance clearly increases, with the opposite effect visible on release. Pushing less hard produces an intermediate response. Because the blood under the skin moves back into its normal place relatively slowly, there is a natural smoothing on the release of approx 100ms, this may be useful for 'debouncing' purposes, avoiding multiple presses being detected when the finger is only pushed down once.

It is also clear that depending on lighting and individual variation, the absolute variance values alter somewhat. A floating normalisation window is therefore employed, with the value of 'pressure' detected being mapped to 0...256, by using previously recorded pressure values as a max and min. A constant minimum pressure range (mr) is used, for the case when the finger is first seen, and only a small amount of data is in the window. This avoids large random fluctuations if the finger is simply placed down and not pressed. The raw to normalised conversion is expressed as:

$$normalised_t = \frac{256 * \left(raw_t - \left(\min_{k=t-windowSize}^{k=t}(raw_k)\right)\right)}{\max\left[mr, \left(\max_{k=t-windowSize}^{k=t}(raw_k) - \min_{k=t-windowSize}^{k=t-1}(raw_k)\right)\right]}$$

This assumes that when the finger is first seen, there is no pressure on it, which is the case in typical use; even if a press is occurring the finger is first seen as the press starts. This conversion, whilst it means that no exact pressure data is available, makes push and release events clearly visible, and allows intermediate pressure values to be acquired. Normalisation is effective as long as the raw variance is altering with finger pressure. It has a compressing effect on the raw curves, which was desirable in our application (Section 5), but may or may not be suitable depending on context.

3.1   Initial Evaluation

In order to test the fingernail algorithm, a test rig was constructed, with the user's finger pushing on an electronic scale which served as a ground truth pressure gauge. The output from the scale was then video recorded along with the output from several brief sessions of pushing and releasing a single finger. The test rig was able to detect a 'weight' of 2kg (a force of approximately 19.6 Newton). In practice, this limit was not a problem, as forces outside this range proved uncomfortable to apply. The scale reported weight with a relatively slow update rate, updating at up to 4 times a second. Measurements from the visual system were taken each time the scale's reported weight changed. The system was run, and the hand moved into view until the hand tracking found the finger, and then the output was recorded for approx 50 seconds.

Single User Reliability. Once the data had been recorded, the raw hue variance data for each test session was scaled in order to make the mean and standard deviations the same as the ground truth. These normalised graphs showed a very good fit to the ground truth data, with a certain amount of clipping at the highest pressures in some tests. These results were analysed using regression analysis, which gave a P value of <0.1% for all subjects. Figure 2 shows 3 different user's normalised pressure outputs plotted against ground truth. These graphs demonstrate the ability of the algorithm to reflect several push release

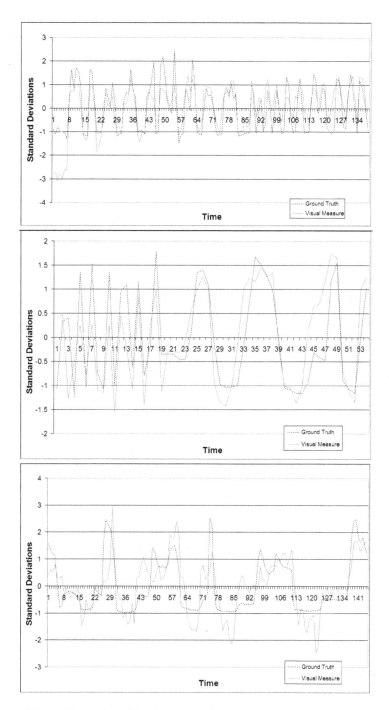

Fig. 2. Examples of Performance of Pressure Tracker over Time

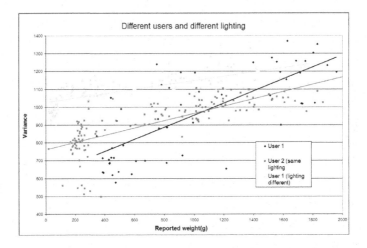

Fig. 3. The Effect of Users and Lighting on Fingertip Variance

cycles accurately. Detecting an initial push is possible, as the minimum pressure range means that an initial push will have a different profile to just touching (the first graph in figure 3 starts by just touching the surface, whereas the second and third graphs start with a push, the visual measure ramps up high straight away. The tracking works at 30 frames per second, limited by the camera frame rate, rather than any processing constraint, which is fast enough to detect quick push and release cycles.

Between User Variation and Lighting Variation. Tests were carried out on different days, in a naturally lit room. This meant that the system was exposed to some lighting variation. To quantify the possible effects of lighting variation, one user was tested on two different days, both times using the same finger.

The variation in lighting had a major effect on the raw variance values from the system, with the same user showing a significantly lower range of variances, which were also significantly higher than their previously recorded values. Multiple users in the same lighting conditions also had differences in the distributions of variance, although these were significantly less than the lighting induced variances. Figure 3 shows some examples of these effects.

These two factors mean that unless very controlled lighting is available, and a training session is undergone for each user, this method is not suitable for providing absolute pressure information, ie. it is not suitable to replace a load sensor. However, when normalised as described above, it can be employed in interfaces where a correlate of pressure, rather than true pressure, is required. It seems likely that colour-based measures can support detection of more fuzzy actions such as pressing, pressing hard, pressing softly etc., as is required in most touch based interfaces.

When Does This Work? Several factors may cause this method to fail. Firstly, nail varnish or gloves will obviously cause the system to fail, as the fingernail

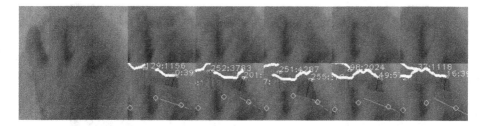

Fig. 4. Grasping and releasing an object. Each frame shows the zoomed in middle finger, and the pressure graphs next to the middle and index fingers.

cannot be seen. Secondly, if the fingernail is very brightly lit by direct sunlight, this may reflect off the nail, making it impossible to see the skin colour beneath it. This was the case during one of the test sessions, with the system failing to work until a curtain was drawn to block the bright rays of sunlight.

The method is reasonably robust to changes in finger orientation. As long as the length of the fingertip can be seen, a correlate of pressure is produced and changes in the hue varaince reflect changes in pressure. If the angle is changed during sensing however, the values can be seen to change slightly. This means that there is potential for use on non-flat surfaces, as long as the finger is not changing in angle massively during a single touch movement. A slight side effect of our simple hand tracking system is that when the fingers are clasped round an object, so the fingernails are out of view, the knuckles and what is visible of the finger above them are detected to be fingertips by the system. When the knuckles are detected as fingertips, the system still responds, as the knuckles are differently coloured to the rest of the finger, and grasping causes the ratio between the knuckles and the part of the finger that is visible to change, thus altering the variance of the detected 'fingertip' (see Figure 4) . Potentially useful data is also provided if the hand is held in the air, and the thumb is squeezed against the bottom of a finger.

4 Skin on Glass

To assess the potential of visual monitoring of skin colour to detect pressure on transparent surfaces, such as windows, glass cabinets, etc., the same approach was applied from the other direction, tracking the finger through a sheet of glass. Changes in skin colour were recorded as the finger was pressed against the glass. It was found that at the point of contact pressure was sensed reliably if normalised as described in Section 3. Intermediate pressures were again detectable, and pushing and not pushing generated distinct output profiles. Sensing through glass may be of particular value as it allows the computer and camera to be entirely enclosed, for example behind a shop window, or inside a glass case, with no exposed electronic parts. It also has an advantage over the fingernail tracking in that it is less susceptible to occlusion, which may be a problem in some uses of the fingernail method.

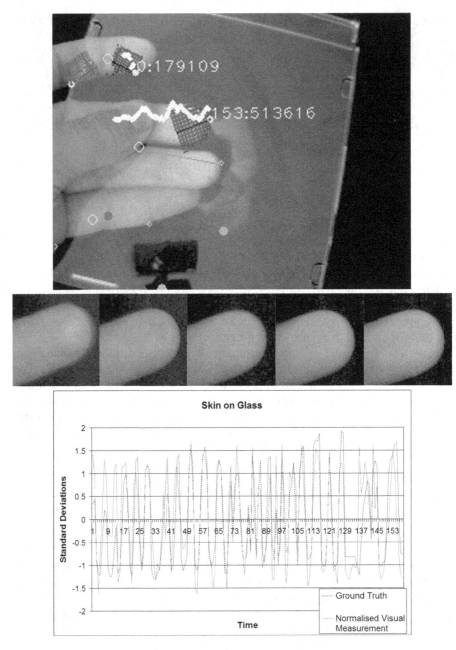

Fig. 5. Sensing pressure through glass - the line of pictures shows the fingertip over a single push sequence

This technique is, however, not quite as reliable as the fingernail-based method in one particular: until the hand is touching the glass, sensing is somewhat erratic. Further research is required, but this is probably the result of the changing distance between the glass surface and user's hand. It seems likely that the fingernail-based method is more reliable because the nail is firmly attached to the surface of the finger, so that the relationship between the fingertip and the surface through which it is viewed remains constant. In the test application, the effect is reduced by only starting to record pressure once the detected fingertip has been in the same position for 3 frames. This means that there is a delay of approx 1/10th of a second before continuous pressure readings begin. It also means that if the hand is held very still in the air in front of an interface, pressure sensing will begin, although it will only break if the hand is very slowly moved directly towards the camera, which proved hard to do in testing. An output from this sensing during two pushes on a rather dirty and reflective sheet of glass is shown in Fig. 5 (this version was tested with a black background, as skin segmentation did not prove a problem in the initial skin on glass tests). The method works well even in sub-optimal conditions. Figure 5 also shows a graph showing the comparison of the skin on glass to the ground truth measurement (as used in Figure 2 for evaluation of the fingernail tracker.) Note that this system uses an identical algorithm to the fingernail tracking, with the normalisation taking care of the smaller absolute variance values seen in this method. It is possible for a user to simply move their hand to the other side of the glass and use the fingernail tracking without any recalibration.

5   Case Study: Rock

The fingernail tracking algorithm was evaluated further in an interactive art installation called Rock. The installation presents a rock in a cage as a pet. A web camera is attached to the cage's top, and a computer and speakers are hidden under a table that the cage is on (see Fig. 6). Rock uses gestural input and audio output to mimic the personality of a small pet rodent such as a guinea pig. It is designed to have quite a timid personality and to be easily frightened. The rock is an extreme test of the behaviour of the fingernail algorithm with a large range of gestures and angles, and provides a testing ground for graceful fallback in situations where it is impossible to sense pressure.

Initially the rock makes a quiet steady heartbeat sound. When the rock is touched it responds by making animal sounds, and the heartbeat changes to signify its level of fear. Touching the rock in different ways can provoke varying responses, for example if touched gently and slowly, it is likely to make quiet purring noises and not be very scared: grabbing at the rock too quickly scares it and makes it snarl or growl.

The rock is designed as an ambient installation, to be left in a gallery or space at an event, and interacted with by people with a minimum of direction. As such, it is designed to attract people to interact with it; this takes two forms. Firstly the heartbeat sound attracts interest to the rock when it is not being interacted with. Secondly, the interaction with the rock is designed to be interesting to onlookers. The interaction is designed so that onlookers can see part of the way that the rock is being interacted with, but so that part of the interaction is

Fig. 6. The Physical Setup of the Rock

not visible to them. In particular, the finger pressure detection is used here and provides an aspect of the interaction that is unclear to onlookers, and designed to intrigue people into interacting with the rock themselves.

5.1 Technology Implementation

The single camera on the top of the cage is the only input mechanism for the rock. The camera is carefully positioned so that it can see all of the bottom of the cage. All the output comes from the speakers, which are positioned so that the sound seems to come from the bottom of the cage.

The computer detects the silhouette of a hand reaching into the cage by use of a simple colour threshold to select pixels which match the colour of the background or the rock. There is deliberately no skin colour detection, or scene based background subtraction, in order to make the system responsive to non-skin objects put into the cage (as long as they are not the same colour as the background or the rock), and also to allow the rock to be moved in the cage without breaking the background model. This makes for a very reliable and simple detection of the hand silhouette when the hand is inside the cage.

The system detects how close the hand is to the rock, and uses this over time to calculate a measure of how fast the person's hand is approaching the rock when they reach into the cage. It also attempts to find the fingertips and detect the average finger pressure on the rock over all the fingertips it can see, by using the algorithm described in Section 3.

These two measures, of approach speed, and pressure are mapped respectively into two variables, 'fear', and 'excitement'. These variables are mapped onto a set of audio samples, and audio processing filters which alter these sounds. The audio samples used were made by one of the authors, and are categorised as to how scared and how excited they sound. The audio processing effects are a mixture of time and pitch shifting, and are used in order to make the sounds sound different every time they are played rather than like a fixed set of samples. Examples of sounds that the rock may make are a low growl if it is scared but not very excited, a high pitched snarl if it is scared and excited, purring sounds if it is not afraid but not very excited and squealing sounds if it is excited and not afraid. A slight element of randomness is added into this mapping; this is designed to make the rock be mostly predictable, but to avoid letting the users be certain how it will respond to a particular gesture. The heartbeat sound continues all the time beneath the animal sounds, getting faster and louder when the rock is more scared.

5.2   Testing the Rock

The rock was exhibited at a recent digital art conference. At this event, it was placed in a corner of a corridor space, where a lot of people were passing by, as an ambient installation during the conference. This allowed us to see the rock interact with approximately 100 people, from various backgrounds including art, architecture, sound design, HCI etc. The rock was running for over 9 hours, and was very successful in this environment; the installation was awarded best paper prize.

Initially, one of the authors was with the rock, introducing it as his pet, in order to entice people to play with it. After a few people had played with the rock, this became unnecessary, as people started bringing back other people to show it. At this point, the rock became more interesting, as the explanations people were creating for its behaviour became increasingly complex and rich. At the end of the event, one of the participants was very attached to the rock and even asked if she could take the rock home. The descriptions of the rock and its personality were very varied, ranging from 'cute' to 'strange' and 'disturbing'.

There were several ways in which people interacted with the rock. Most common initial interactions were poking it, either suddenly, or gingerly reaching in to touch it. In these cases, the technology responded reliably. Once people had

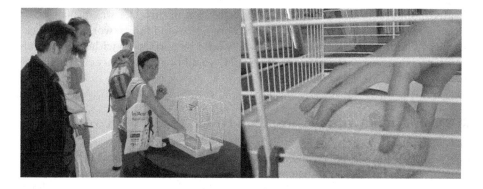

Fig. 7. Interacting with the Rock

realised that the rock was not going to bite them, they explored more complex interactions, such as stroking it (which worked as long as they didn't move their hands too fast), and grasping it. Grasping was interesting, because the effect discussed in Section 3.1 meant that the knuckles were tracked, giving a pressure signal as to how hard the rock was grasped. This meant that in this (relatively common) mode of interaction with the rock, the tracking still worked, although slightly less reliably. A few people did things such as picking up the rock from underneath, waving their hands right in front of the camera, or closing their hand into a fist when touching the rock. In these situations, the pressure tracking broke, and the rock responded to the movements using only the silhouette of the visible part of the arm, which led to slightly unpredictable responses to these particular movements; it was important in the design of the rock's 'personality' that it handled the cases when finger tracking data became unavailable, and still provided some kind of response. The unreliability when presented with these odd gestures was translated in the user's eyes to become a facet of the Rock's personality, for example as it not liking having strange things done to it.

While observing the rock, it was clear that the balance between the unpredictable nature of its response to odd actions, and the predictable response to actions such as stroking gently and holding it, formed a part of the success of the installation. The ambiguity allowed people to spot 'patterns' and create explanations, and meant that whilst people could to some extent learn things about how to control the rock, such as not to grab at it and scare it, or by using gentle touches to make it happy, they were not able to get to a level where they felt they had complete control. One important thing however is that the level of reliability was such that the 'owner' of the rock was able to demonstrate that the rock 'liked' him, and that people were able to learn how to touch it to make it likely to make 'happy' sounds.

The finger pressure sensing method was important in this installation, as it allowed a very expressive mode of interaction with the rock, but without having to augment the rock with sensors. Within the constraints of the cage, this created effectively a wireless, remotely powered, touch sensitive moveable user interface, which was made of seamless stone, with no charging connectors or battery compartments. Alternative ways to create similar effects would have created points at which the audience's suspension of disbelief was broken. For example, a pressure sensor under the rock or cage would fail to work if the rock was lifted, adding sensors to the rock itself would be hard to do without external electronics, battery compartments etc. which would break the concept of it being an organic creature.

6   Using a Bayesian Classifier to Detect Push Events

A key motivation for the development of touch sensitive interfaces is the ability to detect touch events such as contact, pushes, taps and double clicks. To provide an initial indication of the feasibility of detecting such events given colour variance data a bayesian classifier was implemented and used to detect contact

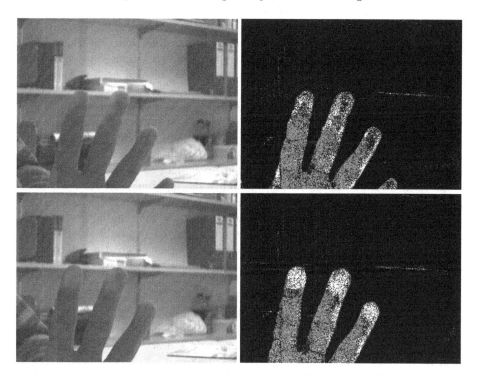

Fig. 8. Skin on glass - hand just touching glass (1), and fingers pushed against (2) - grey pixels are classified as non compressed skin, white pixels are compressed skin

between hand and surface. Colour-based detection and location of human skin is now commonplace in computer vision systems. A number of skin detection techniques have been reported [16,17,18,19], most based upon the work of McKenna et al. [16] which showed that colour spaces exist in which, for a wide range of nationalities and ethnic backgrounds, human skin is tightly clustered. The classifier to detect contact between human fingers and a target surface by identifying compressed flesh adopted a similar approach.

A camera was placed behind a sheet of non-reflective, smear-resistant glass, providing a clear view of the user's hand as s/he interacted with the other side of the surface. The challenge was to use the resulting colour images to recognise the differences between:

- the normal, i.e. uncompressed, skin seen when the user's hand is in view, but not in contact with the glass;
- the compressed flesh that appears when the user touches the glass surface;
- the environment behind the user.

All experiments were carried out in an office/laboratory environment, so the background comprised arbitrary coloured objects. Some of these objects were approximately skin-coloured, but no other people (i.e. no additional real skin) was allowed into the field of view. Six individuals, of mixed age, sex and race took part. Each was first asked to press his/her hand flat onto the glass panel to provide easily identifiable examples of contact, and then invited to press, tap, or otherwise touch the glass at will. Two minutes video of each subject was captured and analysed off-line.

Following [16,18], the well-known hue-saturation-intensity (HSI) colour space was employed throughout. The hue (H) and saturation (S) values associated with human skin are known to cluster tightly, though intensity (I) varies widely. Bayesian classification was used to separate the three classes (uncompressed skin, compressed skin, non-skin) identified above as shown in Fig 8. Models, in the form of approximations to probability density functions for each class were first constructed from manually identified training data. This classification of pixels into tip and non-tip could potentially allow for reliable detection of touch pressure, by detecting the size of the compressed region of the fingertip. Raw colour values were examined to determine whether or not the information required was present, before any features or summary statistics were computed, in the base image data.

When trained on data from an individual's hand, bayesian classification was found to be effective. Contact between fingertip and glass could be reliably detected. However when applying the same algorithm to multiple users, by pooling training data to produce composite colour models, it was found that the variation between users was often equal to the difference between compressed and non-compressed skin for a single user. The experiment therefore demonstrated that variations in individuals' skin colour can better support automatic detection of touch events. As a result, further work on event classifiers will exploit time-based measurements of individuals' finger pressure, similar to those we have used for smooth pressure sensing.

7   Conclusions

We have demonstrated a new correlate of finger pressure which can be measured visually using standard equipment in a wide variety of circumstances. The method detects compression of the fingertip by monitoring changes in the colour of either the skin or the fingernail. Table 1 summarises the main strengths and weaknesses of this approach to pressure sensing.

Table 1. Benefits and Challenges of using Fingertip sensing

Strengths	Weaknesses
No modification of tracking surface required	Viewpoint and occlusion
Quick, easy and cheap setup	Lighting
Smooth pressure sensing	Relies on hand tracking
Potential to support automatic detection of touch events	Not fully 3D
Wide range of surfaces can be augmented	
Multiple touch	

The method allows the addition of an extra dimension of expressiveness to previous vision based hand & finger sensing systems, without requiring complex addons such as multiple cameras, or augmenting the surface in any way. It is inherently multiple touch, as it measures a feature of the pressure on the finger, rather than the pressure on the surface below the finger. It is quick, easy and cheap to setup. The technique extends the range of materials and surfaces available to standard pressure sensing, by allowing touch pads to be created from any relatively firm surface which is visible to a camera. As demonstrated in the Rock example, fingertip pressure sensing does not even require a flat surface, working well when given a bumpy surface. Though further development is required to produce a working system, the colour measures employed here clearly have the potential to support detection of a variety of touch events.

The approach is, like many vision-based techniques, potentially sensitive to camera viewpoint and occlusion and is unlikely to work well in some extreme lighting conditions (very bright sunlight & darkness). It is also reliant on the hand tracking working correctly in order to function; if the tracking fails, no pressure sensing can occur. It is not fully 3D, as it cannot sense pressure when the whole of the fingers are out of view, so applications have to be designed to degrade gracefully if this is a possibility, however it provides useful data in a large range of situations, such as when the fingertips themselves are out of view, as long as the grasping hand and the rest of the fingers are still visible to the system. Also, whilst it works on a wider range of surfaces than most current systems, there clearly is a limit to what surfaces it can work reliably on, for example surfaces such as cushions, gels or liquids will all be impossible to augment.

7.1   Potential Applications

Whilst this technology clearly may be useful in tabletop displays and other common multi-touch interfaces, it has most to offer in the creative, museum and educational sectors. The ability to augment an existing, everyday, physical object would be of particular use to museum, science centres, exploratoria and other similar places where a hands-on approach is encouraged. The skin on glass method of touch sensing provides a useful extra mechanism for objects which are in cabinets and unable to be directly touched. In this situation the hardware would be fully enclosed within the cabinet, which may be an advantage. Augmenting unexpected surfaces in this way has proven interesting and surprising to users in our case study; it is envisaged that in a museum setting, being able to augment the object rather than having a separate interactive display may provide a more direct and engaging experience.

As well as being useful for currently impractical applications, the techniques reported here make pressure and touch sensing available with a significantly lower setup time than existing methods and require no custom equipment; the Rock takes approximately 5 minutes to install and uses a cheap domestic webcam and PC. This means that the proposed method has the potential to be incorporated in mass market entertainment software, for example this could enable innovative interfaces such as used on the Nintendo DS touch screen game console to be created on a larger scale for home users (For example in Warioware Touched, users have to 'rub out' on-screen pictures, stroke dogs, whack moles etc. by using touch gestures).

7.2 Future Work

The work described here has demonstrated the potential of visual monitoring of skin colour to reflect finger pressure in a range of situations. Topics for future research include:

– investigation of alternative methods of capturing changes in skin colour, and their relation to finger pressure. In particular, though the current method is reasonably robust to changes in finger orientation it is not invariant under such changes.
– evaluation of the usability of the approach in a wider variety of application domains and scenarios, focusing on the creative, museum and educational sectors
– techniques for the automatic recognition of single and multiple touch events and gestures. As well as the gestures commonly used in GUI applications such as clicking and dragging, the work with the Rock demonstrated the possibility of detecting more unusual gestures such as grasping and stroking, which may be of interest for those designing applications which do not fit a standard desktop paradigm.With the addition of a more sophisticated hand tracker, it may be possible to further improve the tracking, by tracking touch actions using hand shape as well as fingertip cues, although it is not currently clear whether these may require per-individual training.

Acknowledgements. This work is funded by the EPSRC.

References

1. Synaptics Capacitive sensing technical description, http://www.synaptics.com/technology/tcps.cfm
2. Bérard, F.: The magic table: Computer-vision based augmentation of a whiteboard for creative meetings. In: IEEE workshop on Projector-Camera Systems (2003)
3. Morrison, G.D.: A cmos camera-based man-machine input device for large-format interactive displays. In: SIGGRAPH (2007)
4. Malik, S., Laszlo, J.: Visual touchpad: A two-handed gestural input device. In: ACM Int. Conference on Multimodel Interfaces (2004)
5. Wilson, A.: Touchlight: An imaging touch screen and display for gesture-based interaction. In: Int. Conf. on Multimodal Interfaces (2004)
6. Wacom Graphics tablets, http://www.wacom.com
7. MagicTouch Touch screens, http://www.magictouch.com
8. Synaptics Touch pads, http://www.synaptics.com
9. Dietz, P., Leigh, D.: Diamondtouch: A multi-user touch technology. In: UIST (2003)

10. Schmidt, A., Strohbach, M., van Laerhoven, K., Friday, A., Gellersen, H.W.: Context acquisition based on load sensing. In: Borriello, G., Holmquist, L.E. (eds.) UbiComp 2002. LNCS, vol. 2498, Springer, Heidelberg (2002)
11. Strickon, J., Paradiso, J.: Tracking hands above large interactive surfaces with a low-cost scanning laser rangefinder. In: CHI (1998)
12. Han, J.Y.: Low-cost multi-touch sensing through frustrated total internal reflection. In: UIST (2005)
13. Tosas, M., Li, B.: Virtual touch screen for mixed reality. In: Proc. of ECCV Workshop on HCI, (2004)
14. Benko, H., Wilson, A.D., Baudisch, P.: Precise selection techniques for multi-touch screens. In: CHI (2006)
15. Wigdor, D., Forlines, C., Baudisch, P., Barnwell, J., Shen, C.: Lucidtouch: A see-through mobile device. In: UIST (2007)
16. McKenna, S., Gong, S., Raja, Y.: Face recognition in dynamic scenes. In: British Machine Vision Conference (1997)
17. Yang, J., Fu, Z., Tan, T., Hu, W.: Skin color detection using multiple cues. In: Int. Conference on Pattern Recognition (2004)
18. Zarit, B.D., Super, B.J., Quek, F.K.H.: Comparison of five colour models in skin pixel classification. In: ICCC International Workshop on recognition, analysis and tracking of faces and gestures in Real-Time systems (1999)
19. Störring, M., Andersen, H.J., Granum, E.: Skin colour detection under changing lighting conditions. In: 7th Symposium on Intelligent Robotics Systems (1999)

MAKEIT: Integrate User Interaction Times in the Design Process of Mobile Applications

Paul Holleis and Albrecht Schmidt

Pervasive Computing and User Interface Engineering
University of Duisburg-Essen, Germany
paul@hcilab.org, albrecht.schmidt@acm.org

Abstract. Besides key presses and text input, modern mobile devices support advanced interactions like taking pictures, gesturing, reading NFC-tags, as well as supporting physiological and environmental sensors. Implementing applications that benefit of this variety of interactions is still difficult. Support for developers and interaction designers remains basic and tools and frameworks are rare. This paper presents a prototyping environment that allows quickly and easily creating fully functional, high-fidelity prototypes deployable on the actual devices. With this work, we target the gap between paper prototyping and integrated development environments. Additionally, new interaction techniques can be significantly faster or slower to use than conventional mobile user interfaces. Hence it is essential to assess the impact of interface design decisions on interaction time. Additionally, the presented tool supports implicit and explicit user performance evaluations during all phases of prototyping. This approach builds on the original as well as extensions of the Keystroke-Level Model (KLM) which allows estimating interaction times in early phases of the development with a simulated prototype. An underlying state graph structure enables automatic checks of the application logic. This tool helps user interface designers and developers to create efficient and consistent novel applications.

1 Introduction

Mobile phones have become a ubiquitous computing platform outnumbering desktop computers. A large portion of current mobile phones offer means for third parties to develop custom software for them. Most notably, there are JAVA ME, Symbian OS, and the Windows Mobile platform. Modern phones provide rich ways for interaction, reaching from colour screens, audio output, and keyboard input to gestures, cameras and audio capture. Additionally, more and more such devices include sensors, e.g. for acceleration (e.g. Samsung SGH-E760, Nokia 5500, iPhone). Interaction with physical objects using barcodes is a common feature in many phones and some devices can read smart labels (e.g. the near field communication, NFC, reader in the Nokia 6131). Furthermore, phones can be extended with external sensors connected via Bluetooth, e.g., for GPS, step counting and ECG.

These basic technical capabilities enable developers and interaction designers to create novel interactive experiences using mobile phones in domains such as data access via physical artefacts, context-aware applications and mobile health applications.

J. Indulska et al. (Eds.): Pervasive 2008, LNCS 5013, pp. 56–74, 2008.

Although APIs exist that allow accessing sensor values, it is often a challenge to create sophisticated user interfaces that exploit all these capabilities. In comparison to conventional interaction techniques, there is little established knowledge about how to build compelling applications using these new means. Hence developments often rely on trial and error which can be costly. In most cases, novel experiences require functional prototypes to be built and evaluated. We believe that prototyping and tool support is essential to make this process efficient. Development environments support the implementation on source code level and to some extent the design of the interaction flow (e.g. the NetBeans Visual Editor[1]). There is, however, a lack of tools that support prototyping interactive mobile applications that make use of advanced interaction techniques using internal and external sensors.

Often, the design process is based on paper prototypes after which the actual implementation is started. It is commonly agreed, however, that at least partially working prototypes are essential to efficiently develop interactive applications and to convey and assess new interaction concepts. Including users in this phase is very important for pervasive systems, as show several examples in a special issue on rapid prototyping in IEEE Pervasive Computing [1].

We address the gap between low-fidelity paper prototyping and actual implementations. The MAKEIT framework (short for *Mobile Applications Kit Embedding Interaction Times*) is used to create functional, high-fidelity prototypes for mobile devices supporting advanced interaction techniques. In particular, we focus on the need to easily create and change applications while at the same time providing assistance in keeping projected end user interaction times low. We contribute:

- an integrated development environment for hi-fidelity prototyping of mobile phone applications creating a code framework for the final implementation
- an underlying model based on state graphs validates parts of the application logic and can detect flaws in the navigational structure and suggest alternatives
- an integrated model to estimate task completion times early in the design without needing to deploy a prototype on the actual target hardware platform.

2 Creating Prototypes of Mobile Phone Applications

This section describes the architecture and interface of the development environment that allows quickly and simply prototyping applications for mobile devices. A common screen based interaction process is reflected in the way the MAKEIT tool chain helps designing applications. A state graph data structure represents the possible flow of actions in a program. By creating such a state graph, the designer lays out the functionalities supported by the application, the possible sequences of user actions and the resulting visual behaviour of the mobile device.

Furthermore, the developer is able to adorn defined transitions between states with additional non-functional parameters, such as KLM parameters. The framework then offers the possibility to retrieve predictions of the interaction time of any possible (i.e. defined) sequence of actions by a potential user. These predictions are based on a modelled, deployed version of the application running on a real phone. The system is

---

[1] NetBeans IDE, Mobility Pack *http://www.netbeans.org/kb/articles/mobility.html*

designed to support a variety of interaction techniques as listed below. Some common ones are directly integrated, whereas others can be customized and easily added. For some of those interactions, a detailed discussion can be found in the paper of Rukzio et al. about physical mobile interactions [2].

- **Media Capture.** Capturing audio and video and storing or potentially analysing it is used in many applications.
- **Visual Markers.** Using the camera in the phone, interactions based on markers can be supported. This includes simple recognition of barcodes but also advanced augmented reality applications (e.g. Rohs [3]).
- **Proximity.** Based on proximity, actions can be triggered or application behaviour changed. One example is scanning for Bluetooth devices, e.g. Nicolai et al. [4].
- **Gestures.** Accelerometers built into phones offer many opportunities for interaction based on movements and gestures.
- **RFID/NFC.** To capture the identity of a tagged object, RFID and NFC (near field communication) provide easy means. To implement physical mobile interactions the identifier can then be linked to further content.
- **Location.** Using GPS or cell IDs are widely used to get information about the user's location enabling location based interactive applications; see for example the MediaScapes project by Hull et al. [5].
- **External physiologic sensors.** ECG, pulse rate and oxygen saturation are some examples of sensors that can be used to create applications acting on and to body signals (e.g. Nuria et al. in [6]).

The overall concept is similar to that of paper prototyping. Typical steps are to start with a picture of a mobile phone with an empty screen and then to simulate pressing a hotkey, prepare another picture and draw content into the screen. Next to allow the user to touch an NFC tag and prepare another screen. This process is continued until all important states have been prepared. This is exactly the way this tool works, eliminating the difficulty of keeping track what picture belongs to what action.

2.1 Generating the Application Behaviour

One part of the user interface presented to the developer comprises an image of a modern mobile phone featuring the standard set of keys and an empty display (see Figure 1). The next iteration of the tool will feature skins for specific sets of mobile devices with different screen sizes and button layouts. All keys can be pressed using the mouse generating events to the framework running behind the visualisation. Next to the phone are several buttons that can be used to simulate advanced interactions with the phone. Examples include simple gestures, taking a picture or touching an RFID tag. Since not all of those actions are supported by all phone models and new types of interactions are added as we speak, this list of buttons is automatically generated from an XML properties file, which can easily be extended. Using the controls provided by the mobile phone and the action buttons, the developer can implement actions with a simple click. This triggers a dialog in which the interface designer or developer can specify what the contents of the display will be after the specified action has been executed. It can be a simple string or a URL/filename of a web page or an image which is scaled to fit on the screen. Simple drawings can also be made in place, which is especially useful for people working with graphic tablets.

By repeatedly linking actions to visual elements, a linear sequence of screens can be created which represents the execution of a task in an application; however the majority of applications are more complex requiring richer application logic. This motivates the introduction of the state graph in the following section.

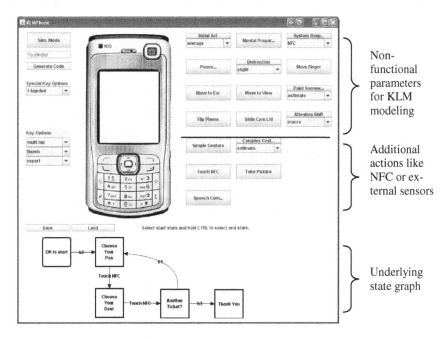

Fig. 1. The keys in the simulated phone and additional interaction techniques can be chosen and the content of its display is controlled by the system

2.1.1 The State Graph

To be able to have a representation of the application logic, we define a state graph $G = (S, A)$. The states of the application that is currently designed represent the set of nodes S. There is an edge $a \in A$ between two nodes S_1 and S_2 if and only if an action has been defined that lets the application switch from S_1 to S_2. All edges are directed from their source to their target node. An edge is also called a *transition* since it describes the transition from its source to its target state. One node can be the source or target of several actions. However, the graph must fulfil the following constraints:

- **Disambiguation Property:** All actions $(a_1, a_2, ..., a_n)$ with the same state S as source must be pairwise disjoint. This means that from one state there cannot be transitions fired by the same action to two different states. Otherwise it would not be clear which strategy should be employed to choose the transition that should be used when the according action is executed. This also implies that between two states no two edges have the same action, eliminating redundancy.

- **Start State Property:** There is a distinguished state called the start state S_S that is a source node, i.e. not the target of any transition. This represents the state the application is in right after it has been started.
- **Reachability Property:** For all states S, there must be a path $p(S_S, S)$. A path $p(S_a, S_b)$ is defined as a sequence of edges that connects S_a with S_b, i.e. a path $p(S_a, S_b)$ exists, if and only if there is an n and edges $(a_0, a_1, ..., a_n)$ with $a_0 = (S_a, S_0)$, $a_1 = (S_0, S_1)$, ..., $a_n = (S_n, S_b)$ and $n \in \{0, 1, ...\}$. Thus, there is no state that cannot be reached from the start state by a sequence of transitions. Note that this is not the same as saying that every node must have an incoming edge (just imagine 2 connected components that are not connected to each other).

An interesting aspect in the system is that these properties are ensured by construction and thus cannot be violated. Thimbleby and Gow [7] describe several aspects that can be derived from an underlying graph model. The diameter, e.g., represents the task that needs the highest number of actions. The Reachability Property implies that there is no unused state. Weaker properties like the reachability of one state from one or more others (e.g. a standby mode) can be checked as described later. The graph can also be used to check whether all actions can be undone and how costly this is.

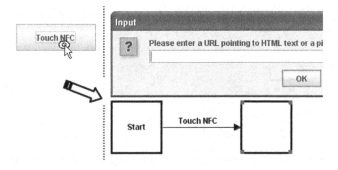

Fig. 2. When triggering the 'Touch NFC' action, a new state is generated and a transition from the start state is added labeled with the action's name

2.1.2 Building the State Graph

MAKEIT provides a visualisation of the set of possible states as well as the transitions triggered by actions. A further part of the user interface presents the state graph described above. Initially, this is only the start state showing an empty phone screen.

The moment an action is triggered, a new node is created in the state graph and an edge is added between the current node and the new node. The edge is labeled with the name of the action (Figure 2). A dialog prompts the developer for the content of the new screen. The new node is automatically selected, indicated by coloured dots in the corners of the rectangle representing the screen of the mobile phone. After specifying the content of the new screen, the next action will continue the sequence and generate another node. This can be used to quickly create a vertical prototype that allows executing defined functionality in detail whereas not all functions that the application will provide when finished are supported.

The creation of the state transitions is not restricted to a linear sequence. When a node of the state graph is selected with the mouse, the defined contents will be updated on the virtual phone's screen and the application is brought into this state. Demonstrating an action can then be done in whatever state the application has been set to. This adds the possibility of leaving a state through different actions. One possible application is to implement different ways to reach the same goal, e.g., press a key, make a gesture or touch a tag. Figure 3 shows the application that the key '8' is used to browse through a list and another one, '5', to activate the selected item.

Adding edges to nodes, i.e. transitions to states, is only limited by the number of different actions allowed for the present state. Following the Disambiguation Property (two edges with the same source node must have different associated actions), transactions that already exist for a specific state cannot create a new edge. Instead, if such an action occurs, the existing transition is fired and the system changes the current state to the target of the edge. Such inputs from the user do not change the state graph. In this way, any sequence of tasks that has already been designed can be walked through and tested. This highly adds to the utility since people often go back to the beginning to recap the task at hand.

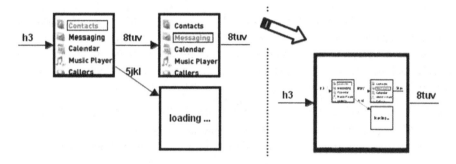

Fig. 3. Reducing the number of visible states by condensing several nodes

2.1.3 Merging States

One of the potential problems with state graphs is that the number of states can grow rapidly. The maximum number of states succeeding a node is only bounded by the number of different actions allowed for this node. However, in our analysis, we found that most applications, besides dynamic screens that are much better implemented in code anyway, do not need many screens. In addition, there are several possibilities to reduce the number of states. One is to **condense** several nodes into a super-node, as is often done to visualise and work with large hierarchical graphs (see Figure 3).

A visually as well as semantically clear approach is based on the observation that applications often return to the same state after different sequences of interactions. Situations in which this occurs afford the merging of equal states. In the case of the visualisation chosen for this project, this means that it must be possible to combine two nodes (shown in Figure 4). We define a **merging** operation $merge(S_1, S_2)$ of two nodes S_1 and S_2 in the same graph as follows:

- for all nodes X such that an edge $e(S_1, X)$ exists, add an edge $e'(S_2, X)$ and copy the properties of e to e'; edges $e(X, S_1)$ is treated analogously
- delete S_1 (and all edges adjacent to S_1, i.e. edges that have S_1 as source or target node) from the graph

The merge operation is defined and executed only if step 1 does not add an edge which would conflict with the Disambiguation or the Root Node Property. By definition, the Reachability Property is not affected by any merge operation.

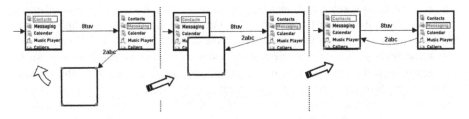

Fig. 4. Merging two states by simply moving one node (empty) over another

Merging states can introduce cycles to the graph which theoretically drastically complicates the automatic calculation of a visually pleasing and planar layout of the state graph. However, in practice, the graphs seem to be fairly easy to layout since most cycles are very short. By moving the nodes in the view, the graph can also be manually adjusted anytime. More importantly, this feature is absolutely essential for many situations like the aforementioned use of a list of items. Scrolling up and down through a list repeatedly generates the same states.

The example in Figure 5 shows a list that can be scrolled by pressing number keys '2' and '8'. The '5' key selects the current item and switches to a state that handles the selected option in the list. This selection method can easily be replaced by, e.g., a gesture without inducing any other change in the graph. This example also illustrates that a node can be the target of several edges as the according state can be reached in

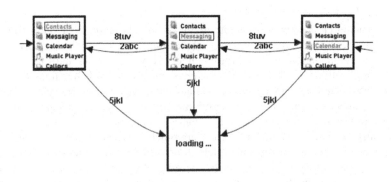

Fig. 5. Designing list scrolling. When an item is selected (key '5'), the same state is reached. Coding will then be employed to show a dynamic screen.

several ways. It also keeps the number of states low by having only one state ('loading ...') that is responsible for displaying a reaction to the selected option. One could also split the node way that pressing the execution key will lead to a different state for each menu entry. Any combination of the two approaches is also possible.

Another example for having several transitions to one state is an exit or error state. Applications may have a dedicated exit state reachable from several points in time. Anytime an error occurs, an error state can be reached which offers fallback solutions. The approach can in general *not* be used, however, for a generic message state (presenting, e.g. a message like "This action is not yet supported") since in most cases the application flow should return to the state that initially triggered the message. This would contradict the Disambiguation Property.

We emphasise at this point that neither the state graph itself nor the tools to create it claim or want to be a full-fledged visual programming language. The idea is to leave the handling of difficult tasks to the places where it can be done best: the source code of the mobile application. By omitting any data exchange between states, the available design space is clearly defined.

The design space of the applications that can be created by using this mechanism only is clearly limited. For example, information cannot directly be passed from one state to the next, and it is not known which steps led to a certain state. Although features like that could be added by using a richer data model, the simplicity of the chose approach suffices to quickly start with and concretely test ideas and different interface and interaction designs. In [8], we added touch sensors to the standard keypad of a mobile phone. Using the MAKEIT framework, we were able to quickly develop and test several variations of a contact list showing preview information when the selection button is touched or an image gallery with zooming by touching. The contact list application with a list of four names, e.g., needs only 4x2 states.

Our approach is to separate components through a defined and communication layer. We deliberately decided for this approach and not for plug-in components, as it is more appropriate for distributed pervasive systems.

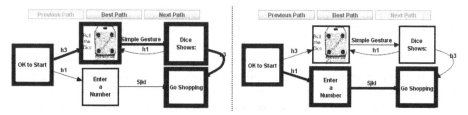

Fig. 6. Two paths from the node 'OK to Start' on the left and the 'Go Shopping' node on the right are highlighted

2.2 Analysing Tasks During Application Creation

One of the important aspects in designing applications is to see and understand if and in what ways a task can be executed with the proposed design. During the design of the flow of the application, i.e. the creation of the state graph, a path finding algorithm can be employed. Selecting a start state S_S and an end state S_e, an algorithm finds all possible paths $p(S_S, S_e)$. Remember that a path is defined as a sequence of directed edges that connects one node with another. In this case, a path also may not contain a node or edge more than once. This implies that a path cannot contain a cycle and that the number and length of all paths is bounded by the number of nodes and edges in the graph. Note that a path does not necessarily exist between two arbitrary nodes. On the contrary, paths ending in the root node appear rarely and some nodes will even be sinks, i.e. not the source of any edge in the graph, e.g. a dedicated exit state. Those sinks can only be the target node of the last edge in a path, but no paths will start from those. However, the Reachability Property of the graph dictates that there will always be a path $p(S_S, X)$ from the root node to any other node X in the graph.

In the graph visualisation, a path is shown by highlighting its edges as well as the source and target nodes of these edges with thick lines (Figure 6). As said, there are potentially several paths between the selected states which can all be browsed and highlighted. Beside the mere sequences of actions leading to the desired state, the paths can be used to provide an analysis of non-functional properties. This (and why there appears a 'Best Path' button in Figure 6) is explained in the following sections.

2.2.1 Adding Non-functional Properties

Non-functional properties are all characteristics that are not directly concerned with the semantics of an element. In the case of the transitions in the state graph, this means attributes of an action like the time necessary to execute it, the effort needed, the pleasure generated, or the privacy affected by it. In the following, we concentrate on interaction time characteristics and build on knowledge about the Keystroke-Level Model (KLM) introduced in the first sections of this paper.

We have already seen that by triggering actions defined in the state graph, a task can be sequentially walked through and the state of the mobile phone is updated accordingly. To be able to additionally incorporate actions necessary to use the operator model of KLM, this part is elaborated in the user interface. After a version of the application has been defined using the state graph, the user can switch to simulation mode. The user interface is then extended with several additional actions. These KLM actions can also be easily configured and new elements can be added whenever new types of interaction are added in future phones using a property file.

In simulation mode, the root node is automatically selected. All actions can then be executed as defined in the state graph. Whenever an action is triggered that has no according edge defined in the state graph, the action is ignored and a warning is issued. Furthermore, the additional actions in this mode can be used at any time, in any state, in any order. Most of these actions have been introduced in one form or the other in the introductory section on the mobile phone KLM we developed. Table 1 gives a quick overview over the meaning of some of the standard operations, see [9]. The general idea of those operations is that additional information about how a task is executed can be gathered and stored. The mentioned actions mostly concentrate on interaction times. Additional options can be specified to calculate interaction times for standard key presses (one thumb or two finger input, multi-tap or predictive methods like T9, novice, average or expert typist).

As a simple example scenario, consider a poster that displays some products and advertises a URL. The task is simply to browse to this given website. A designer

Table 1. Some non-functional operations supported in simulation mode

Initial Act (average, self initiated, ...)	Time necessary to retrieve and look at the phone
Mental Preparation	Time to mentally prepare for the next action
System Response	The time the system needs for computations
Pause	Interrupt for some amount of time
Distraction (slight, strong)	Actions done while being distracted are slowed down on average by some factor
Move to Ear / Move to View	Time needed to move the phone between a state looking at the screen and one close to the ear
Point Somewhere (estimate, Fitts' Law)	Time needed to move the phone to a specific point (e.g. to touch a tag there)

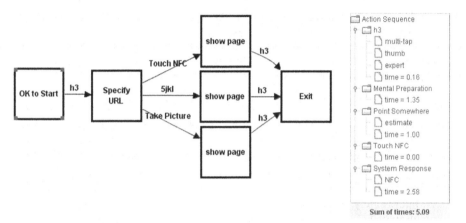

Fig. 7. *Left*: Three different ways of specifying a URL: using an NFC tag entering the URL with the keypad, and detecting a marker using the camera. *Right*: Actions for the NFC interaction from the graph shown on the left.

thinks about implementing one or more of the following three options: enter the URL by hand, take a picture of a marker on the poster or use the phone's NFC capabilities to retrieve the URL from a tag embedded in the poster. A simple state graph that is generated in less than two minutes is shown in Figure 7, left. Since one exit state has been attached to all three interaction methods, selecting the start and the end state will list all three interaction paths.

As next step, the details for each path can be demonstrated. In simulation mode, a separate window shows the action sequence of the currently highlighted path. Here, from the start state, the hotkey 'h3' is pressed and the system prompts for the URL. The act of touching an NFC tag requires four steps: a unit of mental preparation is set to account for the time needed to prepare oneself for the interaction. In the rather coarse modelling of the KLM, this also includes the vague focussing on the target tag (action 'Mental Preparation'). Next, the movement of the phone is done (action 'Point Somewhere'). After the actual reading of the tag ('Touch NFC'), the system needs some time to process that tag ('System Response (NFC)'), see Figure 7, right.

2.2.2 Analysing the Augmented Path

The times for the described actions in the example are: hotkey (0.16 seconds), mental preparation (1.35), pointing (1.00), touching after pointing (0.00), system response time (2.58). This results in a total interaction time of roughly 5 seconds. Those demonstrated non-functional actions (mental preparation, pointing, touching, system response) have now been added to the respective transitions in the graph and need not be re-entered for future calculations of those transactions. The analysis of the other two interaction techniques results in 9.9 seconds (for a short URL of 25 characters such as those produced by TinyURL[2]) and roughly 6 seconds (for a visual marker). Each path between start and end state can be associated with a usability measure like the time the execution of this path would take in real life. The system can then find the 'Best Path' which will be the interaction method that takes the least amount of time. In this example, the algorithm would suggest the NFC interaction. It should be noted at this point that several of the operations like reading NFC tags always result in the same sequence of KLM operators. Those additional non-functional actions can automatically be retrieved and saved. Missing steps, e.g., an anticipated period of mental preparation, this can be easily added to the transition in question.

It is also important to see that the action sequence, augmented with interaction information, can not only be used to compare one sequence to another. We recently used the mobile phone KLM to model different ways of interacting with physical posters. A graphical widget/browser based phone application was tested against one that used NFC tags embedded in the poster. Surprisingly, the model predicted that the text input variant would be considerably faster (2 minutes instead of close to 3 minutes). We ran several tests with different users and found the model to remarkably correct. Interestingly, all users had the false subjective impression that they had been faster with the NFC version. A representation of the modelled sequence of actions is extremely useful to find the parts of the interaction sequence that are responsible for long interaction times. In the scenario under consideration, one of the problems identified was the time lost with checking the feedback of the phone after each single reading of a tag. A proposed solution is that detailed feedback is only given after a series of interactions. This can easily be changed in the state graph of the application by removing the intermediate feedback states and adding a later feedback state.

2.3 Initial User Feedback

To get initial feedback on the prototyping and analysis process, we demonstrated the system to and carried out interviews with 4 experts working in different areas of developing and evaluating pervasive computing applications as well as a couple of students of a user interface master's class. We saw that the main user interface make people try to interact with it at once. Even without initial explanations, they were capable of grasping the idea of generating application logic on the fly. It became obvious that it was not clear that more than linear sequences of actions could be created. After finding out that it is possible to interact with the state graph itself, most people intuitively began to merge states by moving nodes. Actually demonstrating and building the KLM model proved to be more difficult and indicated some necessary refinement in the user interface. All participants saw the

---

[2] TinyURL service, http://www.tinyurl.com

advantage that the interaction is graphical and that arbitrary screen content could be used. Although the more programming oriented users initially asked for more complex visual control structures, they also agreed that shifting complex things to the source code makes sense. They valued the possibility to quickly create prototypes and provide the starting point for more advanced applications without being hindered to implement whatever they want. The environment helps people concentrate on what they can do best: designers can create and test ideas and interaction sequences and developers focus on the coding. The fact that screens could also be drawn in some separate graphics program was valued especially be the design oriented people since when creating paper prototypes, they often assemble images and text using their own tools.

3   Implementation

3.1   EIToolkit – General Underlying Toolkit Support

Implementing applications using many different programs, hardware and software platforms, communication protocols, and programming languages is, in general, difficult. To counter that, we started the open source project EIToolkit[3], a component-based architecture in which each component is represented by a proxy-like object called a 'stub'. These stubs translate messages between a general communication area to the specific protocol of the devices and back. Any component can then register to listen to messages directly addressed to it or broadcast to all. This enables exchanging components on the fly. The system also allows changing the protocol of the messages on a per component basis. The toolkit currently supports a simple proprietary format over UDP or TCP as well as OSC[4] and RTP[5]. The last two are widely used protocols for audio and multimedia systems and streams. Several microcontroller platforms can be connected through existing stubs as well as over a serial connection. Sample stubs are available, e.g. for the media player Winamp or direct MIDI output.

Independently of the MAKEIT application, we integrated KLM semantics into an EIToolkit module. It is practically platform-independent and can be used remotely. Specific control messages choose the type of KLM like for mobile phones or those for another set of controls. After that, queries are sent to the stub presenting information of an action. For a key press of the "2abc" button on a mobile phone, a sample message might contain the ID 'KEY_NUM2' and parameters '1 thumb', 'expert'. The KLM stub browses its known elements and, if available, sends an answer containing a time value back to the sender of the query, e.g. the MAKEIT system.

3.2   Data Structure of the State Graph

For the implementation of the state graph and its visualisation, we adapted code from the Gravisto graph visualisation toolkit[6]. The data structure provided by the toolkit has been adopted without changes. Beside the basic features of graphs with nodes and

---

[3] Embedded Interaction Toolkit (EIToolkit) Project Page, *http://www.eitoolkit.de*

[4] Open Sound Control, OSC: *http://www.cnmat.berkeley.edu/OpenSoundControl/*

[5] Real-time Transport Protocol, RTP: *http://www.cs.columbia.edu/~hgs/rtp/*

[6] Gravisto, Graph Visualisation Toolkit, *http://gravisto.fmi.uni-passau.de*

edges, it provides a mechanism to attach arbitrary data to any of the graph elements (nodes and edges) present in a graph. This data is stored in the form of hierarchically structured attributes of various primitive and composed types. This structure is extremely helpful when several pieces of data have to be managed by the graph. As will be seen in a later section, the graph elements do not only have to store the states and contents of the display, but also much information about the transitions between states. Data about the type of action that triggered the transition as well as detailed information about timing and other model parameters are saved with each edge.

The creation and manipulation tools of Gravisto were adopted to ensure the concordance with the graph properties and to enable additional features like merging states. Also, some visual features have been added to correctly display state images. Gravisto also enables saving a generated state graph to file in a standard graph data format called GraphML[7] which is based on XML and supports custom attributes. A saved state graph can then be loaded without data loss at any time and the connection to the mobile phone visualisation in the user interface is immediately updated.

3.3 Code Generation and Extensibility

The whole semantics of the application is stored in the state graph. Nodes contain the data for states and the contents of the screens. Edges represent actions from one state to another and store information about non-functional parameters associated with transitions. One framework component transforms the state graph into a MIDlet, i.e. a Java program for the J2ME[8] virtual machine which can be compiled, moved to, and run on many modern phones. The created application often needs to be complemented with code changes, e.g. for dynamic screen contents. Thus, project files for the NetBeans Mobility Pack are generated and the program can be extended, compiled and downloaded to a phone and tested there. The manifold features of an integrated development environment can thus be exploited, e.g., syntax highlighting, choosing the target platform and debugging. Of course, this also eases making quick alterations and additions to the code itself like implementing the dynamic content of a screen.

Basically, the state graph is implemented as a set of conditional statements. If an event named a occurs in a state S, the state T is loaded if there is a transition (S, T) labelled with the action a. This is (although not optimal) a common and easily understandable way to program such applications. In a mobile phone application, each screen is represented by an object. We use a custom sub-class of the J2ME class Canvas to write code that can load and draw images as well as render text to the screen. It is a low-level implementation of a screen and can also receive key events from the phone's keyboard (standard keys are treated differently from hotkeys).

Beside number/letter key presses and hotkeys, the current implementation of the framework supports advanced interactions using external Bluetooth sensors/devices as well as those supported by the PMIF framework described by Rukzio et al. in [10]. If interactions with NFC tags have been defined, for instance, code is generated that waits for and acts on the reading of a tag. It is possible to add an ID to the edge representing this action. This transition then is fired only if the ID of the read tag is identical. However, for more complex data stored in the tag, the specification of the seman-

---

[7] GraphML, file format for graphs, *http://graphml.graphdrawing.org*
[8] J2ME, Java Micro Edition Platform, http://java.sun.com/javame/index.jsp

tics is done directly in the code following the principle that the visual design mode should not be overloaded with functionality. The next iteration of the tool will also be able to take into account differences in hardware and software access, e.g. which libraries are used. Currently, the implementation supports S60 phones.

For any other actions – and this includes actions that the user has specified through the properties file – stubs are generated that leave room for the developer to fill it with the concrete code that implements the action. The code generation component uses several template files that contain method stubs and code excerpts. If necessary, these templates can be adapted and extended to work for new interaction techniques like those presented in [8] mentioned before.

The 3 steps to add such touch functionality to the MAKEIT system are:

- add a new action to the transitions.xml file ("Touch")
- add initialization code and specify templates for the code that will handle the new events; specifying, e.g., "$btKeyOn$" will then automatically be replaced by code found in a file "btKeyOn.template"
- add code that shall be executed in the template files, e.g. "btKeyOn.template"

4 Related Work

4.1 Rapid Prototyping Environments

The first of three categories of related works subsumes all kinds of rapid prototyping and authoring frameworks, tools, or methods that can be used to quickly create proto-types of applications to convey or test ideas. The NetBeans visual designer for mobile device applications follows a state based approach as does our project. However, it is restricted in three aspects. First, it is strictly based on the available components like text boxes and lists and does not allow quickly adding free drawings and designs. It also does not directly support advanced interaction methods like RFID tags and cannot integrate non-functional properties like KLM parameters. Focusing on those projects that support in some way or the other mobile or embedded devices as well as more advanced types of interaction (e.g. those requiring sensor input), some shall be mentioned as representatives with no claim for completeness.

The ECT toolkit (Greenhalgh et al. [11]) provides a consistent shared data space across distributed devices. Programming can be done using a visual paradigm. Another recently introduced tool that follows a state-based paradigm is d.tools (Hartmann et al. [12]), implemented as a plug-in of Eclipse. A blueprint of the device to be prototyped can be drawn and widgets representing hardware buttons, sliders, displays, etc. are placed on the drawing. In another editor, a state graph can be created that specifies into which state the device should be transferred on a specific action (like a button press). To our knowledge these projects do not use underlying models that can be exploited for consistency checks or interaction time predictions. In contrast to MAKEIT which generates code that directly and independently runs on a phone, such approaches can suffer from the fact that the prototype depends on the presence of a PC as common gateway and data store. The same holds for several important and useful physical interaction toolkits like the Phidgets [13] that provide readymade hardware UI building blocks for low cost sensing and control implemented as independent components connected to a computer by USB. The Stanford iStuff toolkit [14] offers another set of elements like buttons, microphones and speakers with a communication layer based on a publish-subscribe mechanism. VoodooIO from Villar and Gellersen [15] combines a virtual stage in Flash with a physical stage that allows arranging physical components and material. Although we describe the capabilities tailored for mobile device prototyping, the MAKEIT infrastructure can be extended with moderate effort to connect to these powerful tools.

The Mediascapes project [16] belongs to a well known set of rapid authoring tools for context-sensitive mobile applications. It focuses on enabling non-programmers to design, implement and deploy applications running on mobile devices. Similar approaches have been made by, e.g. Sohn and Dey with iCap [17], a visual language using if-then rules and relations between people, places and things to define an application logic. The programming-by-example or demonstration paradigm has been followed, e.g., by Topiary and DENIM. They allow specifying triggers of actions, which are comparable to the actions used in the MAKEIT environment. Topiary [18] concentrates on location-based applications where regions are drawn on a map and action triggers are set. The DENIM project [19] shows similarities to the approach presented here, letting the designer create transitions between states. The integration of conditionals, i.e. actions that depend on the properties of a state is planned; this would reduce the number of states visible at the same time as does the condensing of states in MAKEIT. The system, however, requires the user to learn several types of gestures, is designed for web page generation, is not open and easily extensible for external components and does not integrate well with later steps in the application development process. It will be interesting to see how a planned more powerful visual programming language will influence the power and usability of the system.

4.2 User Models

To be able to formalise factors describing human users, models are being developed that characterise users in one or more facets important the use of certain application. There are a lot of approaches that differ in the level of abstraction and formalism, granularity, precision, and target application areas and domains. A detailed discussion of general aspects in user modelling in the area of ubiquitous computing can be found in a special issue on User Modelling in ubiquitous Computing [20].

In this paper, we concentrate on user models from the GOMS family. GOMS is one of the first and most prominent of such models and has been introduced by Card, Moran and Newell in 1980 [21, 22]. It defines goals which can be reached by using a sequence of operators that identify unit actions; if there are several methods that can be followed, selection rules are used to disambiguate them. Several extensions and variants have been introduced to make the GOMS model more powerful. However, even the simplest form has proved to be of much value when having to choose between several design alternatives (see, e.g., work by Hinckley [23] and John [24]).

The inventors of the GOMS model had a specific focus on modelling *physical* actions and concurrent or corresponding mental involvement. In the beginning, one of its main uses has been to model tasks on desktop computers. The Keystroke-Level Model (KLM) has then been introduced by Kieras [25] to aid in the development of more precise interaction models in such environments. Its operators describe basic actions like key presses, hand movements between keyboard and mouse, and system response times. A number of projects have successfully validated KLM in many different application areas, for example [26, 27, 28]. In the last years, researchers have also effectively adjusted, extended and updated the original KLM with new operators or different values in order to apply it to different and novel interaction techniques. Manes et al. [29], for example, use it for interactions with car navigation systems. One work extending the original KLM for mobile devices is presented by Holleis et al. in [9]. It adds new operators describing advanced mobile device interactions and modifies some of them for the specific use in mobile phones. This includes standard interactions with number keys and hotkeys as well as novel types of interaction like gestures, visual marker recognition, and reading RFID/NFC tags.

Creating prototypes that allow assessing the usage performance is in general regarded as too cost intensive, especially in the domain of mobile and ubiquitous user interfaces. Providing tools that help to keep track of the expected task completion time is valuable in the design process, as often it is hard to estimate such times. Of course, interaction time is only one of the factors that distinguish one design from another. Still, it can be a decisive aspect in making a justified choice. In situations where users have restricted amounts of time (applications for mobile emergency services or programs used while walking to a station), quick solutions can be a significant advantage. Models such as the KLM make predictions about the time experienced users need to execute specific tasks without any need for actual studies. Hence there is no need to create several functional prototypes that have similar timing characteristics. One of the problems identified to hinder the broad use of such models is the cost of learning and constructing correct models. Creating such models can be very time consuming, error-prone, and different people will come up with at least slightly different models. Tools like CogTool [30] (see below) or MAKEIT are therefore needed to make the use of models more practical.

4.3 Prototyping Tools that Support Underlying Models

Prototyping tools that explicitly support underlying models or semantic checks are hardly available. A range of applications exist that allow incorporating actual user traces into the process of developing a UI prototype. SUEDE [31] and WebQuilt [32] are such examples recording user test data for speech and web UIs, respectively. The major difference to our system is that we do not rely on actual user data but use validated interaction models. This drastically reduces time and cost for reaching decisions regarding projected user interaction times.

Gow and Thimbleby describe MAUI [33], an interface design tool based on a matrix algebra model of interaction. Using finite state machines, he can formally state interface properties using linear algebra. There is currently no support for interaction time analyses or code generation for specific target platforms. A start in providing tool support for developers to model applications is CogTool [30]. It uses storyboards to design an application and then employs a cognitive modelling back-end to generate interaction time predictions. In direct comparison with the MAKEIT environment, one can see that the CogTool provides a visual tool to define advanced user models. In contrast to that, MAKEIT focuses on providing support for the actual implementation by generating source code incorporating non-functional parameters.

5 Summary and Future Work

We addressed the gap between low-fidelity paper prototyping and implementations of mobile phone applications. The MAKEIT framework (*Mobile Applications Kit Embedding Interaction Times*) presented in this paper is used to create functional, high-fidelity prototypes for mobile devices supporting advanced types of interaction. In particular, it focuses on the need to easily create prototypes and aid in evaluating and deciding between different interaction designs. Integrated into MAKEIT is support for a KLM based task completion time analysis of the state graph of the application.

While the state graph eliminates the need to remember the order of paper prototype material, the advantage of paper prototyping to quickly react to unforeseen events during studies remains. The required time is slightly more than for paper prototyping but surely lower than for doing any implementations. Using the state graph approach, several types of errors like creating unreachable states can be avoided. In most design processes, considerations like KLM annotations do not play an important part. We argue that integrating such aspects as early in the process as possible, several changes can be avoided later. An open issue is that changes made to the generated code are not reflected in the state graph and have to be repeated each time the code is regenerated. NetBeans, e.g., solves this by only allowing the user to make minor changes in the code at specific places. This, however, reduces the freedom of the developer.

Future work will further evaluate and improve the concept and user interface with a larger user study and concentrate on simplifying the inclusion of standard controls and widgets in the phone's screen like text input fields and scroll lists. Approaches like those seen in the upcoming Adobe Thermo project[9] aim at exactly this direction by automatically converting drawings of, e.g., a text area to a functional text box.

Acknowledgements

The authors would like to thank Prof. Dr. Franz J. Brandenburg and his research group at the University of Passau, Germany, for developing and providing the Gravisto graph visualisation and editing software.

This work was funded by the DFG ('Deutsche Forschungsgemeinschaft') in the context of the research project Embedded Interaction ('Eingebettete Interaktion').

References

1. Davies, N., Landay, J., Hudson, S., Schmidt, A.: Rapid Prototyping in Ubiquitous Computing. IEEE Pervasive Computing 4(4), 15–17 (2005)
2. Rukzio, E., Leichtenstern, K., Callaghan, V., Holleis, P., Schmidt, A.: An Experimental Comparison of Physical Mobile Interaction Techniques: Touching, Pointing and Scanning. In: Dourish, P., Friday, A. (eds.) UbiComp 2006. LNCS, vol. 4206, pp. 87–104. Springer, Heidelberg (2006)
3. Rohs, M.: Marker-Based Interaction Techniques for Camera-Phones. In: MU3I (2005)

---

[9] Adobe Thermo project, *http://labs.adobe.com/wiki/index.php/Thermo*

4. Nicolai, T., Kenn, H.: Towards Detecting Social Situations with Bluetooth. In: Adjunct Proceedings Ubicomp 2006 (2006)

5. Hull, R., Clayton, B., Melamed, T.: Rapid Authoring of Mediascapes. In: Davies, N., Mynatt, E.D., Siio, I. (eds.) UbiComp 2004. LNCS, vol. 3205, pp. 125–142. Springer, Heidelberg (2004)

6. Nuria, O., Flores-Mangas, F.: MPTrain: A Mobile Music and Physiology Based Personal Trainer. In: MobileHCI 2006 (2006)

7. Thimbleby, H., Gow, J.: Applying Graph Theory to Interaction Design. In: DSVIS 2007 (2007)

8. Holleis, P., Huhtala, J., Häkkilä, J.: Studying Applications for Touch-Enabled Mobile Phone Keypads. In: TEI 2008, pp. 15–18 (2008)

9. Holleis, P., Otto, F., Hussmann, H., Schmidt, A.: Keystroke-level Model for Advanced Mobile Phone Interaction. In: CHI 2007, pp. 1505–1514 (2007)

10. Rukzio, E., Wetzstein, S., Schmidt, A.: A Framework for Mobile Interactions with the Physical World. In: WPMC 2005 (2005)

11. Greenhalgh, Izadi, H.J.S., Mathrick, J., Taylor, I.: ECT: A Toolkit to Support Rapid Construction of Ubicomp Environments. In: UbiSys 2004 (2004)

12. Hartmann, B., Klemmer, S.R., Bernstein, M., Abdulla, L., Burr, B., Robinson-Mosher, A., Gee, J.: Reflective Physical Prototyping Through Integrated Design, Test, and Analysis. In: UIST 2006 (2006)

13. Greenberg, S., Fitchett, C.: Phidgets: Easy Development of Physical Interfaces Through Physical Widgets. In: UIST 2001, pp. 209–218 (2001)

14. Ballagas, R., Ringel, M., Stone, M., Borchers, J.: iStuff: a Physical User Interface Toolkit for Ubiquitous Computing Environments. In: CHI 2003, pp. 537–544 (2003)

15. Villar, N., Gellersen, H.: A Malleable Control Structure for Softwired User Interfaces. In: TEI 2007 (2007)

16. Hull, R., Clayton, B., Melamed, T.: Rapid Authoring of Mediascapes. In: Davies, N., Mynatt, E.D., Siio, I. (eds.) UbiComp 2004. LNCS, vol. 3205, pp. 125–142. Springer, Heidelberg (2004)

17. Sohn, T., Dey, A.: iCAP: Rapid Prototyping of Context-Aware Applications. In: CHI 2004 (2004)

18. Li, Y., Hong, J., Landay, J.: Topiary: A Tool for Prototyping Location-Enhanced Applications. In: UIST 2004 (2004)

19. Newman, M.W., Lin, J., Hong, J.I., Landay, J.A.: DENIM: An Informal Web Site Design Tool Inspired by Observations of Practice. Human-Computer Int. 18(3), 259–324 (2003)

20. Jameson, A., Krüger, A.: Preface to the Special Issue on User Modeling in Ubiquitous Computing. User Modeling and User-Adapted Interaction 15(3-4), 193–195 (2005)

21. Card, S.K., Newell, A., Moran, T.P.: The Psychology of Human-Computer Interaction. Lawrence Erlbaum Associates, Inc., Mahwah (1983)

22. Card, S.K., Moran, T.P., Newell, A.: The Keystroke-Level Model for User Performance Time with Interactive Systems. Communications of the ACM 23(7), 396–410 (1980)

23. Hinckley, K., Guimbretière, F., Baudisch, P., Sarin, R., Agrawala, M., Cutrell, E.: The Springboard: Multiple Modes in one Spring-loaded Control. In: CHI 2006, pp. 181–190 (2006)

24. John, B.E., Vera, A.H.: A GOMS Analysis of a Graphic Machine-paced, Highly Interactive Task. In: CHI 1992, pp. 251–258 (1992)

25. Kieras, D.: Using the Keystroke-Level Model to Estimate Execution Times. The University of Michigan, Unpublished Report (1993), http://www.pitt.edu/~cmlewis/KSM.pdf

26. Bälter, O.: Keystroke Level Analysis of Email Message Organization. In: CHI 2000 (2000)

27. Teo, L., John, B.E.: Comparisons of Keystroke-Level Model Predictions to Observed Data. In: Extended Abstracts CHI 2006, pp. 1421–1426 (2006)

28. Koester, H.H., Levine, S.P.: Validation of a Keystroke-Level Model for a Text Entry System Used by People with Disabilities. In: Assets 1994, pp. 115–122 (1994)
29. Manes, D., Green, P., Hunter, D.: Prediction of Destination Entry and Retrieval Times Using Keystroke-Level Models. UMTRI-96-37. University of Michigan (1996)
30. John, B.E., Salvucci, D.D.: Multi-Purpose Prototypes for Assessing User Interfaces in Pervasive Computing Systems. IEEE Pervasive Computing 4(4), 27–34 (2005)
31. Klemmer, S.R., Sinha, A.K., Chen, J., Landay, J.A., et al.: SUEDE: A Wizard of Oz Prototyping Tool for Speech User Interfaces. In: CHI Letters UIST 2000, vol. 2(2), pp. 1–10 (2000)
32. Hong, J.I., Heer, J., Waterson, S., Landay, J.A.: WebQuilt: A Proxy-based Approach to Remote Web Usability Testing. ACM Trans. Inf. Syst. 19(3), 263–385 (2001)
33. Gow, J., Thimbleby, H.: MAUI: An Interface Design Tool Based On Matrix Algebra. In: CADUI 2004, pp. 81–94 (2004)
34. Rekimoto, J., Schwesig, C.: PreSenseII: Bi-directional Touch and Pressure Sensing Interactions with Tactile Feedback. In: Extended Abstracts CHI 2006, pp. 1253–1258 (2006)

Cooperative Techniques Supporting Sensor-Based People-Centric Inferencing

Nicholas D. Lane[1], Hong Lu[1], Shane B. Eisenman[2], and Andrew T. Campbell[1]

[1] Dartmouth College, Hanover NH 03755, USA
{niclane,hong,campbell}@cs.dartmouth.edu
[2] Columbia University, New York NY 10027, USA
shane@ee.columbia.edu

Abstract. People-centric sensor-based applications targeting mobile device users offer enormous potential. However, learning inference models in this setting is hampered by the lack of labeled training data and appropriate feature inputs. Data features that lead to better classification models are not available at all devices due to device heterogeneity. Even for devices that provide superior data features, models require sufficient training data, perhaps manually labeled by users, before they work well. We propose opportunistic feature vector merging, and the social-network-driven sharing of training data and models between users. Model and training data sharing within social circles combine to reduce the user effort and time involved in collecting training data to attain the maximum classification accuracy possible for a given model, while feature vector merging can enable a higher maximum classification accuracy by enabling better performing models even for more resource-constrained devices. We evaluate our proposed techniques with a significant places classifier that infers and tags locations of importance to a user based on data gathered from cell phones.

1 Introduction

Commercial off-the-shelf mobile devices with embedded sensors (e.g., iPhone, Nokia5500, Motorola PSI) are increasingly common in today's market, and have become a focus of people-centric application development due to their growing ubiquity. In this role, devices are owned by individuals rather than residing in a common administrative domain, and data sourced by sensors on the devices may only be available locally (i.e., no centralized repository with common access). Often, the individually tailored models supporting these new applications are based not only on the raw sensor inputs (e.g., camera, microphone, accelerometer), but also on higher level inferences (e.g., location, activity, mood) drawn from particular sensed data features. Identifying the appropriate data features and best performing models continues to be a subject of intense interest in support of these new applications [18] [16] [17] [15].

Against this backdrop, two main challenges facing the construction of accurate inference models are the lack of appropriate data inputs and the time and effort

J. Indulska et al. (Eds.): Pervasive 2008, LNCS 5013, pp. 75–92, 2008.
© Springer-Verlag Berlin Heidelberg 2008

that must be spent in training a model of sufficient accuracy. The consumer-device-based sensing substrate upon which people-centric applications are built is characterized by heterogeneity in terms of sensing and other resources (e.g., memory, battery capacity). Therefore, the data inputs most useful in generating high accuracy models are not likely to be available on all devices. As an example using a snapshot of current technology, classifiers distinguishing indoor vs. outdoor locations are built using data features from GPS and WiFi sensors [16]. However, GPS and Wifi are integrated into only a relatively small percentage of cell phones on the market today. This heterogeneity often requires users of less capable devices to settle for less accurate models based on other available data features. Figure 1(a) illustrates the result of this situation, showing the experimental performance of a significant places classifier (see Section 4 for implementation and performance details) for four device capability classes (CC): CC1 is Bluetooth only, CC2 is Bluetooth and WiFi, CC3 is Bluetooth and GPS, and CC4 is Bluetooth, WiFi and GPS. Perhaps unsurprisingly, the accuracy of location recognition increases as the sensor inputs from more capable cell phones are used to generate better models. These observations motivate and inspire our proposed *opportunistic feature vector merging* approach with which we seek to push the model performance possible with lower tier devices (e.g., CC1) towards that possible with higher tier devices (e.g., CC4). With feature vector merging, data features from more capable devices are borrowed and merged with data features natively available from a less capable device in the model building stage, allowing the less capable device to generate a higher accuracy model. This borrowing is facilitated by opportunistic interaction (though not necessarily communication), both direct and indirect, between a less capable device and a more capable device in situ. As an example of direct interaction, as two cell phone users follow their daily routines, the cell phone without GPS can borrow GPS data features from the cell phone with GPS as an input to its indoor/outdoor model. An indoor/outdoor model based on GPS feature instances borrowed over a period of time may also be built. In the indirect interaction case, both devices collect data samples according to their respective capabilities. Subsequently, centralized matching between commonly collected features (i.e., not GPS) may provide for a binding between the feature vector collected by the phone without GPS and the GPS features collected by the GPS-equipped phone. The GPS features can then essentially be borrowed via this binding.

Even when devices provide an appropriate set of data features to build accurate models, users may be required to gather a large set of training data (perhaps manually labeling it) before applications using the model outputs work at their peak level. The inconvenience in both the labeling of training data and the time required for model training to complete may act as disincentives to the broad-scale adoption of new people-centric applications [16]. One approach to reduce model training time and effort is to support the sharing of labeled training data among users. Sharing training data has the effect of reducing the per-user training time and labeling effort when building the necessary collection of training data, but is also likely to reduce the accuracy of the resulting models. This is

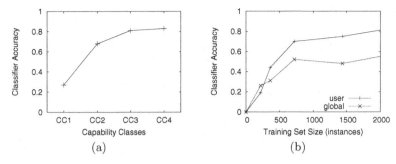

Fig. 1. Classifier performance relative to varying device capabilities and the size of the training data used. In (a), accuracy is plotted for various capability classes (CC): CC1 is Bluetooth only, CC2 is Bluetooth and WiFi, CC3 is Bluetooth and GPS, and CC4 is Bluetooth, WiFi and GPS. In (b), accuracy is plotted against the training set size.

especially true in people-centric sensing systems based on common mobile devices like cell phones. In this context, sensor data features are often limited by the non-ideal set of sensors embedded or interfaced to the cell phones, and also the quality of the training process is difficult to control. Therefore, models in this domain are often more tightly bound to the individual in order to achieve higher accuracy. Consider Figure 1(b), which shows the classification accuracy versus training set size for our significant places classifier. The dashed line curve reflects the accuracy of a model built by merging experimental training data from all participants (see Section 4 for details). The solid line curve in Figure 1(b) shows the average accuracy of a collection of models, built on a per-user basis using only data sourced from each respective participant. For a given value A on the x-axis, for the per-user models, each of the N users provides A instances, while for the global model each user contributes roughly A/N instances. The quantity of per-user training data required in building the global model is low since model training cost is amortized over all the users in the system. However, the accuracy is also consistently low due to the aforementioned problems with global training data sharing in people-centric sensing systems. With our proposed *social-network-driven sharing*, we provide a hybrid approach that builds models based on training data shared within social circles, within which we conjecture group vocabularies and other commonalities lead to more consistently labeled training data and a higher model accuracy, while still reducing the quantity of per user training data required.

The contributions of the paper are: (i) we are the first to propose opportunistic merging of feature vectors between devices to improve model accuracy on lower capability devices; (ii) we propose the sharing of training data and models between devices by leveraging the social relationships between their users; and (iii) we implement and test these two complementary techniques in the context of "significant places" [21] [2] [9], a people-centric service targeting sensor-equipped mobile devices.

2   Related Work

The problem of acquiring suitably labeled training data to build classification models is well recognized, and is addressed in the literature in a number of ways. To the best of our knowledge, there is no existing research targeting feature sharing through opportunistic interaction. This may be due to the fact that feature sharing may add uncertainty to the system and is thus a counter-intuitive approach to improving model accuracy. Opportunistic sharing of data features and models can be viewed as a special case of opportunistic data exchange more generally. As such, sensor fusion [14] in ephemeral proximity-based networks is related, though neither communication within socially connected groups nor the constraints and advantages of sharing to enhance classification accuracy are treated in the general case. Sharing training sets from one user's model to improve the performance of another can be thought of as co-training [22].

The Tapestry system [7] uses a collaborative approach to perform document filtering (e.g., email) based on the reactions/responses of others. The authors of [10] propose what they term collaborative machine learning, which unifies collaborative filtering and content-based filtering. The approach considers both the user's data content, as well as attributes and descriptors, to gain a better idea of the similarities among users, providing better accuracy for document retrieval and recommendation applications. A similar sharing concept is explored in [19], where the authors propose a method for recommendation sharing based on statistical correlations in users' data sets (e.g., music artist playlist). While these approaches enable sharing of what can be considered model training data or classification models, the sharing ignores social group connections. We conjecture our social-network-driven sharing proposal can be integrated into these systems to improve performance (e.g., in Tapestry, only considering annotations created by members of the same social group). Using social connections to guide sharing can be thought of as semi-supervised learning [22].

There are a number of research papers contributing to various aspects of "significant places" applications, including significance learning [13], location clustering [21], and location prediction [2]. We use significant places, representative of emerging applications using sensor-enhanced inferences and targeting mobile devices, to demonstrate the usefulness of our techniques of opportunistic feature vector merging and social-network-driven training data sharing.

3   Proposed Techniques

At a high level, a standard approach to building models involves first sensing available data, extracting and labeling sensed data features that accurately describe states, and then finding a classification technique that provides high accuracy and high confidence classification. In terms of model usage, first the available data is sensed, the necessary features are extracted and fed into the model without labeling, and then the model outputs the inferred label. In Figure 2, we represent these two processes pictorially, and include the stages in each process

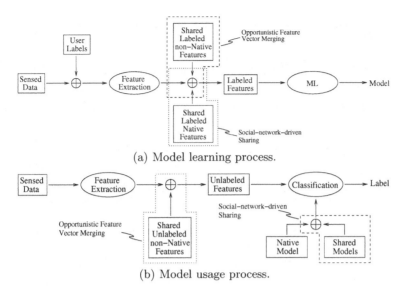

Fig. 2. Typical model learning and usage processes, and how opportunistic feature vector merging and social-network-driving sharing hook into these. In the diagrams, the circumscribed "plus" symbols represent a merging of information (e.g., labeled features). Actions are enclosed ellipses, while objects are enclosed in rectangles.

where our proposed techniques hook in (encircled with dashed/dotted lines). As indicated in the diagram, feature merging and social-based training data and model sharing are complementary techniques that can be composed in both the model learning and usage processes to improve performance. In the following, we discuss in more detail a number of design and implementation challenges, providing a roadmap for future work needed to realize the full potential of our approches. We begin to address these challenges in this work.

3.1   Opportunistic Feature Vector Merging

With opportunistic feature vector merging, we aim to leverage opportunistic interactions (both direct and indirect) between devices with different capabilities to improve the model accuracy achievable on less capable devices. Less capable devices borrow from more capable devices features that allow for the generation and subsequent use of more accurate models than those possible to generate from only natively available data features. Here, the capability of the device can be thought of in terms of sensor configuration, available memory, and CPU/DSP characteristics. Thus, as in the example given in Section 1, opportunistic feature merging can provide desirable vector elements (e.g., those derived from GPS and WiFi data) that are not available natively due to the sensor configuration. Secondly, merging can provide additional data features of native types that may be needed, for example, when the device is not capable of storing a time series of the required size. Finally, opportunistic feature merging can be used to share features extracted from external data that are also available natively, but can not be calculated on the device due to device limitations (e.g., a computationally intensive FFT of microphone data cannot run on a CPU-limited device even though the device has the microphone). A number of questions arise when considering a system design that uses opportunistic feature vector merging, which we explore in the following subsections.

Determining What Features are Sharable. Given the mobile devices available on the market today, the following hardware sensors are available in at least a subset of devices: camera, microphone, accelerometer, 802.11 radio, Bluetooth radio, GPS receiver, cellular radio. The raw sensor data from each of these sources can be processed in many ways, alone and in combination, to extract features useful for model building. However, not all of the features are equally sharable for opportunistic feature merging. For example, two co-located devices, one with a GPS receiver and with an 802.11 radio can likely exchange features from these sensors for mutual benefit. On the other hand, data mined from a user's calendar on one device may not be of much use on another user's device, and may even result in a worse model for the borrowing device. Similarly, raw samples from light sensors separated by even a very small distance by have very different values due shadow patterns, and may not be amenable to sharing. However, it may be useful to share temperature samples even at longer distances since temperature gradients tend to be shallower. While determining which particular features are beneficial to share or not likely depends on the classifier (e.g., how susceptible is the output to inaccuracy in the input), a reasonable guideline is to only share features that are not highly person, device, or location specific. Even if these contribute to a better classifier on their native device, they are unlikely to do so on another user's device.

What are the Feature Sharing Mechanisms. In Section 1, we introduce two types of opportunistic feature merging, depending on whether the interaction is direct or indirect. The feature sharing mechanism for each variant is slightly different. For direct interaction, devices periodically broadcast their available data sources (e.g., hardware sensors) via an available short range radio interface. Advertising only the data sources is preferable to advertising the entire feature set in terms of efficiency, since there are likely many possible features per data source. Additionally, only those data sources that are likely to be sharable (as discussed previously) should be advertised to reduce unproductive feature sharing. Devices that are interested in borrowing reply with a request for all the features available for a given (set of) data source(s). Requesting only the features, rather than all the raw data, saves on communication energy spent by both the lender and the borrower. With direct interaction, models can be used in a distributed way on each mobile device. Over time, it is also possible for a device to collect enough shared feature instances to build models based on shared features, potentially allowing for infrastructureless bootstrapping of the system.

In contrast, feature merging via indirect interaction uses a centralized approach, requiring no direct device peer interaction. All devices collect samples, extract features, and generate models to the best of their respective abilities in situ. Subsequently, when each device transfers its training data/features to a dedicated server, the merging process looks for evidence in the features provided by all users that two or more devices were sensing the same location or event. If so, then these devices are able to share features to generate better models. Indirect sharing is helpful if two devices are co-located but can not communicate locally due, for example, to radio incompatibility. Indirect sharing also allows devices that sense the same event/phenomenon but are never co-located to share data, if the sensed event/phenomenon is relatively constant in the time between the respective devices' visits. Finally, indirect sharing potentially saves on communications costs over direct sharing since no local data exchange is necessary. For example, consider two devices that each have a GPS receiver, but only one has a CO_2 sensor. In this case, the merging process can identify through matching GPS readings that the devices were in roughly the same place at the same time. Then the device without the CO_2 sensor can borrow the CO_2 readings and incorporate them into its training data to generate improved models.

What to do When Shared Features are not Available. One drawback to building models requiring borrowed features is that there is no guarantee a device will be on hand to share the required features when the model is to be used. We address this with two approaches. First, each device generates a collection of models, each relying on different sets of available features. The device uses the model that has the best expected performance (i.e., w.r.t its confusion matrix) given the features available at the time of classification. In the worst case, this will be the model learned only from device-native sources. Second, we build models using algorithms that are more resilient to missing or noisy elements of the feature vector. For example, the KNN imputation method performs better relative to the comparison technique of the LNN classifier [1].

Privacy Concerns in Sharing. Opportunistic feature sharing potentially leaks personally sensitive information (e.g., location trace). One option is to provide the user with the ability to configure the type of data that is sharable, and with whom. Another option is to share features without including any identifiers in the packet payload. However, for direct sharing the MAC address of the short range radio used to share can be logged. Use of disposable MAC addresses is possible [8], but this may limit functionality for certain PHY/MAC technologies. Providing truly anonymous data exchange for ad hoc mobile devices is a focus of ongoing research in the community [5], but is outside the scope of this paper.

3.2   Social-Network-Driven Model and Training Data Sharing

With social-network-driven training data sharing and model sharing, we aim to leverage social connections between device users to reduce the amount of time and effort an average user must expend to train her models while maintaining reasonable model accuracy. These social connections may be short-lived or persistent, and include connections based on proximity, professional groupings, family, friends, people sharing common interests (e.g., tango class), and many others. A number of techniques for mining social graphs from various information sources exist, but a review of this literature is out of scope. In the following, we discuss training data sharing, deferring treatment of model sharing to a later section. As discussed in Section 1, sharing training data generally has the effect of reducing the time and effort of training, but has the undesirable side effect of reducing the accuracy of models generated with this mixed data. Features that have good discriminative power within particular population subgroups, lose effectiveness within larger groups. We propose to allow sharing only within social circles to moderate this reduction in accuracy, while still reducing training time and effort. In the following, we describe a number of challenges to social-network-driven sharing, and discuss the motivation of model sharing between members of the same social group.

Exploiting Social Connections. Previous work [4] [6] suggests ways to mine sensor-based and other data to infer social graphs where the vertices are people or groups and the edges are relationships. Assuming known social graphs, we construct models with training data sourced on the basis of the strength of social connections (edges in the social graph) between the intended target of the model (e.g., the device user) and others. A lower bound on the strength of connection between two users may apply such that sharing does not occur below this threshold. We expect people who are members of the same social groups (such as combinations of cultural, workplace, social, or family groups) will have similar background or other context that translates into similarity in label definitions (i.e., what classes are important and what are the appropriate labels). By exploiting awareness of the social connections between people we build a training set sourced by a variety of people that still produces a model for a particular individual (or group) that approximates the performance of a model built solely from training data sourced from this individual (or group) in terms of both classification accuracy and the understandability of labels.

A number of interwoven social graphs are likely to apply to a given set of individuals. The nature of the inference problem (i.e., the application, or learning technique) may determine which social graph to use when considering which training data to import from other users. In the context of our running example of significant place classification, if a user may provide free-form labels (e.g., colloquial labels for locations), it may be appropriate to incorporate labeled instances from other nodes in her social network with whom she is frequently physically located, under the supposition that a location-specific vocabulary is likely in use (e.g., workplace vernacular, regional dialect). On the other hand, individuals to whom one is extremely close socially (e.g., a girlfriend), may be of less use in sharing location-specific vocabulary if they are frequently physically distant. Similarly, labeling of certain activities or social settings may be more culturally and demographically driven.

Quality and Consistency Issues. A number of challenges arise related to the quality and consistency of shared data instances.

First, the quality of the training instances may vary from user to user due to the care taken when the training data was gathered, the training methods used, and the training environment (e.g., data collected under non-typical circumstances can lead to a model that does not perform well in general). Challenges in repairing ill-labeled data aside, it is difficult even to determine which instances are lower quality. This is especially difficult when the pool of available labels is small and statistical techniques such as anomaly detection are not applicable. Because of this, importing lower quality training data can pollute one's natively collected data, leading to poorer model performance.

When free-form labeling is used, opinions may vary among users on the proper size of label set, the feature support of each label, and the label itself. A related complication is that lexicographically identical labels may mean different things to different people and different labels may mean the same thing to different people. One way to address these issues is to apply structure to the labeling stage such that a fixed set of valid labels, each with a provided definition, is imposed on all users. However, this approach restricts the classifications problems that can be solved, and may result in a model that, though accurate, gives labels that are not well understood by a given user.

Designing Models Robust to Mixed Source Data.   Given the lack of flexibility of structured labeling, we support free-form labeling. While sharing within social circles mitigates labeling consistency issues to some extent, the process of learning models must still be robust to them. Incorporating contradictory instances, where the same class of features is given two or more different labels (by multiple users), leads to a situation where the same class of feature vectors will be mistakenly fragmented into multiple labels. (The impact of this fragmentation is somewhat problem-specific, since a classifier that seeks only to differentiate between logical classes of might perform well even with fragmented features.) We use an unsupervised clustering approach to detecting and correcting this fragmentation in our significant places implementation discussed in Section 4. Instances can then be appropriately grouped regardless of their label, with the introduction of some error due to imperfect grouping. After clustering, a normative label may be applied for consistency.

Social-Group-Based Model Sharing.   In addition to sharing training data, the models themselves are also candidates for sharing. The trigger for borrowing models would be noticing that the performance (e.g., recall, precision) was better in the model of a fellow social group member than in yours for the same feature vector. In this case, either the user's device can check neighboring devices in situ to if they have an appropriate model with better performance (e.g., via an advertise-request-response protocol), or the model sharing can be done in a centralized way on a dedicated server. The rationale for model borrowing between members of a social group in particular is that even though the models may have been learned based on training data labeled by your buddy, your buddy's labels are likely to make sense to you because of your shared membership in the social group. Elements of shared models that may be particularly helpful in improving a user's locally generated model can be permanently incorporated by importing the appropriate training data and relearning the local model. This is beneficial in the online case since performance can be maintained even when the neighbor with the better model is not nearby, and in the offline case it reduces unnecessary processing.

4   Evaluation

To evaluate the impact of opportunistic feature vector merging and social-network-driven data and model sharing on a real people-centric application, we implement a version of the "significant places" classifier (e.g., [11] [6]). We use this as a vehicle to demonstrate the application of our techniques. In the following, we describe the implementation and focus of our variant of significant places, and the experimental data collection methodology, followed by selected performance results.

4.1   Significant Places

A frequently examined classification problem in the literature is that of taking location traces of a user and distilling them into a sequence of visits to places that are significant to her (e.g., home, work, gym). This is used by applications that present historical summaries of the user's daily life [2], or even to determine when a person has taken a wrong turn heading toward home [18]. A generic significant places classifier may be thought of in terms of three main phases. In the first phase, various data features (e.g., visitation frequency and dwell time) of a user location trace are extracted from the raw data and analyzed to identify locations and infer whether they are significant to the user. In the second stage, the significant places are labeled, either by mapping the location feature vector to a set of system-provided labels or by manual prompting of the user to allow for personalized labels. In the third phase, the classifier is run to see how accurately the system can recognize that a user has entered a significant place. A number of proposals (e.g., [21] [11]) exist addressing the first phase of learning models to infer significance. As significance inferencing is orthogonal to our techniques, in our implementation we simplify the first two phases and have the user manually label instances of location feature vectors as significant or not (c.f. the collection methodology in Section 4.2). Based on these labeled instances, we then evaluate the impact of our merging and sharing techniques on the accuracy and label understandability of models built to recognize the labeled significant places.

4.2   Data Collection Methodology

As the sensing, processing and display capabilities of cell phones increase, cell phones provide a unique chance for researchers to understand the real mobile user behaviour and to provide true in situ mobile services. To gather user-labeled significant place instances we use Nokia N80 and N95 smart phones. Both models feature Bluetooth and an 802.11g WiFi interface. The N95 also comes with an integrated GPS receiver. To facilitate user labeling of significant places, we implement and install a PyS60 (Python for Symbian S60) client on each cell phone. The client provides two fundamental services: user labeling and daily trace recording, and sensor sampling. For each significant place, the user enters a new label (or selects a previously entered one). With a button click, the user indicates when she enters and leaves the selected significant place. The client records the label, and the enter and leave times for each significant location visit. From these entries, the client generates a significant location trace for each user. The user is able to review and edit the daily trace to verify its correctness. The sensing daemon runs in the background to sample from the Bluetooth, WiFi and GPS, if available. We use an inter-sampling interval of approximately three minutes, which gives an average battery life of more than 6 hours. The sampling duration is lasts between 30 and 60 seconds, depending on how long the function call to scan the Bluetooth neighborhood takes to return. The following data are captured: GPS - latitude, longitude, altitude, accuracy, time, speed, number of satellites; WiFi - beacon interval, security mode, SSID, BSSID, signal strength; Bluetooth - address, device name, service type.

4.3 Data Analysis Methodology

The inputs to the models we construct are based on a feature vector formed from three types of elements; location, time and social context. Clock, GPS, WiFi and Bluetooth data give rise to the following features, which are also further processed to generate averages and variances. From the clock, we extract day/night, 3-hour block, the duration of visitation, weekday/weekend and, business/after hours. From WiFi, we extract the absence or presence of access points (APs) identified by their MAC addresses, the relative RSSI order among the visible APs, the individual and aggregate RSSI, and other AP statistics that have been previously used to distinguish geographic locations [9] [12]. From social context, we seek to capture the social characteristics of the location. We extract the number of Bluetooth-toting people in the area (assuming one device per person). This is used in concert with a list of the people with whom the individual has social connections (e.g., from Facebook or other social networking sites). Use of Bluetooth and WiFi features allows us to distinguish between adjacent locations that may have very similar GPS features. We use the Weka machine learning workbench [20] for our analysis, specifically the default configuration of the bagging algorithm applied to the decision tree module, REPTree. All models are trained on a randomly selected 50% of the data set available for it. In the following, we describe initial performance results achieved with models based on a proof-of-concept implementation of our sharing and merging ideas. We leave a deeper investigation of the design space for later work.

4.4 Performance Results

In an experiment run over 12 days, data we collect from 13 phone users (four Nokia N95 and nine N80 cell phones) using the collection methodology outlined above comprises 14375 labeled instances of 62 uniquely labeled locations. We run post-collection validation via manual checking and participant interviews to verify the integrity of the data set. All phone users are members of, or are socially connected to the Computer Science Department at Dartmouth College. Participant ages range from 24 to 49; one user of the 13 is female. We also gather results from a survey (described subsequently) that includes the 13 phone users and an additional 8 survey-only participants. These latter fall in the same aforementioned age range and have the same departmental connection; one of the additional 8 is female. We present results demonstrating the potential impact of the opportunistic feature vector merging and social-network-driven sharing.

Feature Vector Merging Performance. We generate models, "merge" and "no merge", from experimental data, and examine the impact of performing direct sharing of features based on different device capabilities. Sharing of features is done on the basis of Bluetooth connectivity. Whenever two devices in the experiment detect each other in their Bluetooth neighborhood then feature sharing is enabled. An exchange of feature vector elements occurs when possible, giving participant nodes a richer feature vector they would otherwise have based on native sensors. Although all Nokia N80 and N95 phones have WiFi and all N95 phones have GPS, to emulate four distinct capability classes of devices for some devices in the experiment the WiFi on the N80 phones and the GPS on the N95 phones is ignored as needed to support allowing four different classes to be emulated. We build the models as follows: a single model is generated for each user during the evaluation. This model is trained using all the feature vectors available, even those that are intermittently available via sharing. This results in numerous feature vector instances with missing elements, since sharing is not continuously available. We do not explicitly handle missing data within execution of our model (e.g., using a model swapping technique), but instead use a machine learning technique (bagging) innately robust to the missing data. Models are built on a per-user basis using training data specific to the user and user's device, and based on his or her own opportunities for merging.

Figure 3(a) shows a comparison of these two models. It reports the average classification accuracy for each of the per-user models generated. Accuracy is plotted against the phone capability class. In each of these classes the performance is reported for all phones being limited to this operating level or lower. The plot shows that with feature sharing, we can always gain an advantage in

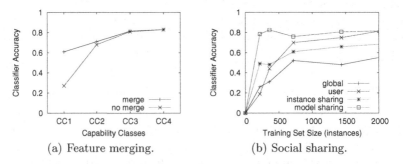

(a) Feature merging.   (b) Social sharing.

Fig. 3. Performance Plots

model accuracy, except for capability class CC4 devices since those already have all the sensors natively. In our campus environment and predominantly indoor significant places, WiFi is the most powerful feature to share to improve accuracy, as indicated in the large increase between CC1 (Bluetooth only) and CC2 (Bluetooth and WiFi). In environments where WiFi features are less available, we expect shared GPS-based feature elements to be the most helpful.

Social-Network-Driven Sharing Performance. We generate four models from experimental data, including two that incorporate sharing to support model generation, "instance sharing" and "model sharing", and two that do not, "global" and "user". With these models, we investigate the impact of sharing on classification accuracy with respect to the amount of training data provided by each user. In all cases, models are trained using a randomly selected 50% of the data, with the balance used for performance testing. The device population comprises the following mix of capability classes: 5 Bluetooth only; 4 Bluetooth and WiFi; and 4 Bluetooth, WiFi and GPS.

As discussed in the Introduction, the "global" model is generated by pooling training data from all participants, with each user contributing roughly the same amount to the pool. The "user" model is generated on a per-user basis using only training data sourced from the user herself.

The "model sharing" approach generates per-user models as in the "user" approach, but then multiple models are tested before settling on a label output for a particular instance. The decision to apply another model or settle on the current result is based on estimated accuracy for the generated label. The choice of whose per-user models to choose for a given classification task is driven by social connections between users, prioritizing social connections that are logically related to the classification task. In so doing, models are applied according to a hierarchy of social groupings. Users' models within a group are ranked arbitrarily in our implementation, but the strength of personal social ties within a group can also be considered when deciding the order of model application. The application of models terminates either when a confidence threshold is reached (to improve classification accuracy), or if a certain maximum number of models is applied (to limit overhead). Lastly, with "model sharing", we always test the "global" model (global sharing) as well, and the result with the highest confidence among all the tested models becomes the final output label.

With "instance sharing", per-user models are built, but for a given user the training data is sourced from the user and from people within the user's social networks. As with "model sharing", a social group hierarchically is constructed considering the purpose of the classifier and the groups' potential impact in this regard, and intra-group ranking is also handled in the same way. In "instance sharing", training data instances are accumulated iteratively, considering one user per step, until the overall required number of training instances L is assembled. At each step i, the user is tapped to provide up to L/i instances. The goal, if K steps are taken to accumulate L instances, is to have each user provide L/K instances. At any point, if a user can not contribute the desired L/i instances, randomly chosen instances from the global pool are chosen, but are removed from the overall required L if they are no longer needed as filler.

The social groups present in our experimental user population and used for the sharing-based models are: "students", enrolled students at any college; "Dartmouth", enrolled students at Dartmouth College; "batch", grouped according to the year arriving at Dartmouth; "founders", founding members of SensorLab that have worked together since the inception of our research group; "SensorLab", all members of the SensorLab research group; "CMC", all members of the CMC Lab research group; "Chinese", have a strong social tie including a daily lunch group; "Facebook", social connections as defined within Facebook; "basketball", participants in a local summer basketball club; "town", those with a common town of residence; "European", those with a European origin; "non-U.S.", those with any non-U.S. origin. We order these groups according to the degree to which we expect them to improve our significant places classifier. Participants in the study are members of multiple different social groups.

The rationales for a few of the ranking decisions are as follows. We rank "Facebook" above "Dartmouth" since we expect Facebook friends to use common names for specific locations more so than does the general pool of Dartmouth students. The same logic leads us to rank the "members" ahead of "students". Group rankings may fluctuate seasonally. For example, the "basketball" group meets regularly, but only during the summer - familiarity (e.g., common experience, shared stories, shared vocabulary) decays over the rest of the year. Conversely, the "Chinese" group meets every day at noon for lunch, so the social ties remain strong throughout the year.

Figure 3(b) shows the classification accuracy versus training set size for each type of model. For a given value A on the x-axis, for the per-user models, each of the N users provided A instances, while for the global model each user contributes roughly A/N instances. For the sharing-based models, we assign equal weights to all social groups; the group hierarchy is flat. Each of the M users involved (i.e., through common social group membership) contributes A/M instances. The figure demonstrates the advantage of sharing only within social groups rather than globally as the model accuracy curves for both instance sharing and model sharing are always above that of the global model. Additionally, we see the advantage in terms of model learning time (i.e., required training data set size) that both instance and model sharing provide. We find that social-based model sharing achieves a higher maximum accuracy than training instance sharing for our data set. As expected, the per-user model outperforms instance sharing as the amount of available training data becomes large enough.

Classifier Performance Details. Figure 3 shows the sensitivity of the model accuracy to both the richness of the feature vector and the availability of training data, accuracy alone does not provide the full picture of the model performance. In Table 1, we present additional performance details (true positives rate (TPR), false positives rate (FPR), precision and recall) for each of the classifiers we use (i.e., the average performance across all classes). For the results shown here, the training set size is fixed at 719 instances.

Table 1. Classifier statistics

Model	User (avg)	Global	Feature Merging	Model Sharing	Instance Sharing
TPR	0.598	0.383	0.617	0.721	0.389
FPR	0.563	0.349	0.565	0.652	0.304
Precision	0.691	0.496	0.712	0.807	0.544
Recall	0.598	0.383	0.617	0.721	0.389

4.5   Survey Results

To understand the impact of social-network-driven model and instance sharing on the understandability and appropriateness of the model output labels, we survey 20 participants concerning the outputs of the sharing-based models used in the experiments described in Section 4.4. In this survey, we focus on determining the participants' depth of understanding of shared labels, and their feeling of the appropriateness of these labels when shared socially.

In Table 2, we report statistics on the level of comprehension people from different social groups have of labels produced by members of their own versus other social groups. Survey participants are asked questions to determine their level of understanding regarding 8 different labels. For each label, users are asked to identify to where they think a label refers when given the label provider's name and the label itself. The understanding is categorized as "strong", "weak", or "none" depending on how accurately the label is positioned on a map; "strong" if the exact location is indicated, "weak" if a location in the vicinity is indicated, and "none" otherwise. Label providers are not asked about their own labels.

Comprehension levels are shown in Table 2 for the dominant social groups ("SensorLab" and "CMC") that produced the most labels in our experiments. Members of the same social group share a better comprehension of each other's labels on average, compared both with members of the other group and the average population. For example, on average members of "SensorLab" stated they had a "strong" comprehension of 75% of labels generated by members of their own group, but no comprehension of 53% of the labels generated by "CMC" members. These results indicate that a model based on global sharing

Table 2. The level of comprehension people from different social groups have of labels produced by members of their own or other social groups. Members of the same social group share a better comprehension of each other's labels on average.

| Group | Strong | | Weak | | None | |
	"SensorLab" Labels	"CMC" Labels	"SensorLab" Labels	"CMC" Labels	"SensorLab" Labels	"CMC" Labels
"SensorLab"	0.75	0.32	0.09	0.15	0.16	0.53
"CMC"	0.40	0.55	0.05	0.03	0.55	0.43
All	0.48	0.34	0.14	0.31	0.38	0.49

Table 3. The level of appropriateness of selected labels as viewed by different social groups. Social connections can strongly impact the perceived appropriateness of a label, an important motivation for social-based instance/model sharing.

	Place:Label		
	SensorLab lab:'Lab'	CMC lab:'Lab'	Orient Restaurant:'Ori'
Groups	("SensorLab")	("CMC")	("Chinese")
"SensorLab"	2.10	1.00	0.83
"CMC"	1.25	1.75	1.25
"Chinese"	0.80	1.20	1.20

is likely to perform poorly in terms of understandability, in addition to accuracy (Figure 3(b)), underscoring the importance of social-based sharing.

To determine the statistical significance of the results in Table 2, we run a χ^2 test with a threshold of 0.05, and calculate $\chi_\alpha^2 = 5.9915$. First, we test the null hypothesis that comprehension of the labels provided by the "SensorLab" group is independent of group membership. The null hypothesis rejected with $Q = 14.401$. In the analogous test for the comprehension of labels provided by "CMC" members, we calculate $Q = 6.3068$, again rejecting the null hypothesis, concluding that the "CMC" members' better understanding (relative to that of "SensorLab" members) of labels provided by fellow members is statistically significant. These results give statistical credence to the notion of social-group-based sharing.

Table 3 presents results from the same survey on the appropriateness of labels provided by selected individuals for particular places. Given a place, survey participants rate four possible labels (each taken from labels generated by the 13 phone experiment participants) to describe the place on a scale from 0 to 4 (0 means "not appropriate"). Table 3 shows selected results for three (place,label) combinations. Generally, the table shows that the perceived appropriateness of a given label can be strongly impacted by social connections, as reflected in the higher values along the diagonal. For example, at least one member of each of the two laboratory groups ("SensorLab" and "CMC") included in the user set use the label 'Lab' to refer to their respective lab. Members of each lab think this label applies most appropriately to their own lab (i.e., average rating of 2.10 and 1.75 for their own versus 1.25 and 1.00 for the other lab). "Chinese" comprises those that often go together for lunch at the Orient restaurant. The table shows that "Chinese" members are more likely than "SensorLab" members (though not more so than "CMC" members) to find the diminutive 'Ori' acceptable. The lack of distinction between between "SensorLab" and "Chinese" for this label may be due to the existing overlap in group membership. These results support the use of socially shared labels in the significant places test application.

5   Conclusion

As the sensing and computation capabilities of commercial devices such as cell phones increase, the development of people-centric applications augmented with sensor inputs will also accelerate. To facilitate the wide-scale adoption of these applications, we have proposed two techniques aimed at both increasing the accuracy of feature classification used by these applications, reducing the burden on the user in terms of providing labeled training data. We have demonstrated the efficacy of both opportunistic feature vector merging and social-network-driven sharing in the context of "significant places", a useful classification process for people-centric sensor-enabled applications. Our results underscore the opportunity and importance of leveraging the inevitable device heterogeneity that results from the evolution of technology, and the importance of taking social relationships into consideration when sharing in support of model building.

Acknowledgment

This work is supported in part by Intel Corp., Nokia, NSF NCS-0631289, and the Institute for Security Technology Studies (ISTS) at Dartmouth College. ISTS support is provided by the U.S. Department of Homeland Security under Grant Award Number 2006-CS-001-000001. The views and conclusions contained in this document are those of the authors and should not be interpreted as necessarily representing the official policies, either expressed or implied, of the U.S. Department of Homeland Security.

References

1. Acuna, E., Rodriguez, C.: The treatment of missing values and its effect in the classifier accuracy. In: Classification, Clustering and Data Mining Applications, pp. 639–648 (2004)
2. Ashbrook, D., Starner, T.: Using gps to learn significant locations and predict movement across multiple users. Personal and Ubiquitous Computing 7(5), 275–286 (2003)
3. Bishop, C.M.: Pattern Recognition and Machine Learning (Information Science and Statistics). Springer, Heidelberg (2006)
4. Choudhury, T., Pentland, A.: Sensing and modeling human networks using the sociometer. In: ISWC 2003: Proc. of the 7th IEEE Int'l Symp. on Wearable Computersp, Washington, DC, USA, p. 216 (2003)
5. Cox, L.P., Dalton, A., Marupadi, V.: Smokescreen: flexible privacy controls for presence-sharing. In: MobiSys 2007: Proc. of the 5th int'l conf. on Mobile systems, applications and services, pp. 233–245. ACM, New York (2007)
6. Eagle, N., Pentland, A.S.: Reality mining: sensing complex social systems. Personal Ubiquitous Comput. 10(4), 255–268 (2006)
7. Goldberg, D., Nichols, D., Oki, B.M., Terry, D.: Using collaborative filtering to weave an information tapestry. Commun. ACM 35(12), 61–70 (1992)
8. Gruteser, M., Grunwald, D.: Enhancing location privacy in wireless lan through disposable interface identifiers: a quantitative analysis. In: WMASH 2003: Proc. of the 1st ACM Int'l workshop on Wireless mobile applications and services on WLAN hotspots, New York, NY, USA, pp. 46–55 (2003)
9. Hightower, J., Consolvo, S., LaMarca, A., Smith, I., Hughes, J.: Learning and recognizing the places we go. In: Beigl, M., Intille, S.S., Rekimoto, J., Tokuda, H. (eds.) UbiComp 2005. LNCS, vol. 3660, pp. 159–176. Springer, Heidelberg (2005)

10. Hofmann, T., Basilico, J.: Collaborative machine learning. In: From Integrated Publication and Information Systems to Virtual Information and Knowledge Environments, pp. 173–182 (2005)
11. Kang, J.H., Welbourne, W., Stewart, B., Borriello, G.: Extracting places from traces of locations. SIGMOBILE Mob. Comput. Commun. Rev. 9(3), 58–68 (2005)
12. Krumm, J., Hinckley, K.: The nearme wireless proximity server. In: Davies, N., Mynatt, E.D., Siio, I. (eds.) UbiComp 2004. LNCS, vol. 3205, pp. 283–300. Springer, Heidelberg (2004)
13. Liao, L., Fox, D., Kautz, H.: Location-based activity recognition. In: Advances in Neural Information Processing Systems 18, pp. 787–794. MIT Press, Cambridge (2006)
14. Luo, H., Luo, J., Liu, Y., Das, S.K.: Adaptive Data Fusion for Energy Efficient Routing in Wireless Sensor Networks. IEEE Trans. on Comp. 55(10), 1286–1299 (2006)
15. Marmasse, N., Schmandt, C., Spectre, D.: Watchme: Communication and awareness between members of a closely-knit group. In: Davies, N., Mynatt, E.D., Siio, I. (eds.) UbiComp 2004. LNCS, vol. 3205, pp. 214–231. Springer, Heidelberg (2004)
16. Miluzzo, E., Lane, N.D., Eisenman, S.B., Campbell, A.T.: Cenceme - injecting sensing presence into social networking applications. In: Kortuem, G., Finney, J., Lea, R., Sundramoorthy, V. (eds.) EuroSSC 2007. LNCS, vol. 4793, pp. 1–28. Springer, Heidelberg (2007)
17. Patterson, D.J., Liao, L., Fox, D., Kautz, H.A.: Inferring high-level behavior from low-level sensors. In: Dey, A.K., Schmidt, A., McCarthy, J.F. (eds.) UbiComp 2003. LNCS, vol. 2864, pp. 73–89. Springer, Heidelberg (2003)
18. Patterson, D.J., Liao, L., Gajos, K., Collier, M., Livic, N., Olson, K., Wang, S., Fox, D., Kautz, H.A.: Opportunity knocks: A system to provide cognitive assistance with transportation services. In: Davies, N., Mynatt, E.D., Siio, I. (eds.) UbiComp 2004. LNCS, vol. 3205, pp. 433–450. Springer, Heidelberg (2004)
19. Shardanand, U., Maes, P.: Social information filtering: algorithms for automating word of mouth. In: CHI 1995: Proc. of the SIGCHI conf. on Human factors in computing systems, New York, NY, USA, pp. 210–217 (1995)
20. Witten, I.H., Frank, E.: Data mining: practical machine learning tools and techniques with Java implementations. Morgan Kaufmann Publishers Inc., San Francisco (2000)
21. Zhou, C., Frankowski, D., Ludford, P., Shekhar, S., Terveen, L.: Discovering personally meaningful places: An interactive clustering approach. ACM Trans. Inf. Syst. 25(3), 12 (2007)
22. Zhu, X.: Semi-Supervised Learning Literature Survey. Tech. Report UW-Madison 1530 (2005)

Microsearch:
When Search Engines Meet Small Devices

Chiu C. Tan, Bo Sheng, Haodong Wang, and Qun Li

College of William and Mary, Williamsburg VA, USA
{cct,shengbo,wanghd,liqun}@cs.wm.edu

Abstract. In this paper, we present Microsearch, a search system suitable for small devices used in ubiquitous computing environments. Akin to a desktop search engine, Microsearch indexes the information inside a small device, and accurately resolves user queries. Given the very limited hardware resources, conventional search engine designs and algorithms cannot be used. We adopt information retrieval techniques for query resolution, and propose a space efficient algorithm to perform top-k query on limited hardware resources. Finally, we present a theoretical model of Microsearch to better understand the tradeoffs in system design parameters. By implementing Microsearch on actual hardware for evaluation, we demonstrate the feasibility of scaling down information retrieval systems onto very small devices.

1   Introduction

Interacting with our physical environment is a key component in many pervasive computing applications [1,6,7,24,26,22]. A typical system design usually involves a combination of simple beacons and a more powerful backend server. For example, a simple RF beacon can be embedded into a file binder and programmed to continuously emit a unique ID. Information regarding the documents found in the binder is stored in the backend sever. A user accesses this information by obtaining this ID and returning it with his query to the backend server. Since each ID is unique, the backend server can retrieve all the data associated with this particular binder and resolve the query. A similar process is executed when a user updates information about that binder.

Hardware improvements, which we will elaborate later, allow us to consider a different design paradigm which does not utilize a backend server. Instead of embedding a simple RF beacon into an object, we can embed a more powerful device. Information previously kept on a server will now be stored directly on this device. User queries will also be resolved by the object itself. This new paradigm reduces cost by eliminating the network of backend servers as well as long range wireless infrastructure needed for a user to communicate with the backend server. Short range protocols such as Bluetooth can be used for communication between a user and an object. Storing data on the object itself also simplifies ownership transfer. The physical act of handing over a binder

J. Indulska et al. (Eds.): Pervasive 2008, LNCS 5013, pp. 93–110, 2008.
© Springer-Verlag Berlin Heidelberg 2008

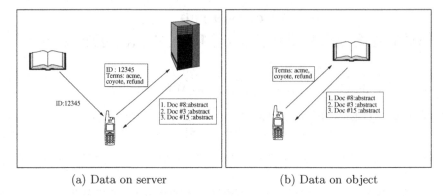

(a) Data on server   (b) Data on object

Fig. 1. (a) Typical design utilizing backend server. (b) Different paradigm without use of a server.

implicitly completes ownership transfer since any data can only be obtained when the user has physical access to the object. Fig. 1 illustrates the two approaches.

In this paper, we describe Microsearch, a search system designed for small embedded devices. We use the following example to illustrate how Microsearch can be used. Consider a collection of document binders. Each binder is embedded with a small device running Microsearch. Each device contains some information about the documents found in that binder. When a user wishes to find some documents, he can query a binder using some terms, i.e. "acme,coyote,refund", and Microsearch will return a ranked list of documents that might satisfy his query. Also included in the reply is a short abstract of each document to help him make his decision. Later, the user decides to add some notes to a document. Through input devices such as a digital pen [19] or PDA, the user can store notes into each binder. Microsearch will index the user input for future retrieval.

Microsearch is designed to run on resource constrained small devices capable of being embedded into everyday objects. One example of such hardware is manufactured by Intel [16] which has a 12MHz CPU, 64KB of RAM, 512KB of flash memory, and wireless capabilities, all packaged in a 3x3 cm circuit board. Larger storage capacity can also be engineered to store more data. In this paper, we use the terms "mote" and "small device" interchangeably.

Similar to desktop search engines like Google Desktop [15], Spotlight [2] or Beagle [4], Microsearch indexes information stored within a mote, and returns a ranked list of possible answers in response to a user's query. We envision that Microsearch can be an important component in physical world search engines like Snoogle [28] or MAX [31].

The challenge of designing Microsearch lies in engineering a complete solution that can run efficiently on a resource constrained platform. Desktop search systems typically require large amounts of RAM to perform indexing. Similarly, query resolution algorithms usually store intermediate results in memory while resolving a query. With just kilobytes of RAM to spare, it is impossible to port existing solutions directly onto motes. In addition, mote hardware uses flash memory for persistent storage. Unlike conventional disk, flash memory requires additional processing for I/O operations. Conventional flash file systems [30,29] cannot be used for this purpose due to the limited hardware resources. This necessitates a different storage design.

We make the following contributions in this paper. (*a*) We provide a system architecture that effectively utilizes limited memory resources to store and index different inputs. (*b*) Our architecture incorporates information retrieval (IR) techniques to determine relevant answers to user queries. (*c*) Since conventional IR techniques are designed for more powerful systems in mind, we introduce a space saving algorithm to perform IR calculations with limited amounts of memory. Our algorithm can return the top-k relevant answers in response to a user query. (*d*) A theoretical model of Microsearch is presented to better understand how to choose different system parameters. (*e*) Finally, we implement Microsearch on an actual hardware platform for evaluation.

The rest of this paper is as follows: Section 2 contains related work, and Section 3 describes the Microsearch system design. Section 4 covers our search algorithms, and Section 5 presents the theoretical model of Microsearch. Section 6 contains our evaluation, and Section 7 concludes.

2   Related Work

Desktop search engines are a mainstream feature found in most modern operating systems. In general, these search engines collect metadata from every file, and store the metadata into an inverted index, a typical data structure used to support keyword searches [10]. Information retrieval algorithms [18,11,12,13] are then used to determine the best answer to a query. Our work draws from the basic principals of IR to rank query results.

A counterpart to Microsearch is PicoDBMS [23], a scaled down database for a smart card. PicoDBMS allows data stored inside the smart card to be queried using SQL-like semantics. The main design difference between our work and PicoDBMS is that PicoDBMS uses a database design. Their approach works well in a specific domain like storing health care information, where rules regarding structured inputs with specified attribute terms can be enforced, and users, e.g. doctors and nurses, are assumed to be well trained in the system. Microsearch on the other hand uses a search engine design which allows for unstructured inputs without enforcing pre-specified attributes, and a natural language query interface. The differences between the Microsearch and PicoDBMS can be summed up as the differences between a search engine and a database.

Other embedded search systems can be found in sensor network literature [32,20,9]. Sensor networks are a collection of small, embedded devices usually deployed to collect environmental data such as temperature readings or soil humidity values. While sensor systems share a similar hardware platform as Microsearch, they are primarily concerned with indexing and processing numeric data. There appears to be no way for existing sensor search systems to index textual data. In addition, query processing in sensor networks typically returns a range query results or min/max values on collected data. Since the data is numeric, there is no concept of relevancy or ranking. Microsearch differs from sensor systems in that it handles textual in addition to numeric data, and uses IR algorithms to reply to queries.

3   System Architecture

We begin by describing the inputs to Microsearch. We assume that a user uploads information to Microsearch via a wireless connection through a suitable interface like a PDA. Microsearch requires every user input to consist of two segments, a *payload*, and a *metadata*. The payload is the actual information the user wishes other people to download. The metadata is a description of the payload data, and is used to determine whether a payload is relevant to a user's query. Both the payload and metadata are user generated.

The metadata is essentially a list of terms describing the corresponding payload. Microsearch requires each term, known as a *metadata term*, to be accompanied by a numeric value, known as a *metadata value*, indicating how important *that* term is in describing the payload. A metadata using n metadata terms to describe a payload can be represented as $\{(term_1, value_1), \cdots, (term_n, value_n)\}$. For a text based payload, the simplest method to determine the metadata value for a term is to count the number of occurrences of that term in the payload. Metadata values for non-text based payloads can be defined by the user.

3.1   Microsearch Design

Microsearch maintains two data structures in RAM: a buffer cache, and an inverted index. The buffer cache is used to temporarily store and organize data before writing to flash to improve overall performance. The inverted index is used to track and recover the stored data. In general, when receiving an input file, Microsearch stores the payload into flash memory, and the metadata into the buffer cache. This continues as more inputs are sent to Microsearch until the buffer cache is full. Selected metadata entries are then organized and flushed to flash memory to free up space in the buffer cache, and the inverted index is updated.

Receiving an Input: Upon receiving an input file, Microsearch first stores the metadata into RAM, and then writes the payload directly to flash memory. The starting address of the payload in flash is returned and added to each metadata entry for that payload. With this payload address, Microsearch can recover the entire payload if needed. Each metadata entry in the buffer cache now becomes a tuple , $(term, value, address)$, consisting of a metadata term, a metadata value, and payload address. For example, consider Microsearch writing a payload to flash memory location $addr_3$. All the metadata associate with this payload becomes, $\{(term_1, 3, addr_3), \cdots, (term_n, 2, addr_3)\}$.

As mentioned earlier, flash memory is used as permanent storage for user inputs. Microsearch writes data to flash memory using a log structure style write which treats the entire flash memory as a circular log, always appending new data to the head of the log. A pointer indicating the next available location in flash memory is kept by Microsearch. Log-style writes have been found to be suitable for flash memory [14]. Since writes are performed on a page granularity, Microsearch will always attempt to buffer the data into at least a single page before writing to flash.

Buffer Cache Organization: As more input files are sent to the buffer cache, the buffer cache becomes a collection of metadata entries which describe the different input files stored in the mote. There is no longer the concept of a set of entries belonging to a particular metadata. Instead, metadata entries which have the same metadata term are grouped together. For instance, two payloads stored in address $addr_3$ and $addr_8$ may share the same term $term_1$. Thus, inside the buffer cache, they will be grouped as $\{(term_1, 3, addr_3), (term_1, 8, addr_8)\}$.

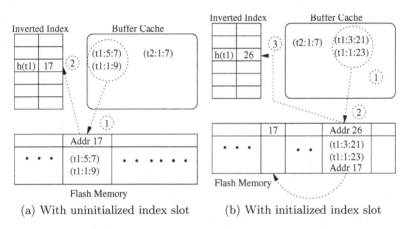

(a) With uninitialized index slot   (b) With initialized index slot

Fig. 2. (a) Buffer eviction with uninitialized index slot: 1) Flushes tuples from buffer cache, 2) Copies address of metadata page, $addr_{17}$, into inverted index. (b) Buffer eviction with initialized index slot: 1) Copies previous metadata page address from inverted index. 2) Flushes tuples from buffer cache. 3) Copies new address, $addr_{26}$, into inverted index.

Inverted Index: An inverted index is commonly used in search engine systems to recover archived information. A conventional inverted index has every slot on the inverted index correspond to a different term. Each slot stores a pointer to a list of documents or web pages containing that term. By matching a given query term with the inverted index, one can recover all the documents or webpages containing that term.

Microsearch uses a modified inverted index which differs from a conventional design in two ways. First, Microsearch uses a hash function to map multiple metadata terms to a certain slot in the inverted index. This results in a smaller inverted index which uses less RAM but is slightly inaccurate. We discuss how Microsearch resolves this inaccuracy in the next section. Second, Microsearch has each slot in the inverted index store the flash address of a page in flash memory containing a group of metadata terms which hash to the same slot. This flash page is known as a *metadata page*. An inverted index slot which already has metadata terms hashed to it is considered *initialized*.

Buffer Eviction with Uninitialized Index Slot: When the buffer cache reaches full capacity, tuples will have to be evicted to free up space for new entries. Microsearch selects the largest group of tuples, which all share the same metadata term, and applies a hash function to the metadata term to determine a slot on the inverted index. If no metadata term has been hashed to that slot before, that slot is considered uninitialized. Microsearch organizes the group of tuples in the order of their arrival into the buffer cache, and writes the metadata pages into flash memory. If the group of tuples spans multiple flash pages, each metadata page contains the flash memory address of the next page. The address of the *last* metadata page containing the tuples is returned to the inverted index. The inverted index stores this address into the uninitialized slot. The slot is now considered initialized. Fig. 2(a) illustrates this process.

Buffer Eviction with Initialized Index Slot: In the event that an inverted index slot has already been initialized, Microsearch will copy the address found in that slot onto the *first* metadata page of the group of tuples. The group of tuples are written to flash memory as before, and the address of the last metadata page is returned and stored in the inverted index. The inverted index thus will always have the address of the latest metadata page written into flash memory. Since each metadata page in flash memory contains the address location of the preceeding page, every metadata page can be recovered by traversing the links. We consider this *a chain* of metadata pages. Fig. 2(b) illustrates this process.

Data Deletion: Once the flash is reaching full capacity, Microsearch simply erases the oldest data to make room. Deletion in flash memory occurs at a sector granularity, with each section usually being 64KB. A pointer is kept by Microsearch to indicate which is the next sector to erase. The deletion does not affect the working of Microsearch since payloads are always written to flash before metadata. Therefore we will not have "orphaned" payloads that exist in flash memory but cannot be retrieved. The next problem is that of entries in metadata pages pointing to invalid payload that have been deleted. This is solved using the deletion pointer. Since this pointer indicates the next sector to erase, the sector that lie before this pointer must have been just erased. Microsearch disregards entries in metadata pages that point to payloads in the sectors behind the delete pointer since they do not exist anymore.

4   Query Resolution

A user queries a mote by sending a list of search terms and parameter k which specifies the top-k rankings he is interested in. The user receives an ordered list of k possible payload data as an answer. We begin by first introducing a basic query resolution algorithm. The actual space saving algorithm used by Microsearch is presented later.

In the basic algorithm, Microsearch first obtains a set of metadata entries which have metadata terms that match the search terms. Remember that a metadata entry is of the form $(term, value, address)$. With this chosen set of metadata entries, Microsearch then ranks the payload addresses in order of their relevancy, and uses the top ranking addresses to retrieve the payloads to return to the user. Since each payload has a unique flash memory address, this address is used as an identifier for a payload.

To obtain the set of metadata entries, Microsearch first scans all the metadata entries in the buffer cache for metadata terms matching the search terms. Matching entries are then copied to a separated section of RAM. Next, Microsearch uses the inverted index to find matching metadata entries in flash. Microsearch first applies the hash function to each search term to determine the corresponding slot in the inverted index. These slots contain the addresses of the metadata pages in flash memory. Each metadata page contains metadata terms which hash to the same slot. Note that the metadata terms found in the same page do not necessarily have to be the same. They only need to hash to the same slot. Microsearch then retrieves each metadata page one at a time until all metadata pages are read. For each metadata page read, Microsearch compares the actual metadata terms to the search terms, and copies the matching ones to RAM.

At this point, Microsearch has a list of all metadata entries which match the search terms. Microsearch uses a simple information retrieval weighing calculation, the TF/IDF function, to determine how relevant each payload address is in satisfying the user's query. TF refers to the term frequency, and IDF refers to the inverse document frequency. Under the TF/IDF function, the weight of each metadata term of a payload is determined by the product of $TF \cdot IDF$, where TF is the metadata value of the metadata term, and IDF is $\log(\frac{N}{DF})$, where N is the total number of payloads stored within the mote, and DF is the number of payloads which share the same metadata term. The relevancy of a payload, or the score of the payload, is the combined weights of the metadata terms matching the search terms. After determining the score of the each payload address, Microsearch orders them from the highest score to the lowest. Microsearch then uses the top k payload addresses to obtain the actual payloads from flash to return to the user.

4.1 Improving Performance

The basic algorithm first selects all the metadata entries which match the search terms, and then proceeds to eliminate low scoring payload address. This approach requires a large section of RAM to be set aside. A better solution is to eliminate low scoring payload addresses as they are encountered.

There are two difficulties in deriving a better solution. First, Microsearch relies on TF/IDF calculations to determine the relevancy of each payload address. Calculating the IDF requires knowledge of DF, the number of payloads in flash which share the same metadata term. This information can only be obtained by reading in every metadata page from flash and checking the corresponding metadata terms. We cannot maintain a running DF score since each inverted index slot represents the metadata terms which hash to that slot. Without reading in the actual metadata page, we cannot determine what the actual metadata terms are.

Second, even we use only TF score without IDF, a simple elimination scheme does not work. Consider the example when a user queries Microsearch with two search terms x and y, with $k = 1$. For simplicity, we assume that the buffer cache is empty, and x, y hash to different slots in the inverted index, i.e. $hash(x) \neq hash(y)$. We have 10 metadata pages each in flash memory matching $hash(x)$ and $hash(y)$. Now after reading in the first metadata page for x, we obtain 2 metadata entries with x. This means there are two potential payload addresses which can satisfy the user's query. Let us denote these two address as $addr_1$ and $addr_2$. The first metadata page for y does not contain either $addr_1$ or $addr_2$. At this point, even though the user specifies the top-1 answer, we cannot eliminate $addr_1$ or $addr_2$ because we cannot determine whether either payload address actually contains the term y. The reason is that Microsearch does not guarantee that metadata from the same payload are evicted from the buffer cache at the same time. To be sure whether $addr_1$ or $addr_2$ contains y, we have to continue reading in the metadata pages for $hash(y)$ from flash.

4.2 Space Efficient Algorithm

To derive a space efficient algorithm, Microsearch exploits the sequential write behavior of log file system. This sequential behavior ensures that data written to flash memory is always written in a forward order. This means that if payload $p1$ is sent to the mote before payload $p2$, then the flash address of $p1$ will be smaller than that of $p2$.

To describe the space efficient algorithm, we first define some notations. We let t be the number of search terms and a user query is $\{k, \{st_1, st_2, \ldots, st_t\}\}$, where st_i is the ith search term. We denote the inverted index as $InvIndex$, and the latest metadata page to be written to flash memory as the head metadata page. For example, $InvIndex[hash(st_i)]$ returns the address of the head metadata page for st_i. We represent this value as $head[i]$.

We allocate a memory space $page[i]$ for each query term st_i, which is sufficient to load one metadata page from flash memory. We first check the buffer and load the metadata entries whose metadata value is st_i to $page[i]$. If st_i is not found in the buffer, we load $head[i]$ to $page[i]$. Let $\min(page[i])$ and $\max(page[i])$ denote the smallest and largest payload addresses in $page[i]$ respectively. We define a *cutoff* value as

$$cutoff = max(min(page[i])), \forall i \in [1, t].$$

Due to the following lemma 1, we have all necessary information to calculate the IR scores for the loaded index entries, whose payload address is greater than or equal to *cutoff*. The entire algorithm is found in Algorithm 1.

Lemma 1. *For any index entry whose payload address $\geq$ cutoff, if its term field is included in the query terms, it must have been loaded into memory.*

Proof. It can be proved by contradiction. Assume there exists such an index entry whose term is one of the search terms st_i, and payload address is $p \geq cutoff$. In addition, the metadata page it belongs to has not been loaded yet. It means that the contents in $page[i]$ are from some ancestor in the same chain. An important property of metadata page chain is that if page i is an ancestor of page j, then $min(i) > max(j)$. Thus, $min(page[i]) > p \geq cutoff$. It is a contradiction with the definition of *cutoff*.

A k-length array $result[k]$ is used to store the intermediate results which are the candidates of final reply. Every time we get a new IR score, this array will be updated to keep the current top-k results. The processed index entries will be eliminated from memory. When $page[i]$ is empty, we load the next metadata page in the chain from flash memory and repeat this process. Based on the definition of *cutoff*, there must be at least one $page[i]$ becoming empty after each iteration. The algorithm terminates when $\forall i, page[i] = \phi$ and every chain reaches its tail. In this design, instead of loading every metadata page, we load at most one page for each query term. Thus, the memory space needed is at most $O(E \cdot t)$, where E is the size of a metadata page.

Note that in practice we actually traverse each index chain twice, the first time to obtain the DF for the term, and the second time to execute the actual query algorithm. This is done to match the DF definition in the simple TF/IDF scoring algorithm adopted for this paper. If alternative scoring algorithms that do not require this form of IDF calculations are used, this extra traversal can be avoided.

Algorithm 1. Reply Top-k Query:

1: Input: $k, \{st_1, st_2, \ldots, st_t\}$
2: Output: k-length array *result*
3: $head[i] = InvIndex[hash(st_i)]$
4: Scan buffer and each relevant metadata page chain to accumulate the document frequency ($df[i]$)
5: Load relevant index entries in buffer to the buffer page $page[i]$
6: If $page[i]$ is empty, load Flash($head[i]$) and move $head[i]$ to the next page
7: **while** there exists a non-empty $page[i]$ **do**
8:     $cutoff$=max$\{$min$(page[i])\}$
9:     **for** non-empty $page[i]$ and max$(page[i]) \geq cutoff$ **do**
10:        **for** every entry $e \in page[i]$ and $e \geq cutoff$ **do**
11:            $score = $ calScore(e)
12:            **if** $score>$minimum score in $result$ **then**
13:                replace the entry with the minimum score in $result$ by $\{e, score\}$
14:            **for** $j = 1$ to t **do**
15:                remove e from $page[j]$
16:        **for** $i = 1$ to t **do**
17:            **if** $page[i]$ is empty **then**
18:                load Flash($head[i]$) to $page[i]$
19:                move $head[i]$ to the next metadata page
20: return *result*

---

5   Theoretical Model

A key parameter in designing Microsearch is the size of the inverted index. We first present the intuition behind the choice of inverted index size, followed by the theoretical model.

With a smaller inverted index, uploading information into Microsearch is faster. When the buffer cache is full, Microsearch evicts data from the buffer cache into flash memory. Microsearch groups all the metadata terms which hash to the same inverted index slot together for eviction. Recall that writing data to flash memory occurs on a page granularity. In other words, the cost of writing a page into flash memory is the same even in situations where there are not enough metadata terms hashing to the same inverted slot to make up a flash page. A smaller inverted index results in more metadata terms hashing to the same inverted index slot. This increases the probability of more entries being flushed out of the buffer cache each time.

With a larger inverted index, query performance is better. A larger inverted index will have fewer metadata terms hashing to each slot. As a result, the chain of metadata pages in flash memory which map to each inverted index slot is shorter. When replying to a query, Microsearch has to read in the entire chain of metadata pages. A shorter chain of metadata pages means that fewer pages are needed to be read from flash memory, and thus speeding up query performance. The variables used for our model are found in Table 1.

Table 1. System Model Variables

D	# of documents
m	# of metadata per document
t	# of query terms
H	Size of main index
E	Size of metadata page
B	Size of buffer
f_s	Query frequency

Query Performance: Assume there are D number of files stored in the flash memory and each of them is described by m terms on average. Totally, we need store $D \cdot m$ index entries in the flash, which occupy $\frac{D \cdot m}{E}$ metadata pages. Considering a fair hashing, the average length of metadata page chain is $\frac{D \cdot m}{E \cdot H}$. When Microsearch processes a query for one term, based on the hash value of the term, it has to go through one of the metadata page chain twice. One round for collecting the value of DF and the other for finding the top-k answers. Expectedly, Microsearch will need to read $\frac{2 \cdot D \cdot m}{E \cdot H}$ metadata pages from the flash. For a query for t terms, Microsearch has to access t distinct metadata page chains, when $t \ll H$. Thus, it takes at most $\frac{2 \cdot t \cdot D \cdot m}{E \cdot H}$ page reads to reply.

Insert Performance: Insert performance is measured by the number of reads and writes operated during inserting D files. In our scheme, the number of reads is roughly the same as the number of writes. Microsearch only writes metadata pages to the flash in buffer eviction. Thus, the insert performance depends on the number of flushed entries during each eviction. Let x denote the number, i.e., on average, every eviction puts x index entries to the flash. After inserting all the files, $D \cdot m - B$ entries are written to the flash. Thus, we need $\frac{D \cdot m - B}{x}$ writes for them. Next, we give an analysis of deriving the value of x. According to our scheme, x is the most frequent hashed value when the buffer is full. Obviously, x is at least $\lceil \frac{B}{H} \rceil$. For one hashed value h_i, the probability that p entries in the buffer map to h_i is

$$\binom{B}{p} \left(\frac{1}{H}\right)^p (1 - \frac{1}{H})^{(B-p)}.$$

Thus, the probability that at least p entries map to h_i is

$$q = \sum_{j \geq p} \binom{B}{j} \left(\frac{1}{H}\right)^j (1 - \frac{1}{H})^{(B-j)}.$$

The probability that $x \geq p$ is $P(x \geq p) = 1 - (1 - q)^H$. Thus,

$$P(x = p) = P(x \geq p) - P(x \geq p + 1).$$

Therefore, the expected value of x is

$$E(x) = \sum_{i \geq \lceil \frac{B}{H} \rceil}^{B} P(x = i) \cdot i.$$

In total, inserting D files requires $\frac{D \cdot m - B}{E(x)}$ number of writes and the same number of reads.

6 System Evaluation

We use the TelosB mote for our experiments. The TelosB mote features a 8MHz processor, 10KB RAM, 48KB ROM and 1MB of flash memory. An IEEE 802.15.4 standard radio is used for wireless communication. The entire package is slightly larger, measuring $65 \times 31 \times 6$ mm, and weighs 23 grams without the battery.

6.1 Generating Workload Data

A difficulty in evaluating a search system lies in determining an appropriate workload. An ideal workload should consists of traces derived from real world applications. However, since Microsearch-like applications do not yet exist, we cannot collect such traces for evaluation. This also makes generating synthetic traces that approximate user behavior difficult. We generated our workload by observing related real world applications.

We envision that most objects such as a wedding photograph album or a document binder will embed a mote running Microsearch. Since each object has its own mote, each mote does not necessarily have to contain a large amount of unique data. For instance, a large bookshelf may contain hundreds of document binders, with a combined total of thousands of documents. However, each binder may contain only a dozen documents. Since each binder embeds a mote, each mote only needs to index the contents of its own binder. Consequently, none of our workloads consider excessively large number of unique data.

Our evaluation consists of two workloads. The first is the *annotation workload* which represents a user storing many short pieces of information, similar to Post-it reminders or memos, onto a mote. The metadata a user would associate with these type of applications is usually very short. We want a real world application where many users provided annotations, since this closely resembles the metadata we desire. One such application is the annotation of online photographs. We extracted 622 photographs and their accompanying annotations from the website www.pbase.com. This created a set of 2059 metadata terms, an average of 3.3 metadata terms per photograph. We consider each photograph as a unique input, and each photograph's annotation as the corresponding metadata terms. The metadata value of each term is set to 1. Fig. 3 shows the metadata term distribution for this workload.

The second workload is the *doc workload*. This workload represents a mote used for tracking purposes, such as keeping track of the documents inside a binder. We assume that the binder contains academic publications, and the accompanying mote contains the abstracts of all the papers. A user can query Microsearch just like querying *Google Scholar* to determine if a particular paper is inside the binder. To create the doc workload, we extracted 21 papers from the conference proceedings of Sensys 2005, and derived an average of 50 metadata terms for each paper. The metadata terms include author names, paper title, keywords. Metadata values are based on the number of times each term appeared in the paper abstract.

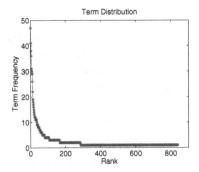

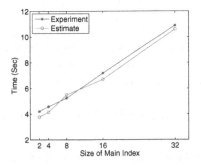

Fig. 3. Term distribution for annotation workload

Fig. 4. Predicted and actual indexing performance

6.2   System Performance

We use the annotation workload to evaluate system performance. The objective is to determine the performance of the two main Microsearch components: indexing the data sent by a user, and replying a user query. Time is the main metric used. In addition, for every evaluation, we present both the actual measured performance, and the predicted performance derived from our theoretical model introduced earlier. The closer the predicted results match the actual results, the more accurate our theoretical model is.

To prepare, we first generate a set of queries by randomly choosing terms from the 2059 harvested annotations. We then divided the set of queries into four groups, with the first group containing queries with one search term, the second group with queries containing two search terms and so on. Each group has a total of 100 queries. We limit the number of search terms to at most four terms, since studies conducted on mobile search conclude that most searches consists of between 2 and 3 terms [8,3,17].

We then inserted the 622 metadata files with a total of 2059 metadata terms into Microsearch. This is equivalent to inserting 622 short messages into the mote. Fig. 4 shows the time taken to insert all the terms into Microsearch. We see uploading information is faster given a smaller inverted index. This is consistent with the intuition given in the prior section.

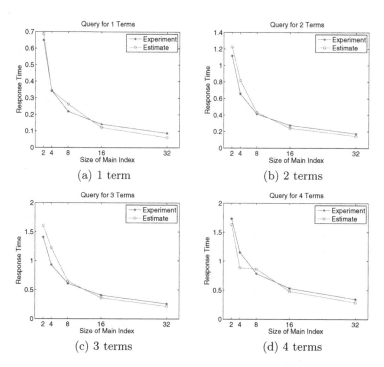

Fig. 5. Predicted and actual query response time. Response time measured in seconds.

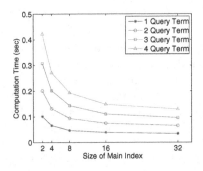

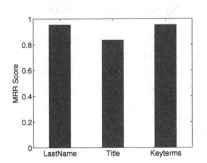

Fig. 6. Processing time overhead of search system processing

Fig. 7. Query accuracy (k=3)

In Fig 5, we show the time taken for Microsearch to satisfy a user's query. As discussed in the theoretical model, we see that a larger inverted index processes queries faster than a smaller inverted index. The predicted query response time is also very close to the measured time. Overall, Microsearch is able to satisfy a user's query in less than two seconds, which we believe is a reasonable time. Fig 6 shows the actual overhead of Microsearch minus the time taken to read from flash memory. We see that the additional time taken to rank the query answers is less than 0.5 seconds.

6.3   Search Accuracy

Shah and Croft [25] suggested using metrics from question answering (QA) research [27] to evaluate search algorithms for bandwidth or power constrained devices. QA is a branch of information retrieval that returns answers instead of relevant documents in response to a query. In QA research, the goal is to return a single or a very small group of answers in response to a query, not all relevant documents. The main evaluation in QA is the mean reciprocal rank (MRR). MRR is the calculated as

$$MRR = \frac{1}{\text{rank of first correct response}}.$$

The first correct response is the top ranked document in the model answer. For example, consider the model answer to a query be the ranked list (A, B, C) and the IR system returns the list of (C, B, A). The first correct answer should be A and the returned answer is 2 spots off. The MRR for this question is thus $\frac{1}{3} = 0.33$. We evaluate the performance of our search system by modifying the guidelines for QA track at TREQ-10 [5]. We consider only the top 3 answers in calculating MRR. If the model answer does not appear within the top three ranks, it has a score of 0.

We use the doc workload to evaluate the accuracy of Microsearch. We first determine a set of queries based on the 21 publications, and their corresponding answers by hand. These questions are divided into three groups, *LastName*,

Title and *KeyTerms*. The queries for the first two categories are terms from the last names and paper titles of the conference proceedings. The queries for the last category are a mixture of terms from last names, titles and abstract keywords.

Our evaluation does not consider deliberately vague queries since it is difficult to objectively quantify what the answer *should* be. Instead, we generated queries which contain terms that are found in multiple documents, but these queries have a clear answer. An example of a query is "underwater sensor storage". There is only one paper containing the term "underwater", and three papers containing the term "storage". Almost all papers contained the word "sensor". The correct answer is should be the only paper on underwater sensors. However, two other papers contain more occurrences of the term "storage". A good search system will be able to rank the most likely result ahead of a less likely one.

Fig. 7 shows the results of our search system for the three categories. For each category, we plot the MRR for the different categories over the average of 21 questions. From the figure, our system returns a MRR of 0.95 for both *LastName* and *KeyTerms*. The MRR for *Title* is lower at 0.83, because some of the paper titles contained very common words like "Packet Combining In Sensor Networks". In all cases, we see that on average Microsearch will return the correct answer when the user specifies $k = 3$.

6.4   Alternative Design

An alternative system design is to not use an inverted index at all. The incoming metadata is buffered and flushed to flash when there are enough entries to make up a full metadata page. Each metadata page will contain a pointer to the previous metadata page in flash. A single entry kept in memory remembers the latest metadata page's location in flash. When querying, Microsearch accesses every metadata page in flash before replying since every metadata page could contain a payload matching the query terms. The intuition is that such a scheme will have a better indexing performance at the expense of worse query performance.

To evaluate, we used a $1KB$ memory limit. The alternative design will allocate all as much space as possible to the buffer cache, and have just one main index entry. Microsearch uses a balanced approach, using an inverted index size of $76B$, and a buffer cache of $944B$. The alternative system takes an average of 6.5 ms to index the metadata in one file compared to the 20 ms for our scheme. Fig. 8 shows the difference in query response time for different number of query terms. Next, we compare the energy consumption between our scheme and the alternative scheme. Since both schemes have to do the same amount of writing for the payload data given the same document set, our comparison only measures the energy consumption of metadata input and query. Let P_w and P_r be the energy consumption for writing and reading one page data in flash memory respectively. Given the input insertion frequency f_u and user query frequency f_q, the energy consumption is determined by the amount of metadata writing during the input insertion period and the amount of metadata reading during the query period. For the simplicity, we ignore the energy consumption of CPU

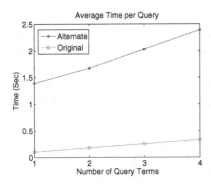

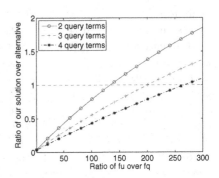

Fig. 8. Comparing alternative scheme with our scheme

Fig. 9. Comparing power consumption of our scheme verses alternative scheme

processing because that part is much smaller compared with the flash memory read and write operations. On a per unit time basis, the energy consumption of our scheme can be expressed as $E_1 = f_u \cdot W_i \cdot (P_w + P_r) + f_q \cdot R_q \cdot P_r$, where W_i is the number of pages written for the metadata in the worst case (when m terms are mapped to m different index entries), and R_q is the number of page read operations required for the query. From Section 5, we have $W_i = \frac{m}{\frac{E}{H}+1}$ and $R_q = \frac{2 \cdot D \cdot m \cdot t}{E \cdot H}$.

Similarly, the energy consumed by the alternative scheme can be expressed as $E_2 = f_u \cdot W_i' \cdot (P_w + P_r) + f_q \cdot R_q' \cdot P_r$, where $W_i' = \frac{m}{E}$, and $R_q' = \frac{2 \cdot D \cdot m \cdot t}{E}$. With the system parameters fixed at $D = 622, m = 3, E = 31$ and $H = 32$, we estimate the energy consumption for both schemes based on TelosB flash memory read and write energy performance presented in [21] (i.e., $P_w = 0.127 \times 256 = 32.5\mu J$, $P_r = 0.056 \times 256 = 14.3\mu J$). To compare our scheme with the alternative, we find the ratio of $\frac{E_1}{E_2}$. Values less than 1 favor our solution while values larger than 1 favor the alternative. To simplify the results, we divide both E_1 and E_2 by f_q, which does not affect the ratio. As a result, $\frac{E_1}{E_2}$ becomes a function of $\frac{f_u}{f_q}$. We plot the energy ratio graph with 2, 3 and 4 query terms respectively. The estimation results are found in Fig. 9. The figure shows that for an average of 2 query terms, the alternative performs better when there are about 140 document insertions to a single query. For an average of 3 and 4 query terms, the alternative scheme performs better only when there are 200 and 260 document insertions to a single query. This suggests that the alternative scheme should be used only when the mote is used to store data and rarely if ever queried.

7   Conclusion and Future Work

In this paper, we present a search system for small devices. Our architecture can index an arbitrary number of textual metatdata efficiently. A space saving algorithm is used in conjunction with IR scoring to return the top-k answers to the user. Our experimental results show that Microsearch is able to resolve a user query of up to four terms in less than two seconds, and provide a high level of accuracy.

In future work we aim to implement security measures such as access control and data encryption into Microsearch and evaluate their performance. We also plan to incorporate Microsearch into our physical world search engine, Snoogle [28], for further evaluation.

Acknowledgments

We would like to thank the reviewers and our shepherd, Nigel Davies, for all their helpful comments in improving this paper.This project was supported by US National Science Foundation award CCF-0514985, CNS-0721443, and CNS-0747108.

References

1. Abowd, G.D., Atkeson, C.G., Hong, J., Long, S., Kooper, R., Pinkerton, M.: Cyberguide: a mobile context-aware tour guide. Wirel. Netw. (1997)
2. Apple, http://www.apple.com/macosx/features/spotlight/
3. Baeza-Yates, R., Dupret, G., Velasco, H.: A study of mobile search queries in japan. In: WWW 2006 (2006)
4. Beagle, http://beagle-project.org/main_page
5. Chen, J., Diekema, A., Taffet, M.D., McCracken, N.J., Ozgencil, N.E., Yilmazel, O., Liddy, E.D.: Question answering: CNLP at the TREC-10 question answering track. In: Text REtrieval Conference (2001)
6. Cheverst, K., Davies, N., Mitchell, K., Friday, A.: Experiences of developing and deploying a context-aware tourist guide: the guide project. In: MobiCom 2000 (2000)
7. Cheverst, K., Davies, N., Mitchell, K., Friday, A., Efstratiou, C.: Developing a context-aware electronic tourist guide: some issues and experiences. In: CHI 2000 (2000)
8. Church, K., Smyth, B., Cotter, P., Bradley, K.: Mobile information access: A study of emerging search behavior on the mobile internet. ACM Trans. Web (2007)
9. Dai, H., Neufeld, M., Han, R.: ELF: an efficient log-structured flash file system for micro sensor nodes. In: SenSys 2004 (2004)
10. Faloutsos, C.: Access methods for text. ACM Comput. Surv. 17(1) (1985)
11. Faloutsos, C., Oard, D.W.: A survey of information retrieval and filtering methods. Technical Report CS-TR-3514 (1995)
12. Frakes, W.B., Baeza-Yates, R.A. (eds.): Information Retrieval: Data Structures and Algorithms. Prentice-Hall, Englewood Cliffs (1992)
13. French, J.C., Powell, A.L., Callan, J.P., Viles, C.L., Emmitt, T., Prey, K.J., Mou, Y.: Comparing the performance of database selection algorithms. In: Research and Development in Information Retrieval (1999)
14. Gal, E., Toledo, S.: Algorithms and data structures for flash memories. ACM Comput. Surv. 37(2) (2005)
15. Google, www.desktop.google.com
16. Intel, www.intel.com/research/downloads/imote-ds-101.pdf

17. Kamvar, M., Baluja, S.: A large scale study of wireless search behavior: Google mobile search. In: CHI 2006 (2006)
18. Kobayashi, M., Takeda, K.: Information retrieval on the web. ACM Computing Surveys 2000 (2000)
19. Logitec, www.logitech.com
20. Mathur, G., Desnoyers, P., Ganesan, D., Shenoy, P.: Capsule: An energy-optimized object storage system for memory-constrained sensor devices. In: SenSys 2006 (2006)
21. Mathur, G., Desnoyers, P., Ganesan, D., Shenoy, P.: Ultra-low power data storage for sensor networks. In: IPSN 2006 (2006)
22. Paradise, J., Mynatt, E.D.: Audio note system
23. Pucheral, P., Bouganim, L., Valduriez, P., Bobineau, C.: PicoDBMS: Scaling down database techniques for the smartcard. In: VLDB 2001 (2001)
24. Rekimoto, J., Ayatsuka, Y., Hayashi, K.: Augment-able reality: Situated communication through physical and digital spaces. In: ISWC 1998 (1998)
25. Shah, C., Croft, W.B.: Evaluating high accuracy retrieval techniques. In: SIGIR 2004 (2004)
26. Starner, T., Kirsch, D., Assefa, S.: The locust swarm: An environmentally-powered, networkless location and messaging system. In: ISWC 1997 (1997)
27. Voorhees, E.M.: Overview of the TREC 2001 question answering track. In: Text REtrieval Conference (2001)
28. Wang, H., Tan, C.C., Li, Q.: Snoogle: A search engine for the physical world. In: Infocom 2008 (2008)
29. Woodhouse, D.: Jffs : The journalling flash file system
30. Wookey. Yaffs: Yet another flash file system
31. Yap, K.-K., Srinivasan, V., Motani, M.: Max: human-centric search of the physical world. In: SenSys 2005 (2005)
32. Zeinalipour-Yazti, D., Lin, S., Kalogeraki, V., Gunopulos, D., Najjar, W.A.: Microhash: An efficient index structure for flash-based sensor devices. In: FAST 2005 (2005)

Identifying Meaningful Places:
The Non-parametric Way

Petteri Nurmi and Sourav Bhattacharya

Helsinki Institute for Information Technology HIIT
Department of Computer Science, P.O. Box 68,
FI-00014 University of Helsinki, Finland
`petteri.nurmi@cs.helsinki.fi`,
`sourav.bhattacharya@cs.helsinki.fi`

Abstract. Gathering and analyzing location data is an important part of many ubiquitous computing applications. The most common way to represent location information is to use numerical coordinates, e.g., latitudes and longitudes. A problem with this approach is that numerical coordinates are usually meaningless to a user and they contrast with the way humans refer to locations in daily communication. Instead of using coordinates, humans tend to use descriptive statements about their location; for example, "I'm home" or "I'm at Starbucks." Locations, to which a user can attach meaningful and descriptive semantics, are often called places. In this paper we focus on the automatic extraction of places from discontinuous GPS measurements. We describe and evaluate a non-parametric Bayesian approach for identifying places from this kind of data. The main novelty of our approach is that the algorithm is fully automated and does not require any parameter tuning. Another novel aspect of our algorithm is that it can accurately identify places without temporal information. We evaluate our approach using data that has been gathered from different users and different geographic areas. The traces that we use exhibit different characteristics and contain data from daily life as well as from traveling abroad. We also compare our algorithm against the popular k-means algorithm. The results indicate that our method can accurately identify meaningful places from a variety of location traces and that the algorithm is robust against noise.

1 Introduction

The location of a user plays an important role in many ubiquitous computing applications. The most common way to represent location information is to use numerical coordinates such as latitudes and longitudes. The main problems with this approach are that the raw location measurements are difficult to use in location-aware applications [1] and that the measurements are seldom meaningful to a user [2]. For example, we do not refer to our home or workplace as a pair of GPS coordinates. A more appropriate way to utilize location information is to use the notion of *place*. A widely used definition for a place is given by Relph, who defines it as a combination of the physical setting, the activities

J. Indulska et al. (Eds.): Pervasive 2008, LNCS 5013, pp. 111–127, 2008.

supported by the place, and the meanings attributed to the place [3]. In this paper, we consider a place as a location to which a user can attach meaningful and descriptive semantics. Thus we focus only on the physical setting and the meanings attributed to a place; see [4] for other definitions of a place.

In this paper we focus on the task of automatically extracting places from discontinuous GPS traces. We consider two kinds of discontinuous traces: traces that have been gathered by sampling the GPS periodically (once every minute) and traces that have been gathered by sampling the GPS whenever the GSM cell identifier changes. Our methodology can be applied also with other kinds of discontinuous GPS traces (e.g, periodically sampled localization traces). As our main contribution we introduce a statistical model for extracting places from this kind of data. The model is based on the non-parametric Bayesian framework[1], more precisely, Dirichlet process mixture models [5,6]. We model data points using multivariate Normal distributions and thus our model can also be understood as an infinite Gaussian mixture model [7]. The main novelty of our approach is that the algorithm is fully automated and does not require any parameter tuning. Another novel aspect of our algorithm is that it can accurately identify places without considering temporal information.

We evaluate our place extraction algorithm using two data sets. The data sets that we use exhibit rather different characteristics: the first data set contains location traces from daily life situations and the second data set contains location traces gathered during a business trip. We also compare the Dirichlet process clustering algorithm against the popular k-means algorithm. Our results indicate that the Dirichlet process model is a good candidate for extracting places as, in both cases, the algorithm produces accurate and compact results. In addition, the Dirichlet process model is robust against noise in the location measurements.

The rest of the paper is organized as follows: Sec. 2 gives background information on why certain locations are meaningful. Sec. 3 introduces related work on place extraction. Sec. 4 introduces our problem setting and presents the statistical model. Sec. 5 presents our experiments. Sec. 6 concludes the paper.

2   Background: Why Some Places Are Meaningful?

There are various explanations to why some places would be meaningful in the first place. For example, environmental psychology [8] examines how people structure their daily activities around common places such as GROCERY STORE, HOME and WORK. Accordingly, this view suggests that meaningful locations correspond to locations around which users relate specific activities. This view has been applied in pervasive computing by Zhou et al. [9].

A complementary view can be given using social identity theory [10]. Social identity theory studies the relationships between the individual and the society, and, more specifically, how an individual's self conceptions relate to the

---

[1] The term non-parametric Bayesian is somewhat confusing as the models actually contain an infinite number of parameters. In this paper we use the term 'non-parametric' to follow its common usage found in the literature; see, e.g., [5].

expectations and norms imposed by the society. Nurmi and Koolwaaij [11] have used social identity theory to argue that some places are meaningful because they act as boundaries between different roles and social categories. For example, WORK is related to being an employee whereas HOME is strongly related to social categories specific to private life. This view is complementary to the environmental psychology view in the sense that it attempts to explain why the structuring takes place.

The places that act as boundaries between different social categories are not the only meaningful places. Consider for example the sentence "let's meet at the same place where we met yesterday". This sentence refers to a location that is meaningful in a specific social context. The data in our setting does not carry sufficient information about the social situation of a user, and for this reason we ignore this kind of places in this paper.

Also various public places can be meaningful, simply because they serve as easily recognizable navigation cues. Zhou et al. [12] conducted a user study that identified five different place categories: generic, well-known public, specific public, personal and activity-based. Of these categories, we focus on the generic (airport, gas store), personal (home, workplace) and activity-based (hobby related) places, as they separate different social categories and activities.

3 Related Work

The main research directions in the analysis of location data are *localization* and *place extraction*. In localization, the goal is to determine the user's location as accurately as possible using whatever location information is available. The most common technique for localization is fingerprinting; see, e.g., [13,14]. The second category, *place extraction*, attempts to find spatial areas that are somehow important to the user. Localization complements place extraction in the sense that it can be used to gather accurate location traces that place detection algorithms can use. In this paper we focus exclusively on place extraction.

Approaches for extracting places from location data can be categorized based on the source of location information. The most common approach has been to use continuously gathered GPS traces. The algorithms for GPS traces are typically based on distance and time-related heuristics. For example, Marmasse et al. [15] use signal loss and distance between successive measurements to identify buildings. Meaningful places are then obtained based on the frequency of visits to the specific buildings. Ashbrook and Starner [2] use a cut-off parameter to determine whether a user stays long enough within an area that has a predefined radius. If the duration of the stay exceeds the value of the cut-off parameter, the location is identified as a place. Toyama et al. [16] present a variation of this work that employs multiple radius parameters to detect meaningful locations at different granularities. Zhou et al. [17] use a modified DBScan algorithm and temporal preprocessing to extract places. The temporal preprocessing ensures that the places are really visited frequently enough and the modification to the DBScan algorithm is needed to cope with signal errors. Other approaches for GPS data are presented, e.g., in [18,19,20,21].

The main problem with the GPS-based approaches is that GPS signal is not available indoors. In addition, tall buildings can reflect signals and cause signal loss or weak measurements in metropolitan areas. Nevertheless, GPS information is easily available and it requires minimal infrastructure investments. The main problem with place detection algorithms that use GPS traces is that they usually have tunable parameters or cut-off values. The algorithms can easily become sensitive to fluctuations in GPS signals and may require parameter tuning for different GPS receivers and environments; see also [22].

In bounded areas, such as office buildings, campuses, research laboratories or even individual cities, information about the physical location of radio beacons can be used to derive estimated location traces (e.g., [13,14]), from which places can be extracted. For example, Kang et al. [23] first use a customized spatial clustering algorithm to detect clusters from the data. The clusters act as candidate places and they are labeled as a place when the user stays long enough within the cluster. The BeaconPrint algorithm of Hightower et al. uses similarities in fingerprints of the radio environment to detect places [24]. An advantage of these techniques is that they work both indoors and outdoors. However, a disadvantage of these approaches is that detailed fingerprint information is not available on many mobile phones[2] and custom hardware is often needed to obtain the required information. Nevertheless, our algorithm can be also used for location traces derived via fingerprinting techniques.

Aipperspach et al. [22] have used a commercial positioning system to obtain high precision indoor location traces. These traces were then used to extract places within a home. The algorithm that they use is based on Gaussian mixture models, which are a simplified version of the model we use. The main problem with this approach is that obtaining high precision location traces requires costly infrastructure investments, which limits the usefulness of this approach.

Also some work on extracting places from GSM identifiers has been suggested [25,26]. Since the size of GSM cells can be rather large, places extracted from GSM data are necessarily only crude estimates of the true meaningful places. Nevertheless, the major advantage of GSM cell based clustering is that it does not require any additional hardware and that the clustering can be performed on the device without need to ever connect to a server. This option is thus optimal from a privacy perspective.

It is also possible to combine the advantages of the GPS approach with GSM identifier based clustering. Nurmi and Koolwaaij [11] use data consisting of GSM transitions and GPS coordinates at the transition point. This approach is more accurate than the GSM identifier based approach, and requires fewer resources from the device as GPS data is read only when a cell transition occurs. The main disadvantage of this approach is that the system is not able to get accurate location information when the user is indoors. Furthermore, since data is collected only at the transition points, this can cause bias to the results.

---

[2] For example, Nokia phones provide only information about the GSM cell tower to which the phone is currently connected. Accurate fingerprinting, on the other hand, requires information about several GSM towers.

The work presented in this paper offers three advantages over existing work. First of all, our approach is fully automated in the sense that it does not depend on any tunable parameters; most earlier methods require at least specifying the number of clusters beforehand whereas our algorithm is able to infer also this from data. Secondly, our approach requires minimal hardware investments[3]. Finally, the discontinuous nature of the GPS traces makes it possible to gather data for longer periods before the user needs to recharge the device. In practice we have been able to gather data for more than one day without recharging the mobile device.

4   Setting, Statistical Model and Algorithm

This section describes the statistical model and the algorithm that is used to cluster data points. The notation that is used in the paper is summarized in Table 1.

Table 1. A summary of the notation used in the paper

Symbol	Description
y_i	Individual data point
$\mathbf{y}$	The vector $(y_1, \ldots, y_n)$ of data points
c_i	Cluster indicator for data point i
$\mathbf{c}$	Vector $(c_1, \ldots, c_k)$ of cluster indicators
$\mathbf{c}_{-i}$	The vector $(c_1, \ldots, c_{i-1}, c_{i+1}, \ldots, c_n)$
k	The number of clusters
n	Number of data points
$\overline{y}$	Sample mean
$\overline{y}_j$	Mean of data points associated with cluster j
Σ	Sample precision
μ_j	The mean vector of cluster j
S_j	The precision matrix of cluster j
n_j	Number of data points in cluster j
$n_{-i,j}$	Number of data points in cluster j excluding point i
λ	Mean vector for the prior on cluster means μ_j
R	Precision matrix for the prior on cluster means μ_j
β	Degrees of freedom for the prior on cluster precision matrices S_j
W	Inverse scaling matrix for the prior on cluster precision matrices S_j
α	Concentration parameter of the Dirichlet process prior
ϕ	Auxiliary variable that is used for sampling α
π_ϕ	Mixture weight for the distribution used to sample α

Model

The data in our setting consists of (latitude, longitude) pairs that mark the transition point between two GSM cells. We use $\mathbf{y} = (y_1, \ldots, y_n)$ to denote the

---

[3] Mobile phone with an integrated GPS or a phone and a Bluetooth GPS device.

data. Each data point y_i is assumed to belong to a single cluster. Intuitively, this assumption implies that the user cannot be simultaneously at HOME and at WORK. We assume that the number of clusters is finite but unknown beforehand. The variable k is used to denote the number of clusters, and c_i is used to denote the cluster indicator that specifies to which cluster data point y_i is currently assigned. We use $\mathbf{c} = (c_1, \ldots, c_n)$ to denote the vector of cluster indicators over all data points.

The data in each cluster is assumed to follow a multivariate Normal distribution with mean μ_j and precision[4] matrix S_j. We assume that both μ_j and S_j are unknown. The distribution of a single data point y_i is thus given by

$$y_i | c_i = j, \mu_j, S_j \sim \mathcal{N}\left(\mu_j, S_j^{-1}\right). \tag{1}$$

Since the cluster parameters μ_j and S_j are unknown, we need to assign priors for them. The selection of the priors is important as they influence how likely it is that the clustering algorithm creates a new cluster component. In our case we use conjugate priors because they offer a good balance between computational simplicity and clustering performance. The conjugate prior for the multivariate Normal distribution, when both the mean and the precision matrix are unknown, is to assign a Normal distribution on the mean vector and a Wishart distribution on the precision matrix (see, e.g., [27]). Accordingly, we have

$$\mu_j \sim \mathcal{N}\left(\lambda, R^{-1}\right) \tag{2}$$

$$S_j \sim \mathcal{Wi}\left(2\beta, \frac{1}{2}W^{-1}\right), \tag{3}$$

where λ, β, R and W are hyperparameters. Following Rasmussen [7], we use a hierarchical model and assign priors to all hyperparameters. If we want clusters that are on average of specific size, we can fix the values of β and W beforehand. This can be done, for example, by assigning W to be the sample covariance and setting β so that the product βW^{-1} corresponds to the desired coverage[5].

Let $\overline{y}$ denote the sample mean and Σ the sample precision. We assign λ a Normal distribution whose mean equals the sample mean and whose covariance matrix corresponds to the sample covariance, i.e.,

$$\lambda \sim \mathcal{N}\left(\overline{y}, \Sigma^{-1}\right). \tag{4}$$

The distribution of λ has full support over the set of data points. This implies that samples from the prior on cluster means μ_j also have full support over the data points. The prior also implies that values of μ_j that are near the sample mean are most likely. A potential problem with this prior is that it puts more weight on the center (sample mean) of the data points, but this does not necessarily correspond to a place. For example, in large cities people often commute

---

[4] I.e., Inverse covariance.

[5] The product βW^{-1} corresponds to the expectation of the Wishart distribution on the cluster precision matrices.

for a long period of time to get to work. In this case, the sample mean corresponds to the midpoint of the travel route and samples from the prior on cluster means rarely fall near the actual clusters (home or work). Thus, the algorithm can take longer time to convergence. An alternative is to assign λ a uniform distribution over the set of data points.

The matrix R specifies the precision matrix for the cluster means. Intuitively, we would want the expectation of the distribution on R to correspond to the sample precision Σ as in this case the values for μ_j are on average drawn from a distribution that is specified by the sufficient statistics of the data. We also have to ensure that the resulting Wishart distribution is well defined[6]. This can be achieved by assigning the following distribution on R:

$$R \sim \mathcal{W}i \left(2, \frac{1}{2}\Sigma \right). \tag{5}$$

The hyperparameters for the prior on precision matrices are more complicated. We start from the variable β, which defines the degrees of freedom for the Wishart distribution on S_j. We do not want to limit the size of clusters beforehand and hence we need to assign a vague prior on β. However, we also need to ensure that the Wishart distribution over S_j remains well defined. These two goals can be achieved by assigning β a flat, continuous distribution over the interval $[1, \infty)$. In order to achieve this, we consider the variable $(\beta - 1)^{-1}$ and assign a Gamma prior for it:

$$(\beta - 1)^{-1} \sim \mathcal{G} \left(\frac{1}{2}, 2 \right). \tag{6}$$

Samples for $\beta - 1$ follow a flat inverse-Gamma distribution and they are within the interval $(0, \infty)$. Thus the distribution of β is as desired.

For the hyperparameter W, i.e., the inverse scale matrix of the prior on S_j, we assign the following Wishart prior:

$$W \sim \mathcal{W}i \left(2, \frac{1}{2}\Sigma^{-1} \right). \tag{7}$$

The expectation of W equals the sample covariance and, since the expectation of S_j equals βW^{-1}, samples from S_j are on average scaled variants of the sample precision matrix.

Our model specification is lacking a prior for the cluster indicators c_i. We can consider our model as a limiting case of a mixture model where the number of components goes to infinity, and the mixing proportions have been integrated out. Following Neal [28], the prior distribution of c_i can be written in the following form:

$$c_i = j | \mathbf{c}_{-i} \sim \frac{n_{-i,j}}{n - 1 + \alpha}$$
$$c_i \neq q | \mathbf{c}_{-i} \sim \frac{\alpha}{n - 1 + \alpha} \quad (\forall q \in \{1, \dots, k\}). \tag{8}$$

---

[6] A Wishart distribution $\mathcal{W}i(b, W)$ is well defined whenever the $p \times p$ matrix W is positive definite and $b \geq p$ holds for the degrees of freedom parameter b.

Here $n_{-i,j}$ denotes the number of data points that belong to cluster j when the data point i is ignored. The variable α is the concentration parameter of the Dirichlet process prior that, together with the priors on μ_j and S_j, governs the rate at which new clusters are created and $\mathbf{c}_{-i}$ is a vector that contains all other cluster indicators except c_i, i.e., $\mathbf{c}_{-i} = (c_1, \ldots, c_{i-1}, c_{i+1}, \ldots, c_n)$.

The support of the prior on c_i is the countably infinite set $\{1, 2, \ldots, k, \ldots\}$ where k denotes the number of clusters that have currently data points associated with them. For each of the represented clusters $j \in \{1, \ldots, k\}$, the prior assigns a probability mass of $n_{-i,j}/(n - 1 + \alpha)$. A probability mass of $\alpha/(n - 1 + \alpha)$ is assigned for all of the unrepresented clusters combined. Thus, although the number of clusters is potentially infinite, only some of them are represented at a given time and we do not need to make a distinction between the clusters that are unrepresented.

To finalize our model specification, we need to assign a prior on the concentration parameter α. Again, we assign a vague inverse-Gamma prior so that

$$\alpha^{-1} \sim \mathcal{G}\left(\frac{1}{2}, 2\right). \tag{9}$$

This prior results in a flat distribution that has support over $(0, \infty)$.

Algorithm

In order to utilize the model, we need to be able to compute summaries for the parameters from the posterior distribution of the parameters given the data. A standard way to achieve this in a Bayesian framework is to use Markov chain Monte Carlo (MCMC) techniques. In our case we use Gibbs sampling (see [7,28]), which is a MCMC algorithm that sequentially updates each parameter in turn. The updates are sampled from a probability distribution that is conditioned on the values of the other parameters. Thus, when sampling a new value for a specific parameter, we keep the values of all other parameters fixed. Detailed discussion about MCMC is out of scope of the paper and we refer to [29] for more information.

A high-level description of the algorithm is shown in Alg. 1, and the sampling distributions that are needed to perform Gibbs sampling are given in the Appendix. To improve the speed of convergence, we sampled the values of the cluster parameters and hyperparameters nine times as often as the cluster indicators c_i. In other words, we set the threshold value in Alg. 1 to 10.

Two parameters, α and β, cannot be sampled using traditional methods as their conditional distributions do not correspond to any density that is known in closed-form. In order to sample α, we used the scheme proposed by West [30]. In this scheme, the first step is to sample the value of an auxiliary variable ϕ that depends on the number of parameters and the current value of α. After this, the new value of α can be drawn from a distribution that corresponds to a mixture of two Gamma distributions. The sampling formulas are given in the Appendix and we refer to [30] for more details. Sampling β is more complicated.

Algorithm 1. Gibbs sampler for the model

1: **Input: data y**
2: *Initialization:*
3: Compute sufficient statistics $\bar{y}$ and Σ
4: Create a single cluster and assign all data points to it (i.e., $\mathbf{c} = (1, \ldots, 1)$)
5: Draw initial values for the hyperparameters
6: Sample parameters for the first cluster using the priors
7: **repeat**
8:     **if** iterations since last cluster indicator update $<$ threshold **then**
9:         **for** each active cluster component c **do**
10:             Sample new value for μ_c and S_c
11:         **end for**
12:         Sample hyperparameters λ, R, W
13:         Sample β using Adaptive Rejection Sampling
14:         Sample auxiliary variable ϕ from a Beta distribution
15:         Compute mixture weight π_ϕ
16:         Sample α^{-1} from a mixture of two Gamma distributions using ϕ, k and π_ϕ
17:     **else**
18:         **for** each data point y_i **do**
19:             **if** iterations $>$ burnout period **then**
20:                 Store current values
21:             **end if**
22:             Construct the sampling probabilities for the represented clusters given y_i
23:             Create a Monte Carlo estimate for the probability of the unrepresented classes
24:             Sample new value for c_i using the constructed probabilities
25:         **end for**
26:     **end if**
27: **until** convergence

Rasmussen [7] observed that the distribution of $\log \beta$ is log-concave, which makes it possible to use adaptive rejection sampling [31] for sampling new values of β. The formulas required to perform adaptive rejection sampling are also given in the Appendix.

Performance

The performance of the Dirichlet process algorithm depends, among other things, on the number of points and on the spatial distribution of data. When the data is relatively evenly distributed, the cluster indicators mix properly and the algorithm converges rapidly. However, when the data is spread out, i.e., it has long and narrow commuting traces (for example, the Innsbruck dataset in Sec. 5), the mixing is much slower. In general, for a given number of clusters, the cluster parameters converge in few hundred (100 - 500) iterations, but the cluster indicators may require several thousands, or even hundreds of thousands, of iterations to converge. The development of inference algorithms for Dirichlet process models is currently an active research area and many improvements have been recently suggested in the literature [32,33].

5   Experiments

5.1   Datasets

We have evaluated our approach using two different datasets. The first dataset has been collected in the city of Enschede, (the Netherlands) and the second dataset has been collected in Innsbruck (Austria). In the following we briefly describe these two datasets. The datasets are shown in Fig. 1.

Enschede. The first dataset that we consider has been gathered by a single user in the city of Enschede. The test subject lives in the city and the measurements have been gathered over a period of one year. Hence, this dataset is a good representative of location traces collected from daily life situations. The data collection was based on voluntary participation. The data was collected using a Nokia 6680 mobile phone and an external Bluetooth GPS receiver (Emtac S3 BTGPS). The GPS measurements were collected whenever the GSM base station to which the device is connected changed. In total, the data set contained over 19000 location measurements. However, most of the measurements were duplicates and there were only 700 distinct GPS measurements. Most of the duplicates correspond to indoor measurements as commonly used GPS devices return the last known GPS measurement when they lose the signal. Moreover, as the data collection was voluntary, the user mainly collected data during working hours.

Innsbruck. The second dataset that we consider has been collected in Innsbruck during Ubicomp 2007. The data has been collected by a single user

Fig. 1. A visualization of the datasets that we use in our experiments. The figure on the left-hand side shows the preprocessed Enschede dataset and figure on the right-hand side shows the preprocessed Innsbruck data.

using a Nokia N95 mobile phone and a Holux GPSlim 236B Bluetooth GPS receiver. The dataset contains 530 unique measurements. The measurements were collected by sampling the GPS receiver once every minute. The measurements contain both work and tourism related location traces. Hence the setting in the Innsbruck dataset nicely complements the Enschede dataset.

5.2   Experimental Setting and Evaluation Metrics

Before running our algorithm on the location traces, we performed a sanity check that removed unrealistic observations. GPS receivers occasionally give measurements that are suddenly off by several hundreds of kilometers; though, our experience suggests this is extremely rare and occurs mainly on cold starts. Nevertheless, the sanity check ensures that when this event occurs, the faulty data is ignored. As another preprocessing step, we removed all duplicate measurements. While it might seem that we lose information by dropping data, the removal of duplicates does not affect the clustering accuracy of the Dirichlet process algorithm. This is because, when the number of points is small, the spatial distribution of points, i.e., how close neighboring points are to each other, dominates the clustering. In frequently visited regions the spatial distribution is typically compact whereas when the user is commuting the distribution is more spread out.

After removing the duplicates, we ran the Dirichlet process algorithm on the data. For both data sets we ran around 225 000 iterations. From the results, we computed summaries of the mean and precision matrices for the clusters. We also performed post-processing on the results. In the post-processing phase we pruned out clusters that had large variance. From the results we observed a clear threshold as a fraction of the clusters had a relatively small variance whereas the remaining clusters tended to have a larger variance. To select the best cutoff threshold, we used agglomerative clustering on the cluster variances; see Fig. 2. This gave us thresholds that were around 1.0×10^{-5}. Note that

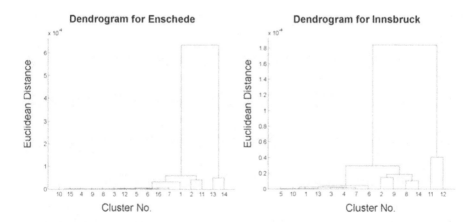

Fig. 2. Dendrograms for cluster variances in the Enschede and Innsbruck datasets

we are considering coordinate units, and this threshold value corresponds to approximately 100 meters. We also removed clusters whose relative frequency (i.e., n_j/n) was smaller than 3% as these clusters are unlikely to correspond to meaningful places.

After the post-processing, we visualized the clusters using Google Earth. For visualization we use the 95% error ellipses, which correspond to the 95% confidence region around the mean of a cluster. We showed the resulting clusters to the user whose data was used. We asked the user to label the clusters and to assess the quality of clustering. Although the evaluation procedure we use is nonstandard for evaluating machine learning algorithms, it provides an intuitive way for evaluating the accuracy of the extracted places. A similar evaluation procedure has also been used in human computer interaction research [9]. To provide a comparison against other techniques, we also repeated the same experiments using the k-means algorithm. When we ran the k-means algorithm, we used the same number of clusters that our algorithm was able to identify from the data and we also performed the same pre- and post-processing steps. The results of our experiments are discussed in the next section.

5.3   Results

Enschede. The results for the Enschede dataset are shown in Fig. 3. The algorithm discovered 16 clusters, of which 4 were considered meaningful after post-processing. The size of the clusters varied from three data points to 282 data points. Although we considered only GSM transition points, the algorithm was able to identify the home and office clusters exactly. In addition to home and work, the algorithm was able to identify a park area. The fourth cluster corresponded to regions around work. Hence, the algorithm was able to detect two partially overlapping work clusters. The k-means algorithm, on the other hand, outputted 6 clusters, most of which were relatively large

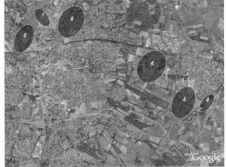

Fig. 3. Results for the Enschede dataset. The figure on the left-hand side shows the results of the Dirichlet process clustering and the results on the right hand side show the results of the k-means algorithm.

Fig. 4. Results for the Innsbruck dataset

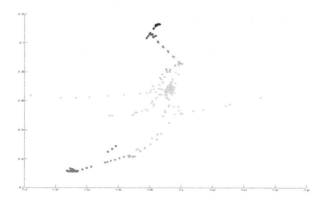

Fig. 5. Altitude plot for Innsbruck data. The darker the color, the higher the altitude.

and meaningless. One of the clusters corresponds to work and one corresponds to home, but both cover a much larger region than the Dirichlet clustering. Since the data collection was based on voluntary participation, the original data consisted mainly of commuting traces and measurements from home and office. However, the results suggest that the Dirichlet clustering is much better in handling noise caused by the irregular sampling of GPS measurements.

Innsbruck. The results for the Innsbruck dataset are shown in Fig. 4. Initially, the algorithm was able to detect 14 clusters. The size of the clusters ranged from 7 data points to 195 data points. After the post-processing step we were left with 5 clusters, all of which were meaningful. One of the clusters corresponded to the hotel where the user was staying during the conference. From the downtown area the algorithm was able to detect two other clusters that were centered around locations where the person had eaten. The remaining places corresponded to locations on top of a mountain (2 places, one corresponds to the location of the Ubicomp banquet). The data did not contain the conference venue, because the person did not gather data during the conference sessions. Again, the results of the Dirichlet process clustering are much more compact than the results of k-means, which identified 7 places from the data (after post-processing). Moreover, the results of the Dirichlet process clustering have a rather clear pruning threshold, whereas the results of the K-means do not.

From the results of Dirichlet process clustering we observe that there are two clusters (Banquet and Hafelkar) that are not as compact and accurate as the other clusters. Both places are on top of mountains (see the altitude plot in Fig. 5), which indicates that changes in altitude cause some problems for the clustering. Though, the Dirichlet clustering suffers less than k-means. Considering how to reliably take into account also altitude information in the clustering is part of our future work.

6   Conclusions and Future Work

In this paper we have introduced a statistical approach for extracting places from discontinuous location traces. Contrary to most of previous research, our algorithm does not have any tunable parameters. We demonstrated the accuracy and robustness of the algorithm using two real world datasets that exhibit rather different characteristics. Our results suggest that Dirichlet processes are a powerful tool for spatial analysis of location measurements and that they can be used to automatically detect locations that are meaningful to users.

In terms of future work, we are currently extending the model to take altitude information into account. In addition, we are constantly collecting more location measurements and we are also planning to compare the algorithm more extensively against other methods suggested in the literature. However, instead of focusing on multiple persons in the same city, we are focusing on comparing the algorithms in cities with different spatial characteristics. Finally, we plan to speed up the converge of the algorithm by considering an improved inference algorithm.

Acknowledgments

The authors are grateful to Wray Buntine for providing insights into Dirichlet processes and Bayesian modeling. The authors acknowledge Jussi Kollin for the implementation of the adaptive rejection sampling algorithm, Johan Koolwaaij for providing us with the Enschede data, and Patrik Floréen for commenting earlier versions of the paper.

This work was supported in part by the IST Programme of the European Community, under the PASCAL network of excellence, IST-2002-506778. The publication only reflects the authors' views.

References

1. Hariharan, R., Krumm, J., Horvitz, E.: Web-enhanced GPS. In: Strang, T., Linnhoff-Popien, C. (eds.) LoCA 2005. LNCS, vol. 3479, pp. 95–104. Springer, Heidelberg (2005)
2. Ashbrook, D., Starner, T.: Using GPS to learn significant locations and predict movement across multiple users. Personal and Ubiquitous Computing 7(5), 275–286 (2003)
3. Relph, E.: Place and Placelessness. Pion Books, London (1976)
4. Turner, P., Turner, S.: Two phenomenological studies of place. In: Proceedings of the 17th Conference on Human Computer Interaction (HCI): People and Computers, pp. 21–35 (2003)
5. Antoniak, C.E.: Mixtures of Dirichlet processes with applications to Bayesian nonparametric problems. The Annals of Statistics 2(6), 1152–1174 (1974)
6. MacEachern, S., Müller, P.: Estimating mixture of Dirichlet process models. Journal of Computational and Graphical Statistics 7, 223–238 (1998)
7. Rasmussen, C.E.: The infinite Gaussian mixture model. In: Solla, S.A., Leen, T.K., Müller, K.R. (eds.) Advances in Neural Information Processing Systems (NIPS), vol. 12, pp. 554–560. MIT Press, Cambridge (2000)
8. Saegert, S., Winkel, G.H.: Environmental psychology. Annual Review on Psychology 41, 441–477 (1990)
9. Zhou, C., Ludford, P., Frankowski, D., Terveen, L.: An experiment in discovering personally meaningful places from location data. In: Proceedings of the Conference on Human Factors in Computing Systems (CHI), pp. 2029–2032 (2005) Late Breaking Results: Short Papers
10. Delamater, J. (ed.): Handbook of Social Psychology. Handbooks of Sociology and Social Research. Springer, Heidelberg (2006)
11. Nurmi, P., Koolwaaij, J.: Identifying meaningful locations. In: Proceedings of the 3rd Annual Conference on Mobile and Ubiquitous Computing (MobiQuitous 2006), IEEE Computer Society, Los Alamitos (2006)
12. Zhou, C., Ludford, P., Frankowski, D., Terveen, L.: Talking about place: An experiment in how people describe places. In: Ferscha, A., Mayrhofer, R., Strang, T., Linnhoff-Popien, C., Dey, A., Butz, A., Schmidt, A. (eds.) Adjunct Proceedings of the Third International Conference on Pervasive Computing (PERVASIVE) (2005)
13. Otsason, V., Varshavsky, A., LaMarca, A., de Lara, E.: Accurate GSM indoor localization. In: Beigl, M., Intille, S.S., Rekimoto, J., Tokuda, H. (eds.) UbiComp 2005. LNCS, vol. 3660, pp. 141–158. Springer, Heidelberg (2005)
14. Chen, M.Y., Sohn, T., Chmelev, D., Hähnel, D., Hightower, J., Hughes, J., LaMarca, A., Potter, F., Smith, I.E., Varshavsky, A.: Practical metropolitan-scale positioning for GSM phones. In: Dourish, P., Friday, A. (eds.) UbiComp 2006. LNCS, vol. 4206, pp. 225–242. Springer, Heidelberg (2006)
15. Marmasse, N., Schmandt, C.: A user-centered location model. Personal and Ubiquitous Computing 6(5-6), 318–321 (2002)
16. Toyama, N., Ota, T., Kato, F., Toyota, Y., Hattori, T., Hagino, T.: Exploiting multiple radii to learn significant locations. In: Strang, T., Linnhoff-Popien, C. (eds.) LoCA 2005. LNCS, vol. 3479, pp. 157–168. Springer, Heidelberg (2005)
17. Zhou, C., Frankowski, D., Ludford, P., Shekhar, S., Terveen, L.: Discovering personal gazetteers: an interactive clustering approach. In: Proceedings of the 12th annual ACM international workshop on Geographic information systems (GIS), pp. 266–273. ACM Press, New York (2004)

18. Patterson, D.J., Liao, L., Gajos, K., Collier, M., Livic, N., Olson, K., Wang, S., Fox, D., Kautz, H.A.: Opportunity knocks: A system to provide cognitive assistance with transportation services. In: Davies, N., Mynatt, E.D., Siio, I. (eds.) UbiComp 2004. LNCS, vol. 3205, pp. 433–450. Springer, Heidelberg (2004)
19. Hariharan, R., Toyama, K.: Project Lachesis: Parsing and modeling location histories. In: Egenhofer, M., Freksa, C., Miller, H. (eds.) GIScience 2004. LNCS, vol. 3234, Springer, Heidelberg (2004)
20. Adams, B., Phung, D., Venkatesh, S.: Extraction of social context and application to personal multimedia exploration. In: Proceedings of the ACM Conference on Multimedia (MM), pp. 987–996. ACM, New York (2006)
21. Liu, J., Wolfson, O., Yin, H.: Extracting semantic location from outdoor positioning systems. In: Proceedings of the 7th International Conference on Mobile Data Management (MDM), IEEE Computer Society, Los Alamitos (2006)
22. Aipperspach, R., Rattenbury, T., Woodruff, A., Canny, J.: A quantitative method for revealing and comparing places in the home. In: Dourish, P., Friday, A. (eds.) UbiComp 2006. LNCS, vol. 4206, pp. 1–18. Springer, Heidelberg (2006)
23. Kang, J., Welbourne, W., Stewart, B., Borriello, G.: Extracting places from traces of locations. In: Proceedings of the 2nd ACM international workshop on Wireless mobile applications and services on WLAN hotspots (WMASH), pp. 110–118. ACM Press, New York (2004)
24. Hightower, J., Consolvo, S., LaMarca, A., Smith, I., Hughes, J.: Learning and recognizing the places we go. In: Beigl, M., Intille, S.S., Rekimoto, J., Tokuda, H. (eds.) UbiComp 2005. LNCS, vol. 3660, pp. 159–176. Springer, Heidelberg (2005)
25. Laasonen, K., Raento, M., Toivonen, H.: Adaptive on-device location recognition. In: Ferscha, A., Mattern, F. (eds.) PERVASIVE 2004. LNCS, vol. 3001, pp. 287–304. Springer, Heidelberg (2004)
26. Meneses, F., Moreira, A.: Using GSM CellID positioning for place discovering. In: Proceedings of the 1st Workshop on Location Based Services for Health Care (Locare), pp. 34–42 (2006)
27. Gelman, A., Carlin, J., Stern, H., Rubin, D.: Bayesian Data Analysis. Chapman & Hall/CRC (2004)
28. Neal, R.: Markov chain methods for Dirichlet process mixture models. Technical Report 9815, University of Toronto, Department of Statistics (1998)
29. Gilks, W., Spiegelhalter, D., Richardson, S.: Markov Chain Monte Carlo in Practice. Chapman & Hall/CRC (1996)
30. West, M.: Hyperparameter estimation in Dirichlet process mixture models. ISDS Discussion Paper #92-A03, Duke University (1992)
31. Gilks, W., Wild, P.: Adaptive rejection sampling for Gibbs sampling. Applied Statistics 41, 337–348 (1992)
32. Jain, S., Neal, R.: Splitting and merging components of a nonconjugate dirichlet process mixture model. Bayesian Analysis 2(3), 445–472 (2007)
33. Daumé III, H.: Fast search for dirichlet process mixture models. In: Meila, M., Shen, X. (eds.) Proceedings of the 11th International Conference on Artificial Intelligence and Statistics (AISTATS), pp. 83–90 (2007)

Appendix: Formulas for the Gibbs Sampler

$$p\left(\mu_j|\mathbf{c},\mathbf{y},S_j,\lambda,R\right)\sim\mathcal{N}\left(\left(n_j\bar{\mathbf{y}}_j^T S_j+\lambda^T R\right)(n_j S_j+R)^{-1},(n_j S_j+R)^{-1}\right)$$

$$p\left(S_j|\mathbf{c},\mathbf{y},\mu_j,\beta,W\right)\sim\mathcal{Wi}\left(\beta+n_j,\left(W\beta+\sum_{i:c_i=j}(y_i-\mu_j)(y_i-\mu_j)^T\right)^{-1}\right)$$

$$p\left(\lambda|\mu_1,\ldots,\mu_k,R\right)\sim\mathcal{N}\left(\left(\bar{y}^T\Sigma+(\sum_{j=1}^k\mu_j^T)R\right)(\Sigma+kR)^{-1},(\Sigma+kR)^{-1}\right)$$

$$p\left(R|\mu_1,\ldots,\mu_k,\lambda\right)\sim\mathcal{Wi}\left(k+1,\left(\Sigma^{-1}+\sum_{j=1}^k(\mu_j-\lambda)(\mu_j-\lambda)^T\right)^{-1}\right)$$

$$p\left(W|S_1,\ldots,S_k,\beta\right)\sim\mathcal{Wi}\left(k\beta+1,\left(\Sigma+\beta\sum_{j=1}^k S_j\right)^{-1}\right)$$

$$p\left(\phi|\alpha,k\right)\sim\mathcal{Be}\left(\alpha+1,n\right)$$

$$p\left(\alpha^{-1}|\phi,k\right)\sim\pi_\phi\mathcal{G}\left(k+\frac{1}{2},2-\log\phi\right)+(1-\pi_\phi)\mathcal{G}\left(k-\frac{1}{2},2-\log\phi\right)$$

$$p\left(c_i=j|\mathbf{c}_{-i},y_i,\mu_j,S_j\right)\sim Z^{-1}\frac{n_{-i,j}}{n-1+\alpha}p\left(y_i|c_i=j,\mu_j,S_j\right)$$

$$p\left(c_i=c^*|\mathbf{c}_{-i},\alpha\right)\sim Z^{-1}\frac{\alpha}{n-1+\alpha}\int p\left(y_i|\mu_j,S_j\right)p\left(\mu_j,S_j|\lambda,R,\beta,W\right)d\mu_j dS_j$$

Here Z^{-1} is a normalizing constant, $\pi_\phi=(k-0.5)/(2n-n\log\phi+k-0.5)$ and c^* represents a new cluster component. The variable ϕ is an auxiliary variable, which is used for sampling the value of α; see [30] for details and derivation.

The conditional distribution $p(\beta|S_1,\ldots,S_k,W)$ is not of standard form and we sample instead values for $\log\beta$ using adaptive rejection sampling. The formulas for adaptive rejection sampling are:

$$\log p\left(\log\beta|S_1,\ldots,S_k,W\right)\propto\log\beta-\frac{3}{2}\log\left(\beta-1\right)-\frac{1}{\beta-1}-k\beta\log 2$$

$$+\frac{\beta}{2}\sum_{j=1}^k\log|S_j|-k\left(\Gamma\left(\frac{\beta}{2}\right)+\Gamma\left(\frac{\beta-1}{2}\right)\right)$$

$$\frac{\partial}{\partial\log\beta}\log p\left(\log\beta|S_1,\ldots,S_k,W\right)=1-\frac{3\beta}{2(\beta-1)}+\frac{\beta}{(\beta-1)^2}+\frac{k\beta}{2}$$

$$-k\beta\log 2+\frac{\beta k}{2}\log|W|+\frac{\beta}{2}\sum_{j=1}^k\log|S_j|$$

$$-\frac{k\beta}{2}\left(\Psi\left(\frac{\beta}{2}\right)+\Psi\left(\frac{\beta-1}{2}\right)\right).$$

Here Ψ is the digamma function, i.e., the logarithmic derivative of the Gamma function.

An Integrated Platform for the Management of Mobile Location-Aware Information Systems

Anthony Savidis[1,2], Manolis Zidianakis[1], Nikolaos Kazepis[1], Stephanos Dubulakis[1], Dimitrios Gramenos[1], and Constantine Stephanidis[1,2]

[1] Institute of Computer Science, Foundation for Research and Technology – Hellas
[2] Department of Computer Science, University of Crete
`{as,zidian,kazepis,dubulak,gramenos,cs}@ics.forth.gr`

Abstract. We present an integrated platform comprising a set of authoring and management tools for mobile location-aware information systems. The development of the platform was targeted in supporting large-scale systems with very crowded use sessions, at the scale of hundreds of simultaneous visitors, addressing information delivery for exhibits with proximity down to a couple / few meters. The key platform features are: (i) spatial content editing with mixed-mode administration, either mobile (on-site with a PDA) or non-mobile (off-site, using a PC); (ii) system-initiated location-triggered information delivery combined with free user-initiated data exploration; (iii) applicable both indoors and outdoors; (iv) very efficient device renting processes through barcode readers; and (v) multiple location sensing technologies, prioritized according to precision trust (includes WLAN, GPS, and infrared beacons). Currently, the platform is being installed at the fifteen main museums and archeological sites of Greece (including Acropolis, Olympia, Delphi, Knossos and Mycenae), encompassing a total of five thousands mobile devices (see acknowledgements).

1 Introduction

Mobile location-aware information systems are capable to deliver position-dependent information over a portable device for users that are primarily on the move. In our work we consider multiple sources for user-location information, including explicit positioning as coordinates in a 2D place (e.g. *X*, *Y* and optionally a *DIR* vector) or implicit positioning as the result of interpretation data coming from sensory modules. The latter is managed by various technologies like special tags (e.g. infrared or radio), sonar methods and computer vision. The former is possible mainly via GPS, for outdoor environments, and WLAN positioning engines, relying on signal fingerprints, for both indoor and outdoor setups. We adopted the dual use of explicit and implicit positioning, while supporting the statically-prioritized (i.e. invariant during runtime) use of location sensing technologies based on the known precision of the generated location data. The reported system is currently being installed at the fifteen major museums and archeological sites of Greece (see acknowledgements), encompassing a total of five thousand mobile devices (PDAs).

1.1 Contributions

The key technical contributions of the reported work, concerning the support for content administration, user navigation, and runtime management of user sessions, are listed below:

J. Indulska et al. (Eds.): Pervasive 2008, LNCS 5013, pp. 128–145, 2008.

☐ Spatial location-oriented data editing with a direct-manipulation editor, offering mixed-mode administration: (a) mobile, on-site, mainly to administer location data; and (b) non-mobile, off-site, mainly to administer typical semantic content.

☐ System-initiated location-triggered information delivery combined with user-initiated on-demand content exploration.

☐ Unified infrastructure applicable both to indoor and outdoor setups.

☐ Very efficient and intuitive device renting facilities through barcode readers.

☐ Multi-channel statically-prioritized location sensing, currently implemented to deploy WLAN positioning, GPS, and infrared beacons.

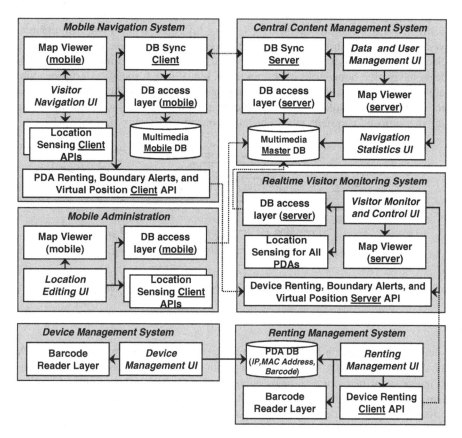

Fig. 1. Overall platform architecture

1.2 Architecture

The overall system architecture is provided under Fig. 1 at two levels of decomposition detail: (i) primary applications and tools (shaded rectangles); and (ii) their respective key constituent components (white rectangles and buckets). Solid arrows indicate intra-process method invocations (e.g. deployment of *Map Viewer* component), while dashed arrows denote inter-process RPCs (e.g. *DB Access Layer*). Also, with underlined labels we mark different versions of a component, such as: mobile / server DB

Access Layer, mobile / server Map Viewer, client / server API categories, and mobile / master DBs. Some other important sub-systems, not to be elaborated in this paper, are also incorporated in the architectural diagram of Fig. 1:

☐ On-demand synchronization of the master DB to the mobile DB on the PDAs (i.e. *DB Sync Client / Server*). While one expects this facility to be offered by the DBMS, we had to implement it from scratch as the mobile edition of the MS SQL Server restricts the size of the mobile DB to at most 100 MB.

☐ Recording data for navigation sessions (e.g. time spent at an information item, information items reviewed, elapsed time of use, etc.) supporting various queries (e.g. most popular information item in a selected period, total time of use for all visitors, average exploration time for visitors, information items with simultaneous visitors up to a threshold, etc). The latter concern the *Navigation Statistics UI*.

☐ Security policy relying on the definition (during content administration) of the legal navigation boundaries over area maps, out of which specific alert procedures are triggered (e.g. PDA locking with message to the user, explicit alert pop-ups on the monitoring console, visitor identification from the PDA and notification from the museum audio system, etc.). The latter concern the *Visitor Monitoring System*.

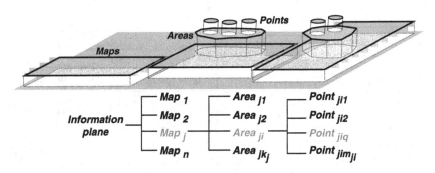

Fig. 2. Split of the information plane to maps, areas and information points

Our platform relies on a generic location-sensing interface enabling sensing APIs to be loaded dynamically (as DLLs). Our method splits the global information plane into independent maps, where maps encompass polygonal information areas, which enclose the actual information points, i.e. the real exhibits (see Fig. 2). In this context, the location sensing interface allows distinct technologies to return either a point (higher precision) within the currently active map plane, or alternatively the identifier of a polygonal area (lower precision) that is associated to a particular physical area (e.g. room, hall, corridor, corner, stares, etc.). Following our approach, the adopted technologies need not be merely point-based, but alternative techniques like infrared beacons or radio tags can be deployed as carriers of area identification information (e.g. an infrared beacon can be programmed to simply emit the logical identifier of an area denoting a specific room).

Effectively, when the latter is combined with typical point-based sensing technologies it helps to resolve possible ambiguities or precision problems, or overcome other types of practical barriers. The capability to support multiple prioritized sensing technologies is crucial, since, in some situations, the particular characteristics of the installation site, or other types of restrictions regarding possible physical interventions, may directly exclude specific technologies. For instance, in our project, we were forbidden to put any type of equipment (i.e. no tags, no power supply) inside archeological sites, except of the wireless network antennas perimetrically installed. Additionally, the prioritized use of location sensing APIs reflects the differing reliability of the position outcome in different technologies.

2 Related Work

Location sensing technologies are the cornerstone of location-aware information systems. Some technologies support indoors localization through specialized, expensive and usually inflexible hardware installations. A typical recent example is the Active Bat system (Harle et al., 2003) relying on signal distance measurements to determine user's position. C-MAP (Sumi et al., 1998) was among the first exhibition-tour systems exploiting the Active Badge System for location awareness. Other systems based on distance signal measurements are the Cricket Location Support System (Priyantha et al., 2000), Spot-On system (Hightower et al., 2000), and EasyLiving (Krumm et al., 2000), the latter with vision methods via motion-tracking cameras.

Recent location sensing systems rely on standard wireless networking hardware, by measuring signal intensity and attenuation to determine a user's location. The RADAR system (Bahl & Padmanabhan, 2002) was amongst the first tracking systems based on IEEE 802.1, while in (Savarese et al., 2002) an algorithm is increasing the precision of the estimated users' positions. A commercial system in this category is the Ekahau Positioning Engine[1] (EPE) supporting laptops, PDAs and other Wi-Fi enabled devices, accomplishing floor, room, and sometimes door-level accuracy, while working indoors and outdoors. In our platform, we deployed EPE as one of the point-based location sensing technologies. The official specifications of the EPE indicate that it is capable to reach an average precision 1 meter, though we observed that in real practice the average precision is around 3 meters. Besides point-based methods, technologies like passive RFID tags or active infrared beacons support proximity-based localization as carriers of land-marking information. Such tags require explicit installation and programming, while they are not very intuitive in use: (a) infrared requires line of sight; and (b) passive radio tags that do not need power-supply require very close proximity, sometimes virtually like physical contact or touch as in MoVIS (Schwieren & Vossen, 2007) - the reason is that radio antennas on PDAs are not powerful due to low-power demands enforced to enable autonomous PDA use for a few hours. Advanced systems like PlaceLab (LaMarca et al., 2005) support metropolitan area coarse-grained positioning (at the level of 20 meters), relying on the variety of preinstalled stationary beacons, ranging from WiFi antennas to Bluetooth tags, roughly estimating users' position in indoor / outdoor urban areas. A probabilistic method to fuse results from various types of sensors for location estimation, relying on particle filters, is proposed in (Hightower & Borriello, 2004); the technique displays increased accuracy as the number of sensors is increased, while having outcomes close to the most accurate of the sensing technologies deployed.

---

[1] http://www.ekahau.com

In our platform, targeting for a unified solution across indoor and outdoor settings, no single technology suffices. Our emphasis is put to enable integration of solutions with acceptable estimations, rather than to introduce a new method for location sensing. Currently, outdoor information systems lack genericity (no indoors), practicality (satellite signal can be lost) and precision at the level of information points (coarse-grained positioning). On the other side, most indoor navigation systems employ tag technologies, like infrared beacons or radio tags, with known issues as previously mentioned. The latter technologies implement context-sensing rather than position tracking, so user monitoring and trajectory recording is minimal. Naturally, better positioning may be gained by placing a large number of tags around; however, this is hardly a globally acceptable option.

Employment of multiple location-sensing technologies has been originally proposed in (Nord et al., 2002), encompassing virtually all sorts of location sensing methods. They propose a resolution policy based on area intersections, however, it is not mentioned how ambiguities are resolved (i.e. when the intersection is empty) and they do not encompass a prioritization of technologies according to trust on localization precision. Bluetooth is also proposed, known to suffer from severe problems: unacceptable stalls upon device discovery (scan inquiry takes around 15 seconds), signal traveling through walls causing ambiguous results (Savidis & Stephanidis, 2005), and significant power demands.

A high-level architecture for redundancy of adopted technologies to derive positioning information is suggested in (Pfeifer, 2005). The idea is to exploit virtually any type of medium from which positioning information can be extrapolated. Our approach is closer to this philosophy, however, not targeted on algorithms to fuse signals for deriving better estimates (i.e. enhanced location sensing), but on ways to make systems deploy reliable sensing technologies with known trust values with the least implementation dependencies (i.e. enhanced software engineering).

3 Mobile Navigation System

The key novel features of our visitor's navigator system to be discussed are: (i) prioritized *multi-channel location sensing*; (ii) combined *system-initiated and user-initiated navigation*, supporting predefined tours; and (iii) smooth map zoom using 3D rendering with *interactive control on the information detail*. The deployment of a WLAN positioning system providing continuous affine location estimations together with RFID tags to get more precise localization is adopted in (Blache et al., 2003), although in the reporting RFID integration was not yet applied. We rejected the use of RFID tags for usability reasons: (i) in typically crowded museum rooms tags are hardly locatable; (ii) since PDA-powered readers require touch-like proximity, a social protocol is needed in case multiple visitors intend for the same exhibit, something that is less preferred due to the significant cultural diversity among visitors; and (iii) they require technical equipment proximate to exhibits, which may not be allowed (e.g. the new Acropolis museum was designed with a glass-rooms, allowing extra equipment to be mounted only on the ceiling corners.

Extensible and Prioritized Location Sensing. To support location sensing, we have implemented an infrastructure supporting multiple concurrent sensing channels as dynamically installed and managed API instances, each given a specific static priority relating to practical precision characteristics (i.e. trust) of its respective location-sensing approach. Such an infrastructure essentially allowed our mobile navigation and administration systems to accommodate dynamically alternative location sensing APIs, in the form of runtime loaded components with an XML configuration file listing the API components to be loaded. Such scalability and extensibility was accomplished by making APIs pertain to the same generic interface, while loaded dynamically. In particular, the statically assigned trust-based priority is taken by invoking a specific method (*Get-Priority* – see Fig. 3). This software architecture approach allows modularly incorporate alternative sensing technologies without modifying the original administration and navigation systems. The super-classes are provided under Fig. 3, defined in C++ for platform generality (the original specification is in C#).

```cpp
typedef unsigned mapid_t;
typedef unsigned areaid_t;
typedef unsigned priority_t;
typedef pair<unsigned, unsigned> point2d_t;
typedef pair<mapid_t, point2d_t> location_t;
class LocationSensingAPI {
   public:
   virtual string          GetId (void) const = 0;
   virtual priority_t      GetPriority (void) const = 0;
   virtual void            SetPollingInterval (unsigned t) = 0;
   virtual bool            IsConnected (void) const = 0;
   virtual void            StartUp (void) = 0;
   virtual void            CloseDown (void) = 0;
};
class PointBasedAPI : public LocationSensingAPI
   { public: virtual location_t GetLocation (void) const = 0; };
class AreaBasedAPI : public LocationSensingAPI
   { public: virtual list<areaid_t> GetAreas (void) const = 0; };
```

Fig. 3. The generic interfaces for dynamically loaded location sensing APIs

There are two derived super-classes for location sensing components, reflecting our classification of alternative technologies in two families: (i) those relying on user-position tracking and estimation (like Ekahau, GPS, radio tags / badges, and vision modules); and (ii) those relying on context marking (land-marking), like infrared beacons and passive / active radio tags. In our system, we referred to the technologies estimating directly user's position as *point-based* methods, while those relying on land-marks as *area-based* methods.

As we discuss latter, this separation is also very important for the mobile administration system where we needed to recognize conflicts when placing distinct landmarking tags: when at a particular position multiple beacons / tags are detected, though carrying different context identifiers, then we have a conflict (implying imperfect placement of the beacons / tags). Up to now, we already employed three specific technologies for location sensing, two of them being point-based and one being area-based, discussed below with increasing priority value:

☐ *WLAN* point-based location sensing, through the Ekahau Positioning Engine, both indoors and outdoors, with precision of 3-5 meters, requiring no line of sight.

☐ *GPS* point-based location sensing for outdoors environments. Average precision is 2-4 meters, requiring visual contact among the GPS card and the satellites.

☐ *TAGS* (currently mostly infrared beacons) area-based location sensing for indoors, and outdoors (when applicable) environments. For infrared beacons the precision at area level is virtually perfect, requiring the receptor to fall inside the active ray-diffusion conic space. Practical barriers concern the required line of sight.

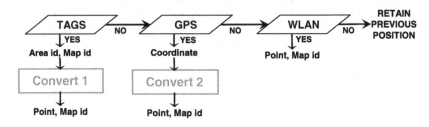

Fig. 4. The location sensing technologies deployed ordered by trust-based priority

The location-sensing pipeline is illustrated under Fig. 4, showing the way the APIs are actually deployed with decreasing priority. One should consider that this sort of processing is generalized for the case of N distinct prioritized location sensing API components. Following Fig. 4 the infrared receiver API is used to check if a signal is detected. The ray actually emits a single number in which we encode an area and a map identifier. From the area id its respective polygon and centre are extracted (indicted as *Convert 1*), the latter is returned together with the original map id as an approximation of the current users' position. It should be noted that the conversion of area identifiers to planar coordinates is not part of the area-based API implementation itself, but is a standard component of the overall location sensing API management logic, that we automatically apply to area-based APIs.

In case no signal is detected and the GPS is on, the current geographical coordinate is taken, used to identify the current enclosing map from the list of maps – maps are stored in the database with their geographical boundaries, and turn the geographical location to a raster coordinate inside this map (indicted as *Convert 2*). This conversion is included in the GPS point-based API implementation, returning the point and the map id as the current user's position. Finally, and alternatively, if the WLAN is on, the local EPE client API is used to inquire the current PDA position and the respective map id. As expected, if none of the previous technologies is active, the old user position is retained. The adoption of this particular implementation style to cope with varying location sensing technologies has been proved to be a key complexity-reduction factor in our project. For instance, although we generally dropped the deployment of Bluetooth tags (beacons) due to practical barriers, we also retained a respective API implementation as there are even at this point in time a couple of cases where we intend to use it as a back-up. In particular, in two specific archaeological sites, there are tombs whose entrances and main rooms are blind spots for both WLAN and GPS, while we do not yet have clearance to install infrared beacons around. In this context, one option we investigate is to install Bluetooth tags using the power for the lights, close to the entrance and down to the floor, to at least be able recognize presence of visitors on site.

Supporting Multiple Navigation Scenarios. Our platform supports the authoring of arbitrary navigation scenarios, i.e. different types of tours that visitors may take, edited as sequences of selected information spots associated with a short descriptive title. During use, the navigator explicitly marks all information spots of the initially selected (by the visitor) navigation scenario on the map, displaying also their relative order within the navigation scenario. The authoring of navigation scenarios is shown under Fig. 5: the left column (Selected Items) is the ordered list of information points (titles) for the currently edited navigation scenario, while the right column (Remaining Items) is the list of all information points (i.e. entire information plane), offering typical editing facilities (add / move / reorder).

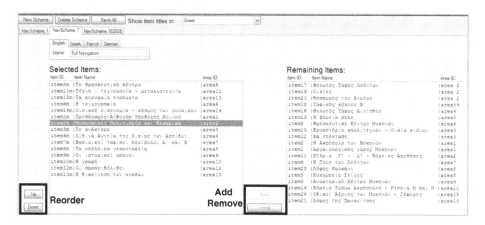

Fig. 5. Authoring of navigation scenarios

Mixed Initiative for Information Presentation. During the requirements analysis phase it came out that whether using a personal guide or navigating with a leaflet, visitors prefer to deviate from predefined paths to visit alternative proximate or distant information spots. Thus, the navigator had to guide users across the scenario, allowing them to freely deviate from it, effectively enabling them to keep track of their overall path. Additionally, experienced guides reported that during tour sessions, many visitors use leaflets or books to review information details for previously visited items, and in some cases even for items to be met later during the tour, since in many situations the exposed items are directly related to each other. This gave us an alternative insight on location-aware information delivery: besides automatic location-based information provision, users should be enabled to freely review all information points, whether visited or not. In our case, the latter is possible either via previous / next navigation buttons, or by pointing directly with the pen over items on the displayed the map. A snapshot of the navigator's map view is provided in Fig. 5, showing how users may interactively control the display of extra details for information items, performing sequential transition among the following display options in a circular manner:

☐ Display no extra detail (default)
☐ Display the order of non-visited items that are part of the navigation scenario(see labels indicated with thick circles in Fig. 6)
☐ Display only the titles for all items

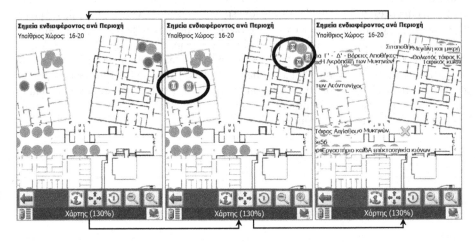

Fig. 6. Controlling level of overview detail for information items

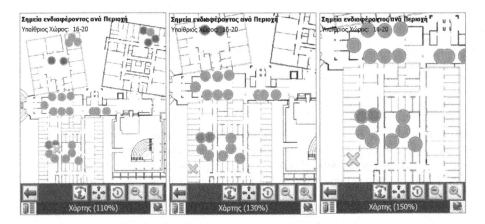

Fig. 7. Real-time smooth zooming. (110%, 130% and 150% are the zoom factors).

The user position is indicated with an X (see Fig. 6, middle of rightmost screen) while color encoding is used to distinguish among visited and non-visited items, with extra encoding for the latter to separate items belonging to the selected navigation scenario from those that do not. Additionally, real-time smooth zooming is supported as shown in Fig. 7; the latter was accomplished by implementing the map rendering functionality using Direct3D. In every map, the number and orders of unvisited items from the navigation scenario is briefed (top part of maps in Fig. 7). In many cases exhibits must to be placed very close to each other, with relative distances that cannot be handled by the precision of the positioning systems. For instance, it is common to place ancient helmets, shields and arcs close to each other, each having a separate information unit. For such scenarios, our platform supports the grouping of multiple information items into a single chunk called an information area, physically being defined by a polygon encompassing the locations of all respective information items.

During navigation (see Fig. 8), once the visitor enters an information area, a menu of all information items is displayed (screen 1). The initial screen of an information item (screen 2) displays a representative image, together with two options, to review textual and multimedia content (screen 3). Video playback with a brief panoramic tour for an ancient castle is sown in screen 5. Besides automatic location-based information delivery, manual exploration of all information areas and points is allowed (next / previous arrows of screen 2). Information elements already reviewed by the visitor are drawn with a tick marker in their respective menu.

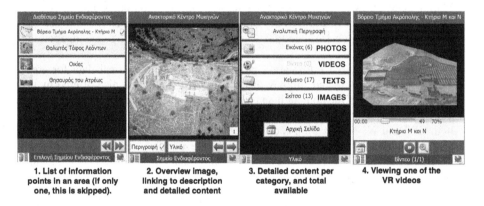

1. List of information points in an area (if only one, this is skipped).

2. Overview image, linking to description and detailed content

3. Detailed content per category, and total available

4. Viewing one of the VR videos

Fig. 8. Snapshots of the mobile navigation system during use

4   Mobile Administration System

The novel feature in this context is actually the *explicit provision of a mobile administration system for location data editing*, except from the traditional non-mobile content management and from-based data entry that is also offered. The support for mobile administration of position data is crucial for indoors and outdoors location-aware information systems relying on fine-grained positioning. While such a facility may seem redundant, assuming the common practice of GIS where content management is done off-site by positioning data over maps, as we explain below, the need for such a tool is mandated by various practical constraints. Firstly, location sensing may display varying accuracies at different physical areas. For instance, within indoor settings, WLAN accuracy is affected by many factors like material, room structure, crowd, and signal interference. During real-life installations, there have been rooms or corridors where we gained 2 meters accuracy, and there have been halls and open rooms where we never got something better than 5 meters. Secondly, the ability to use infrared beacons as wraparounds to overcome the accuracy problems point-based sensing is limited by a number of practical factors, such as light reflections, room structure (ceiling height), signal diffusion, power supply points, and the practical barrier of line-of-sight.

Similarly, when it comes to outdoor environments, the dual use of GPS and WLAN positioning, to rectify GPS and WLAN blind spots, necessitated precise on-site programming and validation of position data. Overall, while performing content administration, authors should be enabled to practically evaluate the actual accuracy of location sensing accomplished during navigation sessions, so as to more accurately define: (a) the physical polygon of an information point that will trigger information delivery (when the user falls inside); and (b) whether multiple information points need to be collected into a single enclosing area (when we cannot get precision down to non-overlapping smaller areas). Additionally, testing of signal collisions (conflicts) among different infrared beacons is supported. The mobile administration system (see Fig. 9) offers the following features:

☐ Map display, showing the spatial distribution of information areas and points, the current administrator position as tracked by the active point-based location sensing technologies on site (WLAN and GPS in our case), while offering smooth zooming and scrolling facilities.
☐ Definition of areas and information points, editing of geometrical data for areas including point editing and "drag & drop" facilities – the latter, also offered by the spatial data editor of the content management, are elaborated in the next Section.
☐ Start trajectory recording and displaying of various user paths (way points) from both GPS and WLAN location-sensing technologies (see Fig. 9, left part).
☐ Testing of infrared tag signals and marking corresponding active areas, detecting conflicts, i.e. multiple signals at a certain position that encode different area identifiers (see Fig. 9, middle part).

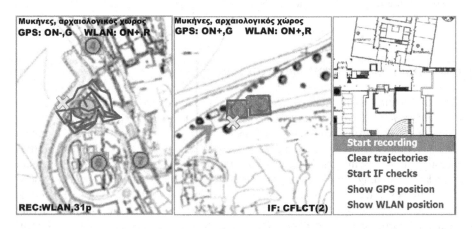

Fig. 9. Mobile administration in use (big arrow in middle part belongs to the map image)

The message displayed on top of the PDA screen explains whether GPS or WLAN are active at the current position (label *ON / OFF*), if position display was chosen (label + / -), and the respective location marker colour (label *G* for green, *R* for red). The message prefixed with an *IF* concerns information for detected infrared signals,

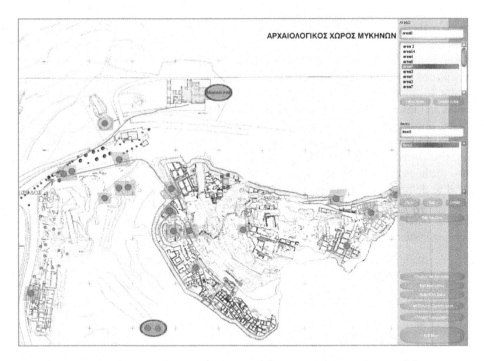

Fig. 10. Spatial content editing (Mycenae site); the horizontal line on top is part of the trespassing limits defined by the administrator for security reasons

CFLCT(2) meaning a conflict because of *2* different incoming signals. Additionally, for infrared signals, the respective areas are also highlighted (see Fig. 9, middle part - areas are drawn with semi-transparent red polygons).When recording user positions (*REC* indication), the sensing system chosen is shown (e.g. *WLAN*), together with the number of different successive positions returned, e.g. *31p*. Finally, the main control menu, activated by clicking on the map, is provided in Fig. 9, right part.

User Interface Automation. A very important remark is that the mobile administration system relies entirely on the dynamically loaded location-sensing API components. For instance, the specific identifiers displayed on the PDA, like *"GPS"*, *"WLAN"* and *"IF"*, as shown within Fig. 9, are not hard-coded in our implementation but are extracted during runtime from the APIs via *GetId()* so as to produce messages like *"GPS*: ON-, G" and *"WLAN*: ON+, R". Moreover, the construction of our mobile administration User Interface is quite automated and parameterized. More specifically, given any point-based dynamically loaded API, following the definitions of the loading configuration file, we automatically add: (i) in the main menu a toggle option to tune position display like *"Show[Hide] <GetId()> position"*; (ii) a toggle option in the *"Start recording"* sub-menu as *"<GetId()> On [Off]"*, and (iii) an option *"<GetId()>"* in *"Clear trajectories"* sub-menu. In a similar way, for area-based loaded APIs we add a toggle option in the main menu to perform area identification (polling) and multiple signal (conflicts) checks as *"Start [Stop] <GetId()> checks"*.

5 Content Management System

They key feature of our content management system is that *content administration is facilitated through spatial data editing*, providing a direct-manipulation graphical editor to administer the semantic content and the geometrical data of information areas and information points directly over the displayed maps. Information entities are firstly positioned over the map using the mobile administration system or the spatial editor of the content management system. Such dual administration mode, to spatially position items both 'on the desk-top' and 'on the move' is not met in other systems. The two methods are used in cooperation as follows: (i) the content management system is used to define an initial approximate positioning and distribution of information areas and information items over the map; (ii) the mobile administration system is deployed later to fine-tune the positioning on-site, through the actual data provided by the location sensing systems.

Fig. 11. Content editing opened from the spatial administration pane

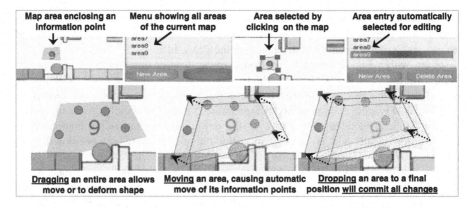

Fig. 12. Direct area manipulation with *drag & drop* facilities

The main window of the content management system is shown during deployment under Fig. 10; together with the map, all respective information areas and information points are also rendered. The control panel at the right side provides operations for opening the content editing forms, for all sorts of information types, as well as to edit maps and navigation scenarios. The content editing panel, for authoring of multimedia and multilingual information elements, is shown under Fig. 11.

The positioning adjustments, apart of typical displacements and polygon editing, may require radical changes, such as moving information points outside particular areas or joining multiple information points together into a new containing area. Under Fig. 12 we show some of the real-time features for editing the geometrical aspects of information areas, in particular selection, and drag & drop. More specifically, when an entire area is moved, all encompassed information points are automatically moved. In case that movement is not cancelled in the middle, the final positions of the information points are committed directly to the underlying content database. Such direct-manipulation facilities, offered by both the desk-top and the mobile versions of the content management systems, proved to be very valuable for practical administration of content spatial data. Item misplacements on maps and imperfect area definitions were far more frequent than originally anticipated, and it turned out that without automatic facilities, any approach relying on manual corrections directly on the database would be clearly impractical for a project of this scale.

6 Device and Renting Management System

Existing location-aware mobile information systems do not deal with the issue of explicit device renting and returning processes. Typically, users are pre-assigned a particular device (organization-wide use) or they are required to input individual information after deployment via on-line forms (sporadic trusted use). The latter are not applicable for protected, ad-hoc, commercial use, displaying high demands for quick servicing, as in museums, galleries and exposition settings. Our platform supports *very fast device management and renting processes* (charging of visitors is optional). It has been design to meet specific requirements coming from the Greek Ministry of Culture: 'the system should support massive inquiries, e.g. incoming groups of 50 to 100 visitors; the delay for renting is considered unacceptable when it exceeds twice the delay of issuing a ticket receipt'.

The option of letting the system run on devices all the time was impractical: it wasted precious WLAN resources (bandwidth), it provided useless data to the visitor surveillance system, and it introduced fake entries ('noise') to the statistics component. So, practically, we had to find an error-prone way for unlocking, application activation, and language selection in less than 15 seconds. In this context (see Fig. 13) we adopted a variant of the process met in typical shopping transactions (right part): (i) WLAN restart is activated by pressing a large on-screen button on the PDA (not shown); (ii) the barcode reader is used to get the PDA's barcode; and (iii) by consulting a database mapping barcode to IP addresses, connection with the PDA is internally established and a message is sent to it for unlocking and launching the information system with the selected target language. The latter required the explicit registration of PDAs (labeled as 'Device management' in Fig. 13), as triplets of barcode, IP and MAC addresses, something that is supported by the device management system.

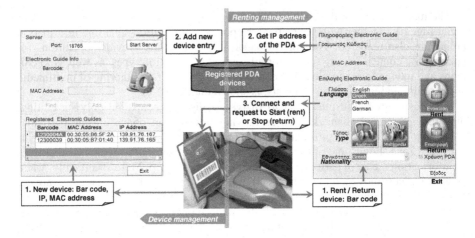

Fig. 13. Device and renting management systems and processes

Our contribution in this context, besides the use of barcode readers as a way for quickly renting the PDAs, is the enhancement of a well-known process by turning the actual purchased products, i.e. the PDAs, to active items capable of internally communicating with the database to self-initialize and self-configure for real use.

7 Discussion

The development of our platform was driven by specific objectives that justify some choices which look suboptimal at a first glance. In particular, we do not adopt the most powerful location sensing methods around (there are commercial solutions with claimed precision down to a few inches). This is due to our primary target: *being able to turn an existing infrastructure to a location-aware information context with minimal technical interventions, very low installation cost, and quick turnaround time.* We assumed as a rationale common denominator for the target environments presence of WiFi indoors and use of GPS outdoors, with availability of the respective chipsets on the PDAs. Also, we decided that digital tags like infrared or radio beacons may be sporadically employed as land-marking emitters. We selectively installed infrared beacons, using a model with up to six LEDs per device, placed at the top corners with a 45 degrees angle downwards (see Fig. 14).

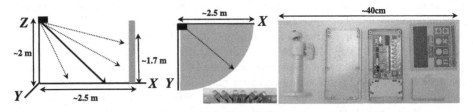

Fig. 14. Typical placement and boxing of infrared beacons in room corners

We focused in producing a tool to augment a variety of controlled environments into location-aware information contexts: exhibitions, organizations, museums, universities, hospitals, hotels, etc. This technical focus was proved to be the decisive factor enabling our platform to be applicable across the diverse museums and archeological sites of Greece. Practically, we have put a separation line with third-party location sensing technologies, treating everything from installation, configuration and calibration, to API licensing as something external to our platform. The only contact side with our system was the need for compliance to specific generic APIs, via which our platform became capable to deploy existing technologies without particular implementation dependencies. In any case, one cannot avoid dealing with the low-level details of such technologies to guarantee maximal gains, since the trust value that is incorporated in the respective location-sensing API should directly reflect real-life experience after performing numerous tests and experiments in the real field.

Problems Faced. Since we had five thousand PDAs across different museums with our software installed, we needed to address the issue of release updating after requested changes and bug fixing. For this purpose we added in the database all executables and DLLs, thus handled automatically by our synchronization system, and implemented a software updater to run locally at the PDA. This way, version upgrading became fully automatic and centralized. In outdoor settings, we observed considerable delays (sometimes tens of seconds) when a group of more than 20 visitors exits a WLAN blind spot; the delay was attributed to connection reestablishment at the system level with the WLAN. We also had some unexpected GPS precision issues at some areas, with accuracy frequently falling down to 8-10 meters. Fortunately, information provision on archeological sites was decided with information spots very distant to each other; however, besides information delivery, a few visitors observed this issue when reviewing their position on the map. Finally, in outdoor settings, having more than hundred PDAs connected to the same access point causes severe delays on WLAN positioning updates; these temporary stalls were bypassed since the GPS has highest trust value. Nevertheless, there are still scenarios were GPS low accuracy intervals appear either at network blind spots or at sites where the sporadic installation of access points turns WLAN positioning quite inaccurate to alternatively trust it.

8   Summary and Conclusions

We have presented key components of an integrated platform for the authoring and uptake of location-aware mobile information systems, putting emphasis on specific novel features reflecting requirements that emerged in the course of large-scale real-life deployment. The development of the overall platform required three years (2004-2007), while authoring and installation for the 15 major museums and archeological sites of Greece started at February 2007, and is completing during May 2008, with pilot use scheduled for summer 2008. Due to the considerable size of the project, both in terms of equipment (five thousands PDAs), as well as in terms of divergence of physical exhibition areas (e.g., hills, tombs, protective roofs, covered or open amphitheatres, halls, corridors, glass rooms, forests, open stadiums, etc.), we had to work in close cooperation with Ekahau for calibration sessions as well as for engine improvements, and with the manufacturers of infrared beacons for optimized customized solutions (both in terms of h/w type, as well as in terms of SDK support). All computing equipment, peripherals, networking and constructions are delivered by SIEMENS.

Amongst the most technically challenging issues was the accomplishment of satisfactory location-sensing across all different settings. In this context, the conclusions from our technical decisions discussed in the paper are: (a) the unified location-sensing infrastructure for indoors and outdoors simplifies maintenance and extensibility; (b) trust-based statically-prioritized multi-channel location sensing solves many precision problems increasing significantly the robustness the position tracking infrastructure, even though it puts an extra authoring overhead; and (c) when tags are introduced to augment the location-sensing approach, they should be programmed to identify locations or areas, i.e. return geometrical information, rather than transmitting internal database keys or indices of particular information items. Regarding content authoring, the support for spatial data editing and mobile on-site editing and adjustment of position data, enabling to query and test location values, proved to be very helpful. The latter is not only due to easier administration of location-dependent content by being on site, but most importantly because of the ability to rectify the frequent precision problems. Our location adjustment tool works on top of, and in cooperation with, the Ekahau calibration system (site survey tool). The latter prepares the ground for EPE location sensing, and the former allows adapting initial positioning of exhibits to the real output of the location system after its calibration phase.

Acknowledgements

Part of this work is funded by the Greek Ministry of Culture, via a subcontract from SIEMENS to FORTH, for installation and deployment of the platform at fifteen museums and archeological sites across Greece, including Acropolis, Olympia Knossos, Delphi and Mycenae. The total project budget is 11 Million Euros, with installations and pilot deployment scheduled to complete before summer 2008.

References

Bahl, P., Padmanabhan, V.N.: RADAR: An In-Building RF-Based User Location and Tracking System. In: Proceedings of IEEE INFOCOM 2002, vol. 2, pp. 775–784 (2002)

Blache, B., Chraiet, N., Daroux, O., Evennou, F., Flury, T., Privat, G., Viboud, J.P.: Position-Based Interaction for Indoor Ambient Intelligence Environments. In: Aarts, E., Collier, R.W., van Loenen, E., de Ruyter, B. (eds.) EUSAI 2003. LNCS, vol. 2875, pp. 192–207. Springer, Heidelberg (2003)

Harle, R.K., Ward, A., Hopper, A.: Single Reflection Spatial Voting: A Novel Method for Discovering Reflective Surfaces Using Indoor Positioning Systems. In: Proceedings of ACM MobiSys 2003, International Conference on Mobile Systems, Applications and Services, pp. 1–14 (2003)

Hightower, H., Want, R., Borriello, G.: SpotON: An Indoor 3D Location Sensing Technology Based on RF Signal Strength, UW CSE 00-02-02, University of Washington, Department of Computer Science and Engineering, Seattle, WA (February 2000)

Hightower, J., Borriello, G.: Particle Filters for Location Estimation in Ubiquitous Computing: A Case Study. In: Davies, N., Mynatt, E.D., Siio, I. (eds.) UbiComp 2004. LNCS, vol. 3205, pp. 88–106. Springer, Heidelberg (2004)

Krumm, J., Harris, S., Meyers, B., Brumitt, B., Hale, M., Shafer, S.: Multi-Camera Multi-Person Tracking for EasyLiving. In: Proceedings of the 3rd IEEE International Work-shop on Visual Surveillance (VS 2000), pp. 3–3 (2000)

LaMarca, A., Chawathe, Y., Consolvo, S., Hightower, J., Smith, I., Scott, J., Sohn, T., Howard, J., Hughes, J., Potter, F., Tabert, J., Powledge, P., Borriello, G., Schilit, B.: Place Lab: Device Positioning Using Radio Beacons in the Wild. In: Gellersen, H.-W., Want, R., Schmidt, A. (eds.) PERVASIVE 2005. LNCS, vol. 3468, pp. 116–133. Springer, Heidelberg (2005)

Nord, J., Synnes, K., Parnes, P.: An Architecture for Location Aware Applications. In: Proceedings of the 35th Hawaii International Conference on System Sciences - HICSS 35 2002, IEEE, Los Alamitos (2002) in CD-ROM

Pfeifer, T.: Redundant Positioning Architecture. In: Computer Communications, vol. 28(13), pp. 1575–1585. Elsevier Science Publishers B.V, North-Holland (2005)

Priyantha, Nissanka, B., Chakraborty, A., Balakrishnan, H.: The Cricket location-support system. In: Proceedings of the ACM MOBICOM 2000, 6th International Conference on Mobile Computing and Networking, pp. 32–43 (2000)

Savarese, C., Rabaey, J., Langendoen, K.: Robust Positioning Algorithms for Distributed Ad-Hoc Wireless Sensor Networks. In: Proceedings of the General Track: 2002 USENIX Annual Technical Conference, pp. 317–327 (2002)

Savidis, A., Stephanidis, C.: Distributed Interface Bits: Dynamic Dialogue Composition from Ambient Computing Resources. ACM-Springer Journal on Personal and Ubiquitous Computing 9(3), 142–168 (2005)

Schwieren, J., Vossen, G.: Implementing Physical Hyperlinks for Mobile Applications using RFID Tags. In: 11th International IEEE Database Engineering and Applications Symposium (IDEAS 2007), Banff, Canada, September 6-8, pp. 154–162 (2007)

Sumi, Y., Etani, T., Fels, S., Simonet, N., Kobayashi, K., Mase, K.: C-MAP: Building a Context-Aware Mobile Assistant for Exhibition Tours. In: Ishida, T. (ed.) Community Computing and Support Systems. LNCS, vol. 1519, pp. 137–154. Springer, Heidelberg (1998)

Calibree[*]: Calibration-Free Localization Using Relative Distance Estimations

Alex Varshavsky[1], Denis Pankratov[1], John Krumm[2], and Eyal de Lara[1]

[1] Department of Computer Science, University of Toronto
{walex,delara}@cs.toronto.edu, denis.pankratov@gmail.com
[2] Microsoft Research
jckrumm@microsoft.com

Abstract. Existing localization algorithms, such as centroid or finger-printing, compute the location of a mobile device based on measurements of signal strengths from radio base stations. Unfortunately, these algorithms require tedious and expensive off-line calibration in the target deployment area before they can be used for localization. In this paper, we present Calibree, a novel localization algorithm that does not require off-line calibration. The algorithm starts by computing relative distances between pairs of mobile phones based on signatures of their radio environment. It then combines these distances with the known locations of a small number of GPS-equipped phones to estimate absolute locations of all phones, effectively spreading location measurements from phones with GPS to those without. Our evaluation results show that Calibree performs better than the conventional centroid algorithm and only slightly worse than fingerprinting, without requiring off-line calibration. More-over, when no phones report their absolute locations, Calibree can be used to estimate relative distances between phones.

1 Introduction

The most widespread localization technology available today is the Global Positioning System (GPS) [7,17]. Although accurate in open environments, GPS does not work well indoors, in urban canyons, or in similar areas with a limited view of the sky. In addition, GPS is installed in only a small portion of the mobile phones in use today. ABI research reported that the number of mobile phone subscribers with GPS equipped devices constituted only 0.5% of the total number of subscribers in 2006, but it estimates that this number will grow to 9% by 2011 [19]. As a result, several alternative localization algorithms have been proposed, including *centroid* and *fingerprinting* [18,3]. The main drawback of these algorithms is that they require off-line calibration in the target deployment area before they can be used for localization.

Calibrating a fingerprinting system is tedious and expensive, involving phys-ically sampling signal strengths at many locations. For instance, a recent effort

---

[*] [kaw-li-bri] is a Russian word for hummingbird.

J. Indulska et al. (Eds.): Pervasive 2008, LNCS 5013, pp. 146–161, 2008.

by Intel Research Seattle to sample the GSM radio environment in the Seattle metropolitan area took 3 months to complete, costing about US\$ 30,000 [3]. If the locations of cell towers are not readily available, centroid methods need the same type of calibration to compute the unknown locations of the cell towers. Another disadvantage of relying on physical sampling is that it gives only a snapshot of signal strengths at a particular time. Cell towers can be added, removed, blocked, renamed, or moved, partially invalidating an expensive calibration run.

In this paper, we present a novel localization technique, called Calibree, that requires no such calibration or maintenance. Calibree takes advantage of a small number of phones with known locations to determine locations of a larger set of phones. Calibree has two stages. In the first stage, Calibree computes relative distances between mobile phones that detect at least one GSM cell tower in common by comparing their GSM signatures. We define a *GSM signature* as a set of GSM cell towers that a phone detects and the signal strengths at which the phone hears these towers. To estimate relative distances, Calibree computes a regression formula in real time, based on a snapshot of GSM signatures and absolute locations from a small number of phones. In the case when no phones report their absolute locations, Calibree reverts back to using the last computed regression formula.

In the second stage, Calibree combines the pairwise distance estimations into a graph, in which nodes represent mobile phones and weighted edges represent likely distances between the phones. If a small number of mobile phones are able to report their absolute positions (e.g., through GPS), these phones are anchored at their known locations. Calibree then computes likely locations for all other phones by modelling the graph as a constraint problem and estimating mobile phone positions in order to minimize overall constraint violations using a mass-spring minimization method [4]. If no phones report their absolute locations, Calibree cannot compute absolute locations, but it can estimate relative distances between pairs of mobile phones. This is useful for gaming and social-mobile applications [16], where knowing a relative distance to another mobile phone is sufficient.

When computing relative distances between phones, Calibree takes into account only the ranked list of cell towers that phones hear sorted by the signal strength. Not using the actual signal strength as part of the relative distance estimation makes Calibree independent of the particular phone model it is running on, as the relative ranking of cell towers has been shown to be independent of the specific phone used [8].

We evaluated Calibree in the University of Toronto campus, located in downtown Toronto, Canada and a quiet residential neighborhood, located on the outskirts of Toronto. The results show that with only a small number of phones having GPS, Calibree outperforms the centroid algorithm and is comparable to the fingerprinting algorithm, achieving up to 147m median error. This result is very promising because Calibree achieves similar accuracy to existing localization algorithms, without requiring off-line calibration. Moreover, Calibree continues to work well and outperforms both the centroid and fingerprinting algorithms when tested on measurements collected inside 20 buildings scattered around the University of Toronto campus. This result shows that Calibree is effective at propagating the absolute location information from phones located outdoors to the phones located indoors. Finally, even when no absolute locations are known, Calibree estimates relative distances between phones more accurately than the centroid algorithm and only slightly worse than the fingerprinting algorithm.

The rest of this paper is organized as follows. We describe Calibree, centroid and fingerprinting algorithms in detail in Section 2 and present our evaluation results in Section 3. Section 4 discusses the differences between Calibree and related research efforts. Finally, we present our conclusions in Section 5.

2   Localization Algorithms

In this section, we describe Calibree, the fingerprinting and the centroid algorithms. We compare performance of these algorithms in Section 3.2.

2.1   Calibree

Calibree is a localization algorithm that estimates locations of GSM phones based on a snapshot of all phones' GSM signatures and absolute locations of a small number of these phones. If no absolute locations are known, Calibree can be used to estimate relative distances between any two mobile phones.

Figure 1 demonstrates how Calibree solves the problem of estimating absolute phone locations. The anchored mobile phones obtain their locations through GPS and feed these locations to Calibree, which uses them to estimate locations of phones without GPS. Calibree has two stages. In the first stage, Calibree computes a regression formula based on GSM signatures and known locations of GPS-equipped phones, and then uses this formula to estimate relative distances between phones without GPS that overhear at least one common cell tower. In

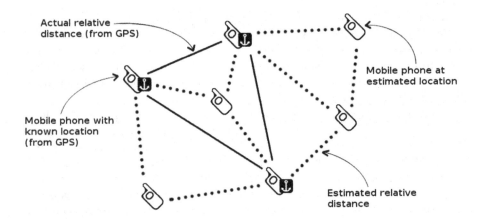

Fig. 1. Absolute positioning of mobile phones using Calibree

the second stage, Calibree uses a graph-based algorithm to estimate locations of phones without GPS. We next describe these two stages in detail.

Estimating Relative Distances. In the first stage, Calibree computes relative distances between pairs of mobile phones based on their GSM signatures. Recall that a GSM signature consists of a set of GSM cell towers that a phone detects and the signal strengths at which it hears these towers. Computing distances based on pairs of GSM signatures involves extracting features from the signatures and feeding the extracted values into a pre-generated formula.

We explored several possible features, including: number of common cells, number of cells not in common, Spearman coefficient, Euclidean distance in signal space, ratio of the number of cells in common to the total number of cells and a boolean variable indicating whether the phones hear the same serving cell.

To identify which features to use, we experimented with a number of different combinations of features, each time recording the median error of relative distance predictions using a given set of features. We found three features that both achieve good accuracy and that are insensitive to a particular phone model. The features are:

Common cells: The number of cell towers that are common to the two GSM signatures.

Uncommon cells: The number of cell towers that are not common to the two GSM signatures.

Spearman coefficient: The Spearman coefficient [12] between rankings of common cell towers by signal strengths.

These features use information about cell towers and relative signal strengths only. Previous studies have shown [8] that these parameters are cell phone model agnostic.

Given GPS coordinates and GSM signatures from a number of phones, Calibree generates a formula for predicting pairwise distances between phones by applying the multiple regression method to the features extracted from the GSM signatures and the distances computed from the GPS coordinates. We experimented with polynomials of different degrees. The evaluation procedure was the same as for selecting the features. We observed that while polynomials of high degrees often suffer from overfitting, a degree two polynomial gives consistently good performance and results in more accurate predictions than a linear function.

Figure 2 shows the general form of the formula that Calibree uses for relative pairwise distance estimations. In this formula, x_i stands for the value of the ith feature. The constants a_{ij}, b_i, and d are fitted from the GPS coordinates

$$Distance(x_1, x_2, x_3) = \sum_{i=1}^{3} \sum_{j=i}^{3} a_{ij} x_i x_j + \sum_{i=1}^{3} b_i x_i + d$$

Fig. 2. The general form of the regression formula for relative pairwise distance estimates

and GSM signatures of phones with GPS. These constants are recomputed each time the graph is built, which makes Calibree implicitly adaptive to changes in cell tower configurations. Once Calibree computes the constants a_{ij}, b_i and d, it is ready to estimate relative distances between pairs of mobile phones. Note that when two mobile phones overhear no common cells, the Spearman coefficient is not defined and the Common cells feature always evaluates to 0. Therefore, Calibree does not estimate relative distance between phones that detect no common cells, but rather assumes that these phones are located far away and lets the graph-based algorithm deal with these cases.

Estimating Absolute Locations. To compute absolute positions of mobile phones, Calibree uses the relative distance estimates obtained from the previous step as well as the absolute positions of a small number of mobile phones with GPS. With this data, Calibree builds a graph, in which nodes represent mobile phones and weighted edges represent estimated distances between mobile phones.

The graph models a geographic coordinate system: each node has a corresponding latitude/longitude coordinate and the distance between nodes is calculated using the Haversine formula [15]. Calibree initializes the coordinates with the actual mobile phone positions for the GPS-equipped phones and with random values for other phones. This initial placement of nodes results in a discrepancy between the weights on the edges and the distances between nodes in the graph. The goal of Calibree is to find a placement of nodes such that the overall discrepancy is minimized. Calibree doesn't change the coordinates of mobile phones with GPS during its runtime since these are known to be very close to correct.

To better understand the problem, imagine that every pair of nodes with an edge between them is connected using a spring with a relaxed length equal to the estimated relative distance between the corresponding mobile phones. As Calibree adjusts the locations of the nodes, it recomputes the lengths of the springs based on the Haversine formula, which calculates the distance between two latitude/longitude coordinates. Calibree's goal is then to find a placement of nodes such that the lengths of the springs are as close as possible to the relaxed lengths of the springs. More formally, if we denote two nodes as x and y, the relaxed spring length as r_{xy} and the current spring length as c_{xy}, Calibree needs to find a node placement that minimizes the error function:

$$Err = \sum_x \sum_y |r_{xy} - c_{xy}| \tag{1}$$

Calibree minimizes this function by iteratively refining node coordinates. Each spring exerts a force on the pair of the nodes that it connects. The magnitude of the force is taken to be the difference between the current and the relaxed lengths of the spring. We denote the direction of the force from node y to node x by a unit vector $unit(x, y)$. The force on node x from node y is then:

$$F_{xy} = |r_{xy} - c_{xy}| \times unit(x, y)$$

The net force on node x from all other connected nodes is just the sum of all individual forces:

$$F_x = \sum_{y \neq x} F_{xy}$$

Once Calibree calculates the net force, it is then ready to move the node in the direction of that force. However, applying the full force on the node would result in oscillations in node positions because many of the current node positions are incorrect. Therefore, Calibree applies only a portion of the original force on the node. The portion of the applied force is controlled by a parameter δ. Finding the right value for δ is important, because large values will result in large oscillations of node positions and consequently Calibree may not reach equilibrium altogether, while small values will result in slow convergence. We experimented with different values of δ and found that a value of 1.0×10^{-8} provides a good compromise between the speed of convergence and no oscillations.

Formally, if we let $coor_x$ be the vector coordinate of node x, the new coordinate after applying the force is:

$$coor_x = coor_x + \delta \times F_x$$

Calibree stops minimizing the error function when the refinement of node coordinates results in a negligible change in the total error Err, controlled by another parameter $tolerance$. For smaller values of δ, Calibree needs to use smaller $tolerance$ values, or otherwise Calibree might terminate prematurely.

A special case occurs when a pair of nodes has no relative distance prediction. This is a result of two mobile phones detecting no common cell towers. In this situation Calibree assumes that the two phones are more than a certain threshold distance away. To compute this threshold we looked at the cumulative distribution function of distances between mobile phones that detect no cells in common and picked the 25th percentile, which turned out to be about $500m$. Pairs of nodes that correspond to mobile phones that detect no common cells therefore have a special spring connecting them that exerts force only if the actual distance between nodes is smaller than $500m$. This is because Calibree does not know how far the two nodes are, but it does know that the nodes are likely to be at least $500m$ apart. Formally, the force between nodes x and y that detect no common cells is calculated as:

$$F_{xy} = \begin{cases} |500 - c_{xy}| \times unit(x, y) & \text{if } c_{xy} < 500 \\ 0 & \text{otherwise} \end{cases}$$

It is possible for Calibree to end up in a local minimum equilibrium, in which node position refinements are small, but the overall error Err is still large. We used an optimization that proved to work consistently well in pushing Calibree towards global equilibrium. With our optimization, when Calibree achieves a local equilibrium state, instead of terminating, it repositions a randomly chosen non-fixed node in the average of the current locations of all its connected nodes. This is repeated several times with different mobile phones.

▷ input: graph G = (V,E) and relative distance estimation function r
▷ output: coordinates of nodes in V
CALIBREE-ABSOLUTE(G, r)
```
 1   Err_cur ← ∞
 2   repeat
 3             Err_prev ← Err_cur
 4             for  each x in V
 5             do
 6                   if x has a fixed location
 7                      then continue
 8                   F ← 0
 9                   for  each y ≠ x in V
10                   do
11                        if (x, y) ∈ E
12                           then F ← F + |r_xy − c_xy| × unit(x, y)
13                           else  F ← F + max((500 − c_xy) × unit(x, y), 0)
14                   coor_x ← coor_x + δ × F
15             Err_cur ← Error(G)
16   until |Err_prev − Err_cur| > tolerance
```

Fig. 3. The pseudo-code of a graph-based stage of Calibree

Figure 3 shows the pseudo-code for the graph-based stage of Calibree. We leave out the above optimization for simplicity. The algorithm receives as input two parameters: (a) G, a graph with a set of nodes V and a set of edges E and (b) r, a pre-computed function of relative pairwise distances between nodes. The algorithm computes a new set of coordinates that minimizes the total error as defined in Equation 1. The outermost loop runs until the error difference between two successive iterations is less than the *tolerance* value. The inner loop keeps calculating the net force exerted on each node and updating their coordinates in the direction of the force. *Error* function on line 15 calculates the current total error of graph G.

CALIBREE-ABSOLUTE, shown in Figure 3, works correctly even when no absolute phone locations are known. In this case, although the orientation of the nodes is arbitrary, the algorithm may be used to estimate relative distances between any two nodes in the graph.

2.2 Fingerprinting

The fingerprinting algorithm [1] relies on the fact that signal strengths observed by mobile phones exhibit temporal stability and spatial variability. In other words, a given cell tower may be heard stronger or not at all a few meters away, while at the same location the observed signal strength is likely to be similar tomorrow and next week.

The fingerprinting algorithm requires a calibration phase, in which a mobile phone moves through the target environment, recording the strengths of signals emanating from radio sources (e.g., GSM cell towers). At the end of calibration, the fingerprinting algorithm creates a mapping from radio measurements to locations where these measurements were observed. Since the fingerprinting algorithm does not model radio propagation, a fairly dense grid of radio scans needs to be collected to achieve good accuracy. The original RADAR experiments, for example, collected measurements of WiFi signal strengths about a meter apart [1]. In our implementation we collected measurements every two meters on average.

Once the calibration phase is complete, a mobile phone can estimate its location by performing a radio scan and feeding it into the fingerprinting algorithm, which estimates the phone's location based on the similarity between the phone's radio scan and the measurements recorded during the calibration. The similarity of signatures can be computed in a variety of ways, but it is common to use the Euclidean distance in signal space [11,3]. The fingerprinting algorithm then estimates the location of a mobile phone to be the location of the measurement in the mapping with the smallest Euclidean distance in signal space to the radio scan. If a cell tower is not present in one of the measurements, we substitute its signal strength with the minimal signal strength found in this measurement.

2.3   Centroid

To estimate phone locations, the centroid algorithm [3] needs to know the locations of GSM cell towers. However, since this information is typically kept confidential by service providers and it is not available to third parties, the centroid algorithm has to estimate positions of cell towers by reverting to the same physical sampling of the radio environment employed by the fingerprinting algorithm. Once the physical sampling is complete, the centroid algorithm can estimate locations of cell towers in the environment by positioning a cell tower in a location where the signal strength from that cell tower was observed the strongest. In our experiments, we used the same calibration data for the centroid algorithm as we did for the fingerprinting algorithm.

Once the positions of cell towers are known and a mobile phone performs a radio scan, the centroid algorithm computes the location of the mobile phone as an average of locations of cell towers that appear in the radio scan. Typically, giving a higher weight during averaging to cell towers with stronger signal strength yields better localization accuracy.

3   Evaluation

In this section, we describe our data collection process, present our experimental results and then discuss the usage model of Calibree.

3.1   Data Collection

To evaluate the accuracy of our localization algorithms, we collected GSM measurements on the streets of the University of Toronto campus. The university covers an area of approximately $1km^2$ and it is located in the downtown core of Toronto, Canada. We gathered additional traces covering a residential area of similar size located on the outskirts of the city. To test the localization accuracy of Calibree indoors, we also collected several measurements inside 20 university buildings.

To collect the measurements, we used a Pocket PC T-Mobile MDA and an AudioVox SMT 5600 phone, connected to a Holux GPSlim236 GPS via Bluetooth. Both the PDA and the phone ran Intel's POLS [3] data collection software, which gives access to identities and signal strengths of up to 8 GSM cells. We walked through the target area at a speed of 2 meters per second and sampled the radio environment and GPS unit at a rate of one sample per second.

We collected two sets of traces for each area, to be able to train and test our algorithms on different traces. Full traces for the downtown and the residential areas contain about 6000 and 5000 measurements, respectively. Since different network operators use different cell towers, Calibree, fingerprinting and centroid algorithms work only when training and testing traces use the same operator. To support multiple operators, separate traces need to be collected for each operator. We collected all traces using Rogers, a single GSM network operator available in Toronto, Canada.

3.2   Experimental Results

In this section, we compare accuracy with which Calibree, the fingerprinting algorithm and the centroid algorithm estimate absolute phone positions and relative distances between phones.

Absolute Positioning. We trained Calibree "on-line" by randomly picking a number of points from the testing trace, simulating mobile phones with GPS, and using their GSM signatures and known locations to train the regression formula. To test the three algorithms, we randomly picked 50 points from a testing trace, simulating 50 mobile phones, estimated their absolute locations using each of the three algorithms and calculated the localization error using the actual phone locations from the trace. For example, if Calibree picks 25 points to train the regression formula and another 50 points for testing, it will use all 75 points to construct and solve the mass-spring graph. The 25 points that Calibree uses for creating the regression formula do not change their location during the runtime of Calibree and are not included in the calculation of accuracy. To reduce random effects and smooth the graphs, we repeated this procedure 40 times for each experiment. The following experiments use downtown traces unless otherwise specified.

Figure 4 plots the 50th and 95th percentile error of Calibree as a function of the number of phones with GPS. The results show that although the localization accuracy generally improves with the larger number of phones with GPS, the error levels off at 25 GPS-equipped phones. Note that 25 phones with GPS in the area of $1km^2$ is not too many, given that the average population density of Toronto including residential areas is 4000 $people/km^2$ and it is much higher in the downtown area.

Figure 5 and Figure 6 show the cumulative distribution function (CDF) of absolute localization error for the fingerprinting algorithm, the centroid algo-

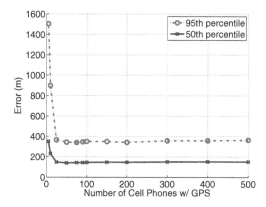

Fig. 4. The effect of the number of phones with GPS on the 50th and 95th percentile localization error of Calibree

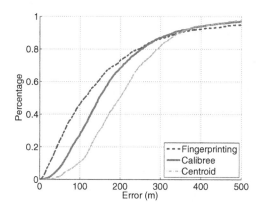

Fig. 5. Cumulative distribution function of absolute localization error of Calibree, the fingerprinting and centroid algorithms, evaluated in the downtown area

rithm and Calibree with 25 phones having GPS, evaluated in the downtown and the residential areas, respectively. In the downtown area, the fingerprinting and centroid algorithms achieved comparable accuracy to previously reported implementations, $112m$ and $200m$ median error, respectively. Calibree achieved $147m$ median error, which is better than the centroid algorithm and slightly worse than the fingerprinting algorithm. In the residential area, the errors are larger for all three algorithms; however, the general picture looks very similar - fingerprinting algorithm and Calibree show good performance, achieving $138m$ and $214m$ median error respectively, while the centroid algorithm does poorly with $335m$ median error. These results are very encouraging because Calibree achieves similar accuracy to existing localization algorithms, without requiring off-line calibration. We note that, with 25 phones acting as real time calibration points, our calibration density is much less than that of the fingerprinting or

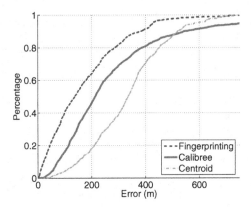

Fig. 6. Cumulative distribution function of absolute localization error of Calibree, the fingerprinting and centroid algorithms, evaluated in the residential area

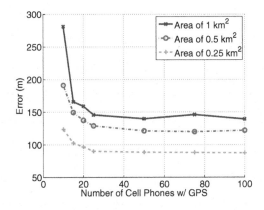

Fig. 7. Median localization error for areas of different size as a function of the number of GPS devices in the area

centroid algorithms, yet Calibree still achieves accuracies in the same range as these much more labor-intensive algorithms.

We conjectured that there is a correlation between the area size under consideration and the number of GPS-equipped phones required to achieve similar localization accuracy. To test this correlation, we experimented with limiting the traces collected to only half and quarter of the original area size. Figure 7 shows the median localization error for area sizes of $1km^2$, $0.5km^2$ and $0.25km^2$ as a function of the number of GPS-equipped phones in the area. The results confirm that it is typically the case that increasing the target area requires more GPS-equipped phones in the area to achieve comparable accuracy. For instance, Calibree achieves $123m$ median error with 10 GPS devices in the area of $0.25km^2$, $149m$ median error with 15 GPS devices in the area of $0.5km^2$ and $147m$ median error with 25 GPS devices in the area of $1km^2$.

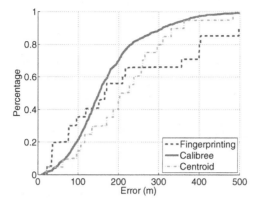

Fig. 8. Cumulative distribution function of absolute localization error for mobile phones located indoors

Finally, we tested the localization accuracy of Calibree, the fingerprinting and centroid algorithms on measurements collected inside 20 buildings of our university. The training of Calibree was performed as explained previously by picking 25 random points outdoors and estimating the regression formula. For testing all algorithms, we used 20 testing points, each collected in a different building. Because we knew where the buildings are located, we marked the ground truth of each of the 20 testing points manually in our trace. Figure 8 shows the CDF of absolute localization error for each of the three algorithms. Calibree achieves better localization accuracy than both the fingerprinting and centroid algorithms, reaching $151m$ median error vs. $165m$ median error for the fingerprinting algorithm and $203m$ for the centroid algorithm. Interestingly, the $151m$ median error that Calibree achieves on indoor measurements is very close to the median error of $147m$ that Calibree achieves on measurements taken outdoors. The results suggest that Calibree is effective in propagating the absolute location information from phones located outdoors to the phones located indoors.

Relative Positioning. In this section, we show that even when no phones report their absolute locations, Calibree is effective at predicting relative distances between phones. Note that although our regression formula computes distances between mobile phones that detect at least one common cell, Calibree is also able to predict distances between phones that have no cells in common. To compute relative positions, the centroid and fingerprinting algorithms first compute absolute phone positions and then calculate relative distances directly. Calibree, on the other hand, was trained using GSM signatures and absolute locations from 25 phones used in previous experiments.

Figure 9 shows the CDF of estimated relative distances between phones for Calibree, centroid and fingerprinting localization algorithms. The results show that Calibree is able to estimate distances between phones with a similar accuracy to that obtained by the centroid and fingerprinting algorithms, without the need to compute absolute locations first.

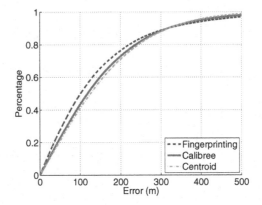

Fig. 9. Cumulative distribution function of pairwise distance estimation errors for Calibree, fingerprinting and centroid algorithms

3.3 Discussion

Although we developed and tested Calibree off-line with stored data, we envision it as a real time Web service in its final form. Mobile clients would transmit their measured signal strengths and, if available, their GPS coordinates, to a central Calibree server. The server would run our algorithm and make the computed, absolute coordinates available to authorized subscribers. Clients with satisfactory GPS availability would not need the Calibree service, because they already know their location. These clients could be enticed to contribute their data by micro-payments, discounted subscriber rates, discounted location data for other users (assuming authorization), or an offer of free position data from Calibree whenever they lose GPS satellite connectivity. For privacy, GPS data and the associated signal strengths could be transmitted to the service completely anonymously, although this would complicate the process of giving compensation for those users. Alternatively, or in addition to regular GPS-equipped users, the service could exploit GPS and signal strength data from taxis, police cars, municipal vehicles, garbage trucks, and delivery vehicles, many of which are already equipped with GPS and cell phones. Cell phone companies and ordinary users could set up static GPS and cell phone stations to transmit absolute coordinates in regions of particular need, although Calibree ideally exploits only mobile users to avoid the need for extra infrastructure.

4   Related Work

The Calibree localization algorithm is related to several research efforts in ubiquitous computing and sensor networks. We next describe key distinctions between these efforts and ours.

4.1   Relative Distance Estimation

Several projects have suggested ways to compute ranging estimates between wireless devices. In SpotON [6], tags use received radio signal strength information as an inter-tag distance estimator. Relate [5] uses a combination of ultrasound and radio communication to infer relative position and orientation between specialized USB dongles. Calibree differs from these efforts in the way it computes relative distances between nodes. Instead of using peer-to-peer measurements between devices, Calibree estimates distances between devices based on measurements of signals from static beacons – cell towers in our case.

The technique Calibree uses for estimating pairwise distances was inspired by the NearMe wireless proximity server [8]. NearMe showed that it is possible to calculate the relative distance between WiFi devices based on their WiFi signatures. In contrast, Calibree applies this technique to GSM instead of WiFi, and it uses the computed distances to find absolute phone locations with help from GPS measurements from a small number of phones. Furthermore, Calibree takes advantage of a network of pairwise distance estimates to refine the location results, while NearMe stopped after computing just individual pairwise distances.

4.2   Graph-Based Location Estimation

Self-mapping [9] is a graph-based algorithm for mapping radio beacon (e.g., WiFi APs or GSM cell towers) locations given a small seed of known beacon locations and a set of radio scans. The main idea behind self-mapping is that if a radio measurement contains two beacons, these beacons are located within twice the maximum transmission range of each other. A better distance estimate may be obtained by using a radio propagation model. Self-mapping combines the estimated distances into a graph and solves for beacon positions using an iterative error minimization algorithm.

A number of related localization techniques have been developed for sensor networks, mainly to improve network routing. Some of these approaches assume that a small number of beacon nodes with known locations are available [13,10] and compute locations of other nodes in the network. Other approaches assume no such knowledge and compute only the relative node locations [2,14].

Calibree applies similar techniques to localize GSM mobile phones instead of radio beacons or sensor nodes. However, Calibree estimates relative distances between phones using a regression formula derived in real time from a set of GSM signatures and their absolute locations. In contrast, self-mapping estimates distances between beacons based on a simple radio propagation model, while sensor network efforts either rely on sheer node-to-node connectivity or estimate relative distances using peer-to-peer measurements of time of flight [10] between sensor nodes. Finally, Calibree uses a different graph-based algorithm for constraint satisfaction: a variation of the Vivaldi algorithm [4].

Vivaldi is a distributed algorithm for predicting communication latency between Internet hosts without requiring explicit round trip time measurements between them. For that purpose, Vivaldi assigns each host a synthetic coordinate such that distances between the coordinates accurately predict the latency between hosts. Vivaldi uses round trip time measurements to estimate relative distances between network nodes, combines these measurements into a graph and then solves the graph constraint system using a distributed version of the mass-spring minimization method. In contrast, Calibree estimates relative distances based on phones' measurements of GSM cell towers and it calculates absolute, not relative, phone positions based on a seed of known locations of GSM signatures measured by devices with GPS.

5 Conclusions

In this paper, we presented Calibree, a novel GSM localization algorithm that does not require the tedious calibration phase that normally accompanies cell tower localization algorithms. Calibree uses a relatively small number of GPS-equipped mobile phones to compute the locations of mobile phones without GPS. Calibree takes advantage of the fact radio signatures are a reasonably good basis for computing the relative distances between mobile phones that detect at least one cell tower in common. Our algorithm combines these relative distance measurements with GPS measurements from some of the phones in an error-minimization procedure to compute the absolute locations of all the phones.

Our experimental results showed that the accuracy of Calibree is comparable to traditional, calibration-intensive algorithms for cell phone localization. Even as the number of cell phones equipped with GPS grows, Calibree will remain relevant, as it works for phones that are located indoors or otherwise unable to detect GPS satellites. Calibree is also an effective technique for computing the relative locations of a group of phones even if none of them have GPS. This can be useful for proximity-based applications and games.

Extensions to Calibree could include a technique to enforce spatial continuity of the inferred locations. As it is, Calibree computes locations based on measurements from a single instant in time. It may be possible to improve accuracy and robustness by smoothing or filtering location estimates across time, using probabilistic motion models. Such models could include path constraints on the mobile nodes, such as a network of streets, railways, and pedestrian paths. Considering both time and path constraints, it may even be possible to compute absolute locations from a sequence of relative locations by finding the unique set of absolute paths that could give rise to the inferred relative paths. Calibree could be extended to deal with the error inherent in GPS. As it is, the algorithm assumes that GPS measurements are always correct, although we know that GPS has its own error characteristics, including occasional outliers. The spring-mass scheme could be easily extended to account for some error in the GPS estimates.

References

1. Bahl, P., Padmanabhan, V.N.: RADAR: An in-building RF-based user location and tracking system. In: Proceedings of INFOCOM, pp. 775–784 (2000)
2. Capkun, S., Hamdi, M., Hubaux, J.-P.: GPS-free positioning in mobile ad-hoc networks. Cluster Computing Journal 5(2), 157–167 (2002)

3. Chen, M.Y., Sohn, T., Chmelev, D., Hightower, D.H.J., Hughes, J., LaMarca, A., Potter, F., Smith, I., Varshavsky, A.: Practical metropolitan-scale positioning for gsm phones. In: Proceedings of the Eighth International Conference on Ubiquitous Computing, Irvine, California (September 2006)
4. Dabek, F., Cox, R., Kaashoek, F., Morris, R.: Vivaldi: a decentralized network coordinate system. In: Proceedings of SIGCOMM, pp. 15–26 (2004)
5. Hazas, M., Kray, C., Gellersen, H., Agbota, H., Kortuem, G., Krohn, A.: A relative positioning system for co-located mobile devices (2005)
6. Hightower, J., Want, R., Borriello, G.: SpotON: An indoor 3d location sensing technology based on RF signal strength. Technical Report 00-02-02, University of Washington, Department of Computer Science and Engineering, Seattle, WA (February 2000)
7. Hofmann-Wellenhof, B., Lichtenegger, H., Collins, J.: Global Positioning System: Theory and Practice, 3rd edn. Springer, Heidelberg (2001)
8. Krumm, J., Hinckley, K.: The nearme wireless proximity server. In: Davies, N., Mynatt, E.D., Siio, I. (eds.) UbiComp 2004. LNCS, vol. 3205, pp. 283–300. Springer, Heidelberg (2004)
9. LaMarca, A., Hightower, J., Smith, I., Consolvo, S.: Self-mapping in 802.11 location systems. In: Beigl, M., Intille, S.S., Rekimoto, J., Tokuda, H. (eds.) UbiComp 2005. LNCS, vol. 3660, pp. 87–104. Springer, Heidelberg (2005)
10. Langendoen, K., Reijers, N.: Distributed localization in wireless sensor networks: a quantitative comparison. Computer Networks 43(4), 499–518 (2003)
11. Otsason, V., Varshavsky, A., LaMarca, A., de Lara, E.: Accurate gsm indoor localization. In: Beigl, M., Intille, S.S., Rekimoto, J., Tokuda, H. (eds.) UbiComp 2005. LNCS, vol. 3660, Springer, Heidelberg (2005)
12. Press, W.H., Flannery, B.P., Teukolsky, S.A., Vetterling, W.T.: Numerical Recipes in C: The Art of Scientific Computing, 2nd edn. Cambridge University Press, Cambridge (1992)
13. Savarese, C., Rabay, J., Langendoen, K.: Robust positioning algorithms for distributed ad-hoc wireless sensor networks. In: Proceedings of USENIX Technical Annual Conference (2002)
14. Shang, Y., Ruml, W.: Improved mds-based localization. In: Proceedings of Infocom (2004)
15. Sinnott, R.W.: Virtues of haversine. Sky and Telescope 68(2) (1984)
16. Smith, I.E.: Social mobile applications. IEEE Computer 38(4), 84–85 (2005)
17. Sprint. Location based services network overview. Technical report (2005)
18. Varshavsky, A., Chen, M., de Lara, E., Froehlich, J., Haehnel, D., Hightower, J., LaMarca, A., Potter, F., Sohn, T., Tang, K., Smith, I.: Are GSM phones THE solution for localization? In: IEEE Workshop on Mobile Computing Systems and Applications (April 2006)
19. GPS-Enabled Location-Based Services (LBS) Subscribers Will Total 315 Million in Five Years, http://www.abiresearch.com/abiprdisplay.jsp?pressid=731

Location Conflict Resolution with an Ontology

William Niu and Judy Kay

School of Information Technologies
The University of Sydney, Australia
{niu,judy}@it.usyd.edu.au

Abstract. Location modelling is central for many pervasive applications and is a key challenge in this area. One major difficulty in location modelling is due to the nature of evidence about a person's location; the evidence is commonly noisy, uncertain and conflicting. Ontological reasoning is intuitively appealing to help address this problem, as reflected in several previous proposals for its use.

This paper makes several important contributions to the exploration of the potential power of ontologies for improving reasoning about people's location from the available evidence. We describe ONCOR, our lightweight ontology framework: it has the notable and important property that it can be semi-automatically constructed, making new uses of it practical. This paper provides a comprehensive evaluation on how ontological reasoning can support location modelling: we introduce three algorithms for such reasoning and their evaluation based on a study of 8 people over 10–13 days. The results indicate the power of the approach, with mean error rates dropping from 55% with a naive algorithm to 16% with the best of the ontologically based algorithms. This work provides the first implementation of such an approach with a range of ontological reasoning approaches explored and evaluated.

Keywords: Ontological reasoning, location conflict resolution, ontological algorithms.

1 Introduction

Accurate location information plays a critical role in context-aware systems. Depending on the application, it may be preferred to have location information presented at different levels of granularity: for example, when Bob's manager wants to have a phone discussion with Bob, she may only want to know if he is at work or not: this may be inferred by his location, being either within the workplace building or not. By contrast, Bob's daughter may want to know a finer grain value for Bob's location—Bob may be happy for her to know his precise location at all times—such as *at the kitchen sink* to have her homework book signed. To take just one other example, a Follow-me-music application may need to model Bob's location accurately at the room level to the deliver desirable service. Being able to determine accurate locations and to tailor the desired grain-size of location to users and contexts is not trivial. This is especially

J. Indulska et al. (Eds.): Pervasive 2008, LNCS 5013, pp. 162–179, 2008.
© Springer-Verlag Berlin Heidelberg 2008

true in a multi-sensor environment, as more uncertainty may be introduced in resolving a location value from multiple location sensors [1,2,3]. The challenges of achieving accurate location modelling and the demands of privacy mean that it is important to address the problem of modelling people's location in ways that enable reasoning over granularity levels and in ways that support accurate modelling from multiple sources.

A number of researchers have tackled the problem of modelling locations with ontologies, for example [4,5,6,7], but few focus on the issues of resolving conflicting context evidence and reasoning across granularity of locations. EasyMeeting [4] supports privacy at different grain-sizes of location by defining appropriate personal privacy policies, but has limited support for conflict resolution. Wishart, Henricksen and Indulska [7] proposes an *obfuscation* approach that can "adjust the granularity of different types of context information to meet disclosure requirements stated by the owner of the context information." The literature, however, did not report an implementation of an actual location ontology in a working prototype.

For conflict resolution for locations, Hightower and Borriello [1] compares the accuracy of three algorithms that uses *Particle filters* to estimate locations. It focuses on physical sensors. By contrast, our infrastructure includes both physical and virtual sensors, and we exploit the potential of an ontology to automatically determine and resolve conflicting location information. Myllymaki and Edlund [2] presents an conflict resolution algorithm to determine locations of a user from the evidence of multiple mobile objects. Indulska et al [3] adopts a similar approach to [2] and their work uses two additional confidence factors: discounting the weights of the sensor sources that previously provided incorrect readings and accounting for *activeness* of each sensor type. Both include a step to filter out location values that spatially contain another one, but the actual underlying approach is not documented.

Previous work, described above, explores various promising aspects of ontological reasoning in context-aware computing. We introduce a new role for ontologies: interpretation of the typically noisy and contradictory evidence available about location. Our implementation of this approach is called ONCOR. At the heart of ONCOR is a location ontology—extending MIBO (Middle Building Ontology) [8]. In this paper, we will refer to that ontology as the *building ontology*.

The rest of the paper is structured as follows, Section 2 outlines common challenges in interpreting sensor evidence inside a multi-sensor environment. Section 3 then introduces and explains the motivation for the design of three algorithms that ONCOR uses to resolve conflicting location values. Then, Section 4 describes the design of our empirical evaluation of those ontological reasoning algorithms, with the results in Section 5 followed by our conclusions.

2   Challenges in Interpreting Sensor Evidence

There are many sources of noise and uncertainty in reasoning about location from the evidence that can be collected by the many available sensor types. As a basis for the design of new ways that an ontology can address these difficulties, we identify three categories of problems in interpreting location evidence sources.

Granularity variance. This category describes the situation where there is a set of evidence, at different granularity levels. For example, a Bluetooth™ sensor with a ten-metre range may detect Bob's phone, giving evidence of his location at the granularity of a wing of the building, Level 1 East, while a login sensor may provide evidence he is at a finer grain location, Room 100. If Room 100 is within Level 1 East, this does not represent conflict and a building ontology has the potential to reason that this is so. Similarly, if Room 100 is in Level 1 West, there is a conflict and a building ontology has the potential to reason that this is the case.

False positive. This occurs when the available evidence is wrong. There are many ways this can happen. One important case occurs with sensors, such as Bluetooth detectors which may detect Bob's phone on two levels of a building, with one sensor on Level 3 providing evidence and another on the floor above also giving evidence. A building ontology may be able to determine that these two pieces of evidence are in conflict. User behaviours may also cause false positive evidence: for example, Bob may leave his phone in Alice's office, giving a stream of evidence that he is still in her office. If Bob then starts using his machine in his office, the activity sensor's evidence of his location conflicts with the evidence from his phone location. A building ontology can be used to infer that this is a conflict.

False negative. This describes the case where evidence is missing. There are many potential causes: for example, a sensor may fail temporarily; there may be network latencies or failures. Importantly, people's behaviours may play a role, for example, when Bob turns off his phone, or its battery fails. One case may present when the Bluetooth sensor on Level 3 West stops delivering sensor readings and the sensors one floor above and below detect the presence of Bob's mobile phone. We may infer that the Bluetooth sensor on Level 3 West has stopped working and that Bob is indeed located between Level 2 West and Level 4 West (i.e. Level 3 West). This may require the ontology to specify the third dimension of the spatial relation.

Certainly, all of these can occur in combinations. For example, a login sensor may provide evidence Bob is in Room 100, while two Bluetooth detectors may give evidence that his phone is both on Level 1 East and Level 2 East. The first two pieces of evidence may have granularity variance, the third is a false positive. An ontology of the building has the potential to support reasoning about the evidence, determining whether it is conflicting. In addition, ontological reasoning has the potential to help in the resolution of conflicting evidence.

3   ONCOR Approach to Location Reasoning

We now describe the way that our ONCOR ontology has been used to explore how ontological reasoning might tackle the challenges arising from the classes

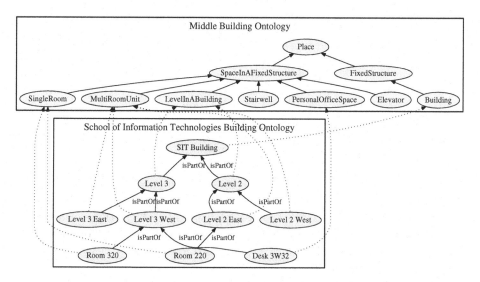

Fig. 1. A sample of the building ontology (bottom) extending MIBO (top). Each un-labelled arrow represents an isA relationship. There is no semantic difference between solid and dotted lines; dotted ones are only for visual clarity. The full building ontology consists of a total of 573 location instances.

of conflict and uncertainty in modelling location from a collection of sensor evidence. First, however, we note that the ONCOR ontology has two parts: a handcrafted, general ontology for buildings (Figure 1 top) and a generated part that captures the structure of a particular building (Figure 1 bottom). We have previously described the way that we created the ontology [8]. A key property of ONCOR is the careful separation of the costly handcrafted but reusable parts and the use of automated analysis of information about buildings to generate the remainder of the ontology for a new building and to make it easy to handle the addition of new sensors. While our previous work explored ways to build the ontology, this paper moves beyond the representation to consider how to exploit ontological reasoning.

We now introduce our three approaches to ontological reasoning about location based on diverse sensor evidence. For each, we first explain the design motivation, then provide an illustrative example followed by some discussion of that approach, its expected power and limitations.

Closest Common Subsumer (CCS). This algorithm is motivated by the goal of determining the finest grain location that is consistent with a set of evidence. For example, if Bob's presence is inferred by sensors in both Level 3 West and Level 3 East with similar uncertainty[1], CCS may find

---

[1] As the focus of this work is on the ontological reasoning, and since this is orthogonal to the reasoning about the arbitrary collections of uncertain evidence, we treat all evidence as equally reliable. However, the Accretion/Resolution approach [9] under-lying this work affords support for a flexible range of such reasoning approaches.

Level 3 as the finest grain location containing both of these. This algorithm uses the location ontology to find the closest common subsuming location: this is similar to the lowest common ancestor concept in graph theory. This algorithm may be valuable in cases where an application requires location at a certain grain-size and, with this algorithm, it is possible to determine if a set of data can give a consistent location at the required granularity. In addition to providing an indication of the level of conflict in data from different sensors, the algorithm can be used to resolve a value for location that is consistent with all available evidence.

Granularity Harmoniser (GH). This algorithm is motivated by the common inconsistency of granularity variance seen in multi-sensor networks. So, for example, if Bob's presence is inferred by sensors in Level 3 and Room 300, GH would return Room 300 as it is contained in Level 3. GH uses a location ontology to determines whether or not a list of locations are all on the direct `isPartOf` ontological path (e.g. Level 1 West `isPartOf` Level 1). If they are all on the direct ontological path, it returns the finest-grained location in the list. Otherwise a conflict is reported, and a designated conflict resolver is used to resolve the inconsistency. Not only can this algorithm effectively harmonise granularity variance, it also reveals other forms of conflicts in sensor evidence that typically occur in a multi-sensor environment. The simplicity of this algorithm also facilitates the important aspect of *scrutability*[2], enabling end applications to provide simple and natural explanations of this reasoning.

Democratic. The assumption underlying this approach is that noisy data tends to be less common than accurate data. So, for example, within the locations of Room 300, Room 400 and Level 3 West, when they are grouped by physical levels of a building, Room 400 belongs to a *minority* group, as the others are all on Level 3. Therefore, it is discarded. This algorithm groups the location values according to the set of subsuming locations at the same level of granularity (e.g. Level 1, Level 2, Level 3). The groups that contain less evidence, or the minorities, are discarded. The democratic algorithm may eliminate some false positive sensor evidence described in Section 2. It may fail if false sensor evidence sources overweigh the genuine ones.

The Granularity Harmoniser (GH) and Democratic algorithms are used more like filters: they do not guarantee complete conflict resolution, but try to filter out certain conflicts. Each algorithm excels, in terms of both accuracy and precision, in different contexts. When precision is within an acceptable range, CCS may be a good candidate for accuracy. When deployed sensors have overlapping location ranges but differing in granularity, GH can be a good filter in the process of interpreting the evidence. Depending on the setup of a sensor infrastructure, the Democratic algorithm may help filter false positive sensor evidence. Algorithm 1 is the pseudocode of an algorithm that uses Democratic and GH approaches as filters.

---

[2] Definition of "scrutable": Capable of being understood through study and observation; comprehensible, http://dictionary.reference.com/browse/scrutable

---

Algorithm 1: An algorithm that adopts the *Democratic* approach

---

Input   : *evidenceList*, each evidence consists of a timestamp and a location
Output: A location, from an evidence source in *evidenceList*
/* Non-finest grain-sizes could be a wing, a level or a building   */
1 **foreach** *grainSize in non-finest grain-sizes in a spatial ontology from coarse-to-fine order* **do**

2   *groups* = group *evidenceList* by *grainSize* to a mapping like {"level 1": $[e_1, e_2 ..]$, "level 2": $[e_n, e_{n+1} ..]$, .. "level k": $[e_m, e_{m+1} ..]$}

3    $maxSize = 0$

4   **foreach** *group, evidenceSources in groups* **do**

5       $maxSize = $ **max**$(|$*unique locations in evidenceSources*$|, maxSize)$

6   **foreach** *group, evidenceSources in groups* **do**

7   **if** $|$*unique locations in evidenceSources*$| < maxSize$ **then**

8   remove *group* from *groups* ;   /* remove the minority */

9   *evidenceList* = evidence sources for each group in *groups*
   /* filter out granularity-variance conflicts   */

10   *resolvedLocation* = **granularityHarmoniser**(*evidenceList*)

11   **if** *resolvedLocation* $\neq$ **null** **then**

12   **return** *resolvedLocation*

/* If conflict still exists, use the *Point* algorithm [10] , i.e.
return the most recent piece of evidence   */
13 **return** **point**(*evidenceList*)

---

4   Evaluation—Experimental Design

In this section we describe the design and setup of an experiment aiming to obtain a gold standard of movements of people inside a building. This is to exploit and evaluate the potential of the ontology: the managing of multiple evidence sources, with varying levels of reliability, range, and characteristics that may potentially lead to conflicting information. Similar experiments have been carried out using robots, e.g. [1]. The clear advantage of robots is the accurate and precise position traces. However, they behave quite differently from real humans—whose locations are what we ultimately want to determine—and their actions might not be generalisable to humans. Hence, we conducted this experiment with actual humans. The word *entry* is used throughout the rest of the paper referring to a user-logged message.

4.1   System Design

Two systems were designed for this study: the School of Information Technologies Interactive Map (SITIM) and the Location Log Feedback system.

SITIM has been designed for simplicity and ubiquity. SITIM allows users to log a location entry with three or less (correct) mouse/stylus clicks: one for selecting a floor level, one for a place and the other one for an intended action.

Tabs are used to allow a larger viewing space and greater clicking area, as well as to provide more flexibility for incorporating additional information, such as inserting supplementary maps.

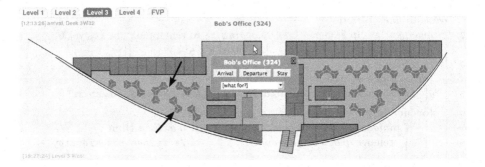

Fig. 2. A screenshot of SITIM when a user, who knows Bob, clicks on Room 324 on the map at the "Level 3" tab

Figure 2 is a screenshot of SITIM after the user clicks on Room 324 on the map at the "Level 3" tab. The system displays a personalised name of the room at the upper-centre region and in the pop-up message. The most recent user-logged and sensor-generated locations are displayed both as dots on the map (pointed out by the arrows in Figure 2) and in text at bottom-left and top-left corners respectively.

System feedback is an important means to engage users and prevent confusion, especially with a non-traditional interface. This is addressed by: using a range of interactive Web programming features, displaying the most recent user-logged entry (e.g. [12:12:26] arrival, Desk 3W32) and sensor-generated locations (e.g. [18:27:24] Level 3 West), and reporting the user's entry capture status (e.g. whether the entry is successfully recorded or not).

In addition to a week-long practice during the pre-experimental period, system design decisions were made to minimise potential user mistakes. These include: allowing users to undo the immediate erroneous entry; allowing the user to log their top 10 most frequently visited places (FVP); and displaying a one-click entry box for **departure** after an **arrival** entry, following the assumption that a user would depart the place they last arrived at. With the introduction of the FVP page and departure floating box, a location can be logged with two and one click respectively.

Participants were asked to review their log at the end of each day. They used the Location Log Feedback page (Figure 3) to review the log to identify inaccurately logged location data. Feedback was given via an online interface that consisted of the logged entries for the day, a list of sensor-generated location data, two multiple choice questions on how *informative* the logged data was for that day and input areas for users to give comments. The two multiple choice questions are for participants to assess the completeness and accuracy of their

(a) ID	(b) Time (gap)	(c) Action	(d) Location	(e) Comments
1	10:55 (0)	arrival (leaving/coming to uni)	Desk 3W32	
2	11:23 (28)	departure (coffee/drinks)	Desk 3W32	
3	11:30 (6)	arrival	Room 126	
4	11:39 (9)	departure	Room 126	
5	11:40 (0)	arrival	Room 125	
6	12:11 (30)	departure	Room 126	should be Room 125
7	12:13 (2)	arrival	Desk 3W32	
8	12:27 (14)	departure (meeting/seminar)	Desk 3W32	seminar and tutoring
9	17:07 (279)	arrival (back to office/desk)	Desk 3W32	
10	20:31 (204)	departure (leaving/coming to uni)	Desk 3W32	

(f) Location Log (total time: 576 minutes)

(1)	(2)	(3)	(4)
74	12:23	Present	Desk 3W32 (Sys)
75	12:24	Found	Level 3 West (BT)
76	12:25	Lost	Level 3 West (BT)
77	12:26	Lost	Desk 3W32 (Sys)
78	12:26	Present	Level 3 West (BT)
79	12:26	Found	Level 3 West (BT)
80	12:27	Found	Desk 3W32 (Sys)
81	12:28	Lost	Desk 3W32 (Sys)
82	12:28	Lost	Level 3 West (BT)
83	12:29	Found	Room 304 (BT)
84	12:30	Lost	Room 304 (BT)
85	12:31	Lost	Level 3 West (BT)
86	16:09	Found	Room 304 (BT)
87	16:09	Found	Level 3 West (BT)

Fig. 3. A sample view of the feedback page. The table to the left shows user-logged entries: (a) is the ID column that numbers each entry, (b) shows time of each logged entry as well as the gap between this one and its preceding entry, (c) shows the action and purpose, if given, of the entry, (d) is the location logged, (e) is for users to give comments for each entry, (f) is the duration for the day and (g) shows the two highlighted rows that are potentially erroneous. The table to the right lists the evidence sources from sensors: (1) is the ID column, (2) is the timestamp of the evidence source, (3) is the sensor message, (4) lists the inferred location as well as the sensor type (i.e. BT for Bluetooth sensors, Sys for activity sensors and Login for login sensors) and (5) shows the highlighted rows, temporally close to the 8th logged entry clicked by the user; it highlights the rows that are less than 2 minutes away (i.e. 2 minutes backward and forward) from the clicked entry with a darker green colour, and those that are less than 20 minutes away with a lighter green colour.

own logged entries. The first question asks them to assess the reliability of the data they logged and the second one asks about the reliability of the logged data after applying corrections they provided.

4.2 Location Modelling and Sensor Infrastructure

Location models, along with user and device models, are kept in the Personis modelling server [9]. Each location in the building is semi-automatically populated into the server by parsing the building maps in Scalable Vector Graphics (SVG) format, including an ID, a MIBO class (see top of Figure 1), its parent location, its child locations and its coordinates on the map.

There is a number of sensors that can be used to monitor people's indoor locations for a range of accuracy and precision, as reviewed in [10]. Our infrastructure is set up to have a representative range of sensor types, taking account of pragmatic considerations, such as minimal maintenance, simple setup and minimal user interaction.

Bluetooth Sensors. For sensing in the range of for roughly 10 metres, they consist of Bluetooth dongles that periodically scan for surrounding Bluetooth-enabled devices and report the list of detected devices. They occasionally fail to pick up some signals in range and may suffer from overlapping detection.

Activity sensors. For sensing at the desk/room grain-size, they are programs installed on the users' machines to report their activity/inactivity based on keyboard/mouse movements and activation of screensavers.

Login sensors. For sensing at the desk grain-size, are programs that monitor users logging in and out of machines in computer laboratories. Since the machines in the laboratories are shared by many people, users normally take extra care in logging off when they are physically away. Login sensors report less frequently than activity sensors, but provide reliable readings of users' presence in the laboratories.

4.3   Experimental Procedure

The study took place in the School of Information Technologies building on the University of Sydney campus. It ran for 10–13 days with a mean of 11 days for each participant. There was an exception for the author participant who had 34 days of logged data. Before the experiment, each participant was given a tutorial on how to use a Tablet PC, the SITIM system and the feedback page. The first week was allocated for the participants to familiarise themselves with the systems and logging. The data collected during this week was excluded from the analysis.

At the end of each day, the participants were reminded by email to verify their logged data and to self-assess the accuracy of it. While users were able to comment on the logged entries any time during the day, the two self-assessment questions were required to be done at the end of the day. The experiment conductor would then review each participant's feedback to ensure reasonable responses.

There were eight participants, including one of the authors, for the experiment: seven males and one female. Their ages were between 22 to 35. There were one undergraduate and seven postgraduate students with Computer Science related majors. All of them regularly worked inside the building.

Logging a location consists of the following steps:

1. The participant selects the tab of the level in the building where they are currently located.
2. Then the participant clicks on the location they want to log on the map.
3. A confirmation message then pops up just below the cursor asking for the participant's intended *action*, which is one of: `arrival`, `departure` or `stay` (see Figure 2): `arrival` and `departure` are the primary actions; `stay` would only be used if one forgets to indicate their arrival on time, i.e. delayed arrival. The participant can optionally indicate their purpose for that action from a drop-down menu. This enables the participant to add semantics to the data, which facilitates understanding of the log at the end of the day.
4. After a location, an action and an optional purpose for the action are selected, a message box would pop up with the information to be sent to the Personis server. The entry is delivered automatically after eight seconds, unless the participant decides to retract the action, by clicking "Undo".

Each participant was asked to log their locations whenever they moved from one place to another inside the building, with a few exceptions: going to the toilet, short trips that normally took less than two minutes (e.g. getting water) and in transit from one place to another.

5 Analysis on User Data and Sensor Data

5.1 User-Logged Data

As described in Section 4.3, each participant was asked to comment on the logged data for any abnormality as well as self-assess it by answering two multiple choice questions at the end of the day. Feedback was mostly on erroneous entries (e.g. wrong locations) and omissions. For the cases when participants were able to provide corresponding corrections, they were manually put into the logged data.

For the self-assessment questions, an answer of 5 indicates the highest reliability with more than 90% of accuracy and 1 is the least reliability with less than 25% of accuracy. The mean scores were 4.6 and 4.9 for participants' views on, respectively, the reliability of their logged data and the reliability of the logged data with their corrections incorporated. Only the days that participants indicated more than 90% of accuracy, which account for 101 out 111 days, are used for error rate analysis for better data integrity.

Then we analysed the actual logged data by examining each pair of consecutive entries. There are three possible logging actions: `departure`, `arrival` and `stay`. Combined with a boolean value of whether two consecutively logged locations are the same, there are 18 different combinations. They are assigned to four different classes of time: stationary, transit, unknown and error.

Stationary time. It denotes the amount of time that the participant was stationary at a place. This category includes two combinations of entries: `arrival` X→`departure` X and `stay` X→`departure` X, where X is a place. Even though there is uncertainty about the time of arrival, the time between `stay` and `departure` for a location still indicates the person being at that location. This is the only category of time taken into account for accuracy calculation.

Transit time. It is the amount of time that the participant was travelling from one place to another. It is represented by `departure` X→`arrival` Y. This category of time is excluded from analysis for two pragmatic reasons: the actual locations during travelling are difficult to determine and verify; and it accounts for a relatively small proportion of time (around 3%, see Figure 4(b)) which outweighs the high uncertainty.

Unknown time. It denotes the amount of time that the location of the participant could not be inferred from the entries. This category is represented by `departure` X→`arrival` X. Possible explanations for this type of entry were: participants went out of the building; they took short trips around their work space; or they failed to log both `arrival` and `departure` of another place. Manual inspection of the data revealed that 90% of the cases could be accounted for by the first two explanations. That leaves the rest of the 10%

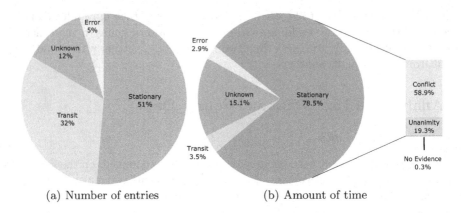

(a) Number of entries   (b) Amount of time

Fig. 4. Mean distribution of the number of entries and the length of time

to be potentially erroneous entries. This class of time is also excluded from analysis as the *actual* destination of the participant is unknown.

Error time. It is the amount of time when the participant made one or more errors in logging an entry. This category of time consists of all 14 other combinations. One example combination is `departure X→departure Y`. This implies that the user failed to put in an `arrival` entry when arriving the place Y. This category accounts for about 4.6% of overall entries and the majority (2.4%) of them imply one human error. It indicates that participants were generally careful when putting in each entry.

Figure 4(a) and Figure 4(b) summarise the distribution of the logged data in terms of the numbers of entries and amount of time, respectively, for each class. So, *stationary* accounts for 51.4% of total number of entries and 78.5% of the time, which is about 6.5 hours from 9am–5pm, working hours. Most of the *unknown* time, which accounts for about 15.5% of the time,was because of participants going out of the building. And there is a relatively small amount of *error* and *transit* time, about 2.9% and 3.5% respectively.

5.2   Sensor-Generated Location Data

A diverse range of sensor and device evidence was gathered during the study: 38414 messages from 16 Bluetooth sensors sensing 16 Bluetooth-enabled devices (5 mobile phones, 8 Tablet PCs and 3 laptops), 13252 messages from 12 activity sensors and 57 messages from the login sensors.

Table 1 summarises the classes of sensor evidence collected during the study in percentage of time. We classify the evidence into three categories: no evidence, unanimity and conflicting evidence. The last category is further divided into the granularity variance conflict and all others. *No evidence* denotes the amount of time that had no sensor evidence inferring the participant's location. Time classified as *Unanimity* means that when there is only one location value from the

Table 1. Classification of sensor evidence in percentage of time

| Participant | No evidence | Unanimity | Conflicting evidence | |
			Granularity variance	Others
A	0.1%	14.4%	71.2%	14.2%
B	0.0%	17.6%	71.6%	10.7%
C	0.3%	51.6%	32.2%	15.9%
D	0.0%	42.6%	48.3%	9.0%
E	4.1%	28.5%	65.0%	2.4%
F	0.2%	21.9%	59.0%	18.9%
G	0.0%	26.0%	73.8%	0.2%
H	0.0%	0.2%	0.0%	99.8%
Average	**0.4%**	**24.6%**	**57.0%**	**18.0%**

sensor evidence, i.e. no ambiguous evidence sources. *Granularity variance*, described in Section 2, represents the amount of time when the ambiguous evidence sources are overlapping in granularity difference. *Others* denotes the percentage of time with all other types of conflicting evidence sources; more than 99% of it was false positives.

The high percentage of granularity variance (57.0%) was because each participant was detected by at least one Bluetooth sensor and one activity sensor when they were using their computer at their work space. Participant C's and D's data have more unanimous evidence than the other three. This is because their Tablet PCs would enter stand-by mode[3] more often, causing their system sensors to be the sole sensing devices. Participant E's higher percentage of *No evidence* time (4.1%) was mainly due to their time spent in a research laboratory outside of the Bluetooth sensor coverage. Because the work spaces for participants A, B, C, F and H could be detected by Bluetooth sensors from different floors of the building—especially for participant H—they had more non-granularity-variance conflicting evidence than Participants D and E. Participant G changed locations least frequently throughout the study; they only stayed at two places during the study: their work space (97%) and a seminar room (3%).

5.3   Algorithms Compared

In this section we compare accuracy of algorithms that use ONCOR and three other algorithms: Point, Time Decay and Bias. We focus on resolving location values across different levels of granularity. In our case, we use four different grain-sizes of locations: Room/Desk (e.g. Room 300, Desk 3W30), MultiRoomUnit (e.g. Level 3 West), LevelInABuilding (e.g. Level 3) and Building. Only the results of the first two grain-sizes are presented in this paper, as they represent the grain-sizes of locations detected by the sensors described in Section 4.2, and are, therefore, more interesting.

---

[3] Each Tablet PC would enter stand-by mode after 30 minutes of inactivity on battery.

Point selects the most recent piece of evidence generated by any sensor. It is the least computationally expensive algorithm for resolving a location value with sensor data. Its simplicity has attracted many systems using single grain-size sensors, such as commercial infrared badge location systems, reviewed in [10].

Time Decay is based on exponential decay of time to weigh each evidence source. Multiple evidence sources for each unique location value are aggregated in favour of the most weighed evidence source for each location value as well as the locations with more repetitions. Equation (1) calculates the exponential decay of each given evidence source based on their timestamp, where the adjusted decay constant (λ) is set to be 0.01. Equation (2) discounts the adjusted weights of evidence sources of other location values from the maximum weight for the current location value, where n is the total number of evidence sources, m is the number of evidence sources of the location value whose weight is being calculated:

$$w_i = N(t_i) = e^{-\lambda t_i} \tag{1}$$

$$TD(w_{1..m..n}) = \max(w_{1..m}) - \frac{\sum_{i=m+1}^{n} w_i}{n}. \tag{2}$$

Bias selects the participant's personal work space if it is found in the evidence sources. Otherwise it returns the most recent evidence source. This algorithm is biased towards the place where the user tends to spend more time.

It is sometimes not possible to resolve the location of desired grain-size with the existing sensors, and this may be caused by system faults or lack of sensor coverage. When a user, for example, is not actively using a machine that either runs an activity sensor or is monitored by a login sensor, then the finest-grained location value for that user is not likely to be generated. Thus, a resolver which estimates the best possible location value that can be achieved is also used. A *best possible* location is defined as the best matched location value—in terms of grain-size difference from the user-logged location—from the list of evidence sources. So, for example, if the user-logged location is Room 100 and the list of possible locations from sensor evidence are Level 1 and Level 3, Level 1 would be the best matched location value. For all cases, when there is no evidence found in the designated time frame, the last resolved location value would be used.

When comparing the resolved location values from sensors against the user-logged location value, both location values are normalised to the desired grain-size whenever possible. For example, if the user-logged location is Room 300, and the resolved value from sensors is Level 3, it would be counted as an erroneous sensor value for Room/Desk and MultiRoomUnit grain-sizes, as Level 3 can not be normalised to a finer-grained location. However, it would be correct for LevelInABuilding and Building grain-sizes, as both Room 300 and Level 3 would be normalised to Level 3 and the Building respectively.

Location Reasoning at Room/Desk Grain-size

Figure 5 shows the error rates for running five algorithms and the Best Possible resolver on the participants' data to resolve for the location at the Room/Desk

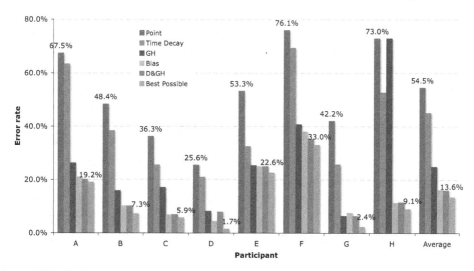

Fig. 5. Error rates for different resolvers reasoning at Room/Desk grain-size

level, in the order of the mean error rates. The x axis denotes the eight participants and their average. The y axis is the percentage of the error rates that each algorithm resolver has on each participant's location data. For example, for participant A, the Point algorithm is able to resolve a location value for that participant when they were in the building with an error rate of 67.5%, the Democratic and Granularity Harmoniser (D&GH) algorithm (see Algorithm 1) reduces it to 20.3% and the Best Possible is 19.2%. The results of CCS (Closest Common Subsumer) are excluded from the chart for its poor performance, which would reduce the visual clarity. It constantly performed more than 40% worse than the Point algorithm.

The ONCOR algorithms—Granularity Harmoniser (GH) and D&GH—generally have lower error rates than Point and Time Decay (TD). Participant H is an exception, because their work space constantly received inter-floor Bluetooth signals (false positive evidence) which resulted in extremely high non-granularity-variance conflict (99.8%). On average, GH reduces the error rates of Point and TD from 54.5% and 45.2% to 24.9% by harmonising granularity variance in sensor evidence. The D&GH algorithm filters out some false positive noise before resolving granularity variance, hence further reduces the error rates. The Bias algorithm performs comparably to D&GH because it favours the participants' work spaces, where they spent most of the time.

Location Reasoning at MultiRoomUnit Grain-size

Figure 6, analogous to Figure 5, illustrates the error rates generated by a list of resolver functions in reasoning about location at the MultiRoomUnit grain-size. CCS is, again, excluded. Note the high error rates on Point (44.9%), TD (24.2%) and GH (44.9%) algorithms for participant H.

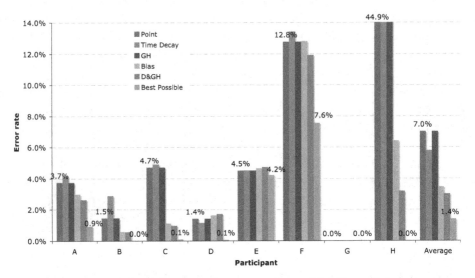

Fig. 6. Error rates for different resolvers reasoning at MultiRoomUnit grain-size

The Point and TD algorithms now have comparable error rates. GH performs the same as Point, because GH only filters out granularity variance before using the Point algorithm for the other conflicting evidence. There are currently two granularity levels in our sensor infrastructure: Room/Desk and MultiRoomUnit, so GH would only differentiate itself from Point when reasoning at the finer grain-size. D&GH has slightly better mean error rates than Bias at this grain-size, mainly due to its ability to filter out more false positive noise. For instance, it is able to filter out the evidence value of Level 2 East from the possible locations of Level 1 East, Level 1 Middle and Level 2 East, which can not be done with the other algorithms. The location values resolved by CCS, in most cases, are too coarse-grained to be useful in this sensor infrastructure.

Participant E and F spent more time away from their computers, usually in a laboratory, the common room, or areas nearby their work spaces. This often prevented the sensors from getting their finest grain locations, which resulted in higher error rates for their best possible results. Bias and D&GH show clear improvements over the other algorithms for participants A, B, C and H because they have more non-granularity-variance conflicting evidence than participants D, E and G.

6 Conclusions

The key contribution of this paper is the exploration of a new role for ontological reasoning in pervasive computing: we have tackled one of the foundation problems, modelling location from a diverse range of sensors, each of which produces evidence at varying levels of noise and uncertainty. We have introduced three algorithms for ontological reasoning about location, explaining the motivation for their design and linking this to the challenges in interpreting sensor evidence.

Our approach takes careful account of pragmatic issues. In the case of the ontology, we have created ONCOR so that, while the core ontology is hand-crafted, it can be extended to a large range of building ontologies. The parts of the ontology that need to be created afresh for each new building are generated semi-automatically. This approach means that there is modest cost in taking the approach to a new building and in altering the infrastructure, as sensors are added or altered. Also important to our approach is that the ontological reasoning is amenable to create simple, natural explanations: this makes it possible for a system to explain its operation to a user. This is critical for user control, for example enabling individuals to select, or tune, the algorithms that work effectively for their behaviour and the classes of evidence available about them.

As the locations were semi-automatically extracted from SVG/XML-based building maps, some geometric properties can be retained in the ontology as attributes (e.g. coordinates and area for each polygon) or relations (e.g. isPartOf, hasPart). Even though we chose to use symbolic location descriptions (e.g. Room 310) rather than coordinates, it is feasible to integrate our current model with a coordinate model, such as that described in [11], provided that the coordinates represent polygons with containment relationships, like our symbolic model. So, for example, we can extract the set of vertices in coordinates for each place when parsing the SVG/XML maps and put them in each place model. In that case, the system can then translate coordinate-based positions with simple computational geometry (e.g. Point-in-Polygon algorithms) into a finest-grained containing symbolic place, and then would still be able to make use of the ontology-based algorithms.

We have implemented our abstract ideas in ONCOR, giving a system and framework for testing our ideas. This has enabled us to see how, in practice, they perform in interpreting the location evidence. This shows that ONCOR is able to resolve location values at different levels of granularity with a semi-automatically generated working location ontology. Our experimental evaluation compared the performance of these algorithms against a gold standard, created by participants in our study.

From the experimental results, GH reduced the error rates of the Point algorithm by over one half on average, from 54.5% to 24.9%, demonstrating the the power of an ontology in resolving granularity variance. D&GH further reduces the mean error rate of GH from 24.9% to 16.1%, showing the ability of the ontology to resolve false positive sensor evidence. In terms of the other type of conflict, false negative, it is yet to be explored.

Even in cases where ontological reasoning does not give minimal errors, it can provide more generic, less context-dependent reasoning in a dynamic environment. By contrast, the Bias algorithm can only work well for people who spend more time at their work space. With an approach like ours, based on ontological reasoning, it becomes possible to reason across granularity levels. There has been considerable work on ontological reasoning and modelling for pervasive environments [3,12,4,7], reflecting the intuitive appeal of such approaches. Our work goes beyond the earlier proposals to the implementation and evaluation of location reasoning across granularity levels to conclude a person's location, exploring and comparing different ontological algorithms. Our empirical study provides insights into the ways these algorithms operate for different people with different behaviours.

Ontological reasoning appears to offer much promise for pervasive computing because it seems to provide a way to deal with key problems, including reasoning about a person's location, based on a diverse set of evidence from different classes of sensors. This paper has demonstrated the ways that a low cost ontological reasoner can be constructed, building on the ONCOR framework, and how it has the potential to reduce the error rate in reasoning about location.

Acknowledgements

We would like to express our appreciation to the Smart Internet Technology CRC for partially funding this project. We would also like to thank all the experiment participants for their time and participation. Finally, we want to thank Bun Chan, Andrew Lum, David Symonds, and the shepherd of our paper John Krumm for valuable comments and insights on this paper.

References

1. Hightower, J., Borriello, G.: Particle filters for location estimation in ubiquitous computing: A case study. In: Davies, N., Mynatt, E.D., Siio, I. (eds.) UbiComp 2004. LNCS, vol. 3205, pp. 88–106. Springer, Heidelberg (2004)
2. Myllymaki, J., Edlund, S.: Location aggregation from multiple sources. In: Proceedings of Third International Conference on Mobile Data Management, 2002, pp. 131–138 (2002)
3. Indulska, J., McFadden, T., Kind, M., Henricksen, K.: Scalable location management for context-aware systems. In: Distributed Applications and Interoperable Systems, pp. 224–235 (2003)
4. Chen, H., Finin, T., Joshi, A., Kagal, L., Perich, F., Chakraborty, D.: Intelligent agents meet the semantic web in smart spaces. IEEE Internet Computing 8, 69–79 (2004)
5. Ranganathan, A., McGrath, R.E., Campbell, R.H., Mickunas, M.D.: Use of ontologies in a pervasive computing environment. Knowl. Eng. Rev. 18, 209–220 (2003)
6. Wang, X.H., Zhang, D.Q., Gu, T., Pung, H.K.: Ontology based context modeling and reasoning using OWL. In: Proceedings of the Second IEEE Annual Conference on Pervasive Computing and Communications Workshops, 2004 (2004)
7. Wishart, R., Henricksen, K., Indulska, J.: Context obfuscation for privacy via ontological descriptions. In: Strang, T., Linnhoff-Popien, C. (eds.) LoCA 2005. LNCS, vol. 3479, pp. 276–288. Springer, Heidelberg (2005)
8. Kay, J., Niu, W., Carmichael, D.J.: ONCOR: Ontology- and evidence-based context reasoner. In: IUI 2007: Proceedings of the 12th International Conference on Intelligent User Interfaces, New York, NY, USA, pp. 290–293 (2007)

9. Kay, J., Kummerfeld, B., Lauder, P.: Personis: A server for user models. In: De Bra, P., Brusilovsky, P., Conejo, R. (eds.) AH 2002. LNCS, vol. 2347, pp. 203–212. Springer, Heidelberg (2002)
10. Hightower, J., Borriello, G.: Location systems for ubiquitous computing. Computer 34, 57–66 (2001)
11. Jiang, C., Steenkiste, P.: A hybrid location model with a computable location identifier for ubiquitous computing. In: Borriello, G., Holmquist, L.E. (eds.) UbiComp 2002. LNCS, vol. 2498, pp. 307–313. Springer, Heidelberg (2002)
12. Strang, T., Popien, C.L., Frank, K.: Applications of a context ontology language. In: Begusic, D., Rozic, N. (eds.) Proceedings of International Conference on Software, Telecommunications and Computer Networks (SoftCom 2003), pp. 14–18 (2003)

Evaluation and Analysis of a Common Model for Ubiquitous Systems Interoperability

Michael Blackstock[1], Rodger Lea[2], and Charles Krasic[1]

[1] Department of Computer Science, University of British Columbia
201-2366 Main Mall, Vancouver, B.C., Canada
[2] Media and Graphics Interdisciplinary Centre, University of British Columbia
FSC 3640 - 2424 Main Mall, Vancouver, B.C., Canada
{michael@cs,rodgerl@ece,krasic@cs}.ubc.ca

Abstract. To support the deployment of ubicomp systems, the ubiquitous computing research community has developed a variety of middleware platforms, meta-operating systems and toolkits. While there is evidence that these systems share certain abstractions, it is not realistic to use the same platform in all environments; systems and applications specialized for specific environments and applications will always be required. In this paper we present a methodology for interoperability that allows developers to innovate and evolve their platforms while allowing others to build interoperable applications. Our approach is based on our design of the Ubicomp Common Model (UCM) and an implementation of this model called the Ubicomp Integration Framework (UIF). Our aim in this work is to provide clear evidence that the UCM unifies the capabilities of ubicomp systems based on an evaluation and analysis of its use in integrating several existing systems into a composite campus environment.

1 Introduction

As Weiser's vision for ubiquitous computing (ubicomp) [1] becomes a reality, we see an increasing number of ubicomp systems deployed in campuses, class rooms [2], hospitals [3], meeting rooms [4], and the home [5]. To support these deployments, the ubicomp research community has developed a variety of middleware systems, meta operating systems [4, 6] and toolkits [7], all exhibiting features and functionality suitable for their target domain. Although there is often commonality in the core abstractions or functionality of these systems, the community is still a long way from agreeing on a common approach and model, and further still from the adoption of a common platform or toolkit. While we believe that in the long term a common platform will be developed, we feel it is impractical for practitioners to agree on such a platform while the ubiquitous systems field continues to evolve. Further, we argue that even in the long term, the use of the same middleware platform in all smart spaces is not realistic as there will always be cases where systems specialized for specific applications and locations will be deployed in particular environments. Given these facts, it is clear that there will always be a variety of ubicomp platforms and hence, there is a need to develop a methodology that supports the integration of these

J. Indulska et al. (Eds.): Pervasive 2008, LNCS 5013, pp. 180–196, 2008.

platforms. This will allow some application developers to continue to create environment-specific applications, while others can create applications to integrate ubicomp systems, or span sites and administrative domains. Further, it ensures that systems developers can continue to evolve their platforms while supporting a growing application developer community.

To address this need we have, over the past two years, developed and implemented the Ubicomp Common Model (UCM), with the primary goal of providing a meta middleware that enables developers to build applications that can span existing ubicomp systems in multiple domains [8, 14]. Our aim in this paper is to provide an evaluation of that model and its implementation and to provide clear evidence that the UCM unifies the capabilities of ubicomp systems for such inter-environment interoperability. Partly this is to support our claim that our approach addresses the needs of those who aim to support interoperability between environments, but also, we feel our work offers valuable lessons for those who develop new ubicomp applications and platforms, or those who wish, like us, to bridge and compose existing platforms. To do this, we describe our experience integrating several representative ubicomp systems [4, 7-9] into a single, integrated smart space using our platform. The Ubicomp Integration Framework (UIF), highlights the ease of integration, performance and use of our core UCM abstractions.

We believe our work is of value to three groups of researchers within the ubicomp community. Firstly, for those who develop ubicomp systems, our work provides a rigorous analysis of a systems model as well as a validated approach to integrating existing ubicomp systems. Secondly, for application level researchers, our work offers an approach that not only allows them to develop applications that make use of existing ubicomp platforms, but also provides a stand-alone platform with validated abstractions and a comprehensive programming model. Finally, by reflecting on several existing platforms and their abstractions and then developing a meta-level model we believe we have synthesized a comprehensive model and abstraction that reflects ubiquitous systems experimentation over the last 6-10 years.

The paper is organized as follows. In Section 2 we review the abstractions that formed the basis for the Ubicomp Common Model. Section 3 then describes the design and implementation of the Ubicomp Integration Framework used in our evaluation with a focus on the integration adapters. In Section 4 we describe our design process and the four representative integration adapters we developed. Section 5 summarizes lessons learned from our integration experience. Section 6 presents related work and Section 7 concludes the paper.

2   The Ubicomp Common Model (UCM)

While there will always be a variety of ubicomp systems designed for certain places and application domains, interoperability is critical for application mobility between smart spaces, public and guest access, and environment composition. Our approach to interoperability is to create a bridge between existing ubicomp systems abstractions and a shared model for ubicomp environments called the Ubicomp Common Model (UCM). This model can be used to design stand alone systems for application development or in gateways and integration frameworks for cross domain interoperability.

The UCM design is based on our survey of several ubicomp systems [9] and first hand development experience [19]. From this work we developed the following set of high level abstractions that we have found to be useful for 'native' ubicomp application development and common to several existing ubicomp systems:

- **Environment.** An environment model is required to encapsulate the available components, types of context and services, and entities in the environment such as users, places and devices. The environment model is often handled by a service discovery system [8], but in some systems, a subsystem that handles more complex models of the environment is provided [5, 10].
- **Entities** are base-level abstractions representing people, places, computing devices and other things such a groups and activities. They can be specialized to environment-specific entities such as game players, living rooms, class rooms, mobile phones and meetings as needed.
- **Entity Relationships** have been shown to be a valuable type of context for discovering computing resources associated with entities in the environment [11, 12]. These include location-based, geometric, social, and activity-related relationships.
- **Context** is relevant information about an entity's situation. Context can include values such as location, temperature, direction, or time, or higher level inferred context such as user activities and goals [12, 13].
- **Services** or functionality often explicitly associated with devices, actuators or software services. Most ubiquitous systems either provide their own service infrastructure or build on existing service oriented systems.
- **Events** that can signal a change of state such as a door closing, a light turning on or a slide change in a presentation. Events can also be signaled or due to entity relationship changes. Several platforms support events as separate abstractions in their own right [4, 6].
- **Data or Content**, like context, may also be related to an entity. Content could include a photo of the user, or documents a group has been working on. Some systems handle content as a type of context while others treat certain content like documents as an entity associated with a time, place or activity (e.g. [4]).

Using these abstractions, we designed the UCM, an *entity-centric* model for both application portability between environments and ubicomp system integration. It is entity-centric in that the context information, computing capabilities, and component information in the model are all associated with a physical or virtual *entity*: a person, place, device, or the enclosing environment itself. The UCM consists of three related aspects called the Environment *State*, *Meta-State* and *Implementation* illustrated in Figure 1. The core UCM is an ontology described using the Web Ontology Language (OWL) [14] along with a set of rules for use in the Jena general purpose reasoning engine [15].

The Environment State includes entities modeled by the supporting system, the relationships between entities and their current *context values*. Context values need not be simple primitive types such as strings and integers, but also more complex data structures described using the Resource Description Framework (RDF). These data structures could indicate a range of values, or an indication of timeliness and accuracy. An example of Environment State RDF is shown in Figure 2.

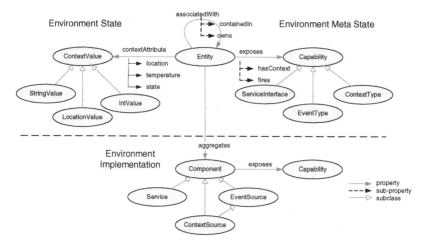

Fig. 1. Environment State, Meta State and Implementation aspects of the Ubicomp Common Model

```
<campus:CampusBuilding rdf:ID="coffeeShop">
  <location:location>
    <location:Position>
      <ucm:name>position</ucm:name>
      <ucm:javaType rdf:datatype="&xsd;string">
        ca.ubc.cs.uif.prototype.types.WorldPosition</ucm:javaType>
      <location:latitude rdf:datatype="&xsd;double">
        49.260537157736785</location:latitude>
      <location:longitude rdf:datatype="&xsd;double">
        -123.24801921844482</location:longitude>
      <ucm:time rdf:datatype="&xsd;long">0</ucm:time>
    </location:Position>
  </location:location>
  <ucm:containedIn rdf:resource="&campus;ubcCampus"/>
</campus:CampusBuilding>
```

Fig. 2. Example RDF describing a *coffeeShop* with static *location* context, and a static *containedIn* relationship with the *ubcCampus* place. The coffeeShop has a static context *campusLocation* context value data structure containing latitude and longitude properties.

Note that the UCM does not define all possible context types or quality; rather it is a core ontology intended for specialization by an integrator or standards group to define the context types for a specific environment or application domain. The interpretation of a given context value data structure will depend on the specialization of the UCM model for a given domain such as a campus, home, office or classroom.

Other systems have shown (e.g. [16]) that pervasive applications must be able to reflect on an environment model to determine the computing capabilities and context available at run time. In the UCM *capabilities* are defined as the *context types, event types*, and *service interfaces*. Applications can use information in the Environment Meta-State to determine whether presence or location context is available for a user, or whether lighting or projection services are available in a given room for example. A context type capability can also include information on the timeliness, accuracy and quality of the events signaled or context values returned by a request.

Inspired by the entity aggregation servers of several existing systems (e.g. [8, 11]) the Environment Implementation aspect links entities to implementation *components* of various types that expose capabilities. *Service* components expose interfaces, *Context Sources* expose context types, and *Event Sources* exposing event types. These capabilities are then inherited by the aggregating entity in the meta-state. The Implementation aspect is used only for integration; implementation components and the entity-component aggregation relationships are not exposed to applications.

Because of space limitations, we refer the reader to a more detailed overview of the analysis and the UCM design in [9] and [17]. In the following section we describe our meta-middleware platform used to evaluate the UCM's suitability for integration and application development: the Ubicomp Integration Framework.

3   The Ubicomp Integration Framework

The Ubicomp Integration Framework (UIF) meta-middleware is an implementation of the UCM to provide a platform for both application developers and ubicomp system integrators. Application developers use the UIF API to build native UCM applications while integrators can create adapters and configure the system to exploit the existing facilities of one or more existing ubicomp systems. This section describes the architecture and implementation of the UIF and integration adapters.

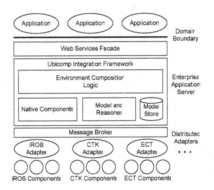

Fig. 3. Ubicomp Integration Framework Architecture

The UIF is a tiered enterprise server application as shown in Figure 3. The system performs three essential functions. (1) It serves as a repository for knowledge about a composite environment model. This "knowledge" consists of information contributed directly by an integrator, ubicomp system adapters at run time, or deduced by an integrated reasoning engine and integration rules. (2) The UIF dispatches method calls from applications to the appropriate adapter or internal components based on the raw and inferred data in this repository. (3) Finally, the system manages event subscriptions for clients of the composite model, ensuring subscriptions are propagated to the components and maintained as long as a component and its integration adapter is available.

The Façade subsystem provides a SOAP-based [18] web service interface to applications for cross-domain interoperability. Application calls to the Façade are delegated to the middle tier. The middle tier contains the Environment Composition Logic

(ECL) subsystem, responsible for maintaining subscriptions for clients and dispatching calls to other subsystems based on queries to the Model subsystem. Queries for entities based on their types, capabilities and static context are handled directly by the Model since this information is maintained in the UIF knowledge base. Method calls to get or set context values, invoke a service, or subscribe to an event are dispatched to a component hosted by the UIF or an adapter. The adapter is chosen based on the component that supplies the chosen entity's capability (context, event, service).

The Model subsystem maintains the current environment model including the UCM itself, specializations of the UCM, entity instances, static context values, capabilities, and component descriptions and their relationships. Based on rules supplied with the UCM and an integrator, the integrated reasoning engine establishes new relationships depending on entity types and context values in the model [17]. The Native Component subsystem hosts internal "native" UCM components instantiated either on startup, or when first accessed by an application. A typical use of a native component by an integrator is to provide a composite service, or a specialized context inference capability for the integrated environment.

Method calls destined for an adapter are dispatched by the Message Broker. Adapters transform the method call to and from the integrated system's data structures and APIs as needed. To support asynchronous events, applications call a `subscribe` Web Services method to supply subscription parameters specific to the event type. The adapter marshals the subscription to the native system and maintains an internal mapping from a UIF subscription to a native subscription. When an event is signaled by the integrated ubicomp system, its adapter marshals the event data to a common UIF *EntityEvent* data structure, and sends it to the UIF. The ECL looks up the associated subscriber and either queues the event for the application or sends it directly using a web service interface.

The UIF was implemented using the JBoss Java 2 Enterprise Edition (J2EE) server [19]. This system is a fairly standard platform used for enterprise application integration. The Model subsystem wraps the Resource Description Framework (RDF) store and general purpose rule-based reasoning engine supplied with the Jena Semantic Web Framework [15]. The initial model of the environment consisting of static entity, context and component descriptions and loaded at start up along with UCM rules and environment specific rules supplied by an integrator. The Broker communicates with Adapters using Remote Method Invocation (RMI) [20] so they can be distributed in the environment. In the following subsection we describe the design of our adapters in more detail.

3.1 Adapter Design

Key to our approach to integration is the use of *adapters* which sit between our model and an underlying ubicomp system. The adapter interface shown in Figure 4 is designed to encapsulate the functionality of an existing ubicomp system. Adapters ensure the integration framework holds the exposed entities and capabilities of the integrated system, maintain component, event subscription and entity identifier mappings between our model and the integrated system, and marshal method calls to and from the integrated ubicomp system on demand. Adapters initiate a connection with the UIF by calling `adapterStarted()`in the `AdapterListener` interface. The `AdapterListener` add/removeComponent and add/removeEntity methods are called to add and remove entities and components to the model as they are discovered in an integrated system. Aggregation links between entities and components may be established by the adapter in the `ComponentInfo` data structure, or specified in an integration rule installed in the framework.

```
public interface Adapter
        extends Remote {
  boolean start(boolean reset);
  void stop();
  boolean check();
  ContextValue getContextValue(
    String componentID,
    String entityId,
    String attribute);
  void setContextValue(
    String componentID,
    String entityId,
    String attribute,
    ContextValue value);
  DataObject invoke(
    String componentId,
    String entityId,
    String serviceType,
    String methodName,
    DataObject[] inArgs);
  int[] subscribe(
    String componentId,
    String subscriberId,
    EventSubscription[]
        eventSubs);
  public void unsubscribe(
    String componentId,
    String subscriberId,
    EventSubscription[]
        eventSubs);
```
(continued...)

```
  String[] getRelatedEntities(
    String componentId, String id,
    String relationship);
  void addEntityRelationship(
    String componentId, String id,
    String entityId,
    String relationship);
  public void addEntity(
    EntityInfo info);
  public void removeEntity(
    String entityId);
}

public interface AdapterListener
        extends Remote {
  void adapterStarted(
    String adapterName,
    Adapter adapter);
  void fireEvent(
    String adapterName,
    String sourceId,
    String subscriberId,
    EntityEvent event);
  String addEntity(
    EntityInfo eInfo);
  void removeEntity(
    String entityId);
  String addComponent(
    ComponentInfo cInfo);
  void removeComponent(
    String componentId);
}
```

Fig. 4. Adapter and AdapterListener interfaces

Several method calls support direct interaction with the underlying system. The `get/setContextValue` calls access context values for the specified context attribute in the integrated system. The `getRelatedEntities/addEntityRelationship` access and update entity relationships. The `invoke` method calls a service associated with an entity in the integrated system and the `subscribe` method supports event subscription Adapters signal events to by calling the listener `fireEvent` method. All of these method calls include the component id, and the entity id of the aggregating entity.

Two method calls, `addEntity` and `removeEntity` are called when an application adds or removes an entity from the model. This can occur when an application registers a new user with the model, or when a new place of interest is added for example. The new entity information is broadcast to all adapters in case they need to update their native model with this new information. Using the adapter interfaces described here, we implemented four adapters to create a composite integrated campus environment as shown in Figure 5. In the next section we report on this experience.

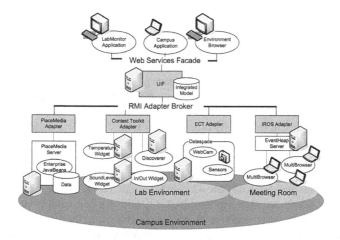

Fig. 5. Integrated environment deployment. The UIF coordinates communication between applications, and distributed adapters.

4 Deployment Experience: An Integrated Campus Environment

To evaluate our model in terms of its completeness for application development and integration we created a prototype deployment and two test applications. The environment deployment emulates an campus-scale ubicomp environment by integrating four existing systems: the MUSEcap platform [21], the Context Toolkit (CTK), [8], iROS [4], and the Equip Component Toolkit (ECT) [7]. The UIF acts as an intermediary between the four ubicomp systems as shown in Figure 4.

Rather than inventing our own unique applications, we aimed to support applications inspired by previous work on the Active Campus Explorer [2] (described in [9])

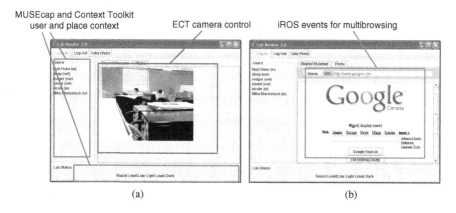

Fig. 6. Lab Monitor Application User Interface. The integrated systems shown provide different capabilities to the application.

and the other systems we integrated. Our "Lab Monitor" application is inspired by the Context Toolkit In/Out Box [13] and the iRoom Multibrowse [22] applications. The Lab Monitor user interface, shown in Figure 6, performs two primary functions. First, it monitors our lab by providing information about who is present (left pane), the current sound and lighting levels (bottom pane), and allows users to take a photo of the lab as shown in Figure 6a. This will allow remote users to see who is present and whether there is a meeting going on for example. Secondly, it allows users to share web pages with others in the lab by broadcasting URLs to other Lab Monitor applications as shown in Figure 6b.

This application makes use of features from each of the four underlying systems. User identity is supplied by our MUSEcap system. User presence in the room is supplied by an In/Out widget from the Context Toolkit (CTK) using an RFID sensor. Sound and light levels are also supplied by CTK widgets and appropriate sensors. To share web pages with other users, it broadcasts URLs using the iROS Event Heap. A web camera is controlled by an integrated Equip Component Toolkit component. This integration was accomplished using four adapter implementations described next.

4.1 Adapter Implementation

To integrate the ubicomp systems using adapters we first determined the appropriate interface for an adapter to access the underlying system. The following table summarizes our adapter functionality categorized by the UCM abstractions.

System/ Abstraction	Context Toolkit (CTK)	Equip Component Toolkit (ECT)	iROS	MUSEcap
Environment Model	Discoverer	Equip Dataspace	ICrafter sub system, and EventHeap	Session interface to database
Entities	Static locations, users	Implied place (lab) where components are located	Host device in ICrafter service description	Place markers, users
Entity Relationships	InOutWidget relates *places* to *users*.	Not supported	Host device con-*tained-in* the meeting room	User *friends*, place marker *ownership*
Context	User *location*, user *presence*, room *sound, light level, temperature*	Component properties (not implemented)	iROS State API (not implemented)	User *location*, user *identity*, *presence*, place marker *location*
Services	Context Widget Services (not implemented)s	Camera Service	Browser service, interaction event service	Chat service
Events	*Relationship changed, context changed*	Property changes (not implemented)	Interaction event	User or place marker *Near event*
Data/Content	(Not supported)	Get photo service method	DataHeap (Not implemented)	Place marker content

The CTK adapter uses the CTK BaseObject class to communicate with the Discoverer and Context Widgets in our deployment. We borrowed the DataspaceMonitor class used by the ECT environment editor applications to communicate with components coordinated by the ECT Dataspace. The iROS adapter uses the Event Heap client API to handle events and make ICrafterService calls. We then added any "missing" or implicit static entities into the model. This included entities like the Lab (place) where the ECT and iROS systems were deployed and the users supported by the CTK components. We then described the components (Service, ContextSource, EventSources) of the integrated systems using our Component model abstractions. These components and their capabilities were added to the model at startup in an RDF file, or by the adapter at run time. Adapters were implemented to maintain component, entity and event mappings, transform method and maintain the composite environment.

Clearly we did not attempt to map all of the available functionality of the chosen platforms. Rather, our efforts focused on exercising our UCM abstractions to gain a better understanding of the integration development process, abstraction mappings and tradeoffs such as adapter complexity vs performance, which we report on next.

4.2 Adapter Complexity

To evaluate how well our UCM abstractions capture those of an underlying system we considered the complexity of adapter development. We found that the development of adapters work became easier with more experience and as previous implementations were refactored for greater reuse. We estimate that the time required to integrate basic functionality (less than 6 components) of a Java-based system was about 2 weeks. This development time depends on the programming model and API, the documentation available, and the capabilities to be integrated. The MUSEcap adapter was created without any code shared by other adapters and is about 1200 lines of code. The CTK, iROS and ECT adapters share about 400 lines of code, and added about 850, 1050 and 550 lines of additional code respectively. Overall we found that the UCM abstractions provided adequate coverage of the underlying systems' capabilities, and adapters were straightforward to develop. We intend to gather more evidence to support both conclusions with a wider study involving additional systems and integrators as the platform is made available to other research groups.

4.3 Performance

Next, we considered the performance and the overhead of the integration framework. Applications such as PlaceMedia and the LabMonitor will poll the UIF for new context values, or to retrieve events using the web services interface. They then call services, send events or set context based on events received or user input. To gain insight on the

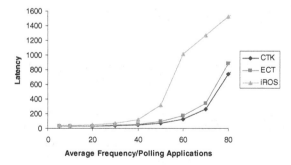

Fig. 7. Average latency vs. average frequency of web services calls by applications. Each application polls the server once per second.

system's responsiveness to application requests, we measured the average time taken to get context supplied by the Context Toolkit, to call a service supplied by ECT or send an iROS event when calling the UIF once per second. We varied the number of polling applications between 5 and 80, and measured the average latency of synchronous web service calls to three integrated systems, the Context Toolkit, ECT and iROS. The results are shown in Figure 7.

In our deployment we hosted iROS, ECT and the CTK on a single 2.13 GHz Pentium Core Duo system with 1 GB RAM, the MUSEcap platform and the UIF in a second 3.4 GHz Pentium D with 2 GB RAM. Simulated applications were run on a tablet PC with 1GB of RAM and a 1.5 GHz Pentium M processor; all machines were on the same LAN. The model consists of 535 data triples; the inference engine uses 278 rules. These tests represent a best case response time; before each test we restarted the system and did not change the model. The system was primed with a light test to cache query results. At higher application loads (60-80), we found that the server response time increases to over one second; applications are making requests faster than the server can respond. Overall we found that the system response is less than 100ms for loads of up to 40 or 50 concurrent applications.

Table 1. Components of UIF overhead for a call to an ECT component through the UIF framework. These average values are based on 3000 samples taken at about 20 per second.

Component	Average time (ms)	Overall Distribution
Web to Logic Tier	1.096982	3.39%
ECL subsystem	0.491013	1.52%
Model Query	0.95558	2.95%
RMI Broker	2.576806	7.97%
Native ECT call	0.010512	0.03%
Internal time taken	5.130892	15.86%
Web Services*	27.21426	84.14%
Total Latency	32.34515	100.00%

* calculated by subtracting the measured average internal time from the latency measured by the application

We then examined the overhead of the UIF system in some detail by instrumenting key subsystems in the framework and measuring the average time taken for an application to call an ECT service through the UIF. As table 1 indicates, we found that the largest component of overhead was related to the use of the web services middleware and network latency taking more than 84% of the average time taken. Internally our system contributed just over 5 ms to the average time taken to execute a call; most of this time was used by the RMI adapter request and adapter marshalling.

Finally we considered the responsiveness of the UIF while undergoing changes to the model managed by the Jena inference engine. The model changes when applications add new users to the model, or when components are added or removed by an adapter for example. In this experiment, summarized in Figure 8, one application adds then removes a *place* entity to and from the model every 10 seconds. We measured the latency of a *getContext* call from 10 other applications made every 2 seconds. The latency of the first few calls after a model change increases to more than 1 second then falls back to under 100ms as shown. After model changes, queries to the model become the largest component of overhead.

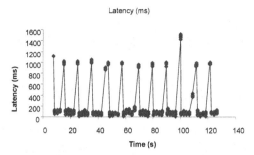

Fig. 8. Model changes trigger forward reasoning, which causes context requests to wait for more than a second until the reasoner has completed forward reasoning and the write lock is released

5 Discussion

Based on the experience and analysis reported in the previous section, we discuss our findings with respect to the use of the core Ubicomp Common Model abstractions, and reflect on the implementation of the Ubicomp Integration Framework.

5.1 Ubicomp Common Model Abstractions

In the process of evaluating the utility of the core UCM abstractions to integrate several systems we have learned a number of lessons web believe will be useful for both ubicomp systems developers and integrators:

A comprehensive and flexible environment model aids application resource discovery. It is important for an environment model to not only contain components (as in the ECT Dataspace, or the CTK Discoverer) but also entities, relationships, context, and entity capabilities. We found that some applications will add and remove entities such as places of interest, or newly registered users to an integrated model.

Maintaining consistency between a composite model and integrated systems' is challenging. Since several abstractions in an integrated composite model such as *entities* and *relationships* are missing or only implicit in an underlying system, it can be challenging to maintain consistency. This is especially the case for dynamic context that needs to be reflected in a composite model for resource discovery. In our system, adapters must add and remove (implied or explicit) entities and components as they are discovered; the UIF infers relationships between them using integration rules.

An entity abstraction is a natural way to aggregate capabilities but *not* components. Based on our experience we have found that it is natural to aggregate capabilities such as service interfaces, context and events types around entities, however we found that there is not a one to one relationship between entities and components: the implementations of these capabilities. More than one entity will often aggregate a component, inheriting its capabilities. For example, a single InOut CTK component was associated with both users and the "place" entity the component served. These n-to-n relationships can present challenges for managing event subscriptions where a single UCM event may be supplied by multiple components.

Make entity relationships explicit as they are an important subclass of context. The Cooltown system highlighted the use of entity relationships to create web links between related entities allowing users to browse their changing environment [11]. We found that it was valuable to make these relationships explicit in our integrated model. Entity relationships supported by iROS in event and service description fields for example, made it possible to find the devices 'contained-in' the 'lab' that the Multibrowse service exposes.

Applications are not only consumers, but also producers of context and events. While most systems manage context derived from sensors in the environment, we have found that it is common for applications to not only consume such context, but produce it. For effective integration, application-supplied context must be propagated to the underlying system for use by native applications. Applications are also a source of events; the Lab Monitor application, like Multibrowse [22], can send user interaction events to other UIF applications and iROS services.

Most ubicomp systems share a common set of events. While several systems have highlighted the importance of event abstractions [4, 6], we have also found that several systems share certain event *types*. Context Tookit update events, like ECT component property changes, are signaled when context values change. When new components are added or removed from a system, the environment model (e.g. Discovery subsystem, Dataspace) will signal applications in case they rely on their capabilities. So far we have found the following high level event types to be common between systems: *Context/relationship changed, entity added/removed, capability changed*. Based on our experience, the consistent implementation of these canonical events will reduce the need for applications to poll for changes allowing applications to more readily respond to changes in the environment.

In general we found that the UCM abstractions were a superset of the systems' we integrated. This is not surprising since we attempted to develop unified abstractions based on these systems and others. While we found few abstraction mismatches, we did find it necessary to compensate for *missing* abstractions either in the adapter implementation or the UIF system configuration. We came to realize that there are a range of approaches to environment integration: One is to compensate for missing abstractions in underlying system(s). Another is to provide information about the integrated system's capabilities without any compensation for missing abstractions. In the former case, the integration system can provide information about implied entities, interpret context data to create and maintain missing entity relationships, and support composite services. In the latter case, the integration system can simply provide a mechanism for accessing the *existing* capabilities of an underlying system. An integrator may elect to compensate for some missing abstractions such as static entities but not others. Our aim here is to support the full range of integration approaches since we integrate several systems with varying capabilities into a single composite environment. To achieve this, a flexible model for ubicomp environments such as the UCM is required.

5.2 Ubicomp Integration Framework Implementation

In this section we reflect on the ease of application development, performance and the use of the Ubicomp Integration Framework as a stand alone system.

Application Development. Our experience in using a single API to interact with multiple systems has several advantages. Developers need only learn and use one set of abstractions, and only one API instead of four or more. This should reduce the learning curve and increase the portability of applications. However, these benefits come at a cost: the performance overhead associated with the use of meta-middleware like the UIF and the development of flexible adapters to maintain the integrated model and marshal method calls to and from the integrated systems. In a typical deployment, we expect that UCM application developers will be largely isolated from the cost of implementing adapters since they can be created independently.

Performance. In section 4.3 we reported mixed results on the overall performance of the UIF system. On one hand, the *internal* performance of the system was adequate, but the overall performance factoring in the cost of web services middleware, network latency, and the use of an inference engine may seem discouraging. However, since we used off the shelf components for model management, reasoning and web services, we are encouraged by these results! With some additional optimizations these issues can be readily addressed. For example, with a suitable caching scheme and background reasoning it should be possible to trade off query response times for freshness of the environment model. By choosing light weight protocols, and by providing APIs to batch more than one context or service call at once, the cost of web services calls can be reduced. Based on our experience with web-based UCM/UIF applications, we have found that a single server-based application can serve multiple users, reducing the load on the integrated model.

The UIF as a Stand Alone System. In our design of the UIF, we aimed not only to support abstractions of an underlying system, but to compensate for *missing* abstractions. To this end, some of the missing functionality of an underlying system can be implemented directly using the UIF. For example, an integrator can add static entities and relationships found to be useful abstractions but missing from systems such as ECT or only implicitly supported in iROS event fields. "Native" UCM services can broadcast messages to users by calling single users messaging services. Based on our experience a system designed around the core abstractions of the UCM may not only serve as an integration platform, but could serve as the basis for a reference ubicomp system implementation. We aim to explore this possibility in collaboration with other practitioners in the ubicomp systems community who have begun to use our platform.

6   Related Work

Addressing interoperability within and across smart spaces is an ongoing challenge that continues to be investigated by both research and standards groups. Component and service-level operability have been addressed by standards groups such as the Open Systems Gateway Initiative (OSGi) [23] for example. The ReMMoC [16] system isolates mobile applications from the heterogeneity of available service infrastructures. Similarly, Friday et al. [24] described the requirements for an infrastructure to hide the heterogeneity of various service platforms. Unlike service oriented approaches, the UCM provides not only a service interface, but an interface to additional abstractions found to be useful such as *entities* and *context*.

SpeakEasy/Obje [25] uses mobile code and a small set of agreed upon interfaces to address data interoperability where components will download the code needed from another to translate one data format to another. The UCM focuses on control flow interoperability using an intermediary such as the UIF. The PatchPanel provided control level interoperability by intercepting and translating messages relayed using the iROS Event Heap [26]. The UCM is designed to provide a uniform API across environments as a whole, not just translate messages between event sources and sinks.

Other researchers have proposed large scale, global infrastructures for ubiquitous computing, to allow applications to move seamlessly between environments. The Context Fabric proposed a global infrastructure for querying and subscribing to context [27]. The Nexus Project proposed to unify environment models into a global federation for location aware application access by integrating various sensor and information sources [28]. More recently researchers have proposed the use of Grid technologies to support wide area ubiquitous computing [29]. Unlike these systems the UCM aims to unify the core abstractions required for interacting with *individual* smart spaces independent of their implementation. Once this is achieved, the more ambitious goal of federating smart spaces should be more attainable.

Ubicomp systems aim to provide a complete and easy to use programming model for application developers. This model can vary from a consistent way to find and access available distributed context sources [8], to an API for accessing a high fidelity model of an augmented physical world [5, 10]. Our integration model aims to provide the necessary set of abstractions required to support both simple and higher fidelity environment models according to the capabilities of an integrated system.

Recognizing that a common understanding of the types and quality of context available is a key requirement for interoperability, researchers such as Henrickson et al. have begun to formalize models for context independent of the implementation [30]. More recently, several groups have used semantic web standards such as the Web Ontology Language (OWL) [14] to model context as relationships between entities and context values [31, 32]. Unlike these models and their supporting systems the UCM aims to unify the abstractions of *existing* ubicomp systems. In our work aim to facilitate a degree of application portability using a single API, while maintaining the native APIs of these systems for environment-specific applications.

7 Conclusions

In this paper we have presented our evaluation of the Ubicomp Common Model, a core set of abstractions for ubicomp environment interoperability based on both an analysis of existing systems [9] and implementation experience [21]. We provided evidence of the UCM's completeness for application development, and demonstrated the feasibility of integrating existing ubicomp systems with the UCM. Overall we found that adapters were not overly complex to implement, and reported that while there are some performance tradeoffs, they can be readily addressed. Finally we presented several lessons learned related to the use of our abstractions for ubicomp systems integration and application development. In future work we aim to continue to address some of the tradeoffs of integration highlighted here, advance the design of the UCM and apply it to other integrated environments to address interoperability between current and future ubicomp systems.

Acknowledgments. The authors would like to thank colleagues in the UBC MAGIC Lab, Adrian Friday and Aiman Erbad who provided valuable feedback.

References

1. Weiser, M.: The computer for the 21st century. Scientific American 265, 94–104 (1991)
2. Griswold, W.G., Shanahan, P., Brown, S.W., Boyer, R., Ratto, M., Shapiro, R.B., Truong, T.M.: ActiveCampus: Experiments in Community-Oriented Ubiquitous Computing. Computer 37, 73–81 (2004)
3. Bardram, J.E., Hansen, T.R., Mogensen, M., Soegaard, M.: Experiences from Real-World Deployment of Context-Aware Technologies in a Hospital Environment. In: Dourish, P., Friday, A. (eds.) UbiComp 2006. LNCS, vol. 4206, pp. 369–386. Springer, Heidelberg (2006)
4. Ponnekantia, S.R., Johanson, B., Kiciman, E., Fox, A.: Portability, extensibility and robustness in iROS. In: PerCom 2003, Dallas-Fort Wirth (2003)
5. Brumitt, B., Meyers, B., Krumm, J., Kern, A., Shafer, S.A.: EasyLiving: Technologies for Intelligent Environments. In: Proceedings of the 2nd international symposium on Handheld and Ubiquitous Computing, Springer, Bristol (2000)
6. Roman, M., Hess, C., Cerqueira, R., Ranganathan, A., Campbell, R.H., Nahrstedt, K.: Gaia: a middleware platform for active spaces. SIGMOBILE Mob. Comput. Commun. Rev. 6, 65–67 (2002)
7. Greenhalgh, C., Izadi, S., Mathrick, J., Humble, J., Taylor, I.: ECT: a toolkit to support rapid construction of ubicomp environments. In: Workshop on System Support for Ubiquitous Computing (UbiSys 2004) at Ubicomp 2004, Springer, Nottingham (2004)
8. Salber, D., Dey, A.K., Abowd, G.D.: The context toolkit: aiding the development of context-enabled applications. In: Proceedings of the SIGCHI conference on Human factors in computing systems, ACM Press, Pittsburgh, Pennsylvania (1999)
9. Blackstock, M., Lea, R., Krasic, C.: Toward Wide Area Interaction with Ubiquitous Computing Environments. In: Havinga, P., Lijding, M., Meratnia, N., Wegdam, M. (eds.) EuroSSC 2006. LNCS, vol. 4272, Springer, Heidelberg (2006)
10. Addlesee, M., Curwen, R., Hodges, S., Newman, J., Steggles, P., Ward, A., Hopper, A.: Implementing a sentient computing system. IEEE Computer 34, 50–56 (2001)
11. Kindberg, T., Barton, J., Morgan, J., Becker, G., Caswell, D., Debaty, P., Gopal, G., Frid, M., Krishnan, V., Morris, H., Schettino, J., Serra, B.: People, places things: Web presence for the real world. In: Third IEEE Workshop on Mobile Computing Systems and Applications Monterey, California (2000)
12. Bardram, J.E.: The Java Context Awareness Framework (JCAF) - A Service Infra-structure and Programming Framework for Context-Aware Applications. In: Gellersen, H.-W., Want, R., Schmidt, A. (eds.) PERVASIVE 2005. LNCS, vol. 3468, pp. 98–115. Springer, Heidelberg (2005)
13. Dey, A.K.: Providing Architectural Support for Building Context-Aware Applications. College of Computing, PhD Thesis. Georgia Institute of Technology (2000)
14. Web Ontology Language (OWL) Overview, http://www.w3.org/TR/owl-features/
15. Jena, a semantic web framework for Java, http://jena.sourceforge.net/
16. Grace, P., Blair, G.S., Samuel, S.: A reflective framework for discovery and interaction in heterogeneous mobile environments. SIGMOBILE Mob. Comput. Commun. Rev. 9, 2–14 (2005)

17. Blackstock, M., Lea, R., Krasic, C.: Managing an Integrated Ubicomp Environment using Ontologies and Reasoning. In: 4th IEEE Workshop on Context Management and Reasoning (CoMoRea) 2007 at PerCom 2007, New York (2007)
18. SOAP Version 1.2 Part 0: Primer. W3C Recommendation (June 24, 2003), vol. 2006, W3C (2003), http://www.w3.org/TR/2003/REC-soap12-part0-20030624/
19. JBoss Home Page, vol. 2006 (2006), http://www.jboss.com/
20. Remote Method Invocation (2003), http://java.sun.com/j2se/1.4.2/docs/guide/rmi/
21. Finke, M., Blackstock, M., Lea, R.: Deployment Experience Toward Core Abstractions for Context Aware Applications. In: Kortuem, G., Finney, J., Lea, R., Sundramoorthy, V. (eds.) EuroSSC 2007. LNCS, vol. 4793, Springer, Heidelberg (2007)
22. Johanson, B., Ponnekanti, S., Sengupta, C., Fox, A.: Multibrowsing: Moving Web Content Across Multiple Displays. In: Abowd, G.D., Brumitt, B., Shafer, S. (eds.) UbiComp 2001. LNCS, vol. 2201, Springer, Heidelberg (2001)
23. Open Services Gateway Initiative Alliance (OSGi), vol. 2007, http://www.osgi.org/
24. Friday, A., Davies, N., Wallbank, N., Catterall, E., Pink, S.: Supporting service discovery, querying and interaction in ubiquitous computing environments. Wirel. Netw. 10, 631–641 (2004)
25. Newman, M.W., Sedivy, J.Z., Neuwirth, C.M., Edwards, W.K., Hong, J.I., Izadi, S., Marcelo, K., Smith, T.F.: Challenge: Recombinant Computing and the Speakeasy Approach. In: Proceedings of Mobicom 2002, Atlanta, Georgia USA (2002)
26. Ballagas, R., Szybalski, A., Fox, A.: Patch Panel: Enabling Control-Flow Interoperability in Ubicomp Environments. In: PerCom 2004, Orlando, Florida, USA (2004)
27. Hong, J.I.: Context fabric: Infrastructure support for context aware systems. In: CHI 2002 extended abstracts on Human factors in computing systems, ACM Press, Minneapolis, Minnesota, USA (2001)
28. Hohl, F., Kubach, U., Leonhardi, A., Rothermel, K., Schwehm, M.: Next Century Challenges: Nexus - An Open Global Infrastructure for Spatial-Aware Applications. In: Fifth Annual International Conference on Mobile Computing and Networking (Mobicom 1999), Seattle, WA (1999)
29. Storz, O., Friday, A., Davies, N.: Towards 'Ubiquitous' Ubiquitous Computing: an alliance with the Grid. In: Dey, A.K., Schmidt, A., McCarthy, J.F. (eds.) UbiComp 2003. LNCS, vol. 2864, Springer, Heidelberg (2003)
30. Henricksen, K., Indulska, J., Rakotonirainy, A.: Modeling Context Information in Pervasive Computing Systems. In: Mattern, F., Naghshineh, M. (eds.) PERVASIVE 2002. LNCS, vol. 2414, pp. 167–180. Springer, Heidelberg (2002)
31. Chen, H., Finin, T., Joshi, A.: An ontology for context-aware pervasive computing environments. Knowledge Engineering Review 18, 197–207 (2003)
32. Gu, T., Pung, H.K., Zhang, D.Q.: Toward an OSGi-Based Infrastructure for Context-Aware Applications. IEEE Pervasive Computing 3, 66–74 (2004)

A Context-Aware System that Changes Sensor Combinations Considering Energy Consumption

Kazuya Murao[1], Tsutomu Terada[2], Yoshinari Takegawa[3], and Shojiro Nishio[1]

[1] Graduate School of Information Science and Technology, Osaka University
1-5 Yamadaoka, Suita-shi, Osaka 565-0871, Japan
[2] Graduate School of Engineering, Kobe University
1-1 Rokkodai, Nada, Kobe, Hyogo, 657-8501, Japan
[3] Organization of Advanced Science and Technology, Kobe University
1-1 Rokkodai, Nada, Kobe, Hyogo, 657-8501, Japan
{murao.kazuya,nishio}@ist.osaka-u.ac.jp,
{tsutomu,take}@eedept.kobe-u.ac.jp
http://www-nishio.ist.osaka-u.ac.jp/index-e.html

Abstract. In wearable computing environments, a wearable computer runs various applications using various sensors (wearable sensors). In the area of context awareness, though various systems using accelerometers have been proposed to recognize very minute motions and states, energy consumption was not taken into consideration. We propose a context-aware system that reduces energy consumption. In life, the granularity of required contexts differs according to the situation. Therefore, the proposed system changes the granularity of cognitive contexts of a user's situation and supplies power on the basis of the optimal sensor combination. Higher accuracy is achieved with fewer sensors. In addition, in proportion to the remainder of power resources, the proposed system reduces the number of sensors within the tolerance of accuracy. Moreover, the accuracy is improved by considering context transition. Even if the number of sensors changes, no extra classifiers or training data are required because the data for shutting off sensors is complemented by our proposed algorithm. By using our system, power consumption can be reduced without large losses in accuracy.

Keywords: Wearable computing, wearable sensors, context awareness, power consumption.

1 Introduction

The downsizing of computers has led to wearable computing attracting a great deal of attention. Wearable computing is different from conventional computing in three ways[1]: (1) Hands-free operation: information can be obtained without manual operation because the computer is worn. (2) Power always on: the computer is always available because the power is always on. (3) Daily-life support: daily activities can be supported because the computer is worn all the time. Along with the progress in wearable computing, recently, many context-aware systems with various kinds of sensors have been introduced, such as systems with an electromyograph [2], electrocardiogram [3], GSR (Galvanic Skin Reflex) [4], and hand-made devices [5]. In particular, one of

J. Indulska et al. (Eds.): Pervasive 2008, LNCS 5013, pp. 197–212, 2008.

the purposes in the Porcupine project[5] is reduction in power consumption. A switch-ball device takes the place of an accelerometer. One switch ball outputs binary data depending on whether it is tilted or not, and nine switch balls go in all directions. Power consumption is very low because of its simplicity, but the accuracy is significantly inferior to that of an accelerometer. This is because an accelerometer has better resolution than that of other devices.

Context-aware systems are applied to many services: health care[4], recognition of workers' routine activity[6], and support of assembly and maintenance tasks[7]. A health-care system[4] recognizes situations of life habits in real time using a heat sensor, GSR sensor, accelerometer, electric sphygmograph, GPS, geomagnetic sensor, and gyroscope. The system recognizes contexts and advises the user about how to make improvements in one's life.

A nurse's routine activity recognition system[6] supports his/her routine work. They have to memorize what they did in a day to communicate with each other and not make a mistake such as giving a dose of medicine needlessly. However, the system seems messy and mistakes might occur. This system recognizes nurses' activities with an accelerometer and their locations with RF-ID receivers.

In the above examples, the accelerometer plays an important role. We consider that the accelerometer is best among current sensors for recognizing behavioral contexts, but the architectures for using accelerometers are not optimal, especially in terms of power consumption. Though the number of sensors in conventional systems are predetermined and fixed, if some sensors can be turned off flexibly, that leads to a reduction in power consumption without much deterioration in accuracy.

In this paper, we propose a context-aware system that changes the combination of accelerometers considering energy consumption. Previously, we have developed the CLAD (cross-linkage for assembled devices) device, which is a relay device between wearable sensors and a wearable computer. CLAD manages the power supply to the sensors[8]. By utilizing CLAD, the proposed system can manage sensors to achieve a high accuracy of activity recognition with a low energy consumption.

This paper is organized as follows. Section 2 describes advanced research contributing to this system. Section 3 presents the system structure. The performance of our system is discussed in Section 4. Finally, Section 5 concludes our research.

2   CLAD

We have proposed CLAD[8] which is a relay device positioned between a wearable computer and wearable sensors. CLAD manages the connected sensors to achieve (1) flexible power supply control for energy saving, and (2) flexible error control for achieving sufficient sensed-data accuracy. The CLAD prototype is shown in Figure 1. The size of CLAD is W76 × H13 × D70 mm, and the size of the sensor is W45 × H12 × D12 mm.

CLAD has its own power source and manages connected sensors. The voltage and current to detect power shortages and overcurrents are monitored . Each sensor has a microcomputer (CPU) to process commands from CLAD. Information about the sensor (type, accuracy, output range, start-up time, operating voltage, and operating current) is stored in the CPU. CLAD has the following characteristics.

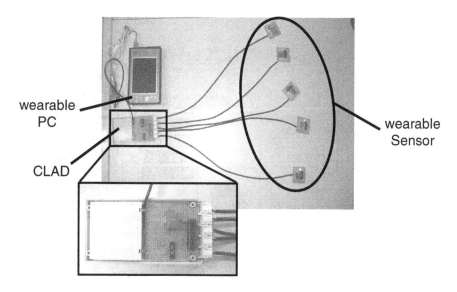

Fig. 1. CLAD prototype

- **Alternative device retrieval and changeover**
  CLAD detects sensor anomalies from consecutive outlying data points and sensor data interruptions, for example. In such cases, CLAD identifies an alternative device by referring to the sensor profile information, and CLAD activates it.
- **Power-supply control**
  CLAD always monitors its internal power source. If CLAD detects a power shortage, power consumption is reduced by stopping the power supply to some of the sensors on the basis of a user-defined policy.
- **Overcurrent detection**
  If an overcurrent is detected, CLAD stops all power supplies for safety.
- **Error detection**
  CLAD detects problems such as outlying data and dying sensor batteries. CLAD notifies the PC of such problems, so applications can deal with them individually such as by displaying a message recommending a battery change.
- **Pseudo data generation**
  When a sensor is turned off and there is no alternative device, CLAD generates pseudo data from learned data and the correlation to other sensors. This function improves operational reliability.

The most distinctive function of CLAD is the pseudo data generation. Generally, there are three answers in response to missing data.

- Listwise deletion
  No sensed data is used when at least one piece of missing data is included. In our assumption, a data complementation is used in case a sensor has broken down. This method cannot be used because missing data comes consecutively in that situation.

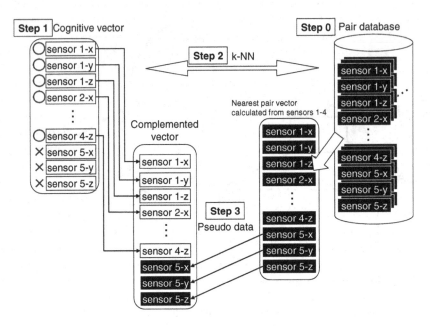

Fig. 2. Pseudo data generation

- Pairwise deletion
  Sensed data is used after removing only missing data. However, a change in sensed data dimension is caused, which requires several restrictions on context recognition algorithms. Therefore, this is not an appropriate answer as a generalized mechanism.
- Imputation
  Sensed data is used after complementing missing data with other values. Doing that does not change the dimension of sensed data, so the user of CLAD need not consider the data complementation.

Considering these characteristics, CLAD uses the imputation for data complementation. An example of pseudo data generation for a context-aware system with five accelerometers is shown in Figure 2. This example supposes that sensor 5 is shut off by a breakdown. The pseudo data is generated as follows.

Step 0. Construct pair database
CLAD has already collected sensed data (pair vectors) for all contexts and constructed a database of pair vectors (pair database).

Step 1. Acquire cognitive vector
When the input contains missing data for some reason such as sensor breakdown, the missing data is removed, and we call the remaining data a cognitive vector.

Step 2. Extract pair vector from pair database
The system finds the pair vector in the database that is nearest the cognitive vector by using the k-NN (k-nearest neighbor) method.

Step 3. Extract pseudo data from pair vector
The data for sensor 5 (missing data) is replaced with that of the extracted pair vector. Then, a complemented vector is generated and will be used as input of a context-aware system.

In pseudo data generation, the distance is calculated among working sensors between cognitive vector $X = (x_{1x}, x_{1y}, x_{1z}, \cdots, x_j, \cdots, x_{5x}, x_{5y}, x_{5z})$ and pair vector $P_i = (p_{i_{1x}}, p_{i_{1y}}, p_{i_{1z}}, \cdots, p_{i_j}, \cdots, p_{i_{5x}}, p_{i_{5y}}, p_{i_{5z}})$ $(i = 1, \cdots, N)$. The subscripts: $1x$ or $5y$ indicate x-axis of sensor 1 or y-axis of sensor 5, and each component such as x_{1x} is a scalar value. N is the number of samples in the pair database. If our mechanism uses Euclidean distance for calculating the distance between a cognitive vector and pair vector, classifying the contexts when the data of working sensors for two contexts are nearly equal and only missing data differs is difficult. Therefore, we focus on the correlation among worn sensor values, and the k-NN method achieves more accurate data complementation by using the correlation. We use the Pearson product-moment correlation coefficient:

$$correlation(x, y) = \left| \frac{\sum_{i=1}^{N}(x_i - \overline{x})(y_i - \overline{y})}{\sqrt{\sum_{i=1}^{N}(x_i - \overline{x})^2 \sum_{i=1}^{N}(y_i - \overline{y})^2}} \right|, (x \neq y).$$

Generally, an absolute value of 0.0 - 0.2 for the correlation coefficient means there is scarcely any correlation, 0.2 - 0.4 means some correlation, 0.4 - 0.7 means good correlation, and 0.7 - 1.0 means strong correlation.

This method applies the k-NN method to all working sensors and uses the sum of the Euclidean distance divided by the correlation coefficient defined as correlated distance d. The correlation is calculated from variance of the pair data. Data of sensor m is complemented with data of sensor m in the pair vector whose $d_{m,i}$ is minimum, as the following equation shows.

$$d_{m,i} = \sqrt{\sum_{j \in working} \frac{\{x_j - p_{i_j}\}^2}{correlation(x_m, x_j)}}$$

In this method, Euclidean distances among strongly correlated sensors carry much weight and scarcely correlated sensors carry little weight. At last, we find the nearest pair vector $P_{I=argmin_i(d_i)}$, and the system outputs the complemented cognitive vector $C = (c_{1x}, c_{1y}, c_{1z}, \cdots, c_j, \cdots, c_{5x}, c_{5y}, c_{5z})$.

$$c_j = \begin{cases} x_j & (j \in working) \\ p_{I_j} & (j \in malfunctioning) \end{cases}$$

Someone might think that using multiple classifiers for each sensor combination is as practical as our approach. However, an advantage of our approach is that it works independently of classifier. The data of a classifier is always assumed to be complete, and a classifier does not require any configurations. If a better classifier is found in the future, integrating it with our proposal would be easy.

3   System Structure

The purpose of pseudo data generation is to manage hardware errors of sensors (missing data) to maintain the accuracy of context recognition. On the other hand, even when no sensor breaks down, power consumption can be reduced by turning off redundant sensors. Therefore, we focus on the event when cognitive context (context to be recognized) and required accuracy level differ according to situations and applications. We propose a context-aware system, which achieves low battery consumption by considering the situation. In this section, we describe the details of our system and how to reduce power consumption on the basis of the situation. Please note that we have already published a paper on pseudo data generation in [8]. When multiple sensors are loaded for a context-aware system, a result in [8] has demonstrated that unnecessary sensors appear thanks to pseudo data generation. This paper has constructed it as a system. In addition, that we consider the followings for a better contribution.

3.1   Required-Accuracy-Based Power Saving

Required accuracy is different according to the situation. For example, while the highest accuracy is always required in fine-grained services, some users prefer low power consumption (long battery lifetime) in daily activities. In detail, we set a threshold of accuracy. In a serious situation (aerospace, battlefield), we set the accuracy at 90%. Then, the best sensor combination is the least number of sensors needed to satisfy the threshold. On the other hand, in a normal situation, the threshold is set at a lower value. In this way, setting a threshold, we flexibly arranged the trade-off between accuracy and power consumption compared to how the conventional system would have worked only at full power.

However, turning off sensors simply leads to low power consumption and low accuracy. Hence, subsequently, we propose mechanisms to reduce power consumption while maintaining accuracy.

3.2   Context-Granularity-Based Power Saving

Conventional context-aware systems require many sensors to recognize contexts with high accuracy. However, in life, not all trained contexts will be a choice. In detail, while a health-care system needs to recognize many detailed contexts, an information-presentation system on an HMD (Head Mounted Display)[9] just has to judge whether there is movement. Recognizing such easy contexts with fewer sensors is possible.

In this paper, we define *context group* which is a subset of trained contexts. For example, given situations shown in Figure 3, Situation 1 is used in an application that needs to know whether the user is moving. When a user is forbidden by a doctor to exercise strenuously, Situation 2 is used for an application to alert the user in case of high levels of activity. Besides, Situation 3 is used for a health-care application to calculate calorie consumption by recognizing detailed contexts. This method works as follows. First, a user selects a situation according to his/her circumstances or active applications. Second, our system finds the sensor combination whose number of active sensors is least while fulfilling the threshold of accuracy in the same manner as that described in

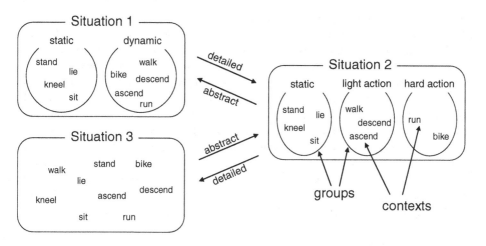

Fig. 3. Context groups

Table 1. Context transitions

Previous context	Possible context
walk	walk, run, stairs, bike, lie, kneel, sit, stand (all contexts)
run	walk, run, stairs, bike, stand
stairs	walk, run, stairs, stand
bike	walk, bike, stand
lie	walk, lie, kneel, sit, stand
kneel	walk, lie, kneel, sit, stand
sit	walk, lie, kneel, sit, stand
stand	walk, run, stairs, bike, lie, kneel, sit, stand (all contexts)

Section 3.1. If there is no situation that the user needs, he/she can define a new situation by regroup contexts. For example, when a user wants to know the context of whether another user is dead, he/she makes *lying*, *kneeling*, and *sitting* a group and makes other contexts another group. When the former context-group lasts for a long time, you may judge if a user is in a critical condition. Judging life and death plays an important role in a wearable system. Detecting death is efficient for military purposes and elderly citizens living alone. Using only one sensor to recognize contexts in Situation 1 is sufficient. By turning redundant sensors off and by complementing data for them, we achieve a low-power-consuming context-aware system with any classifier and training data.

3.3 Context-Transition-Based Power Saving

Focusing on transitions in a person's actions, people basically continue the current context, and that restricts the next context that occurs. A context transition from the result of our preliminary evaluation by 5 people (3 men and 2 women) with 9 contexts (*walking, running, descending steps, ascending steps, bicycling, lying, kneeling, sitting,* and *standing*) is shown in Table 1. From Table 1, the candidates of context after *bicycling* are expected to be "go on riding a bike" or "get off a bike". *Lying* and *kneeling* do not happen often in life. For using these characteristics first, we list context candidates from all the contexts shown in Table 1. Second, a classifier is trained for all previous contexts. When a user trains a classifier for recognizing *walking*, training data includes only *walking*, *running*, *stairs*, and *standing* (see Table 1). The other contexts are trained likewise. Finally, when a user is *bicycling*, the system recognizes contexts using the trained classifier for *bicycling*. In this way, restricting candidates of possible contexts based on the current context achieves a high recognition accuracy. This means that our system requires fewer sensors, and power consumption can be reduced. When the number of cognitive contexts have increased, this mechanism becomes more effective. In addition, context transitions are automatically constructed by using a record of daily activities with sensors on at full power.

3.4 Algorithms for Context Recognition

There have been many kinds of algorithms for recognition. Our context-aware system uses Support Vector Machine (SVM)[10] as a classifier. We also implemented several classifiers such as Memory Based Reasoning (MBR) and Self-Organizing Maps (SOMs)[11]. The tendency of evaluation results is the same among all classifiers, and SVM achieves the best total accuracy among them, so we use SVM for the explanation.

SVM is a classification algorithm that often provides competitive or superior accuracy for a large variety of real-world classification tasks[10]. Consider the problem of separating a set of training data $(\boldsymbol{x}_1, y_1), (\boldsymbol{x}_2, y_2), \cdots, (\boldsymbol{x}_J, y_J)$ into two classes, where $\boldsymbol{x}_i \in R^N$ is a feature vector and $y_i \in \{-1, +1\}$ is its class label. Supposing that the classes can be separated by the hyperplane $\boldsymbol{w} \cdot \boldsymbol{x}_i + b$ and no knowledge about the data distribution is given beforehand, the optimal hyperplane is the one with the maximum distance to the closest points in the training dataset. We can find the optimal values for w and b by solving the following problem:

$$\min \frac{1}{2}||\boldsymbol{w}||^2$$

subject to $y_i(\boldsymbol{w} \cdot \boldsymbol{x}_i + b) \geq 1, \ \forall i = 1, \cdots, n.$

The factor of 1/2 is used for mathematical convenience. By using Lagrange multipliers $\lambda_i(i = 1, \cdots, n)$, the expression is rewritten in this way:

$$\max \sum_{i=1}^{N} \lambda_i - \sum_{i,j=1}^{N} \lambda_i \lambda_j y_i y_j \boldsymbol{x}_i^T \boldsymbol{x}_j, \qquad \text{subject to } \sum_{i=1}^{N} y_i \alpha_i = 0, \ \lambda_i \geq 0.$$

That results in a classification function

$$f(\boldsymbol{x}) = sign\left(\sum_{i=1}^{n} \lambda_i y_i \boldsymbol{x}_i \cdot \boldsymbol{x} + b\right). \tag{1}$$

Most of the λ_i take the value zero. Those $f(\boldsymbol{x}_i)$ with nonzero λ_i are so-called support vectors, all of which are on each hyperplane. In cases where the classes are not separable, the Lagrange multipliers are modified to $0 \leq \lambda_i \leq C, i = 1, \cdots, n$, where C is the penalty for misjudgement. This arrangement is called *soft margin* and is the reason SVM performs well.

The original optimal hyperplane algorithm proposed by Vapnik was a linear classifier. To obtain a nonlinear classifier, one maps the data from the input space $\mathbb{R}^N$ to a high dimensional feature space by using $x \rightarrow \Phi(x)$. However nonlinear classifiers were created by applying the kernel trick to maximum-margin hyperplanes. Assuming there exists a kernel function $K(x, x') = \Phi(x) \cdot \Phi(x')$, a nonlinear SVM can be constructed by replacing the inner product $x \cdot x'$ by the kernel function $K(x, x')$ in Eq. 1. Commonly used kernels are polynomials $K(x, x') = (\gamma x \cdot x' + c)^d$, the Gaussian Radial Basis Function (RBF) $K(x, x') = exp(-\gamma||x - x'||^2)$, and the sigmoid $K(x, x') = tanh(\gamma x \cdot x' + c)$.

We have examined the kernels while changing their parameters: penalty C: 5,000, 50,000, and 500,000; γ in RBF and sigmoid: $0.0001, 0.005, 0.001, 0.01, 0.1$, and 1; and constant c in RBF and sigmoid: 0, 0.1, and 1. No kernel exhibited better performance than that of linear classification, and a C of 50,000 exhibited the best performance. The extension of a 2-class SVM to the N-class can be achieved, e.g., by training N SVMs, one class will be separated from the others.

4 Evaluation

In this section, we evaluate our system on the basis of accuracy and power consumption.

4.1 Evaluation Environment

To evaluate our system, training data and test data were captured by five different test subjects who wore five sensors: both wrists, both ankles, and hip. They acted according to the scenario shown in Table 2. Each instruction is very simple. Instructions have a high degree of freedom in activity, such as stopping halfway or walking to talk to other people. This scenario includes the following nine basic activities: *walking, running, ascending steps, descending steps, bicycling, lying, kneeling, sitting*, and *standing*[5]. The former four activities are dynamic and the latter five are static. The worn sensors were three-axis accelerometers[12]. The sampling frequency was 20 Hz. The algorithm for context awareness is Support Vector Machine (SVM) described in Section 3.4. Raw data and hand-labeled contexts of two test subjects in the scenario are shown in Figure 4. As shown in the figure, though general actions are similar to each other, detailed actions are different. The subject of the upper part of the graph in the figure sometimes stops while walking. On the other hand, there is little change in contexts for the subject of the lower graph. In addition, before riding on a bicycle, the subject in the upper graph stands, and the subject in the lower graph walks. In this way, the data used in a evaluation contains various characteristics, so this data is suited for the evaluation.

Generally, using a context-aware algorithm, raw data would not be used but preprocessed for extracting the feature values to grasp the meaning of sensed data. Supposing time $t = T$ now, the constructed context-aware system uses mean $\mu_i(T)$ and variance $\sigma_i(T)$ for 20 samples of 15-dimensional sensed data (cognitive vector) $c_i(T)$ ($i = 1, \cdots, 15$) retraced from time $t = T$.

$$\mu_i(T) = \frac{1}{20} \sum_{t=T-19}^{T} c_i(t)$$

$$\sigma_i(T) = \frac{1}{20} \sum_{t=T-19}^{T} \left\{ c_i(t) - \mu_i(t) \right\}^2$$

Characteristic vector $Z(T)$ is normalized using the following equation for 30-dimensional vector $X(T) = [\mu_1(T), \cdots \mu_{15}(T), \sigma(T) \cdots \sigma_{15}(T)]$, where M and S are the mean and the standard deviation of X, respectively.

Table 2. Scenario performed in evaluation

	Instruction: Go to buy a juice at the co-op by bicycle
Outdoor phase	Laboratory → down stairs → to bicycle shed through corridor → to co-op by bicycle → buy juice from a vending machine → back to the lab.
	Instruction: Read a journal and rest. Then, go upstairs for a job
Indoor phase	look for a journal on bookshelves → read the journal on a chair → take a rest on a sofa → recall a job and run upstairs → back to the lab.

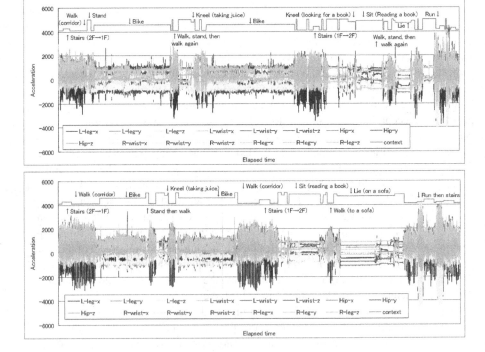

Fig. 4. Raw data and hand-labeled context of test subjects

Table 3. Power consumption @ 5.18 V

Hardware	Power consumption $[mW]$
CLAD only	92.204
Inactive sensor	11.396
Active sensor	40.922

$$Z(T) = \frac{X(T) - M}{S}$$

After this conversion, the mean and variance of $Z(T)$ become 0 and 1, respectively.

The logged data in the scenario were manually labeled, 20% of which becomes training data and the data for complementing while the remaining 80% of the data is used for testing. The amount of the data used for complementing is much less than that in testing, so our proposal makes a significant contribution without using all possible data sets of all remaining sensors. In addition, the pair database is easy to construct because its data need not be labeled.

4.2   Results

First, we measured power consumption of our hardware: CLAD and sensors. The results are shown in Table 3. Each inactive sensor consumes 11.4 mW as a standby power requirement. "CLAD only" means the power consumption for CLAD itself without any sensor. According to this table, 297 mW are consumed in full-power operation (5 active sensors and CLAD).

Evaluation of Context Group. The first result is the accuracy of the context groups described in Section 3.2. The results are plotted in the group × group confusion matrices shown in Figure 5. These results were obtained with five active sensors and without any complementing. Each cell indicates the number of positives per activity (with the true positives diagonally), the accuracy indicates the percentage of true positives over each activity. The matrix makes the difficulty of each context clear: which context is easily recognizable. As you see, the accuracies are vastly different by a context: *bicycling* and *lying* are high, but *descending* and *kneeling* are low. For this result, the clear point is that a more abstract group achieves a better classification percentage.

As a second result, the accuracy in changing the complementing method for each context-group is plotted in Figure 6. The horizontal axis indicates 31 combinations of active and inactive sensors ($\bigcirc$ means active, a blank means inactive). The vertical axis indicates the accuracy of context recognition. The partitions in the graph indicate a border between active sensors. As mentioned above, the more abstract a situation is, the more the accuracy increases. As sensors are turned off, the accuracies decreases, but their decreases are small due to the complementing mechanism, as described in Section 2. For a comparison, we show the accuracy without our complementing. In this case, inactive sensor data is replaced with an average of the other active sensor data. If not complemented well, the decreases are significant[8]. For this result, in Situation 1 with more than one sensor, the accuracies are the same as that at full power. Situation 2

Accuracy

			Accuracy
Static	22561	2339	90.61%
Dynamic	2564	53835	95.28%

(a) Situation 1: 92.94% on average (not over all data but contexts)

Accuracy

				Accuracy
Static	22346	1675	879	89.75%
Light action	1571	23694	673	91.35%
Hard action	474	821	32707	96.19%

(b) Situation 2: 92.43% on average (not over all data but contexts)

Accuracy

										Accuracy
Walking	17513	75	102	155	308	12	68	147	1578	87.75%
Running	132	2001	118	98	0	0	0	0	13	84.72%
Descending	580	13	2340	20	0	0	0	0	46	78.02%
Ascending	489	14	15	2457	5	0	0	0	0	82.45%
Bicycling	304	4	6	23	31141	0	0	35	127	98.42%
Lying	4	0	0	0	0	5684	0	44	28	98.68%
Kneeling	130	0	0	22	138	0	1841	21	168	79.35%
Sitting	147	0	0	3	35	46	20	7183	147	94.75%
Standing	835	51	23	41	160	0	223	51	7856	85.02%

(c) Situation 3: 87.69% on average (not over all data but contexts)

Fig. 5. Confusion matrices for each situation

exhibits the same tendency as that of Situation 1. Though Situation 3 also has the same tendency, the accuracies on the whole are worse than that of other situations because of the cognitive complexity. In short, the power consumption can be reduced by turning off sensors while maintaining the accuracy, and the accuracy increases with an appropriate situation. Optimal sensor combinations in each situation are shown in Table 4. The tolerances of accuracy are supposed to be 94, 90, and 87%. We assume that the tolerance is the accuracy decided by the user or application; under severe conditions, tolerance will be high, or tolerance may be low for a long battery lifetime in daily life. In each situation with each tolerance, our system selects the fewest number of sensors so that the accuracy of a combination satisfies the tolerance. In the present circumstances, we need to determine an optimal sensor combination for each situation by actual measurement in the same manner as that shown in Figure 6. Power consumption is calculated from Table 3. (e.g., with four active sensors, the power consumption becomes $92.2 + 40.9 \times 4 + 11.4 \simeq 267[mW]$.) The reduction rate is the percentage of power consumption

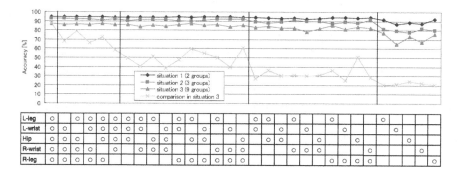

Fig. 6. Accuracy vs. sensor combination in each situation

Table 4. Optimal sensor combinations and their power consumption

Tolerance	Situation	No. of sensors	Combination of active sensors	Accuracy [%]	Power consumption [mW]	Reduction [%]
	1	3	L-wrist, Hip, R-leg	94.30	238	19.9
94%	2	5	ALL SENSORS	92.72	297	0
	3	5	ALL SENSORS	87.38	297	0
	1	1	R-leg	92.03	179	39.8
90%	2	2	R-leg, R-wrist	91.50	208	29.8
	3	5	ALL SENSORS	87.38	297	0
	1	1	R-leg	92.03	179	39.8
87%	2	2	R-wrist, R-leg	91.50	208	29.8
	3	3	L-leg, Hip, R-leg	87.08	238	19.9

that is reduced compared to that in full power. Note that if no combination achieves the tolerance, the system works with five active sensors. Even with 94% tolerance, power consumption is 20% reduced in Situation 1. Moreover, with 87% tolerance, not all five sensors are not required in all situations.

Evaluation of Context Transition. The accuracy of context recognition considering the human context transition in Table 1 is shown in Table 5. These results were obtained with five active sensors. According to the result, the accuracy was improved for all contexts. For example, when a user changes his/her action from *bicycling* to *walking*, the system made 75 mistakes for *running* and 147 mistakes for *sitting* without considering transition. However, considering the context transition, *running* and *sitting* were excepted from the context candidates. By removing unimaginable contexts, from *bicycling*, *walking* was recognized to be 91.74% (3.99% improved). Accuracies when context transition is applied in all sensor combinations are shown in Figure 7. The environment is Situation 3 (9 contexts). Each axis is the same as that of Figure 6. According to Figure 7, the accuracies in all combinations were improved (2.55% on average). A combination of a smaller number of sensors, which has not been selectable because of low accuracy, becomes selectable, e.g., an accuracy at full power before applying

Table 5. Change in accuracy by context-transition

Previous context	Next context	Accuracy Before	Accuracy After
run	walk	87.75	90.49
	run	84.72	87.10
	descend	78.02	82.31
	ascend	82.45	84.21
	bicycle	98.42	98.47
	stand	85.02	88.17
stairs	walk	87.75	92.32
	run	84.72	88.03
	descend	78.02	84.35
	ascend	82.45	85.79
	stand	85.02	89.31

Previous context	Next context	Accuracy Before	Accuracy After
bicycle	walk	87.75	91.74
	bicycle	98.42	98.58
	stand	85.02	88.89
lie kneel sit stand	walk	87.75	93.19
	lie	98.68	99.24
	kneel	79.35	91.14
	sit	94.75	97.53
	stand	85.02	87.52

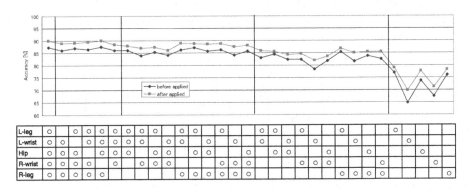

Fig. 7. Accuracy vs. sensor combination before and after applying context-transition

context transition (87.38%) is overtaken by that of 3 sensors after applying context transition (88.91%).

Finally, we consider a combination of all mechanisms. A context-granularity-based method and a context-transition-based method can co-exist. Considering the context-transition of context groups in this paper is difficult. Static and Dynamic groups can change to each other in Situation 1. Static, light action, and hard action groups can also change to each other. However, when there are more contexts to recognize, there will be many context groups. In such a case, by using our proposals at the same time, restricting transitions between context groups results in a better performance. Further evaluation and power measurement is part of our future work.

5 Conclusion

We have constructed a context-aware system that changes sensor combinations considering the energy consumption. By assuming the granularity of cognitive contexts differs according to situations, we defined "context group" by including some similar contexts.

In addition, we focused on a transition in human actions to improve the accuracy by reducing the number of the candidates of possible contexts. The proposed system changes the granularity of cognitive contexts of a user's situation and manages the power supply on the basis of an optimal sensor combination. From the evaluation, clearly, not all sensors are needed to recognize required contexts according to situations. As a result, our system has achieved a reduction in energy consumption. The advantage of our system is that even if the number of sensors changes, the system does not require any extra classifiers and training data because the data for sensors that have been shut off is complemented by our proposed algorithm.

As future work, we plan to propose a mechanism for automatic change of the current situation. In our current system, we have to change the situation by hand or another device. The system may be able to decide the current situation by using co-occurrence information among contexts. In addition, context transition is applied according to a binary decision. There is a method limiting context with conditional probability such as in a Bayesian network. Such probabilistic approaches have flexibility, but they have the weakness of unexpected events such as change of context, which rarely happens. This problem is our ongoing study. Furthermore, we think our approach is applicable to wireless sensors that use sleep commands. We also plan to evaluate power consumption of wireless sensors.

Acknowledgements

This research was supported in part by a Grant-in-Aid for Scientific Research (A) (17200006) and Priority Areas (19024046) of the Japanese Ministry of Education, Culture, Sports, Science and Technology, and by the IPA Exploratory Software Project entitled "Development of a Rule Processing Engine for Constructing Wearable Applications."

References

1. Miyamae, M., Terada, T., Tsukamoto, M., Nishio, S.: Design and Implementation of an Extensible Rule Processing System for Wearable Computing. In: Proc. of the 1st IEEE Intl. Conference on Mobile and Ubiquitous Systems: Networking and Services (MobiQuitous), pp. 392–400 (August 2004)
2. Toda, M., Akita, J., Sakurazawa, S., Yanagihara, K., Kunita, M., Iwata, K.: Wearable Biomedical Monitoring System Using TextileNet. In: Proc. of the 10th IEEE Intl. Symposium on Wearable Computers (ISWC 2006), pp. 119–120 (October 2006)
3. Shen, C.L., Kao, T., Huang, C.T., Lee, J.H.: Wearable Band Using a Fabric-Based Sensor for Exercise ECG Monitoring. In: Proc. of the 10th IEEE Intl. Symposium on Wearable Computers (ISWC 2006), pp. 143–144 (October 2006)
4. Ouchi, K., Suzuki, T., Doi, M.: LifeMinder: A wearable Healthcare Support System Using Users Context. In: Proc. of the 2nd Intl. Workshop on Smart Appliances and Wearable Computing (IWSAWC 2002), pp. 791–792 (July 2002)
5. Laerhoven, K.V., Gellersen, H.W.: Spine versus Porcupine: a Study in Distributed Wearable Activity Recognition. In: Proc. of the 8th IEEE Intl. Symposium on Wearable Computers (ISWC 2004), pp. 142–149 (October 2004)

6. Naya, F., Ohmura, R., Takayanagi, F., Noma, H., Kogure, K.: Workers Routine Activity Recognition using Body Movement and Location Information. In: Proc. of the 10th IEEE Intl. Symposium on Wearable Computers (ISWC 2006), pp. 105–108 (October 2006)

7. Stiefmeier, T., Ogris, G., Junker, H., Lukowics, P., Tröster, G.: Combining Motion Sensors and Ultrasonic Hands Tracking for Continuous Activity Recognition in a Maintenance Scenario. In: Proc. of the 10th IEEE Intl. Symposium on Wearable Computers (ISWC 2006), pp. 97–104 (October 2006)

8. Murao, K., Takegawa, Y., Terada, T., Nishio, S.: CLAD: a Sensor Management Device for Wearable Computing. In: Proc. of 7th Intl. Workshop on Smart Appliances and Wearable Computing (IWSAWC 2007) (June 2007)

9. Ho, J., Intille, S.S.: Using Context-Aware Computing to Reduce the Perceived Burden of Interruptions from Mobile Devices. In: Proc. Conference on Human Factors in Computing System (CHI 2005), pp. 909–918 (April 2005)

10. Vapnik, V.: The Nature of Statistical Learning Theory. Springer, Heidelberg (1995)

11. Kohonen, T.: Self-Organizing Maps. Springer, Heidelberg (1996)

12. Wirelss Technologies, Inc.: http://www.wireless-t.jp/

Providing an Integrated User Experience of Networked Media, Devices, and Services through End-User Composition

Mark W. Newman[1], Ame Elliott[2], and Trevor F. Smith[3,*]

[1] School of Information, University of Michigan, Ann Arbor, MI 48109
mwnewman@umich.edu
[2] IDEO, 100 Forest Ave., Palo Alto. CA 94301
ame.elliott@mac.com
[3] Transmutable Networks LLC, 4742 42nd Ave SW #326, Seattle, WA 98116
trevor@transmutable.com

Abstract. Networked devices for the storage and rendering of digital media are rapidly becoming ubiquitous in homes throughout the industrialized world. Existing approaches to home media control will not suffice for the new capabilities offered by these digitally networked media devices. In particular, the piecemeal interaction provided by current devices, services, and applications will continue to engender frustration among users and will slow adoption of these technologies and the more sophisticated pervasive technologies that will surely follow them into the domestic environment. To address this challenge, we present OSCAR, an application that supports flexible and generic control of devices and services in near-future home media networks. It allows monitoring and manipulation of connections between devices, and allows users to construct reusable configurations to streamline frequently performed activities. A lab-based user study with 9 users of varied backgrounds showed that people could use OSCAR to configure and control a realistic and fully operational home media network, but that they struggled when constructing certain types of reusable configurations. The results of the study show that users were enthusiastic about adopting a system like OSCAR into their own media-related practices, but that further research and development is needed to make such systems truly useful.

Keywords: End-user composition, domestic technology, universal remote control, home media network.

1 Introduction

Networked devices for the storage and rendering of digital media are rapidly becoming ubiquitous in homes throughout the industrialized world. Today's devices, such as personal video recorders (e.g., [20]), media rendering devices (e.g., [19]), portable

---

* All work was conducted while authors were employed at the Palo Alto Research Center (PARC) http://www.parc.com

J. Indulska et al. (Eds.): Pervasive 2008, LNCS 5013, pp. 213–227, 2008.

media players (e.g., [1]), and electronic picture frames (e.g., [4]), to name just a few, will soon be joined by further waves of devices with even greater built-in networking capabilities. It is reasonable to view these collections of devices as an early beachhead in the advancing front of pervasive computing in the domestic environment and beyond. Given that future generations of technology will almost certainly be layered atop today's technology [8, 18], it is our view that the successful integration of media networking into the practices and preferences of home users will be critical to the ultimate success of the multiple overlapping visions of the "smart" or "aware" home [11, 14]. The currently emerging "digital" home is characterized not yet by it's ability to sense and react to the presence and patterns of its occupants but by its potential to place a wide range of functionality at the fingertips of its users.

This rapid emergence of networked home media devices has been driven by a confluence of factors. On the one hand, data networks in the home are becoming more powerful and are growing to include not only traditional computing devices like desktop and laptop computers, but also media-oriented consumer electronics devices such as those listed in the previous paragraph. At the same time, media itself is being transformed into a digital commodity that can be accessed on demand in a variety of ways from a variety of sources, both inside and outside the home network.

In this paper, we describe a system whose goal is to cut through the entanglement of dealing with growing and changing networks of devices and media in the home environment. We present the design and evaluation of OSCAR (see Fig. 1), an end-user tool for device and media control and composition. In the next section we discuss previous research on the design of technology for the home and derive guidelines for the design of networked media, devices, and controls in such environments. Following that we present OSCAR and describe its functions and user interface. A user study involving nine users drawn from the local community is then described and its results analyzed to assess the effectiveness of OSCAR and explore avenues for further research. We then present related work and conclude.

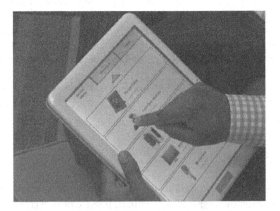

Fig. 1. OSCAR allows end-users to discover, connect, and control media devices and services in a home network, as well as create re-usable compositions for quick access to common functions

1.1 Designing for the Home

A number of studies have attempted to understand the impact of digital technology on domestic life and project the most promising avenues for future development. These studies have revealed the home as the site of multiple overlapping activities that unfold across time and involve the coordination of different resources and actors. Venkatesh, et al. have described the home as a set of overlapping "centers" [25] (earlier called "sub-environments" [24]) that have differing relationships to the technical "space" of the home. Household occupants appropriate both "technical" (e.g., computers, networking equipment, televisions) and "non-technical" (e.g., doors, tables, mantelpieces) resources in various ways to support their multiple practices, as has been described for communication [5], household coordination [21], work [26], and entertainment [10], In addition, these resources are accreted over time rather than all at once [8, 18] and are often repurposed into different roles multiple times throughout the course of their useful life [10].

Taken together, these studies paint a picture of the home as a site where members of individual households compose resources in creative ways to accomplish the particular patterns of their own household's version of daily existence. In keeping with this image of the home, we have focused our efforts on supporting end-user composition of varied resources in the media domain. It should be noted at this point that we do not intend to equate "media" strictly with "entertainment." Returning to Venkatesh's "centers," we can see that media technologies are (or are becoming) central to household activities such as "communication," "work," "information," and "learning," and likely will play an increasing role in other activities as well. Our goal, therefore, is a generalized system and user interface for creating, monitoring, and controlling media-oriented devices and services in the interest of a variety of activities.

1.2 Near-Future Home Networking Scenario

The following scenario illustrates both the benefits and challenges of near-future home media networks with respect to managing resources to accomplish multiple overlapping activities.

Alice is sitting in her living room on a Saturday afternoon reading news on her laptop. She decides she would like to listen to some music, so she navigates to her favorite online music service and arranges to have some music streamed directly to her living room speakers. A short while later, the doorbell rings. Engrossed in the news, she does not wish to get up, so she directs the webcam above the front door to send its output to a digital picture frame that is mounted on the wall next to her. Seeing a delivery person on the screen, she remembers that she is expecting a package, so she connects her laptop's microphone to the intercom speaker next to the front door to say "Hold on, I'll be right there." The delivery person's "OK" is heard through the living room speakers as Alice leaps off the couch to head for the door.

The experience presented in this scenario is one of convenient, seamless access to a variety of resources both within and without the home. The benefit to Alice is that she is able to connect and control her available devices and services with little effort and minimal advance planning. There are a number of challenges to realizing such an integrated user experience.

As discussed earlier, the devices and networking technologies to accomplish each part of this scenario are rapidly coming to market. There is some uncertainty about whether such devices will provide sufficient interoperability guarantees to work together, but others have been addressing this problem (e.g., [9, 23]) and we assume their eventual success as the baseline for the current project. What remains is to provide the user interface for effecting and controlling compositions. By providing a single integrated user experience for interacting with each device individually as well as the network as a whole, we endeavor to overcome the problem of *piecemeal interaction*.

"Piecemeal interaction" describes the experience of using different applications, often with very different user interface styles, to interact with and control the different devices and services with which one interacts. In the scenario above, this would occur if Alice needed to use one application to control her streaming music and a different one to connect the webcam to the picture frame. Much of interacting with today's technology is characterized by piecemeal interaction. Different applications, different devices, and different software platforms have different user interfaces and in many cases each has to be mastered by users in order to get things done. This situation is poised to become worse as networked devices and services proliferate into the homes and daily lives of more and more people. Solving the problem of piecemeal interaction is critical to the ultimate realization of the visions of calm, well-integrated experiences of computation that characterize the enterprise of pervasive computing. As we shall describe in the next sections, OSCAR is an end-user tool for composition and control of networked devices and services that overcomes piecemeal interaction to provide an integrated user experience of interacting with multiple devices.

2 The OSCAR User Interface

OSCAR was designed as a next-generation prototype of a universal remote control for composing and controlling networked devices in the home. It consists of software running on a touchscreen-based tablet device such as the one shown in Fig. 1. The form factor was chosen because it is portable and touch-operated, and thus comfortable to use while seated on a couch or easy chair, yet large enough to afford users an uncluttered view of all the controls and information needed to carry out complex configuration and control interactions. While our design focused on the tablet form factor, we believe OSCAR's functions can easily be replicated on other devices such as laptops, desktops, or smartphones.

The tablet used for our prototype features a 30.7 cm (12.1 in) LCD screen operated via touch input, runs Windows XP Tablet PC Edition, and has an 802.11b network interface. As OSCAR was designed to simulate a new, unfamiliar device with new, unfamiliar capabilities, it was made to use the entire screen and to hide all of the OS widgets and controls so that users were largely unaware that they were interacting with a computer application running on a conventional PC.

For our prototyping efforts and user studies, we created a testbed that consisted of a simulated "home." Our home was contained entirely in one large room, with areas marked off for the "living room," "kitchen," and "front door." The home was populated with a number of networked devices (e.g., TV screen, digital picture frame, security webcam, speakers in several room) and services (e.g., software-based collections of music and photos), all of which were live and accessible to OSCAR.

Both OSCAR and the testbed devices and services were implemented atop the Obje Framework [10], which is a mobile-code based interoperability framework previously developed in our lab at PARC. The dependence on Obje does not limit the generality of OSCAR's contribution, as the solutions provided by OSCAR are applicable with little modification to a number of more widely available interoperability platforms such as UPnP [23], Jini [27], and Zeroconf [13]. All that is required for OSCAR is the existence of discoverable networked services that implement standardized interfaces for providing and accepting data streams.

OSCAR provides users with three basic capabilities: (1) browse, select, and control individual devices; (2) connect devices, services, and content together; and (3) create, edit, and invoke reusable service compositions. We will describe each in turn.

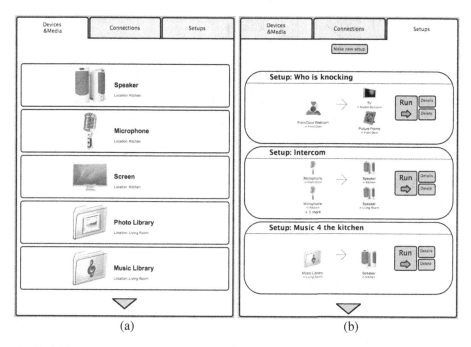

Fig. 2. OSCAR allows users to browse and select among all devices and media sources that have been discovered on a home network. Users employ the Devices & Media List (a) to select a device or media item to obtain its user interface, connect it to other items, or use it as part of a reusable configuration called a *Setup*. After a number of Setups have been created, the Setups List (b) can be used as a starting point for carrying out common activities.

2.1 Browse, Select, and Control Individual Devices

OSCAR presents a list of all devices it has discovered (see Fig. 2a), and the user can select one in order to view its details. The details include the control user interface that is downloaded automatically and displayed to the user. The details also show any connections or *setups* that involve this component. In addition to allowing the user to manipulate the control user interface, the user can choose to create a new connection or setup based on this component.

2.2 Connect Devices, Services, and Content Together

OSCAR allows the user to make connections among providers and consumers of data. The user selects either endpoint of the desired connection first, and is then prompted to select among a restricted subset of compatible endpoints in order to complete the connection. After the connection is constructed, OSCAR presents a control panel

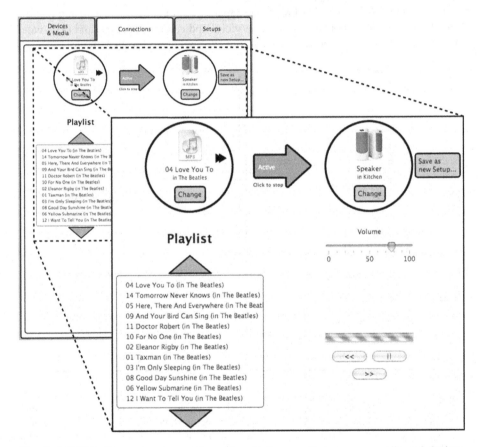

Fig. 3. OSCAR allows users to monitor and control connections among media and devices, including both device-to-device connections and media-to-device connections. For each connection, the user can monitor and change the status of the connection (e.g. from "Active" to "Stopped"), access the controls for the individual devices and/or media-rendering services involved in the connections, or replace either the source or destination with any other device or media on the network by pressing *Change* and selecting from among the options presented.

screen that allows the user to monitor and manipulate the connection (i.e., start, stop, and restart) and also presents the user with a single, collected view of the user interfaces for each of the components involved in the connection. Referring to the scenario presented earlier, Alice can choose to create a new connection using the den picture frame, at which point she is prompted to select a source for the connection. After the front door camera is selected, Alice is presented with a screen that allows her to pause or restart the camera connection, and also provides user interfaces for controlling the settings on the camera and picture frame.

Content items such as media files or documents are presented as first-order entities in OSCAR, which means they can be connected with devices and services directly (see Fig. 3). Thus, a connection between a streaming movie that is being served by a remote video-on-demand service and a local TV display would be constructed and managed in exactly the same way as a connection between a security camera and the TV. Collections that contain multiple media sources (e.g. music files or digital images) can be used as sources for a connection in OSCAR. In those cases, OSCAR automatically generates a playlist and provides the user with controls for navigating among the items in the list. For example, Alice can browse through her Music Library aggregate to find music to listen to, and she could select the *Beatles* subfolder (also an aggregate) as the source. After picking the den speakers as the sink, the first song begins to play while the remaining songs are loaded into the playlist and presented to Alice along with controls to skip to the next song or choose a different song in the list.

2.3 Create, Edit, and Invoke Reusable Compositions

Being able to connect arbitrary devices and media together is important to allow users to create unplanned connections, to freely reconfigure devices, and to take advantage of new or transient resources like recently purchased equipment or portable devices that normally live outside the home. After a period of use, however, it is likely that most users will find regular patterns of connections that they wish to re-use on a regular basis. OSCAR supports the notion of *setups*, which describe how components are to be found, selected, and connected together in order to carry out a routine activity such as "See who's at the front door," or "Listen to NPR in the kitchen."

A setup consists of source and a destination "slots" (see Fig. 4). Each slot contains a query that is executed when the setup is invoked in order to generate a set of candidate components. Each slot also contains a selection rule that dictates how the active component or components will be selected from among the candidates at invocation time. Selection rules include "present candidates to user and prompt for selection," "choose at random," and "sort candidates by one or more criteria and then pick the highest ranked component(s)." When the setup is invoked, or "Run," the source and destination queries run and the selection rules are applied. After both source and destination slots have been populated with a playlist or a single component, a connection is made between them.

Eventually, most of the household's common patterns of activity will be encapsulated in a Setup, and the household members will be able to use the *Setup List* (see Fig. 2b) as a convenient access point for all of their home's functionality.

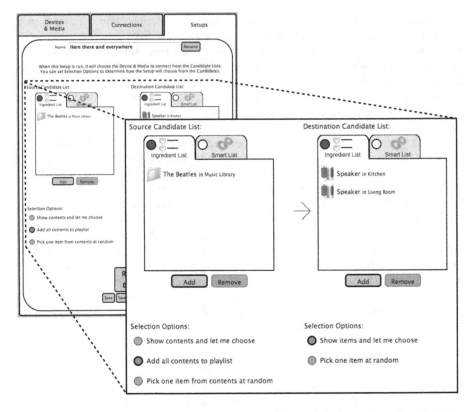

Fig. 4. OSCAR allows users to create reusable compositions of devices and media called *Set-ups*. Each Setup consists of a *Source* and a *Destination*, and each Source and Destination in turn consists of a list of *Candidates* and a *Selection Option*. The list of candidates specifies the media source and/or devices that can be selected for the relevant role when the Setup is later *Run*. The Selection Option determines how the Setup will choose from among the candidates for a given role when the Setup is Run.

3   User Study

The OSCAR design process consisted of a number of phases, including the generation of personas and scenarios; development of a paper prototype followed by an expert evaluation; development of a medium-fidelity mockup prototype followed by a second expert evaluation; and the development of an initial interactive prototype followed by a usability study with 9 users. Space does not permit us to describe this process or its results in detail, but the resulting system and user interface was described in the previous section.

In this section, we describe and report findings from a final user study that was conducted to assess OSCAR's usability as well as to probe users' perceptions of the desirability of integrating OSCAR's functionality into their own media practices and to gain insights for future design. Although this was the "final" user study conducted as part of the OSCAR project, the study was designed to contain both summative and formative aspects. The summative goals were to assess the usefulness of the functions provided by OSCAR (e.g., making ad hoc connections among devices and creating reusable "setups" for encapsulating common activities) and to assess the usability of the basic approaches taken by OSCAR to presenting those functions (e.g., presenting *setups* as bipartite constructs consisting of source and destination with candidate lists and selection options). The formative goals consisted of exploring avenues for further design by understanding the breakdowns experienced by users when carrying out tasks and by engaging with users to understand how OSCAR might be used within the contexts of users' existing practices. In order to study these various aspects, we observed users carrying out a number of tasks, administered a questionnaire, and conducted an in-depth follow-up interview.

3.1 Participants

Nine participants were recruited from the local community by an external focus group recruiting firm. In order to understand how OSCAR would be used by less computer-savvy individuals, users were screened such that none were professional programmers or system administrators. Only one high-tech worker (a mechanical engineer) was included in the sample, the remainder represented a variety of professions including hotel clerk, real estate broker, homemaker, and carpenter. Other than the mechanical engineer (ME), no users reported any regular use of computing beyond email, web, and basic office applications, and only two users (the ME and one other) reported having primary responsibility for setting up and maintaining their own home networks (if they had one). Users were also screened such that all were either regular (n=4) or avid (n=5) consumers of media as determined by the number of hours of TV watched per week, CDs purchased per month, and movies watched per month. Infrequent consumers[1] of media were excluded. Gender and age were distributed fairly evenly across participants (gender=5m/4f; age range=24-51, mean=35.6). None had seen or received any information about OSCAR before the study.

3.2 Study Sessions

Each participant individually came to our lab for a 90-minute session. The basic physical configuration used in the study is shown in Fig. 5. After a brief preamble in which participants were introduced to "their house" and its devices, they were handed OSCAR and asked to perform the four multi-part tasks shown in Table 1. Users received no training in the usage of OSCAR beyond the description "Imagine you just purchased this device at a local Circuit City [a popular US consumer electronics store]. All you know that it is operated with your finger and that it is supposed to allow you to control all the devices in your home." During completion of the tasks, users were asked to think aloud. After the completion of all tasks, we asked users to

---

[1] Infrequent media consumers were those who watched less than 10 hours of TV/wk, purchased less than 2 CDs/month, and watched less than 2 movies/month. Digital downloads were not screened for, though several users reported at least occasional downloading.

Fig. 5. The study setup used for the OSCAR user study. *Top left:* the two test observers with a participant. *Top right:* A participant using OSCAR. *Bottom left and right:* the testbed room, showing the "living room," "kitchen," and "front door".

Table 1. Participants in the OSCAR user study carried out four multi-part tasks using the OSCAR client to connect and control devices in the OSCAR testbed environment

TASK	INSTRUCTIONS
1	Play the welcome message on the Living Room Speakers.
2	Show a picture from your recent trip to Australia on the Living Room TV. Then show a different photo from the same trip.
3a	Someone has just rung the doorbell. See who it is by displaying the image from the webcam outside the front door on the picture frame just inside the front door.
3b	Now make it so that you or someone you live with can easily do this again, without having to redo it from scratch. Give it a name so that you will remember what this does.
3c	Now make it so that when the doorbell rings, you can decide to either show the image from the webcam on the picture frame OR the living room TV.
4a	Someone you live with is more motivated to clean when they are listening to music. Make a recipe that will allow them to play all of the songs by the Beatles on the Kitchen speakers.
4b	The person you made this for asks you to change this so that they can listen to other music, too, and do it any room of the house. Change the recipe so that they can pick the artist and the speakers when they activate the recipe.

complete a questionnaire indicating on a 5-item Likert scale their level of agreement or disagreement with 16 statements regarding OSCAR's usability and usefulness. Questions 1-10 were derived from the System Usability Scale [2], and the remaining six were devised by us to assess users' overall acceptance of OSCAR. Following the questionnaire, we interviewed users to gain further insight into their experiences with and assessments of OSCAR. Two team members were present for each session and participated in all observations and interviews. Each session was videotaped and reviewed for understanding critical incidents and selected interview responses.

3.3   User Study Results

Subjective results. Participants' responses to the test questionnaire indicated a positive response to OSCAR, in particular to statements like "I would find this system very useful in my own home," ("strongly agree": n=5, "somewhat agree": n=4) and "I would like to have this system if it were available ("strongly agree": n=4, "somewhat agree": n=5). These statements of overall acceptance were made despite the fact that participants gave OSCAR a fairly mediocre score in terms of usability. The composite SUS score of 63.3 out of 100 (stdev=11.46, max=87.5, min=47.5) indicates that users were not impressed with OSCAR's usability. Nevertheless, they expressed enthusiasm for incorporating OSCAR into their own media systems, warts and all.

Task Performance. The amount of help required by each user to complete each task is shown in Table 2. The results show that users were able to complete nearly all tasks without significant help. In only one case was a user completely unable to complete a task (3a) without a direct intervention by the test observers. In 12 out of 63 task attempts a small amount of help was required. We defined a "small amount" of help as any comment by a test observer that revealed a system state ("it's waiting for you to do something") or called attention to a particular UI element ("what do you think 'Run' would do in this case?")

Most users required a small amount of help to complete Task 4b. Referring again to the task instructions in Table 1, recall that Task 4b asked users to modify the Setup they had created in Task 4a and then test it out. There were two interrelated issues that gave users difficulty when completing this task: selecting the appropriate candidate devices/media sources for inclusion in the Setup, and choosing the correct selection options. Taken together, this can be expressed as the difficulty of specifying list/rule combinations. Interestingly, mastery of these issues was also required for the completion of Task 3c, which was completed without help by all but one user. The differences between 3c and 4b were twofold: (1) 3c dealt only with device-device connections, whereas 4b required users to connect a media source (song) to a device (speakers) and (2) 3c only required users to specify a list/rule combination for the destination slot, whereas 4b required them to specify such combinations for both the source and destination.

Analysis. Drawing from the difficulties users experienced with Task 4b as well as observations and comments made during the study sessions, we were able to see a few areas where users experienced problems using OSCAR.

Some of the problems experienced derived from straightforward user interface design problems, such as a modal dialog box that users did not perceive was waiting for them to provide input. Such issues could be easily fixed with another design iteration. In addition, there were a couple of overarching issues that point to more fundamental challenges in designing end-user composition systems for the home.

1. *Users were unsure how to create Setups that would produce the desired results.* In fact, in some cases they remained uncertain even after they had created a "correct" solution. There were two particular issues that caused apprehension among users: (a) defining list/rule combinations and mapping decisions made during Setup creation (e.g., "Show me and I will choose") with behaviors that would occur when the Setups were "Run;" and (b) creating compositions involving one or more aggregations of media sources (e.g., song files) and understanding how those aggregations would be used during the setup. While incremental UI redesigns might be able to ameliorate these problems to some extent, they derive from the inherent difficulty of designing rules that will react to future states to produce desired outcomes. This is a style of thinking that is familiar to programmers but much less familiar to non-programmers. In order to address this issue, we believe that users must be provided with means to conduct rapid, lightweight experiments within OSCAR to view the results of their Setup designs before committing to "Run" them. This could be accomplished, for example, by implementing a "Test" function to sit alongside the "Run" function in the Setup Details screen.

2. *Users believed they correctly accomplished the task when they had achieved only a partial solution.* This occurred largely because they were able to produce the effect they believed they wanted (e.g., hearing the Beatles "Yellow Submarine" on the living room speakers) without having created the general solution we had requested (e.g., create a Setup that will allow your roommate to listen to the Beatles in any room in the house). While this stems in part from the artificiality of the study setting and in part, perhaps, due to a failure to communicate the tasks effectively, we believe it points to an unanticipated use of our system that may be desirable in the end. Users were satisfied with their ability to accomplish their immediate goals, but would perhaps become motivated to master the Setup functionality upon later realizing that

Table 2. The amount of help required by each user to complete each task in OSCAR2. Users were able to complete most tasks with no help, but many users required at least some minor help to complete Task 4b.

		participant									?	!
		1	2	3	4	5	6	7	8	9		
task	1										0	0
	2										0	0
	3a			!							0	1
	3b					?		?			2	0
	3c					?					1	0
	4a	?							?		2	0
	4b	?	?	?	?	?	?		?		7	0
											12	1

Key:
<blank> = success: user completed task with no help
? = mild help: revealed system state or called attention to UI element
! = intervention: told user to take particular action(s)

they were repeating the same configuration operations time and again. By maintaining a history of previous actions, OSCAR could present users with heuristically-generated starting points for their Setups (e.g., playing several individual songs by the same artist would suggest a Setup playing all the artist's songs) or even automatically generate Setups based on past behavior in a manner similar to programming by demonstration systems (e.g., [6, 15]). Thus the work done initially to create ephemeral connections among media and devices could be leveraged to aid the users' later attempts to stream-line their interactions with their media environment.

4 Related Work

Most users today control their media devices by means of remote controls, often be-ing forced to use multiple devices' remotes in concert. A relatively small number of users have availed themselves of the best mass-market solution currently offered by the industry: *universal remotes*. While they provide a single point of control for inter-acting with multiple devices, a significant limitation of such devices is that they are cumbersome to set up initially and the process of adding a new device to control can be quite painful as well. Some universal remotes like the Logitech Harmony [3] have significantly eased the pain of the initial setup by allowing programming codes to be downloaded into the device directly from the a centralized location (e.g., the Logitech website). They have also improved the user experience by allowing single button presses to send commands to multiple devices in order to set up the whole system to carry out an activity like "Watch a DVD," or "Listen to CD." Even so, none of these devices can adapt to new devices without being explicitly told. More broadly, the Harmony and its peers are not capable of making ad-hoc connections among net-worked services—it can only activate connections among devices that are already hard-wired together (e.g., a DVD player connected to a TV through a stereo receiver). It is also designed to only make device-device connections, and has no notion of in-teracting with content. As media becomes virtualized and capable of being aggregated and served by large-scale content services, it will become increasingly important for users to be able to interact with content as a first-order entity.

A number of research projects have looked at how to support end-user *program-ming* for the creation of different styles of ubiquitous computing applications in the home such as sensor-triggered actions [12], context-aware rules [7], and capture-and-access applications [22]. OSCAR differs from these systems primarily in that OSCAR provides a unified interface for creating spontaneous, ad hoc connections as well as long-lived "programs." Additionally, OSCAR, unlike these systems, provides access to the control user interfaces for each device, thus combining direct control, ad hoc connections, and creation of reusable configurations.

At a high level, Huddle [17] shares OSCAR's goal of providing an integrated user interface for interacting with multiple devices. Huddle allows devices to provide rich user interface descriptions that can be aggregated with other devices' user interfaces to present a coordinated UI for multiple devices. However, OSCAR's focus is differ-ent. Whereas Huddle requires an explicit XML-based system-wide "wiring diagram" to reason about content flows, OSCAR employs dynamic discovery to allow ad hoc connections among devices with little or no advance setup. In brief, Huddle is limited by the same factors that limit commercial industrial remotes: it cannot create ad-hoc connections and does not directly support content-to-device interactions.

The Speakeasy Browser [16] introduced the notion of Activity-Oriented Templates that allow users to easily invoke commonly-used compositions of devices, media, and services based on their current context. The present work builds upon the concepts introduced in [16] by adding the crucial ability for users to create and edit compositions, as well as providing insights from a detailed study with users representing a range of technical skill.

5 Conclusion

Home media technology is undergoing a sea change, in which standalone devices with custom remote controls are being replaced by networked services that can be combined with each other and with Internet-based media services in varied ways. Existing approaches to home media control will not suffice for these new capabilities.

In this paper, we described OSCAR—an end-user composition tool for home media networks that builds upon Obje's user experience goals and extends them by allowing the construction of reusable compositions for common tasks.

A user study involving 9 users with varied backgrounds showed that people could use OSCAR to configure and control a realistic and fully operational home media network, but that they struggled with certain aspects of the UI—especially constructing reusable configurations. Users reacted positively to OSCAR in terms of their desire to use such an application in their homes.

References

1. Apple Computer. Apple - iPod touch, http://www.apple.com/ipodtouch/
2. Brooke, J.: SUS: A quick and dirty usability scale. In: Jordan, P., Thomas, B., Weerdmeester, B., McClelland, I. (eds.) Usability evaluation in industry, pp. 189–194. Taylor and Francis, London (1996)
3. Carnoy, D.: CNET editors' review: Logitech Harmony 880, http://reviews.cnet.com/Logitech_Harmony_880/4505-7900_7-31337419.html
4. Ceiva Logic Inc. Learn More About the CEIVA Digital Photo Frame, http://www.ceiva.com/lmore/dpr/dpr.jsp
5. Crabtree, A., Rodden, T., Hemmings, T., Benfort, S.: Finding a Place for UbiComp in the Home. In: Dey, A.K., Schmidt, A., McCarthy, J.F. (eds.) UbiComp 2003. LNCS, vol. 2864, pp. 208–226. Springer, Heidelberg (2003)
6. Cypher, A.: Eager: Programming Repetitive Tasks by Example. In: Proc. CHI 1991, New Orleans, LA, pp. 33–39 (1991)
7. Dey, A.K., Sohn, T., Streng, S., Kodama, J.: iCAP: Interactive Prototyping of Context-Aware Applications. In: Fishkin, K.P., Schiele, B., Nixon, P., Quigley, A. (eds.) PERVASIVE 2006. LNCS, vol. 3968, pp. 254–271. Springer, Heidelberg (2006)
8. Edwards, W.K., Grinter, R.E.: At Home with Ubiquitous Computing: Seven Challenges. In: Abowd, G.D., Brumitt, B., Shafer, S. (eds.) UbiComp 2001. LNCS, vol. 2201, pp. 256–272. Springer, Heidelberg (2001)

9. Edwards, W.K., Newman, M.W., Sedivy, J.Z., Izadi, S., Smith, T.F.: Challenge: recombinant computing and the speakeasy approach. In: Proc. Mobicom 2002, Atlanta, GA, pp. 279–286 (2002)

10. Grinter, R.E., Edwards, W.K., Newman, M.W., Ducheneaut, N.: The Work to Make a Home Network Work. In: Proc. ECSCW 2005, Paris, France, pp. 469–488 (2005)

11. Harper, R. (ed.): Inside the Smart Home: Ideas, Possibilities, and Methods. Springer, London; New York (2003)

12. Humble, J., Crabtree, A., Hemmings, T., Åkesson, K.-P., Koleva, B., Rodden, T., Hansson, P.: Playing with the Bits User-configuration of Ubiquitous Domestic Environments. In: Dey, A.K., Schmidt, A., McCarthy, J.F. (eds.) UbiComp 2003. LNCS, vol. 2864, pp. 256–263. Springer, Heidelberg (2003)

13. Internet Engineering Task Force (IETF) Zeroconf Working Group. Zero Configuration Networking (Zeroconf), http://www.zeroconf.org

14. Kidd, C.D., Orr, R., Abowd, G.D., Atkeson, C.G., Essa, I.A., MacIntyre, B., Mynatt, E., Starner, T.E., Newstetter, W.: The Aware Home: A Living Laboratory for Ubiquitous Computing Research. In: Streitz, N.A., Hartkopf, V. (eds.) CoBuild 1999. LNCS, vol. 1670, pp. 191–198. Springer, Heidelberg (1999)

15. Kurlander, D., Feiner, S.: A History-Based Macro by Example System. In: Proc. UIST 1992, Monterrey, CA, pp. 99–106 (1992)

16. Newman, M.W., Sedivy, J.Z., Neuwirth, C.M., Edwards, W.K., Hong, J.I., Izadi, S., Marcelo, K., Smith, T.F.: Designing for Serendipity: Supporting End-user Configuration of Ubiquitous Computing Environments. In: Proc. DIS 2002, London, England, pp. 147–156 (2002)

17. Nichols, J., Rothrock, B., Chau, D.H., Myers, B.A.: Huddle: Automatically Generating Interfaces for Systems of Multiple Connecting Appliances. In: Proc. UIST 2006, Montreux, Switzerland, pp. 279–288 (2006)

18. Rodden, T., Crabtree, A., Hemmings, T., Koleva, B., Humble, J., Akesson, K.-P., Hansson, P.: Between the dazzle of a new building and its eventual corpse: assembling the ubiquitous home. In: Proc. DIS 2004, Cambridge, MA, pp. 71–80 (2004)

19. Roku Labs. Roku - SoundBridge, http://www.rokulabs.com/products_soundbridge.php

20. TiVo. What is TiVo? http://www.tivo.com/whatistivo/index.html

21. Tolmie, P., Pycock, J., Diggins, T., MacLean, A., Karsteny, A.: Unremarkable Computing. In: Proc. CHI 2002, Minneapolis, MN, USA, pp. 399–406 (2002)

22. Truong, K.N., Huang, E.M., Abowd, G.D.: CAMP: A Magnetic Poetry Interface for End-User Programming of Capture Applications for the Home. In: Davies, N., Mynatt, E.D., Siio, I. (eds.) UbiComp 2004. LNCS, vol. 3205, pp. 143–160. Springer, Heidelberg (2004)

23. UPnP Forum. UPnP Device Architecture. UPnP Forum (2000)

24. Venkatesh, A.: Computers and New Information Technologies for the Home. Communications of the ACM 39(12), 47–54 (1996)

25. Venkatesh, A., Kruse, E., Shih, E.C.-F.: The Networked Home: An Analysis of Current Developments and Future Trends. Cognition, Technology, and Work 5(1), 23–32 (2003)

26. Vitalari, N., Venkatesh, A.: In-home Computing: A Twenty Year Analysis. Telecommunications Policy 11(1), 65–81 (1987)

27. Waldo, J.: The Jini Architecture for Network-centric Computing. Communications of the ACM 42(7), 76–82 (1999)

Overcoming Assumptions and Uncovering Practices: When Does the Public Really Look at Public Displays?

Elaine M. Huang[1, 2], Anna Koster[2], and Jan Borchers[2]

[1] Social Media Research Lab
Motorola Labs
1295 E. Algonquin Road
Schaumburg, Illinois 60196 USA
elainemayhuang@gmail.com
[2] Media Computing Group
RWTH Aachen University
Lehrstuhl Informatik 10
52056 Aachen, Germany
anna.koster@rwth-aachen.de, borchers@cs.rwth-aachen.de

Abstract. This work reports on the findings of a field study examining the current use practices of large ambient information displays in public settings. Such displays are often assumed to be inherently eye-catching and appealing to people nearby, but our research shows that glancing and attention at large displays is complex and dependent on many factors. By understanding how such displays are being used in current, public, non-research settings and the factors that impact usage, we offer concrete, ecologically valid knowledge and design implications about these technologies to researchers and designers who are employing large ambient displays in their work.

Keywords: Large displays, ambient displays, public settings, qualitative studies.

1 Introduction

Large displays have been a topic of research and platform for design and study since the emergence of pervasive computing as a field. Research and design using large displays has been extensive, spanning from private use [6, 10], to semi-public use in locations such as classrooms or workplaces [7, 8, 11, 15], to public use in places such as train stations and cafes [4, 5, 17, 18, 19]. In this latter category, there is a growing body of work that seeks to take advantage of large displays for the purpose of displaying awareness and other types of non-critical information to individuals in public areas. Research prototypes such as the Hello.wall ambient information system [14], and interactive public ambient displays [16] are built upon the idea that passersby will engage in explicit interactions with large display applications after first being drawn to them as ambient displays in the environment. Brignull and Rogers created the Opinionizer prototype that allowed party guests to post opinions to a large display from a nearby laptop [2].

J. Indulska et al. (Eds.): Pervasive 2008, LNCS 5013, pp. 228–243, 2008.

The decision to make use of a large display in designing systems and applications, particularly those intended for public or semi-public use, embodies a certain set of assumptions; it is generally assumed that such displays will tend to attract and hold the attention of passersby and that people in the area will be drawn to read or view content shown on them. It is often also assumed that a large display surface will facilitate and encourage use or viewing by groups or multiple individuals simultaneously. Despite extensive work in creating and evaluating individual research systems within the field of pervasive computing, even some in naturalistic deployments [3, 9, 12], a basic understanding of the effectiveness of using such displays to draw viewers and how people respond to them is still lacking. Systems are designed in part with the goal of attracting viewers and users, but evaluations focus largely only on the actions and responses of people who use them, with less attention to the population that fails to be drawn to the displays or whose interest the system does not capture. Additionally, evaluations tend to focus on individual systems or prototypes, and consequently it has been difficult to draw a comprehensive picture of the general appeal and success of large public displays. Therefore, it is still largely unknown whether large displays hold the appeal and power of attraction that they are often assumed to. To what extent do assumptions about the value of using a large display hold true? Do people look at large displays in public situations, and if so when and under what circumstances? What aspects of the displays and the environment affect attention?

Much of the work of evaluating such displays has been conducted using research prototypes either in a research setting, or limited public deployment. In this work we seek to understand how people use and react to large displays in public settings by examining *current and public* (non-research, non-prototype) large ambient information displays showing non-critical information in a variety of settings. We report on the findings of field observations of 46 large displays located in three mid- to large-sized cities in Western Europe. The aim of this work is to offer researchers and designers concrete, ecologically valid knowledge about the use of large ambient displays in public settings based on actual practices that can be used to ground and inform the design and deployment of future large display information systems.

2 Scope of the Research

In this study, we looked primarily at displays intended to provide ambient or non-urgent content for a variety of purposes, including informational, advertising, artistic, or entertainment purposes in a variety of public settings. This work examines the sorts of large displays and display content readily available for viewing in three fairly "typical" mid- to large- sized cities in Western Europe, comprising of mostly commercial LCD and plasma flat panel displays, some front and rear projected displays, and one large electronic billboard. It should therefore be noted that our research did not include settings similar to New York's Times Square or Tokyo, in which there is a dense population of extremely large electronic signage or for which the displays in the environment are a primary source of attraction for the area. The displays we examined were ubiquitous and integrated into their settings, but are of the type readily found in most cities. We therefore cannot generalize how our findings might apply to more extraordinary display settings, such as Times Square.

This work does not consider "reference displays" that provide critical information, such as airport and train schedule and status displays. Although we did conduct observations in sites that contained such displays, we did not conduct formal observations of them specifically outside of the context of other displays in the environment. Additionally, we did not observe displays that were being used to show conventional television programming such as broadcast news or sporting events. We chose to exclude these displays from our analysis for several reasons. In addition to excluding them for the purposes of maintaining a tractable scope for this work, we also felt that these two classes of displays are novel primarily only in form factor, now using flat panel LCDs or plasma screens rather than conventional monitors or analog signs. However, the content itself and its placement in the environment is not new; this content and information has previously been available in mostly the same style and presentation but on other form factors. The types of ambient information displays on which we focused either added new content to an environment, or presented it in ways that differed significantly from previous incarnations, eg. advertisements with video, animation, or sound as compared to conventional signage.

We observed only "naturally occurring" displays, meaning we did not deploy any displays for the purposes of observations. We were therefore limited to the types and forms of content and environments that were available in these cities. The vast majority of the large displays we observed were non-interactive, with only two exceptions, and our reported findings therefore pertain almost entirely to non-interactive displays. When we refer to interaction with displays, we are therefore not referring to human manipulation of interactive elements of a display, but human action with regards to the display, including glancing at a display while walking by without changing direction or speed, slowing down or stopping to look at a display while walking by, pointing or gesturing toward the display, discussing content of the display with others, or other activity involving the display.

3   Method and Challenges

We performed field observation in 24 sites in three cities in central Europe. Many of these sites contained multiple instances of large displays or different types of large displays. In total we conducted observations of 46 large displays across the sites. We conducted observations in a wide variety of contexts, including train stations, bookstores, a travel agency, a library, main buildings of public universities, a cafeteria, a museum, groceries, banks, and a department store. Each site visit lasted at least 60 minutes, and as long as 180 minutes. Although there were several sites that we were only able to visit a single time, we conducted multiple observation sessions when possible, varying the days or the week or time of day during which we observed.

Because of the public nature of the sites, we did not use video recording, opting instead for field notes and still photographs with a camera phone or small digital camera when appropriate. Although all of the data in the study was collected by two researchers, in all cases except for one, observation sessions were conducted by a single researcher working alone. The exception to this was a single observation session conducted by both researchers to ensure that the observation and note-taking methods were being conducted consistently.

We generally focused attention on a single display within a site throughout an entire observation session, except in cases where displays were in such close proximity that it did not make sense to or was not possible to observe them separately. We attempted to be as inconspicuous as possible, positioning ourselves close enough to the displays to see nearby interactions but far enough so as to not draw attention to the display. In most cases, such as retail locations, the number of people within viewing range of the displays was small (eight or fewer people in the immediate vicinity), or people were merely passing by, allowing us to observe all potential viewers at once for glances at or interaction with a large display.

In particularly crowded locations in which people tended to linger rather than pass through, such as a busy cafeteria during a lunch hour, we found that it was not possible to observe the population as a whole. In these situations, we created a "micro-shadowing" technique that entailed observing an individual or small group of individuals (such as a party sitting at a café table) for 5-10 minutes at a time before moving onto another individual or small group. The vast majority of situations that we observed were sufficiently sparsely populated that we did not need to employ micro-shadowing; it was employed at only four sites. Micro-shadowing made it possible for us to systematically conduct focused observations of behaviors within densely populated sites, but we recognized its limitations for our purposes as well. The more populated a site, the less likely it would be for us to "catch" relevant interactions, such as glancing at, pointing at, or discussing content; we realized that it would be possible using this method to miss important interactions. This method was therefore intended as a way of sampling, rather than a way of gathering comprehensive data about behaviors at a site.

In order to refine our observation method and determine the extent to which it was feasible to gather information in this fashion, we conducted some trial observations. Conducting observations in this fashion proved to be effective in catching glances and interactions, but presented several challenges and had limitations as well. We found that it was generally easy for us to determine when someone turned to look at a display or when someone was reading content. Additionally we were able to observe very brief glances by people who did not turn their heads or otherwise change body position to look at the displays It is, however, very likely that we were not able to catch all such instances of these momentary glances. Additionally, we were aware that the micro-shadowing technique had limitations as well; this method of observation offered insight about how people looked and responded to large displays but could not be used to catch all instances of glancing and interaction in a site.

Our data collection was qualitative in nature, looking for glances, gestures, and other responses to displays as well as details of the content, environment, and nature of the audience. However, whenever possible we did try to count to see roughly how long activities lasted. Additionally, in situations where it was possible we counted how many people looked at a display and how many did not. This was only possible under certain limited circumstances, for example when we were observing a display in a shop window and watching passersby on the sidewalk. It was less possible in places like cafes, department stores, and museums where people moved around in a space and it was not always clear when and how often they were within viewing distance or how many people were in the space. These limitations in our ability to observe and record comprehensively and the variations in traffic and behaviors across sites also make it difficult for us to accurately aggregate or average data across sites. We therefore cannot present any totals for phenomena witnessed across the study, or meaningful averages per site or display. Instead, when possible, we present some of these numbers in reference to single sites or displays; these figures should not be assumed to be hard statistical evidence of general practices, but as illustrative examples to give ideas about frequency of activities and the amount of traffic in an environment and serve to ground the more general conclusions drawn across the 46 sites.

4   Comparative Case Study

Before presenting the general findings of this work, we offer a comparative case study of two observation sites that serves to illustrate some of the ways in which people glance at large displays and factors affecting attention to them. We discuss the general patterns of behavior and environment apparent in this case study in greater depth after describing and comparing these two sites. These examples are revealing in that they serve to illustrate several of the common phenomena and patterns that we observed across the various sites of our study.

Travel Agency A is located within a major train station in a mid-to-large size European city. The office is enclosed in glass and customers enter through a doorway to access the office. The office has a counter before which customers queue to speak with a representative. The walls up until about eye level have racks of travel brochures and there are also freestanding racks in the middle of the space that offer postcards and brochures. On the wall next to where people queue for the counter, there is a flat panel display of approximately 40" in diagonal that displays advertisements for vacations and travel specials, placed above head-level above the racks of brochures. The advertisements consist of professional-looking graphics with supplemental text and are shown "screensaver-style"- displayed for several seconds before switching to a new ad. Some of the advertisements have animation or video, but the majority of them are still images.

Travel Agency B is situated within a large grocery store in a mid-size European city. The office is an alcove with a large opening onto the well-trafficked aisle leading in and out of the grocery store. The "doorway" to the office is almost as wide as the office itself and is completely open during the hours when the travel agency is open, and covered by a pull-down metal gate when the office is closed. At one side of the office is a flat panel display of approximately 40" that is placed on a stand slightly below eye-level and angled outwards to the grocery store. The office contains a desk where a representative sits to help customers and the walls are lined in travel brochures. A large rack of colorful flyers for travel specials stands in front of the opening to the office, and similar flyers are also hung below the display. The display shows advertised travel specials in the form of text listings of destinations and prices over a background with palm trees on it. The specials are shown several to a page in screensaver-style.

Fig. 1. Travel Agency A, a busy enclosed space featuring a large display advertising travel specials and paper travel brochures

Fig. 2. Travel Agency B, an open space off of a well-trafficked grocery story entranceway, featuring colorful photocopied flyers and a large display advertising travel specials

After hour-long observations at both sites, we found that although the displays were similar in content, domain, and intent, there were several marked differences. Because of the nature of the spaces in which they were located, the goals of people n the spaces differed. The people in the viewing area of Travel Agency A were there because they were intentionally seeking travel information; they had made a conscious decision to enter the office and the display was therefore reaching a somewhat targeted audience. In comparison, the display in Travel Agency B was broadcasting information to coincidental passersby- the grocery store customers who were walking by the travel agency on their way out of the store. In both locations, we found that people's glances at the large display were rare and lasted approximately 1-2 seconds. Glances at Travel Agency B were relatively more frequent, with 17 out of 105 people looking towards the display, whereas only three of the approximately 50 people observed in Travel Agency A glanced at the large display. In both cases, people looked at the large display only after first browsing or glancing at brochures and flyers in the area, sometimes for several minutes. In the case of Travel Agency B, the display was angled to face people leaving the store more than to face people entering the store. All glances that we observed were by people on their way out of the store.

5   Findings

In general, we found that the technology and content being widely used was relatively simple. The set of public displays for ambient information that we found deployed throughout these cities consisted almost entirely of non-interactive vertical displays consisting of announcements for services, events, resources, "fun facts," or products, as well as more abstract artistic content. Examples include a schedule of upcoming lectures in a university, advertisements for gift certificates at a department store, announcements of book signings at a bookstore, information about financial planning outside a bank, and abstract black and white video imagery in a university building atrium. Forty of 46 of the displays were plasma or LCD screens ranging from about 40" to 50" in size, as well as a few projected displays and other forms of large screens. Most of the displays showed a cycle of several items with or without animation that played in a loop; items usually consisted of a still image, or an image with some minor animation, such as text sliding onto the screen. Occasionally items included short clips of video. We were at first surprised to find that seven of the displays showed single still images (eg. an advertisement for a newspaper at a bookstore, a picture of an animal at a museum) that did not change, animate, or update the entire duration of our observation.

Over the ten months of observation, we were able to conduct longitudinal observations of seven of the sites, visiting them as many as four times to observe them at different times of the day or week, and see how their content had changed over time. The majority of the displays showed the same types and format of content with regular updates throughout the observation period. Six of the displays that originally showed only a single still image switched to showing a cycle of still advertisements on a loop. Two displays that had originally hung near the checkout counter of a large grocery store were moved to the top and bottom of the store's escalator very shortly after our study began and their content correspondingly changed from showing advertisements for specials in the store to advertisements for small local businesses. Other than these examples, we did not notice any significant changes to the displays other than updates with more current information.

In the following sections, we present our general findings regarding practices surrounding large displays and what factors we have found affect and contribute to these activities.

5.1   Brevity of Glances

In nearly all cases, we found that users paid attention only very briefly to the displays, if at all. When people turned their heads to glance at the display, we found that they usually only looked in the direction of the display for one or two seconds. Beyond that, there were extremely few incidents of people slowing down as they passed the displays, and only a few extremely rare occurrences of people actually stopping or changing their walking path to look at the display content. On very rare occasions people would stop to look for as long as 7 or 8 seconds, e.g., after observing 88 people walk by a large display outside a bank, we saw one instance of this occurring. Displays that showed video content tended to capture the eye somewhat longer; although passersby did not frequently stop to watch the video, many did continue to look at the display for a few more seconds as they walked past, following it with their head until they were too far past it to look at it comfortably. Previous laboratory studies suggest that glances of more than 800ms suggest that the glances are intentional on the part of the passersby [13], which is promising for these technologies from an attentional standpoint. This does, however, suggest that the design of these technologies should take this expectation into consideration. Given the general brevity of glancing, we found that there was often an incongruity between the intent of the display content and people's actual actions. Many of the displays showed a few sentences of text at a time in the form of product description, a fun fact, a description of a service and a corresponding URL, or a description of an upcoming event. Considering what we observed, it is unlikely that passersby are actually reading the content in its entirety. Based on this, it seems that upon looking a display, people make extremely rapid decisions about the value and relevance of large display content, and that content that requires more than a few brief seconds to absorb is likely to be dismissed or ignored by passersby.

Fig. 3. Large displays in positioned well above passersby's heads in a variety of location attract few glances

5.2 Positioning of Displays

Displays were generally either located at approximately eye height or positioned considerably above the head, sometimes near the ceiling (Fig. 3). Both of these positions seemed intended to draw attention, the former likely intended to catch the eye easily and the latter likely intended to more visible from a distance or from a greater range of locations within the space or by more people simultaneously.

Our observations showed that the eye-position was far more effective at attracting glances from passersby, while people rarely looked up at displays located above the head. This contrast is apparent in the travel agency case study, and held true in general across the sites that we observed. For example, in one department store, there were seven large plasma displays located throughout the building, mounted at inconsistent heights, all showing similar content about products and services available at the store. Though glances at the displays were all generally brief, lasting about 1-2 seconds, those items located at eye level received a fair number of glances, while we did not observe anyone look up at the displays mounted near the ceiling at this site. Several other sites, such as a bookstore and a university building, offered the same opportunity to observe the same type of display showing the same content at different heights, and confirmed this finding. In another case, projected displays high up in a well-trafficked atrium of a public university building that displayed information about upcoming talks and events attracted almost no glances from passersby, despite being very physically large. During a one-hour observation period, we watched over 100 passersby, and saw only four turn their heads up to look at the content. Only one person actually paused to read the content for more than 1 or 2 seconds. The finding that displays were likely to attract more attention at eye-level than high up seemed to apply regardless of whether the content was for advertising, education, artistic, or informative purposes, as well as regardless of whether it was image, text, video, or some combination thereof.

Fig. 4. A display located significantly below eye-level unsurprisingly receives almost no glances and is often obscured from sight by passersby

Incidentally, we observed only one instance of a large display positioned significantly below eye-level; this display was outside a Middle Eastern restaurant and showed video of the Middle East as well as of Middle Eastern food preparation. This display not only received no glances during our observations, it was often obscured from sight by people in the area (Fig. 4).

5.3 Content Type

The types of content we observed on display were varied, including art, educational content, advertising, fun facts, news and current events. Advertising was most common but took many forms, from ads for local businesses, products, upcoming events, or services. It should be noted that advertisement was not always in the form of attempts to sell goods and services to consumers; they also included digital ads for free movies at universities, upcoming talks and lectures, and the existence of a rooftop garden and kids' reading room for customer use in a bookstore. In general, our observations did not offer any conclusive evidence that people were more likely to pay attention to certain type of content over another. Findings regarding brevity of glances, positioning of displays, and the other factors described below applied to most of the different types of content we observed on the displays.

5.4 Content Format and Dynamics

Although we were not able to draw any concrete conclusions regarding how people's attention varied based on types of content, we did find that format of content played a role in people's responses. In general, people found video to be more attractive than text, animated text, or still images. While glances at video often proved to be brief as well, we saw more instances of people craning their heads to look at the displays to walk by or on a few occasions stopping briefly, while they rarely did so for the sake of reading text. In one example, an advertisement on a display outside of a bank showed a short movie clip of a biplane flying over a landscape. A man fixed his gaze on the display while walking by and eventually stopped for 3 or 4 seconds to watch the video. When the display content switched to showing animated text, the man walked away. We witnessed this pattern on other occasions as well; when the content of a display was a mixture of video and still or other forms of content, people tended to glance less during the moments when video was not being displayed. Moments when video content switched to other forms of content also corresponded to people turning away from the displays or ceasing to look at them. Additionally we witnessed some rare instances of long engagement with video; an electronics shop had a large display in a window that showed colorful video clips of bouncing balls, animals, and other subjects of a more artistic than informative nature. On two occasions, we witnessed people who were walking by while eating fast food stop in front of this display and watch the video until they were finished eating before continuing walking. We observed no similar activity with other forms of content on large displays.

Interestingly, given the choice of digital information in the form of still content that changed periodically or information in the form of physical artifacts such as conventional signage or brochures, people generally were more drawn to the physical signage and spent longer looking at it, as illustrated in the travel agency comparative scenario. We witnessed a similar phenomenon in a university building, where students would spend time browsing paper ads for upcoming events on a physical bulletin board, but did not watch a nearby large display that showed a cycle of still advertisements for upcoming events. It seems that while people are drawn to spend several seconds watching video on a large display, they sooner look at still content on paper than on the digital displays. Our observations lead us to believe that this is because people prefer a *dynamic* experience while engaging with information and content in such settings. Video offers a steadily changing stream of content, and we observed that when browsing paper flyers or bulletin boards in the vicinity of large displays, people browsed at varied rates, skipping past items that were not of interested and focusing longer on others, maintaining control over what they looked at. Screensaver-style information displays that imposed a temporal aspect on browsing over which people had no control rarely caught or held the attention of people in the vicinity.

5.5 Catching the Eye

One assumption often made about large displays in the decision to employ one is that they are eye-catching and naturally attract attention. In our observations, however, we found that people were more likely to look at them if there was something else nearby that caught their attention first. For example, a bookstore window display contained a large display with advertisements, some soccer merchandise, and a poster with some photographs of soccer players on it. In all but two instances of glancing at the display, passersby first stopped to look either at the poster or the merchandise before turning their attention to the display. At another site, a long case facing outwards from a bank had a row of decorative household items, followed by a large display showing advertisements for bank services. We observed approximately 80 passersby and found that nearly all of the people who glanced at the display came from the same direction; they started by looking at the items while walking by and then glanced at the display at the end. We did not notice the reciprocal behavior in the other direction; while people walking in the other direction often looked at the household items, their attention was rarely caught first by the display. This suggests that large displays may not be as eye-catching as they are often assumed to be, and play a secondary role in attracting attention when in the vicinity of other objects.

While it appears that other items in the area of a large display draw the eye to the display, we also observed that this was dependent to some extent on the arrangement of the artifacts. Items needed to be arranged such that they were either very close to another, or along some contiguous path of sight based on the direction in which the passersby were moving, as illustrated above in the example of the bank. Furthermore, the role of height once again came into play; even when displays and objects were placed near each other, having them at differing heights did not encourage viewing. For example, in a department store, a set of mannequins were placed such that the clothing being sold was at about eye-height, but displays placed directly over them showing fashion videos and advertising services and specials at the store were not viewed by the people who looked at the clothing. In the case of Travel Agency A, although brochures were placed directly below the display, the display itself received little attention from people looking at the brochures. In the case of Travel Agency B, people walking by looked at the flyers, and then sometimes looked at the display, which was nearby albeit a few feet away, positioned at roughly the same height, and along the direction of movement of the passersby.

5.6 The "Captive" Audience

In our study, we observed that there were some situations in which people faced a display for an extended period of time as a result of social norms and practices, held "captive" before a display. Examples of such a situation included displays that were located at the top and bottom of escalators; because it is standard practice to face the direction of the escalator's movement, they were therefore also standing and facing the display while coming towards it. In several instances, a large display was located on a back wall behind a store cashier counter, such that people waiting in line to pay for items were facing the display as a result of the accepted social practice of facing forward while queuing. We found, however, that these situations did not promote more glancing or longer glances, even though the audience was "captive." In the case of one particular bookstore, displays behind a cashier did not advertise products for sale, but rather displayed literature trivia and "fun facts" as well as information about upcoming free events and free services at the store. Although the content was colorful and attractively designed, the display received almost no glances from customers waiting in line; they instead focused their attention on other merchandise nearby, such as small toys on the counter, the items in their hands, or on watching the cashiers ring up other customers.

Interestingly, in one department store, we noticed that some displays at ends of escalators did receive occasional lingering glances. These were small black and white displays that showed the content of the security video; i.e., real-time video of that particular escalator. This speaks again to the power of video to attract attention, perhaps in conjunction with the "captive" audience, and as well to a potential interest in a display that shows the viewer back to himself. Works such as [1] have touched upon the appeal of using images of the viewer on large displays, and may warrant further investigation as a technique for drawing attention to public ambient information displays.

5.7 Small Displays vs. Large Displays

In a few locations, we had the opportunity to observe how people responded differently to the same content on different sized displays in public locations. Interestingly, we found that people seemed to linger at smaller displays for a longer period of time. In a university setting, a building entrance hall had a large display showing event information and building information on the wall. This hall also had some small ATM-type kiosks with conventional-sized screens showing this same information. The smaller screens were interactive, also giving access to a university information system. But in addition to observing people actively interacting with the kiosks, we found that people waiting in the lobby also stood at the kiosks and watched the changing content, whereas they did not do this with the corresponding large display. Similarly, in an exhibit in another university building atrium, a black and white artistic video was being displayed on both an extremely large projected display and a standard-sized iMac computer. Both of these setups had a leather bench before them where people could sit and watch the video. With the large display, we found that passersby in the atrium would occasionally turn their heads to glance at the display, and people occasionally sat on the bench briefly, but not to look at the display. The small display did not attract many visitors either, but we found that those who did sit down generally sat for an extended period, watching for several minutes at a time (Fig. 5).

Fig. 5. People in an atrium stop to sit and watch video on a conventional monitor although the same content is available nearby on a very large projected display with similar seating

These observations suggest that small displays may encourage or invite prolonged viewing in public spaces to a greater extent than large displays, possibly because people are more used to or more comfortable with looking at small screens for a extended period of time. The use of a smaller display may also create a more private or intimate setting within the greater public setting that leads a viewer to feel less exposed and therefore encourages a longer interaction and greater comfort with displays within a public space.

6 Implications, Design Recommendations, and Conclusions

This work presents a broad picture of behaviors that occur around large displays deployed within a variety of public settings for a wide range of purposes. We have uncovered findings regarding how their use is affected by the format of their content and situation and presented suggestions for increasing the visibility of displays and improving the match between people's behavior and content. It should, however, be noted that there remains research to be done within the field of pervasive computing on how experiences with such displays should be tailored depending on the specific intent of the displays. For the purposes of brand awareness, for example, market studies have shown that brief viewing may be sufficient for increasing awareness and sales of a product [20]. Product advertisement, however, is merely one of many potential purposes for which such displays are being designed for research and commercial deployments. For some of the more information intensive content we saw in our study, such as talk abstracts or artistic installations, the target user experience may go beyond short glances. Below we present design recommendations based on the general findings of our study; we suggest that these recommendations be taken within the context of the intended purpose of the application.

The findings we presented above generally suggest that attention to large displays in public settings is difficult to attract and hold. Despite this, our observations have revealed situations in which people are more likely to look at them and brought to attention the factors that affect attention to them. In the table below, we explicitly summarize some of the design recommendations that stem from our findings:

Table 1. Summary of recommendations for the design of large public displays

Finding	Recommendations
Brevity of glances	• Assume that viewers are not willing to spend more than a few seconds to determine whether a display is of interest • If the intent of the content is to be informative, present it in such a way that the most important information be determined in 2-3 seconds • Avoid using more than minimal text; even two or three brief sentences are not likely to be read
Positioning of displays	• When possible, position displays close to eye-height to encourage glances • If theft or vandalism are concerns, consider other ways to protect a display or make it inaccessible than putting it above arm's reach
Content format and dynamics	• Make content continually dynamic to keep user attention longer • Avoid abrupt changes in content to encourage continued viewing • Design to give users some degree of control over what information to view
Catching the eye	• Consider the direction of people's movement within a space when deciding where to situate displays • When choosing where to situate displays, take advantage of other objects in the environment to draw attention to displays, rather than relying on the large display to be the eye-catcher • When possible, consider ways in which the area surrounding the large display can be enhanced to maximize attention and increase the chances of glancing
Small displays vs. large displays	• Design to balance feelings of exposure and privacy within a public space by considering multiple display sizes and how they affect the viewer experience, perception, and comfort.

In addition to the implications and recommendations presented here, the more general recommendation that we can draw from this study is that in order to design content and applications that are most likely to serve their intended purpose, setting and audience should be taken into account whenever possible while creating the content, application and presentation. While this conclusion may seem to be of an obvious nature, it seems clear from our observations that the vast majority of large displays in public areas were designed with an eye towards who the target audience was and what the intent of the display was, but with less an a focus on how people would be moving within a space and how other activities within or aspects of the space might affect use of the display. The choice of specific setting within an environment appears to have been decoupled from the design process, thus yielding suboptimal situations, lower utility, and less attention.

The results of this work suggest that the ultimate position and context of the display should be taken into account during the design phase rather than after the fact. Additionally the design of the context itself can have substantial impact on how much attention the displays receive, and when possible, it should be considered how the surrounding environment can be designed or taken advantage of to draw attention to the displays, rather than assuming that the displays themselves will attract passersby. Finally, content itself should be carefully designed in such a way that does not assume that people are willing to engage for more than a few seconds before deciding whether they are interested; non-urgent, ambient information should be able to be conveyed at a glance.

Acknowledgments

The authors would like to extend appreciation to the Alexander von Humboldt Foundation for supporting this work. Thanks as well to Khai Truong and Eric Lee for their feedback and assistance on earlier drafts of this paper, and the Pervasive 2008 reviewers and committee for their valuable suggestions and feedback.

References

1. Agamanolis, S.: Designing Displays for Human Connectedness. In: O'Hara, K., Perry, M., Churchill, E., Russell, D. (eds.) Public and Situated Displays: Social and Interactional Aspects of Shared Display Technologies, Kluwer, Dordrecht (2003)
2. Brignull, H., Rogers, Y.: Enticing People to Interact with Large Public Displays in Public Spaces. In: Proceedings of INTERACT 2003 (2003)
3. Brignull, H., Izadi, S., Fitzpatrick, G., Rogers, Y., Rodden, T.: The Introduction of a Shared Interactive Surface into a Communal Space. In: Proceedings of CSCW 2004, pp. 49–58 (2004)
4. Carter, S., Churchill, E., Denoue, L., Helfman, J., Nelson, L.: Digital Graffiti: Public Annotation of Multimedia Content. In: Extended Abstracts of CHI 2004, pp. 1207–1210 (2004)
5. Churchill, E., Nelson, L., Denoue, L.: Multimedia Fliers: Informal Information Sharing With Digital Community Bulletin Boards. In: Proceedings of Communities and Technologies (2003)

6. Czerwinski, M., Smith, G., Regan, T., Meyers, B., Robertson, G., Starkweather, G.: Toward Characterizing the Productivity Benefits of Very Large Displays. In: Proceedings of INTERACT 2003 (2003)

7. Fass, A., Forlizzi, J., Pausch, R.: MessyDesk and MessyBoard: Two Designs Inspired by the Goal of Improving Human Memory. In: Proceedings of Designing Interactive Systems 2002, pp. 303–311 (2002)

8. Huang, E., Mynatt, E.: Semi-Public Displays for Small, Co-Located Groups. In: Proceedings of CHI 2003, pp. 49–56 (2003)

9. Huang, E.M., Mynatt, E.D., Trimble, J.P.: Displays in the Wild: Understanding the Dynamics and Evolution of a Display Ecology. In: Proceedings of the Fourth International Conference on Pervasive Computing 2006 (2006)

10. MacIntyre, B., Mynatt, E., Voida, S., Hansen, K., Tullio, J., Corso, G.: Support For Multitasking and Background Awareness Using Interactive Peripheral Displays. In: Proceedings of UIST 2001, pp. 41–50 (2001)

11. McCarthy, J., Costa, T., Liongosari, E.: UniCast, OutCast & GroupCast: Three Steps Toward Ubiquitous, Peripheral Displays. In: Abowd, G.D., Brumitt, B., Shafer, S. (eds.) UbiComp 2001. LNCS, vol. 2201, Springer, Heidelberg (2001)

12. McCarthy, J., McDonald, D., Soroczak, S., Nguyen, D., Rashid, A.: Augmenting the Social Space of an Academic Conference. In: Proceedings of CSCW 2004 (2004)

13. Müller, H.J., Rabbitt, P.M.A.: Reflexive and voluntary orienting of visual attention: Time course of activation and resistance to interruption. Journal of Experimental Psychology: Human Perception and Performance 15, 315–330 (1989)

14. Prante, T., Röcker, C., Streitz, N., Stenzel, R., Magerkurth, C., Alphen, D., Plewe, D.A.: Hello Wall - Beyond Ambient Displays. In: Dey, A.K., Schmidt, A., McCarthy, J.F. (eds.) UbiComp 2003. LNCS, vol. 2864, Springer, Heidelberg (2003)

15. Terrell, G.B., McCrickard, D.S.: Enlightening a Co-Located Community with a Semi-Public Notification System. In: Proceedings of CSCW 2006 (2006)

16. Vogel, D., Balakrishnan, R.: Interactive Public Ambient Displays: Transitioning from Implicit to Explicit, Public to Personal, Interaction with Multiple Users. In: Proceedings of UIST 2005, pp. 137–146 (2005)

17. http://www.infocooler.com/

18. http://newsroom.accenture.com/press_kits.cfm?presskit_id=34

19. http://www.nova.ethz.ch/

20. http://www.economist.com/business/displaystory.cfm?story_id=10431119

Gaming Tourism: Lessons from Evaluating REXplorer, a Pervasive Game for Tourists

Rafael Ballagas[1], André Kuntze[2], and Steffen P. Walz[3]

[1] Nokia Research Center, Palo Alto, CA, USA
tico.ballagas@nokia.com
[2] RWTH Aachen University,
Media Computing Group, Aachen, Germany
[3] ETH Zurich, Computer Aided Architechtural Design Group,
Zurich, Switzerland
walz@arch.ethz.ch

Abstract. REXPLORER is a mobile, pervasive spell-casting game designed for tourists of Regensburg, Germany. The game creates player encounters with spirits (historical figures) that are associated with significant buildings in an urban setting. A novel mobile interaction mechanism of "casting a spell" (making a gesture by waving a mobile phone through the air) allows the player to awaken and communicate with a spirit to continue playing the game. The game is designed to inform visitors about history in a fun manner. The results of a formative evaluation are explored to inform the design of future serious pervasive games.

1 Introduction

Games have the unique ability to captivate and engage their audience. The field of serious games leverages this ability to help inspire, educate, and train their target user base [19,23]. In REXPLORER, the serious game concept is applied to the domain of tourism, combining education and entertainment to help visitors engage with the history and culture of their destination through location-based gameplay.[1]

REXPLORER is specifically targeted at the "tour guides are boring" crowd, focusing on tourists ranging in age from 15-30 that grew up playing video games at home. It is not designed as a tour guide replacement, but instead as a new way to acclimate tourists to their surroundings and raise interest in the history and culture of the city. REXPLORER is a part of the Regensburg Experience (REX) museum in Regensburg, Germany, extending the visitor experience beyond the museum walls. Regensburg is a UNESCO world heritage site and the best-preserved medieval city in Germany, mostly untouched by widespread bombings in WWII. The game was launched in Regensburg as a permanent tourist offering in July of 2007.

---

[1] A video overview of REXPLORER is available at: http://wiki.caad.arch.ethz.ch/Research/REXplorer

J. Indulska et al. (Eds.): Pervasive 2008, LNCS 5013, pp. 244–261, 2008.

2   System Overview

The game operates as a rental service; tourists rent a special device (see Fig. 1) from the tourist information office for a 12 Euro fee.[2] Through an short introductory movie, players are informed that the device is a paranormal activity detector that communicates with spirits in the historical city center of Regensburg.

Players can awaken and communicate with spirits by casting spells. A spell is invoked by waving the wand-like detector through the air. The gesture recognition process is supported primarily through camera-based motion estimation as in [2,25]. As motion samples are collected, they are rendered to the screen to allow players to see their gesture progress (see Fig. 2). REXPLORER is the first pervasive and mobile game to enable magic wand style spell-casting.

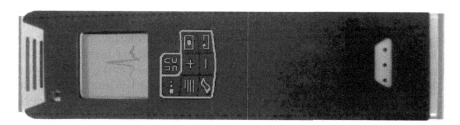

Fig. 1. The REXPLORER "detector" consists of a Nokia N70 mobile phone and a GPS receiver packaged together in a protective shell. A soft and stretchable textile overlay with a zipper on the back transforms the standard phone keypad into an 8-key game interface. For example, the camera button is indicated by a small camera icon, covers two physical phone keys (key '3' and '6') to create larger buttons on the simplified keypad.

Fig. 2. The player casts a spell by drawing a magic symbol in the air. Gesture progress is indicated to the player through both audio and visual feedback.

---

[2] During an initial promotional period, the service rented for six Euros. Discounts are also provided for students.

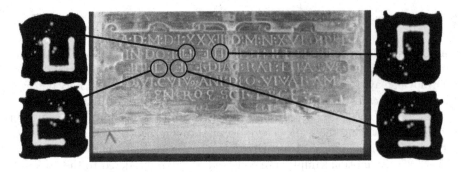

Fig. 3. A child's gravestone inscribed with a secret language serves as inspiration for the gesture vocabulary of REXPLORER

The spell vocabulary consist of symbols inspired by a mysterious secret language from a historical artifact. The artifact is a gravestone (see Fig. 3) located in the Regensburg cathedral, and archeologists have not yet been able to decipher the text. Drawing the symbols in the air excites medieval elements (wind, fire, earth, and water) and establishes a communication channel to the spiritual world. Players are introduced to the symbols and spell-casting through the instructional movie in the tourist information center at the time of rental. Additionally to facilitate game play in the city, a souvenir brochure (see Fig. 4) is provided to the players that contains a map, and brief game instructions. The brochure also contains a reference legend explaining the functionality of the buttons on the detector, as well as gesture symbols and the elements to which they correspond.

During the game, players encounter different spirits located at significant buildings. The spirits reveal their "cliff hanger" stories related to important events and periods in the city's history, and send the players on different quests. Points are rewarded for encountering new characters and completing quests, thereby influencing players movement by leading them from site A to B.

As the players progress through the game, their interactions, pictures, and GPS path are recorded and stored on the mobile phone flash memory card. When the device is returned to the tourist information office at the end of the game, the player data is automatically uploaded to a custom blog server using MetaWeblog APIs [26] (see Fig. 5).[3] The tourists are then emailed a URL of a souvenir travel blog customized to show their personal experiences in the city. Travel blogging is an emerging trend [4], and the automatic construction of the REXPLORER travel blog lowers the threshold of documenting the trip. The blog uses Google Map APIs[4] to display the users' path and the points of interest they visited on an interactive map (see Fig. 6). Players are also encouraged to take

---

[3] The blog server can support real-time blog generation by communicating directly with the phone, but at the time of deployment, costs of mobile data plans pushed the rental fee higher than our desired price-point.

[4] http://code.google.com/apis/maps/index.html

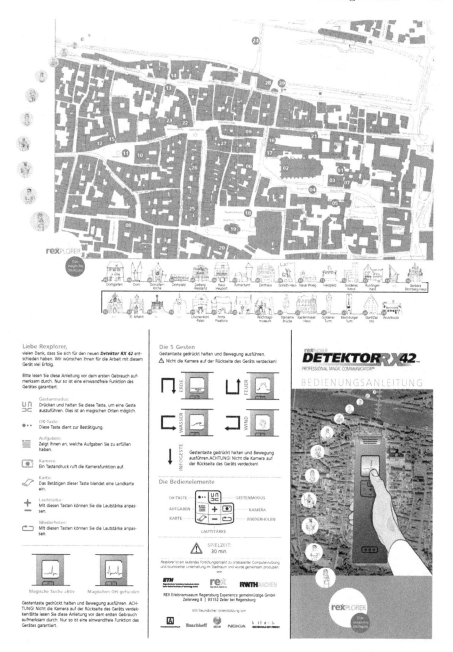

Fig. 4. (Top) The front of the souvenir brochure has a large map with points of interest marked. (Bottom) The back of the brochure displays a legend for device buttons and gestures. The brochure is distributed with the detector during the rental process.

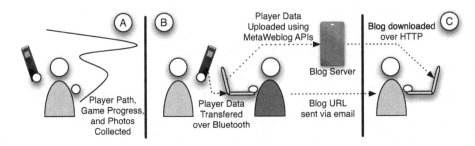

Fig. 5. A system overview of the REXplorer blogging process. (A) While playing the game, the system records the players' photographs, game progress, and path. (B) At the end of the game, the player returns the rental detector, and his data is transferred via bluetooth to a computer in the tourist information office and then automatically uploaded using MetaWeblog APIs to the blog server. A URL to the newly created blog page is then sent via email to the player. (C) After the player returns home, he can review his game experiences and easily share his memories with family and friends.

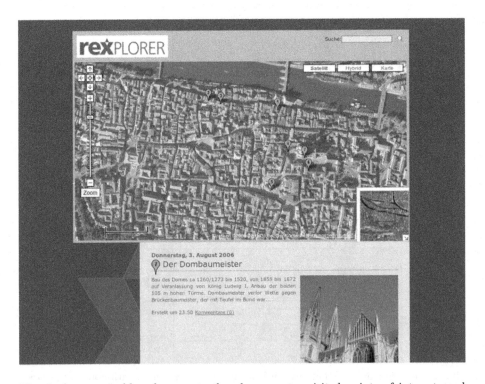

Fig. 6. A souvenir blog documents the player route, visited points of interest, and player-generated content (tourist photographs). The blog is accessed from home through a standard desktop web browser after the visit. Clicking on a point of interest in the map brings the visitor to in-depth historical information with external links and a bibliography for them to explore and learn more.

pictures during their visit and these photos automatically appear on the blog with their location marked in the map. The blog provides a nice summary of their experience to share with friends and family. Perhaps more importantly, it helps players to explore history in more depth after their visit by providing summary text, images of each site, as well as links to further historical information.[5]

2.1 Gameplay Scenario

Anna and Peter are a young couple visiting Regensburg on a day trip. At the tourist information office, they notice REXPLORER advertised as a city-experience game, and decide to try it out. They rent the detector (see Fig. 1) and a souvenir brochure directly at the tourist information office. Then, they are shown a three-minute movie introducing them to the paranormal activity, the mysterious symbols, and their task as a scientific assistant to help solve the mysteries of the city.

As they leave to start playing, Anna is holding the detector and Peter is in charge of the brochure. They turn the corner and reach their first historical building. Anna selects the building through a device menu[6] to tune the detector to the right frequency. In response, the detector emits a heartbeat vibration indicating the location has paranormal activity. From the introductory movie, Anna knows that there is a spirit here that she can awaken by casting a spell.

Peter flips over the brochure map, looks at the different gestures, and points to "wind" for Anna to try. After glancing at the legend to get an idea for the gesture shape, Anna holds down the gesture button and waves the device through the air, just as she saw in the introductory video. As she moves the device, she sees her gesture progress on the detector screen (see Fig. 2) and hears the gesture mode audio sample. Once the gesture is complete, she releases the button, and a short "tornado" video with audio playback confirms that she has successfully completed the wind gesture.

A figure is shown on the detector screen and a spirit begins to speak to the players:

> REXPLORER! *It's nice to see you. I am a salt trader. People like me used horses to pull heavy ships, full of expensive salt, up the river Danube to Regensburg until around 1820 A.D. Usually, the excursions last 4 weeks at a time. Yep, my life is tough and dangerous. Thieves plague the salt trading routes, but I have a loving wife who constantly*

---

[5] Example blog (in german): http://www.rexplorer.de/blog/johannes27/

[6] In the original design, location tracking was used to automatically activate the excited heartbeat of the detector upon approaching the buildings. After months of trying to get GPS to work satisfactorily in the medieval urban canyons, followed by unsuccessful attempts at recruiting local store owners to host bluetooth beacons, we finally resorted to manual location selection to create a reliable user experience that we could launch. It should be noted that the GPS is still used for players to check their current location, to record the traversed path for the blog, and to add location tags to the players' images.

prays in a nearby church for my safe return. Only the fire of her love keeps me alive. Would you be willing to deliver a message to my woman? Then show me the appropriate gesture.

After listening carefully to the text, Anna understands that she must cast the "fire" spell to accept the quest. She looks at Peter and asks: "Which one was fire, again?". Peter shows her the gesture legend, and Anna successfully completes the fire gesture to accept the quest. Then she hears:

I thank you from the bottom of my heart! It pleases me that you are willing to deliver my love letter to my wife at the St. Ulrich Church near the Cathedral. Oh! My colleagues are already waiting for me at the river. Good luck! Take care of yourselves.

Peter looks on the brochure map and quickly finds the next location. He looks to Anna and asks: "Where are we now?" She presses the map button on the detector which shows them their current position and the destination of their open quest. After orienting themselves, they start walking towards the St. Ulrich Church to complete their mission.

3 Related Work

The role playing game Frequency 1550[7] blends Internet and mobile phone gameplay with location-based puzzles to supplement the city history curriculum at the Montessori school in Amsterdam. Specifically Frequency 1550 is of interest in our context, as it demonstrates how to convey site specific knowledge with the help of game mechanics. Both De Souza e Silva & Delacruz [11] and Thomas [21] describe a number of other relevant projects, examining potential uses of pervasive gaming for educational purposes. These theoretical approaches are interesting for the REXPLORER gameplay, which aims at conveying knowledge about touristic sites.

Similar to REXPLORER, site-specific narratives and spatial storytelling - that is, connecting site A with site B through a story - are eminent features in both History Unwired [14] and "The Voices of Oakland" [13]. History Unwired was tested during the 2005 Biennale of Contemporary Art in Venice around one of Venice's less-traveled neighborhoods, involving location-aware smartphones and interactive art pieces at sites which are embedded into the tour. Voices of Oakland provides an audio-based mixed reality experience for a cemetary, bringing the stories of the cemetary inhabitants to life in a structured and guided fashion. History Unwired and Voices of Oakland are not games, but innovative and entertaining linear walking tours. Contrary to REXPLORER, the the designers of these systems decided for linear storytelling, where users had few opportunity to "choose their own adventure", which is an important feature in the non-linear gameplay of REXPLORER.

---

[7] http://freq1550.waag.org

Archeoguide [22] leverages user context, like many other context-aware tour guides [1,10], to enhance the tourist experience by finding information relevant to the current tourist situation. The articles and audio commentary available are informative and can be accessed in a non-linear fashion, but fall short of creating an engaging dramatic narrative such as History Unwired, Voices of Oakland, or REXPLORER.

Sharing the Square [8] allows city visitors to share their experiences through photographs, voice, and location information to other remote participants. Although the system did recommend online media related to the site, the focus of the project was around sociability and collaboration around physical places. It also did not provide site-specific dramatic narrative like REXPLORER and others.

Norrie et al. [18] use interactive paper maps to help tourists during festivals in the city of Edinburgh, Scotland. Tourist pull up audio information about festival events, by pointing at them using a special digital pen in a printed calendar or pointing at the various venues directly on the printed map. REXPLORER does use maps, not as a way to directly access content, but as a navigation tool. REXPLORER uses both a plain paper map and an on-screen digital map to leverage the strengths of each in terms of navigation.

In an educational game, Savannah [5], children role play lions, practicing hunting, and thereby learning about prey behavior in wildlife habitats. Environmental Detectives [16] embeds high schoolers into an authentic situation where teams of players representing different interests have to locate the source of pollution by drilling "wells" and "sampling" with handheld computers.

Our own previous work on REXPLORER has examined the persuasive elements of pervasive games [24]. Additionally, the player-centered design process used to develop REXPLORER is examined in [3] documenting the stages of prototyping activities used over the the three year development effort. This paper is the first to systematically evaluate REXPLORER from a human factors standpoint.

4   Evaluation

During the design of REXplorer, we carried out playability tests designed for formative evaluation. This paper focuses on the formative evaluation of an advance prototype of the game prior to its release. Formative evaluation [12] helps identify problems in the interface so that they can be corrected as a part of a human-centered iterative design process. The insights gained from this evaluation motivated significant design changes in REXPLORER. These insights can also help inform the design of future pervasive games and interfaces for the tourist domain.

The evaluation was structured as an interactive play session followed by a focus group interview (sometimes referred to as a Product-Interactive Focus Group [17]). We had 18 participants in our study between the ages of 18-45. 2 participants played REXPLORER alone, and the rest played in pairs resulting in a total of 10 playing sessions. The playing sessions were coordinated such that

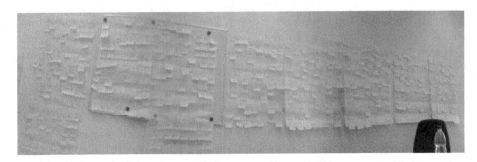

Fig. 7. Affinity diagram with 1000+ direct quotes from play sessions and focus group interviews

2 playing sessions would happen concurrently and then the different groups of players would come together at the end for a focus group interview (consisting of 3-4 participants). We videotaped all 10 play sessions and the corresponding 5 focus group interviews.

The analysis of the video data was performed using grounded theory affinity analysis [7,15]. Relevant direct quotes from the video material of both the playability test and the focus group interview were transcribed and transferred to a sticky note. A bottom-up affinity diagram was constructed by identifying and clustering similar or related items (see Fig. 7). The clusters helped identify opportunities for design improvement, as well as strengths in the current design.

The affinity method originates from the field of anthropology [20] as an inductive method for the holistic integration of qualitative data, and is useful to examine the interrelationships between phenomena. Beyer and Holzblatt [7] adapted and popularized the affinity method (sometimes referred to the B-H method) in the design and HCI communities. The B-H method suggests the placement of abstract research observations on individual sticky notes to assist affinity clustering. Grounded theory affinity analysis, on the other hand, attempts stay as close as possible to the raw data and delay interpretation or abstraction until after affinity clustering. During grounded theory analysis, direct user quotes are placed on sticky notes without any abstraction from the researcher. The grounded theory method has been used successfully to evaluate mobile technology prototypes, such as in the work of Bentley and Metcalf [6].

The original interviews were conducted in German, the quotations listed below are translated by the authors. The names of the original subjects have been changed.

5   Results

The findings are presented in themes directly derived from affinity clusters identified during analysis.

5.1   Focus of Attention

One of our explicit design goals of REXPLORER was to keep the focus of the players' attention on the beautifully-preserved medieval architecture and not on the handheld device. We made several design decisions to support this goal. The game feedback was explicitly designed to be audio-centric. Some visuals were used to complement the audio, but we tried to deemphasize these by (1) selecting a device with a small screen format and (2) selecting a motif that consisted of black and white, rough outline sketches with few fine details to give the players an impression at a glance. As a side note, the high contrast of the monochrome representation also promoted visibility on the screen in bright sunshine situations.

The players behavior during the play session (PS) showed mixed success in this regard, for example in PS3 and PS1 the players tended to glance around the environment while listening carefully to the text. However, Gabi from PS4 stated: "It was a shame that we had to concentrate so much on the display to listen to what the little people had to say." This statement indicates that the player still felt obligated to look at the screen despite our design efforts.

We also noticed that some users got so immersed into the game experience that they neglected standard safety precautions. One group stumbled into a clearly marked construction zone, because they were both so focused on the handheld display. Hannah and Irene from PS5 perceived the play session as a competition between the teams and started running from building to building to fulfill more quests and score more points. At one point, they ran in front of oncoming traffic, almost getting run over. We did not explicitly intend competition, but of course, the scoring mechanism in the game hints at possibility of competition. Luckily no one was hurt, but the incident highlights the potential dangers that game immersion can bring while in a public setting. The main takeaway for future pervasive games is that player safety issues can arise due to time-constrained competition or player immersion.

One design suggestion that resulted from the safety issues was to remove the time constraint in the game so that people didn't feel rushed. However, the time constraint exists because of the limited battery life on the device. Bluetooth, and heavy camera use are severe battery drains, but the features that these technologies supported were deemed too critical to sacrifice. Instead, safety warning statements were included in the introductory movie and the handheld map. It should also be noted that most of the REXPLORER game area resides on pedestrian-only areas of the city, but there are a few important historical buildings that are on busy streets.

5.2   Non-linear Game

Another way that REXPLORER differentiates itself from a standard city tour is that the players have freedom to choose their own path and their own pace. This aspect of the game was frequently brought up during the focus group interviews. Ebony stated, "It is great that I have the freedom to choose the flow of the game... I can take a break whenever I want." Danny imagined that he could do daily things between playing like "buying cigarettes or stay put for a little while."Adriane took a break to buy an ice cream and then kept on playing, ice cream in hand, without any problems. These statements demonstrate that competition wasn't an important part of the experience to all players, which is an important takeaway for future pervasive game design.

The path selection aspect was also important to allow players to develop strategies in how they fulfilled their quests. Jackleen stated, "When we wanted to complete the first quest, we walked by the [Golden] tower. At that point, we decided to finish our assignment first, instead of taking on a new one. Then at some point we had enough, because the game kept sending us so far away, and we didn't want to go so far. Then we decided to complete a different quest instead." Here the players recognized that they could more efficiently plan their paths by taking on numerous quests. During their playing session, Hannah and Irene made use of the status button to view the open quests where they discovered that they had two open quests in adjacent locations, so they chose to head that direction first.

Another important discovery from this session was that we discovered a negative phenomenon of what we termed the *ping-pong* effect; that is, with some quest ordering, it was possible to get assigned a quest that sent the player back to a location that they directly came from. Leading players back around areas they had already seen was intended, thereby trying to help them orient themselves in a city and recognizing markers and milestones. However, the phenomenon of direct backtracking happened much more often than we had anticipated, partly because there are multiple possible outgoing quests at each station and the random selection of the assigned quest. For example, during their playing session the Irene stated "Oh, we need to go back there." and Hannah exclaimed "Oh noooo!". Hannah raised the point again in the focus group interview after the game "It was really dumb to go up one street and then have to turn around and go directly back - that really disturbed us... because we were just there." In a different interview, Danny brought up a similar point, "As a tourist, it can get really nerve-racking when you are always sent back and forth - 5 or 6 times within a 500 m radius for an hour." In response, we made changes to the quest network to try to minimize the occurrence of ping-pong routes. Another design suggestion that resulted from this observation was to use the quest history in determining the issued quest, but the quest network changes seemed sufficient to address the problem.

5.3   Balancing Education and Entertainment

The fundamental goal in creating the game was to inform players about the history and culture of Regensburg in a playful manner. We carefully selected the historical buildings and characters used in the game under the consultation of local tour guides and local history experts. To ensure that our stories were engaging and historically accurate, we hired a professional travel journalist to help us construct the dialogue of the characters with the oversight of our content experts. The dialogue blended historical fact and narrative together to bring life to the characters and relate their problems to the player. In addition, we hired professional voice actors and used professional recording studios to make the voices high quality, interesting, and engaging.

The result was well received by our audience. Nancy said: "The characters are great... the way they told the stories." Calvin stated: "The characters created a wonderful atmosphere, the other [referring to an audio guide used previously] was just bland tourist information." He later stated: "The quests... they were nicely packed in a story that was entertaining and nice and that motivated me to complete them, also the things that make you smirk and stuff, that was nice..." In a different interview, Bart said, "Yeah, I also found it entertaining. I found the stories and the way they were told very interesting, it was something very special, actually, because when you try to learn something about the city, you typically don't hear something like that." Jackleen stated, "The characters were contructed with so much love and everything fit so well together with respect to the voices – that was really great!" Adriane said, "Sometimes I simply listened to the stories again, because I thought the historical things were so interesting." This statement not only speaks positively about the content, but it also brings up an interesting use of the repeat button which was designed to be used in the case of interruptions.

However, some of our users felt that the content didn't contain enough information about the city. Ebony said, "I think its great because you can participate in the action... but when I'm ready to be informed about the city... then I would like to have more information." Hannah stated, "When someone is interested in knowledge, then he would tend toward a guided city tour." This feedback emphasizes that we are actually trying to bring learning to a new audience that doesn't typically enjoy the standard guided city tour. However, other statements demonstrated that we still could improve our content. Daniela said, "[I was interested in] more the facts, and less the people. I was actually not interested in the character's stories at all. Naturally, what they were saying was funny and all..." Danny stated, "Your standing in front of some building worth seeing, that would be part of some tour, but it doesn't say anything about it!" The comments highlight that some of our users felt that the stories were too character-centric and should focus more on the buildings themselves.

One design suggestion that came out of this was to extend the dialogue to incorporate more building information. However, some other statements indicated that this might not be the right direction. Bart said, "I found that the storytelling duration of the characters to actually be good. I mean, there was never a point where I stood and thought: 'Yeah, when is he finally going to stop talking?'" Although a positive statement, it points out that the attention span of our audience is not very high. Extending the dialogue is also problematic in that our stories were constructed from the characters' perspective. Coverage of the different historical epochs of the city was achieved by moving from character to character with each character covering a specific time period. When describing a building and it's significance, it is often important to cover several historical periods. To address this, we added an additional audio track focused on the historical backgrounds of each building. These building descriptions were narrated by the voice of the detector (which had it's own personality and voice) and not tied to a specific time period. Interested players could access this information when near a building using a newly introduced i-gesture. The i-gesture was not required for game play and was purely for information purposes.

We also examined what memorable takeaways people had from the experience. Even directly after the playing session, raw historical facts were difficult for users to recall in the interview. Nancy said, "Once you've fulfilled a quest and arrive at the next station, you've already forgotten the historical facts." However, people did seem to takeaway the connections between the characters in the quest network. When asked what he remembered Calvin responded, "The drunk and his wife – the names I don't remember any more – they fit so well in terms of atmosphere." Here he was referring to a quest that involved a drunk who was upset that his wife was having an extramarital affair, and as a quest the players were tasked with reminding the wife of the penalty for infidelity in the middle ages. People also seemed to retain the link between the characters and the locations. Jackleen stated, "I can still remember each individual character. There was where he lived... the association with the places [and characters], I really think that I'll remember that." Kacee stated, "The next time I walk by one of these buildings, then I'm going to think 'that's were that lady was'." These statements indicate that the game actually altered the perception of the space for the players. Although, they had a hard time remembering names or dates, they did build important spatial connections to different social roles in the historical context. These mental connections may provide a springboard to leverage their spatial memory for reflection through their personalized weblog interface. This multi-stage approach of informing users both during the game and after the game in a customized overview of their experience should be a design pattern for future educational pervasive games to follow.

5.4   Gesture Recognition

Spell-casting was a key component of gameplay, and was required to interact with the characters. By some of our participants the gesture recognition system worked fairly well. Aaron stated, "what I found was really good was even when you made a round 'C', the device would still recognize it - really high tolerance in any case." Other players expressed that the gesture recognition system was not working as they expected. Hannah stated, "With the symbols there: water, wind, fire, and earth... that really didn't work... for me, weird drawings kept showing up on the display." Here she is expressing she felt that there was too large of a mismatch between her gesture trace and her actual motion. Danny suggested, "I think there should be an option on the device where you don't need to gesture. Instead, you can press a button." But Bart said, "If it just showed fire and you only had to push fire, than that would be too boring." Calvin stated, "We had fun with the fact that it was difficult to draw the gestures. If it always works, then it's just boring. It can't be too easy." Nancy followed with, "It was funny somehow", referring to the way it became a recurring joke between them when they failed to gesture correctly. The main takeaway is that technical limitations can sometimes be cast as game skill elements, adding to the enjoyment of the experience.

We knew going into the evaluation that the motion estimation was error prone, but we thought that we had adequately compensated for it by creating a gesture recognition system that was very forgiving to gesture noise. During internal testing, most gestures were being recognized. However, in the field, many people had problems. Upon closer inspection of the video data from the play sessions, we noticed that many people were interrupting their gestures halfway through because they assumed they wouldn't be recognized. This is a problem of mismatched expectations from the users regarding the gesture recognition system. Ironically, if they had finished the motions, the gesture recognition system would probably have recognized the correct gesture. In an attempt to address the mismatched expectations, we focused on improving the on-screen feedback to better resemble the target symbols. We employed simple filtering techniques of the on-screen feedback and restricted motion along a Manhattan grid. These filtering techniques drastically improved the resemblance of the on-screen gesture visualizations to the target gesture traces.

One of the things that we were especially looking out for in our study was the acceptance of the players to perform the unconventional gesture motions in a public setting. Mable said, "I didn't notice people looking at me at all... you are really just concentrated on that part and on the story and all that stuff." Irene said, "The people were looking, but there weren't standing there with an open mouth or anything." Danny said, "For me it varied - I felt a little stupid when I had to make the gesture 5 times in a row." Interestingly, Danny was one of the players who played by himself. It was never explicitly stated by any of our subjects, but we noticed in the play sessions with more than one person, the presence of a second person seemed to validate the actions of the person doing the gesture for onlookers.

Even though the players were comfortable performing the gestures in public, it did create a public spectacle in some cases. Calvin said, "I found it funny in public to see how a whole lot of people that were walking by, staring so intently." Nancy followed with "I totally didn't even realize [they were staring]", and Calvin responded with, "you were also so concentrated". Kacee stated, "It is also very confusing for passerbyers 'hey, what is he doing there?' " During PS4, a bus driver got distracted by Gabi performing a gesture and collided with a construction fence resulting in a loud crash as the side passenger window burst into pieces. This shows that the public spectacle of the game can be dangerous not just for the players, but also for the surrounding public in some situations. Interestingly, Fae and Gabi barely looked up from the handheld device and just went right back to playing, not noticing that they might have caused the accident.

5.5   Issues Playing in Public

We specifically designed REXPLORER to support the shared experiences and shared memories that are important to tourists. One of the design decisions intended to support this was using the phone loudspeaker instead of headphones so that a group of people could easily share the audio. Also, the device shell is specifically designed to increase audio volume; the audio engineer doing the final mix also worked with the final shell to maximize the mix for the corpus.

Although people were comfortable performing gestures in public, some people felt like the audio was disturbing others. Ebony said, "it's naturally funny what they are saying and stuff, but then the people stare at you... and that is unpleasant." Some people asked for headsets, Ebony said "Headphones would have been great... I mean when you're not a group, but when you are alone. I mean, it would have been more comfortable for me if I had headphones." Others pointed out a second benefit of headphones, "Yeah because, first of all, you don't disturb other people, and second of all, you don't hear the environment." However, Fae pointed out "[headphones] would be certainly dangerous". Her point resonates even more given that we already have a problem with too much immersion; cutting out environmental sounds would probably complicate the issue further. Additionally Lacy pointed out, "We were doing a lot of talking amongst ourselves once the characters stopped speaking", indicating that personal headphones might have interfered with natural conversation between the players.

5.6   Collaboration within the Group

The game brochure was very effective at facilitating collaboration. Even though there was a map built into the device, many groups would use the brochure map to choose their next destination. If they were lost in the unfamiliar space, the map built into the device helped them locate themselves, but the large map tended to be used for route planning. For example, after hearing a quest during PS4, Fae (with the map) says, "That's were we need to go!", while pointing at the paper map to show Gabi the destination. This collaborative use of paper maps is expected and consistent with previous ethnographic studies of map usage. [9]

Collaboration was also present in the process of deciding which gesture to perform. For example, in PS3 Ebony asks, "How does that gesture go again?", and instead of pointing at the brochure, Daniella references the gesture legend and says, "Like so", while acting out the gesture in an instructional manner.

The use of multiple props (the detector and paper brochure) also had an unexpected result in that players in groups tended to take on specific roles. Nancy commented, "A map is good when you go out as a couple, where everyone has something in there hands, and everyone feels like they are participating, and you can always switch." Here, Nancy is describing the role split between navigation with the map, and a game management with the detector. The additional role was very important to the players, and almost all of the playing sessions with multiple players swapped roles regularly. Using multiple props to facilitate player roles is an important design pattern that should be employed in future pervasive games.

6   Future Work

This paper focuses on insights gained from a formative evaluation before the official launch. Future work will discuss further insights gained from analysis of actual play data. Unfortunately, the blog was not part of the play experience during this prototype phase. We are currently analyzing blog usage after the launch, and intend to publish the findings as future work. For future improvements of the game play experience, combining GPS data with other localization technologies including WLAN, and GSM cell data may improve accuracy enough to realize the original game design that included automatic detection of player proximity to historical buildings.

7   Conclusions

The method used to evaluate this work deserves some reflection. Grounded theory affinity analysis is an extremely time intensive process; for every hour of video recorded it took teams of 2 people 3 hours to transcribe. Before any clustering could be done, the data needed to be transfered to sticky notes, which is also time intensive. However, the quality of the results justified the required effort. The insights gained from the affinity clustering were helpful and surprising, even to the people involved in the video transcription process. The concrete qualitative statements presented collectively were very effective at building consensus among the design team and convincing stakeholders of the proposed design changes. In these scenarios, having the quotations from real user scenarios directly in the affinity clusters helped as a quick reference to justify claims and communicate the severity of issues that had previously been seen as only minor. Future pervasive games should be encouraged to incorporate grounded theory affinity analysis in the playtesting evaluation process.

Serious pervasive games have the potential to change the way we live and learn. By exploring the human factors issues in an ecologically valid context, we were able to gain important insights about the needs of tourists and the effectiveness of a game as an informative medium. In addition, issues surrounding staging a game in a public setting were brought to light. These insights were used to motivate important design changes as a part of a human-centered iterative design process. We hope that REXPLORER can serve as an inspiring example and the lessons learned through the design process will help spur further development of future pervasive games to promote learning and playful exploration.

References

1. Abowd, G.D., Atkeson, C.G., Hong, J., Long, S., Kooper, R., Pinkerton, M.: Cyberguide: a mobile context-aware tour guide. Wireless Networks 3(5), 421–433 (1997)
2. Ballagas, R., Rohs, M., Sheridan, J.G., Borchers, J.: Sweep and Point & Shoot: Phonecam-based interactions for large public displays. In: CHI 2005: Extended Abstracts of the SIGCHI Conference on Human Factors in Computing Systems, pp. 1200–1203. ACM Press, New York (2005)

3. Ballagas, R., Walz, S.: REXplorer: Using Iterative Design Techniques for Pervasive Games. In: Magerkurth, C., Röcker, C. (eds.) Pervasive Games, Springer, Heidelberg (2007)

4. Bamford, W., Coulton, P., Edwards, R.: Space-time travel blogging using a mobile phone. In: Proceedings of the International Conference on Advances in Computer Entertainment Technology, pp. 1–8 (2007)

5. Benford, S., Magerkurth, C., Ljungstrand, P.: Bridging the physical and digital in pervasive gaming. Commun. ACM 48(3), 54–57 (2005)

6. Bentley, F.R., Metcalf, C.J.: Sharing motion information with close family and friends. In: CHI 2007: Proceedings of the SIGCHI Conference on Human Factors in Computing Systems, pp. 1361–1370. ACM Press, New York (2007)

7. Beyer, H., Holtzblatt, K.: Contextual Design: Defining Customer-centered Systems. Morgan Kaufmann, San Francisco (1998)

8. Brown, B., Chalmers, M., Bell, M., MacColl, I., Hall, M., Rudman, P.: Sharing the Square: Collaborative Leisure in the City Streets. In: ECSCW 2005: Proceedings of the European Conference on Computer Supported Co-opertative Work, pp. 427–429. Springer, Heidelberg (2005)

9. Brown, B., Laurier, E.: Designing Electronic Maps: an Ethnographic Approach. In: Map Design for Mobile Applications, Springer, Heidelberg (2004)

10. Cheverst, K., Davies, N., Mitchell, K., Friday, A., Efstratiou, C.: Developing a context-aware electronic tourist guide: some issues and experiences. In: CHI 2000: Proceedings of the SIGCHI Conference on Human Factors in Computing Systems, pp. 17–24. ACM Press, New York (2000)

11. de Souza e Silva, A., Delacruz, G.C.: Hybrid Reality Games Reframed. Potential Uses in Educational Contexts. Games and Culture 1(3), 231–251 (2006)

12. Dix, A., Finley, J., Abowd, G., Beale, R.: Human-Computer Interaction. Prentice-Hall, Inc., Upper Saddle River (2004)

13. Dow, S., Lee, J., Oezbek, C., MacIntyre, B., Bolter, J.D., Gandy, M.: Exploring spatial narratives and mixed reality experiences in Oakland Cemetery. In: ACE 2005: Proceedings of the 2005 ACM SIGCHI International Conference on Advances in Computer Entertainment Technology, pp. 51–60. ACM Press, New York (2005)

14. Epstein, M., Vergani, S.: Mobile Technologies and Creative Tourism. In: AMICS 2006: Proceedings of the 12th Americas Conference on Information Systems, Association for Information Systems (2006)

15. Glaser, B.: Basics of grounded theory analysis: emergence vs forcing. Sociology Press (1992)

16. Klopfer, E., Squire, K.: Environmental Detectives—The Development of an Augmented Reality Platform for Environmental Simulations. Educational Technology Research and Development (2005)

17. Lee, Y.S., Smith-Jackson, T.L., Nussbaum, M.A., Tomioka, K., Bhatkhande, Y.: Use of product-interactive focus groups for requirement capture and usability assessment. In: Proceedings of the 48th Annual Human Factors and Ergonomics Conference. Human Factors and Ergonomics Society, New Orleans, LA, pp. 2461–2465 (2004)

18. Norrie, M., Signer, B.: Overlaying Paper Maps with Digital Information Services for Tourists. In: Proc. ENTER 2005 Conference on Travel and Tourism Technology, pp. 23–33. Springer, Heidelberg (2005)

19. Sawyer, B.: Serious Games: Improving Public Policy through Game-Based Learning and Simulation. In: Foresight and Governance Project, Woodrow Wilson International Center for Scholars Publication 1 (2002)

20. Scupin, R.: The KJ method: A technique for analyzing data derived from Japanese ethnology. Human Organization 56(2), 233–237 (1997)
21. Thomas, S.: Pervasive learning games: Explorations of hybrid educational gamescapes. Simulation & Gaming 37(1), 41 (2006)
22. Vlahakis, V., Karigiannis, J., Tsotros, M., Gounaris, M., Almeida, L., Stricker, D., Gleue, T., Christou, I.T., Carlucci, R., Ioannidis, N.: Archeoguide: first results of an augmented reality, mobile computing system in cultural heritage sites. In: VAST 2001: Proceedings of the 2001 Conference on Virtual Reality, Archeology, and Cultural Heritage, pp. 131–140. ACM Press, New York (2001)
23. Walz, S.P.: A spatio-ludic rhetoric: Serious pervasive game design for sentient architectures. In: Game set and match II. Proc. of the 2006 International Conference on Computer Games, Advances Geometries and Digital Technologies. Episode Publishers, Rotterdam, NL (2006)
24. Walz, S.P.: Pervasive Persuasive Play: Rhetorical Game Design for the Ubicomp World. In: Fogg, B.J., Eckles, D. (eds.) Mobile Persuasion: 20 Perspectives on the Future of Behavior Change, Stanford Captology Media, Palo Alto (2007)
25. Wang, J., Zhai, S., Canny, J.: Camera phone based motion sensing: interaction techniques, applications and performance study. In: UIST 2006: Proceedings of the 19th annual ACM Symposium on User Interface Software and Technology, pp. 101–110. ACM Press, New York (2006)
26. Winer, D.: RFC: MetaWeblog API (2003),
    http://www.xmlrpc.com/metaWeblogApi

Opportunities for Pervasive Computing
in Chronic Cancer Care

Gillian R. Hayes[1], Gregory D. Abowd[2], John S. Davis[3], Marion L. Blount[3],
Maria Ebling[2], and Elizabeth D. Mynatt[2]

[1] Department of Informatics,
Bren School of ICS,
University of California, Irvine, Irvine, CA USA
[2] GVU Center & School of Interactive Computing,
Georgia Institute of Technology, Atlanta, GA USA
[3] T.J. Watson Research Center,
IBM Research
Hawthorne, NY USA

Abstract. While changing from a predominantly terminal to an increasingly chronic condition, cancer is still a growing concern. Accompanying this change are new opportunities for technologies to support patients, their caregivers, and clinicians. In this paper, we present an in-depth study of cancer communities. From this exploration, we define and describe the concept of a personal cancer journey. We examine lessons and design opportunities across this journey for sensing and context-awareness and capture and access applications.

Keywords: Healthcare, cancer, qualitative methods, sensing, applications.

1 Introduction

One in two men and one in three women in the United States today will be diagnosed with cancer [1]. At the same time, more "people are *living* with cancer, not just dying of it or beating it."[1] Chronic cancer care represents a significant domain challenge for pervasive computing researchers, because the needs of patients, survivors, clinicians, friends, and family are both unique and evolving. The same patient may experience multiple recurrences with differing symptoms, multiple treatment plans with differing side effects, and so on over the course of years. Furthermore, they are experiencing these issues while trying to *live* with cancer rather than letting cancer be their lives.

We set out to explore how cancer patients, caregivers, medical staff, social workers, researchers and other professionals adopt technologies, with an eye towards the potential for pervasive computing in this domain. During this work, we uncovered the framework of a journey, which we use to reveal how technology use crosses clinical and temporal boundaries. Others have addressed notions of a chronic illness trajectory [9] and certainly, inherent to diagnoses of cancer, there are notions of disease progression,

---

[1] Quote from a patient who had lived four years past her prognosis at the time of the interview.

J. Indulska et al. (Eds.): Pervasive 2008, LNCS 5013, pp. 262–279, 2008.

as denoted by the use of *stages*[2] in describing cancer. The chronic cancer journey, however, represents a different framework that warrants separate consideration and helps to reveal user needs in the face of a branching, complex set of experiences while living with a disease. In this paper, we outline findings from a qualitative empirical study of the needs of chronic cancer patients, their support networks, and medical personnel. We also present lessons and design opportunities for pervasive computing.

2 Related Work

Extensive literature exists on technologies for healthcare, both commercial and in research [12]. A complete review of these works is out of the scope of this paper. Here we present a sampling, describe how the space has been explored, and outline the novel contributions of this investigation.

The American Telemedicine Association asserts that "home telehealth (including remote monitoring) should be used as a part of a coordinated, comprehensive care program designed to reduce healthcare costs ... and improve clinical outcomes" [4]. A model of healthcare including telemedicine thus increases patient and caregiver involvement in medical care. For example, Mamykina *et al.* explored the ways in which individuals with diabetes understand and monitor their blood glucose levels in response to various environmental stimuli [18]. The Personal Medical Unit [5] and Personal Care Connect [6] provide potential technological platforms for individual management of sensed and reported health information. Other efforts, such as the Digital Family Portrait [22] and CareNet [8], have focused more on quality of life issues such as social interaction and physical activity. A common theme across all of these projects is collaboration, such as in Computer Supported Coordinated Care [7].

Physical and cognitive disabilities often accompany chronic conditions, either temporarily as with "chemo brain"[3] or permanently due to diminished function inherent to the condition (*e.g.*, as in Alzheimer's at the end of life or developmental disabilities at the beginning). Thus, assistive technologies contribute to the works related to chronic cancer care. Dawe outlined ways in which assistive technologies are and are not adopted by families of children with permanent disabilities [10]. These guidelines can also be helpful in considering adoption of technology for other chronic conditions. In cancer care, for example, use of wheelchairs, transfer boards, lifts, and other physical assistance tools are common, particularly as physical abilities degrade.

Eysenbach explored "cybermedicine," including web pages, on-line communities, and other "medicine in cyberspace" [13]. He differentiates telemedicine as driven by a "technological push" while cybermedicine is defined by a "consumer pull." He also challenges researchers to "develop and evaluate interventions that can maximize the positive effects of the Internet" [14].

---

[2] Staging is a complex process that accompanies all cancer diagnoses. Staging systems describe how far a cancer has spread and group people by prognosis and treatment. Staging applies to almost all cancers except some types of leukemia. Cancers are classified from I to IV in roman numerals, with IV being most severe and including metastases.

[3] "Chemo brain" is the notion amongst members of the cancer community that individuals can experience temporary reduced cognitive functioning as a reaction to chemotherapy treatment.

The work presented in this paper contributes to the state of the art in two significant ways. First, we are exploring cancer as a broad problem, whereas many previous works have focused on only a subset of the entire cancer community, such as the medical staff in hospitals. Second, the present analysis includes an examination across all phases of the disease. Relevant literature and commercial products provide a base for our new focus of research to develop a full model for the ways in which pervasive computing technologies can be and currently are used to support chronic cancer care.

3 Methods

The goal of this work is to understand the effects and potential of pervasive computing on the entire cancer ecosystem[4]. We employed an exploratory, qualitative empirical approach, adapted from contextual inquiry [16]. We used participant and direct observation [23], collected artifacts related to cancer, and conducted in-depth interviews.

3.1 Participant and Direct Observation

For eighteen weeks, we immersed ourselves in the culture of the cancer community. We did not limit our study to any particular type of cancer nor did we limit consideration to a type of patient, survivor, caregiver, clinician or other professional. The decision to proceed with this breadth first approach did not come lightly. We examined those issues that were most similar and common across not only the thousands of possible types of cancer but also across other types of chronic care situations found in the literature.

We started our cultural immersion into the cancer community online, by visiting educational web sites (n=42). These sites were sponsored by cancer treatment centers, hospitals, non-profit organizations and prescription drug manufacturers. We subscribed to cancer- and caregiver-related electronic mailing lists (n=12), often receiving and reviewing hundreds of emails each day. These lists covered a variety of topics, from those dedicated to specific types of cancer (*e.g.,* the Kidney Oncology list) to those dedicated to specific stages of cancer (*e.g.,* bcmets for metastatic breast cancer) to those dedicated to specific types of people (*e.g.,* lists specific to daughters of cancer patients). Some of these latter lists request that you fit certain criteria to subscribe (*e.g.* daughters of mothers with breast cancer). In those cases, we only subscribed to lists that were also personally relevant out of respect for these policies. Although this limitation potentially narrowed our sample size, we were still able to view a wide variety of lists and believe that the ethical requirements of the research warrant this tradeoff.

We also conducted fieldwork, both participating in some cases and observing in others. One member of the research team conducted the majority of the fieldwork, with this individual recording detailed field notes, taking pictures, and presenting those to the rest of the group for discussion at weekly meetings. Field sites included:

- Cancer treatment centers, both interviewing and observing during infusion sessions;
- Cancer screening sessions at hospitals and clinics, with one team member not only recording field notes but also participating in screening activities;

---

[4] The cancer ecosystem includes patients, caregivers, doctors and other medical staff as well as epidemiologists, records keepers, social workers, and others affected by cancer.

- cancer libraries, in which we actively searched for information, recorded field notes and observations of individuals likewise searching, browsing, and consuming information, and interacted with librarians and nurses assigned to these libraries;
- support centers, in which we observed and actively participated in educational seminars and support groups; and
- hospitals, including waiting areas, cafeterias, and treatment and diagnosis areas[5].

3.2 Artifact Analysis

We collected and analyzed hundreds of artifacts from many sources, including hospitals, support centers, patients, and caregivers. These artifacts ranged from published books and pamphlets to homemade information organization tools (*e.g.,* notebooks) to medical journals to on-line support group archives. Taken together, these artifacts provide a basis for understanding the relationships between the physical legacy of human life and the reported and observed internal and external states of our participants. Where possible we included the text of these artifacts in a manner similar to the inclusion of interview transcripts as described in detail in the analysis section.

3.3 Interviews

Twenty-one people participated either in person or by phone (seven people). The interviews lasted one to two hours each. Participants included seven patients and survivors, four medical professionals, four social workers, one hospital health data manager, one home health manager, and four family members. Twelve participants were from the greater New York City area, three from small cities in Alabama, three from small towns in the Mid-West region of the U.S., one from rural Vermont, one from outside of Washington, D.C., and one from Boston, MA. All patients and survivors had been diagnosed with cancer at least two years before the interview, some as long as seven years.

When in person, interviews were conducted at a place of the participant's choosing, usually homes or offices. One patient asked that the interview take place during her chemotherapy treatment. The interviews were open-ended and conversational in nature by design to uncover those issues most significant to the participants. They typically occurred as one-on-one sessions, but in one case, two social workers and the director of hospice care participated as a small group. Following initial data analysis, as described in 3.4, we debriefed with participants, sharing with them their interview transcripts and further probing them about emergent themes. We also shared an early draft of this manuscript and solicited feedback on the results of the work, incorporating that feedback into later analysis and design work.

3.4 Analysis

Interviews were recorded and transcribed with participant permission. When recording was not feasible (four interviews), copious field notes were taken to document participant

---

[5] Chemotherapy is treatment of disease with chemical substances, primarily cytotoxic drugs used to treat cancer. Infusion refers to a common way to inject chemotherapy, intravenously. Infusion centers also serve non-cancer patients who require intravenous drug treatment.

comments. In every case, the researcher conducting the interviews took field notes during and shortly after the events. The transcripts, field notes, and collected artifacts from the observation phase of the study were then analyzed to create a grounded theory [24] about the cancer experience. After two passes of inductive or "open" coding through the data to determine general themes, we then created a coding scheme centered on fourteen major themes, each with two to ten sub-themes (see Table 1 for list of major themes and a single exemplar sub-theme for each). Using this coding scheme, we then completed two passes through the data using axial and deductive coding to demark any potential variants from the emergent themes and any interconnections between them. These themes run across each stage of the cancer journey and thus do not map directly to sub-sections in the Results section but rather are included across them all.

Table 1. Major Themes and Exemplar Sub-Themes from Coding Scheme

Major Theme	*Exemplar Associated Sub-Theme*
Environment	Physical cues in the environment designed for/effective in creating a particular gestalt
Sense of belonging	Roles within a community
Choice of activities	Adoption of new practices, hobbies, activities
Working together	Ability and willingness to ask and answer questions
Support network	Relationship dynamic with patient
Self-concept	Aesthetic and esteem
Information access	Information access preferences
Finances	Cost of new technologies and techniques
Monitoring	Legal, ethical, and societal pressures and norms
Quality of life	Complementary or peripheral care
Medication and treatment	Tension between autonomy and compliance/adherence
Current and new uses of technologies	Caregiver/patient responsibilities for technology
Attitudes regarding prevention and screening	Attention to body and signals and intuition
Epidemiology	Availability and quality of epidemiologic information

From these data, we created design briefs, including lists of the stakeholders and potential users and of the high level features. Each brief then detailed the ways in which these stakeholders, users, and features would likely interact. We used the design briefs in engineering and prototyping discussions and iterated on them based on feedback during these sessions. These designs have not been further tested nor completely developed. We present a subset of these designs in this paper, those that are most directly related to pervasive computing, as a means for provoking further design and development in this area rather than shrink wrapped completed concepts.

4 Results

All interview participants used a metaphor similar to a "journey with six explicitly using the word "trip" or the word "journey." Thus, the concept of a personal journey with cancer became a significant backdrop for investigation. They also all commented that each journey is special and unique to each individual, but that commonalities exist.

> *"...recovering from cancer is like pregnancy... everyone goes through the trip a little differently."*   – Stage I survivor

Building on staging of cancer diagnoses and the chronic illness trajectory noted by Corbin and Strauss [9], we probed this journey metaphor. Participants reported it to be significantly different for them from these other ways of describing cancer's impact. Whereas staging and disease trajectories all map to a unidirectional non-branching path, a journey allows for divergent, convergent, and even circular paths. Given the now chronic nature of cancer, and its common disappearance, reappearance, and constant threat to health, the journey metaphor maps more appropriately.

The data from this study indicate major commonalities across each unique journey expressed in five major phases. These phases are: screening and diagnosis, initial information-seeking, acute care and treatment, no evidence of disease, and chronic disease and disease management. In this section, we lay out significant findings of each phase. We describe the phase itself and indicate how technology is used currently. In section five, we describe the lessons from across these phases and indicate new opportunities for design.

4.1 Screening and Diagnosis

The screening and diagnosis phase begins with an individual experiencing some impetus to get "checked." Often, participants reported they were simply participating in a standard prevention or screening measure. During the screening activities in which we participated, other people awaiting their tests commented they were "doing the right thing." For others, there might be obvious and/or acute symptoms. For example, a common symptom of brain tumors is a bloody nose. These symptoms often only appear after the cancer is advanced, and people can and do live with cancer for years without a diagnosis. Finally, many people also request screening measures because of less acute symptoms or simply an intuition that something is wrong.

Currently, computing provides basic information during this phase. Some physicians and medical staff reported using the Internet to get the most current recommendations for screening from organizations like the American Cancer Society. Individuals can also find information online about opportunities for free screenings.

The time just after a diagnosis of cancer is characterized by the feeling of a "roller coaster of emotions" as diagnoses are changed and new information is presented. Participants reported that the diagnostic information shared during this phase could be extremely overwhelming. Multiple opinions are often sought, and each physician may request his or her own diagnostic tests. The volume of data builds, often resulting in conflicting or complementary but different diagnoses and plans of action.

> "...well, everything looked okay...Well, then no it wasn't okay, but then it wasn't so bad and then it was so bad...she had...a positive reading for breast cancer, and then they did a bunch of other tests and... she had the metastases in her spine ..."   – Husband of Stage IV patient

It can be very difficult to comprehend this information when under the type of duress invoked by a cancer diagnosis [19]. Participants reported relying on a combination of sources to get information on everything from which physicians to see to what their particular symptoms and diagnoses might mean. They often contacted friends and family by phone and email looking for advice and referrals. Those who were Internet savvy also searched online for reviews of physicians and basic disease information.

4.2 Information-Seeking

The information-seeking phase generally begins as soon as a diagnosis is made and continues for one to several weeks. During this phase, newly diagnosed patients often reported seeking multiple opinions and therefore getting even more tests and reports. All the participants, from patients to caregivers to medical staff to social workers, commented that during the weeks immediately after diagnosis, nearly everyone in the support network begins rapidly and aggressively searching for information. They reported using web sites, books, magazines, and other print information as well as both online and offline conversations with others on the journey. The collected information may support consideration of treatment plans and decision-making.

Cancer, although one word, is thousands of diseases, and available information can be overwhelming. Furthermore, the stress of the diagnosis can negatively impact individuals' abilities to learn [19]. Thus, physical cancer libraries, such as those we observed at treatment and community support centers, often are intentionally decorated in soothing colors with light music playing in the background as well as staff on call to assist. In the online environment, people can find much more information and often search out details available few other places. The personal assistance of friends, family, or these staff members and the soothing atmosphere, however, can be absent. Participants repeatedly reported, therefore, that although the Internet and other computing resources offered a lot of information, it was often difficult if not impossible to sort through it all.

> *"... one of the problems that I had on the Internet ... was, I would get so many hits that just going through them to find those that were helpful... was awkward and time consuming."*   – Husband of deceased patient

Participants reported joining online mailing lists related to cancer during this time. Those who previously belonged to mailing lists on other topics (*e.g.*, hobbies) reported joining the most, but even some with no previous experience online joined and/or reviewed list archives. This rapid joining and reading of mailing lists resulted in a deluge of information. In turn, participants reported spending large amounts of time determining what was relevant and important from the different lists and deciding which lists they would continue to monitor. They also reported creating physical binders and virtual folders to organize the massive quantities of information collected.

4.3 Acute Care and Treatment

Once a treatment plan is in place, acute care and aggressive treatment begins. The medical team, patient, and support network implement a plan that may include multiple chemical treatments as well as physical treatments such as radiation and surgery. Medical staff members monitor closely the patients' reactions to these treatments. There are recommendations and tables of suggested dosages by which the physicians determine the treatment plans, but, as one caregiver put it, "...it appears to me like most of the treatment protocols are a, I'll call it an Easter egg or a trial and error. You just try something, and if it works you continue that, and if it doesn't work, you go try something else."

In-office tests and patient tracking supports much of the hypothesis testing and adjustments to treatment plans. Medical teams use a mix of quantitative results (*e.g.,* blood tests) and qualitative discussions about patient symptoms and side effects. The visits at which these discussions take place, however, are usually less frequent than the treatment sessions themselves. Furthermore, oncologists may get very little time talking with patients. To compound the matter, these relationships are usually very new, given that most people do not know oncologists until they need one. To combat the subjective and variable nature of this approach, some medical practices have begun attempting to quantify symptoms. For example, one medical practice we encountered during this study uses a tablet PC-based detailed questionnaire called the SOS Patient Monitor [17]. The electronic solution provided them the ability to administer dynamic, personalized surveys and easily view this data over time in varied formats.

During this phase, changes also take root in the personal lives of patients and their support networks. All of the patients and caregivers we interviewed reported an adjustment in life to focus on activities that addressed core needs in their personal lives. Some patients stopped working; others moved to more remote areas to spend more time with family. Simultaneously, extended social networks also may change. Participants reported sharing information with more people than they ever believed they would.

"I didn't even know that I knew that many people."   – Stage IV patient

"...everybody wants to call and say 'Okay what happened today? Any news today?' And how many phone calls can a person make?" – Social worker

Many patients commented that although they felt loved by their friends and family members calling or emailing and asking for status updates, these calls could also be a burden. They might come at a time that is inconvenient. These calls also often come in succession requiring repetition of news, information that is sometimes very painful to relay. To manage this huge flow of information in from the medical staff and other sources and back out to support networks, some patients and their caregivers develop personalized web sites, either through their own efforts or through services (see for example, www.caringbridge.org and www.lotsahelpinghands.com). Those on the receiving end of this information also reported struggles with current practices. They noted that waiting for posts to websites or blogs meant they were not as up-to-date as they wanted to be. They would have to wait until the patient was at a computer with network access and felt well enough to type and upload photos and other information.

Another primary concern during this phase is obtaining an appropriate level of patient involvement in and understanding of treatment. Even for those patients who do not want to know the details of their diseases and treatments, many physicians believe it is imperative for them to obtain some level of knowledge and maintain some level of involvement. Compliance (the taking of medication appropriately when first prescribed) and adherence (continued compliance) are major issues for prescribing physicians. However, patients are often not intentionally non-compliant.

"...it's not at all a non-compliance issue on the patient's part. It's just an uninformed patient..."   – Social worker

4.4 No Evidence of Disease

If the acute treatment phase goes well, and the cancer was at an early stage, patients are sometimes deemed to be "cured" or to have "no evidence of disease" (NED). Unlike some other phases we describe, NED is also a medical descriptor. Some people choose the NED designation because it denotes that recurrence of the cancer is of concern and that it may be hiding in the body while remaining undetectable. This concern contributes to a culture of continued monitoring and use of medical treatments and holistic remedies to reduce chances of recurrence.

> *"Once you have it, the age of innocence is over. You feel vulnerable the rest of your life...it's like terrorism.... We're always told don't change the way you live your life, but always be on the watch."*
>
> – Cancer survivor, three years NED

Survivors still visit their oncologists for regular tests, the frequency of which decreases with time. The potential for an acute event leading back to the diagnosis phase raises concern levels, and thus symptoms may be tracked for recurrence. One patient who experienced a recurrence noted that the risk may persistently be on their minds:

> *"Every pain that you have, where most people just say 'oh my knee hurts' you think 'Oh my knee hurts, I wonder if it's in my bones.'"*

Support for NED survivors must sit between vigilance and undue concern. Hence, many survivors reported having difficulty with certain support groups, both online and off, once they had lived with the threat of recurrence for a long period of time. Returning to these groups, when acquaintances originally diagnosed at the same time had passed away made things extremely difficult. On the other hand, NED survivors often "give back" to the community. Frequently, email messages from "newbies" in the communities we monitored were answered with words of encouragement from someone "on the other side." Many survivors also reported giving lectures at support groups, fundraisers, and so on as well as volunteering and socializing with patients and others. Most NED survivors reported taking time out to remain in these communities in many cases. It should be noted, however, that many reported being "superstitious" and not wanting to declare themselves "cured" or to act as models for others for fear of a recurrence and so sometimes waited or needed extra encouragement to get involved in cancer communities again.

4.5 Chronic Care and Disease Management

When the possibility of a patient ever gaining an NED status disappears, patients move into chronic care and disease management. Unlike in some chronic conditions (*e.g.,* diabetes) but similar to others (*e.g.,* Parkinson's disease), those dealing with chronic cancer care assume that the cancer is eventually a terminal condition.

> *"Stage IV is terminal...the disease will take us out and it's simply a matter of when."*
>
> – Patient living with Stage IV for six years

During this phase, quality of life becomes a more significant metric of success. Patients reported attempting to maintain hope and a sense of "normalcy" while adjusting to the inevitable terminal nature of their diseases.

> *"...I just think if we lose hope, we die... So, you just have to find the joy in the little rewards."*   – Stable Stage IV patient

During this phase, physicians and patients often opt to change the treatment strategy, concentrating on managing the disease rather than attempting to cure it. This strategy often involves using one treatment at a time, as opposed to treatments during the acute care phase, in which patients usually experience as many approaches (chemical, surgical and radiological) as close together in time as possible without killing the patient.

> *"...you don't want to use up the tools in your toolbox, because we only have a limited number...you want to draw out whatever treatment you're on as long as possible ..."*   – Stage IV patient

These treatments, like those during the acute phase, are closely monitored for reactions and side effects as well as efficacy. Different than treatments during the acute phase, however, there is an ever-present assumption that all treatments will fail eventually. Thus, the work becomes to monitor for signs of treatment failure (*e.g.*, medical indicators such as blood counts or physical indicators such as fatigue) so that a new plan can be put in place before too much damage is done.

> *"...only by testing very rapidly, they find out if the medication's actually working... you hope that if it's not working, it doesn't get too serious too quickly."*
> – Husband of stage IV patient

Monitoring and testing can be a huge challenge in this phase. The desire is to catch any changes as soon as they are recognizable, but at the same time, patients may stay in this phase for a long time and do not want to spend their lives in hospitals. Augmented home tests with networked communication to physicians address this tension. For example, one caregiver described the ways in which his wife was tested regularly at the physician's office for a particular side effect that had emerged for some patients:

> *"...they would monitor the nerves...by applying shocks and monitoring what the nerves were doing... they also had tests of coordination where... my wife would pick up thing... they would redo the where they would wire her up type test more frequently if the coordination test suggested adverse things ..."*

Cancer statistics and epidemiological information, such as cancer clusters and other important data, are hard to gather and only reported annually, as required by law. In more "connected" areas where treatment facilities and hospitals are common, communication between the hospitals assists in understanding these phenomena. Information can be passed through doctors, records managers, or other staff who have either an established rapport with one another or an official association with each other's hospitals.

In rural areas, the need is acute. Hospitals are few and far between. One patient commented that doctors stay only a brief time, often only working the time required for loan forgiveness. Without connected, digital records, it is hard if not impossible to look for the kind of higher level information across multiple patients that can support the discovery of trends in both occurrence and treatment on a large scale.

> *"...what if you had ... 47 women ... in one area that had a specific kind of cancer... and you had a cancer cluster, but how would you know that if you have 47 different files and you live in an area where doctors come and go?"*

– Stage IV patient in a rural area

5 Lessons and Design Opportunities

The opportunities for pervasive computing across the chronic cancer journey are vast. Some of the approaches undertaken for other domain problems can be reappropriated to address these issues in new and innovative ways. Other considerations, however, require rethinking pervasive computing, including sensing, systems, and applications, in light of chronic care for cancer. As described in the Methods section, we created applications design briefs and conducted initial tests with them in iterative design sessions. These briefs included a brief overview of the concept, a bulleted list of necessary and ideal features, a detailed list of potential users and stakeholders, and in some cases, sketches and early conceptual mockups of the design. We present these concepts and recommendations not as a task list for pervasive computing researchers but as design inspiration for those who might take these results and incorporate them into the technologies of the future.

The cancer journey is deeply personal. It is exhausting, overwhelming and often transformative. Certainly, other pervasive computing scenarios must also assume significant changes in the "user" while engaging a set of technologies. The chronic cancer problem, however, is of particular interest in this respect, because the impetus for accessing these technologies initially and the need to maintain and adapt them over time is inherently tied to the cancer journey. New technologies must accompany people on this journey while accommodating huge shifts in uses needs, motivations, energy levels and goals. In this section, we describe the lessons drawn from our findings, including discussion of detailed design briefs, and the technological opportunities they indicate across all of the stages. We group these possibilities, considerations and recommendations into two major pervasive computing sub-areas previously identified as core classes of applications for the future of ubiquitous computing: sensing and context-awareness and capture and access [2].

5.1 Sensing and Context-Awareness

Sensing and context-awareness present opportunities for supporting screening and diagnosis, symptom and side effect management, and to abate the risk for recurrence. These technologies can be used to deliver customized medical advice based on data gathered over time and can support individuals across multiple phases of the journey.

Pre-diagnostic Screening and Monitoring
Medical professionals often suggest using self-screening techniques (*e.g.,* breast self-exams), but people often are not motivated to or may not know how to conduct these tests. They may also struggle to find opportune times for them. One design concept that

had particular traction in our design discussions focused on reminding users when and how to conduct self-screening activities. As an example, many physicians currently distribute educational cards that describe the breast self-examination procedure alongside visual aids. These cards may be created in a form factor that allows them to be hung from a door or by the shower. Although patients and clinicians alike generally found these to be helpful, they noted that they are obtrusive and may only be helpful for people with very fixed routines who can, for example, spend an extra few minutes in the shower each morning conducting an exam. On the other hand, our suggestions of incorporating such screening recommendations and instructions into mobile devices were highly appealing. Already, in support of other daily medical needs, such as taking a vitamin or prescription medicine at the same time each day, the mobile phone has become the platform of choice for many individuals for setting reminder alarms. The same features of the phone that make it an ideal health platform for these types of reminders, would support reminding of screening activities. Furthermore, mobile devices can provide even richer information than the static cards by nature of their interactive capabilities.

Another opportunity for pervasive computing that resonated during design sessions focused on location-based and context-aware applications. These services could make use of sensed data to notify individuals of professional screening activities, which are often underutilized simply because they are hard to find. Many professional screening activities, such as a physician visually scanning a patient's skin for any abnormalities, take only a few moments to complete. Knowing about them and traveling to the location where they are offered, however, can be a much larger activity. Thus, in the same way that location-based services advertising sales or menus for particular restaurants have been touted as a good way to get people to frequent those establishments, so too can these services encourage people with a few moments to spare to take the time to stop in at a screening event when they are nearby.

Finally, even people who are highly motivated to participate in both self and professional screening activities may encounter a situation in which the screening criteria are not appropriate for their needs. Cancer, like other diseases, inhabits an inherently individualized human body and thus presents in a range of ways. Morris and Intille suggest *embedded assessment* as a way to recognize declining health related to aging on an individual basis [20]. Our findings suggest that such an approach could be used to indicate when a screening or diagnosis activity might be necessary before noticeable symptoms arise. For example, in the case of skin cancer, one physician noted that how often he wants to check an individual's skin is highly dependent on how often they are in the sun, the inherent properties of their skin, and in what other activities they regularly engage. Sensing that collects that data and indicates an appropriate screening schedule for a given individual based on both their baseline data and their activities would be a huge improvement on current practices.

Support During Treatment

While being treated for cancer, patients are at risk for deterioration in physical and mental functioning, often in unexpected ways. For example, many patients undergoing chemotherapy lose access to online communities, because the treatment makes their fingertips so sensitive they cannot type. Assistive technology offers some relief for these symptoms, but many patients do not recognize the need for them until the symptoms have become severe.

Assistive technologies that automatically deploy and adjust as abilities shift over time could provide appropriate time-sensitive support. For example, one idea proposed in our design briefs included key-logging software to recognize changes in an individual's typing patterns and automatically adjust the accessibility features of the computer for that user. In discussing this design with various stakeholders, the idea garnered much support, but further suggestions also emerged for use of voice recognition technologies and the creation of new assistive technologies that would be individually useful for particular side effects of chemotherapy and cancer.

In addition to painful and irritating side effects like loss of feeling in fingertips, patients are at risk for dangerous and life-threatening side effects, particularly when treatment plans are not followed properly. There have been numerous pervasive computing applications focused on compliance and medication reminding. These projects, however, often focus on the routine of drug taking, and could benefit from a more holistic view of the patient. Sensing changes in the physiological state of patients could support just in time medication recommendations. Also, provision of additional information to the patient may facilitate patient problem solving and understanding as to why their actions produced particular results. Mamykina *et al.* noted that reflection of this type of data back to diabetes patients contributed to their ability to move their locus of control inward [25]. Similarly, cancer patients may benefit from these types of interactions with data about their own treatments and side effects, and applications of this variety should be explored further.

Throughout their treatments, even when patients are perfectly compliant, physicians monitor closely for damage done by the treatments or by cancer. For example, some patients must come all the way into the office to do simple tests, such as the test for neuropenia that involves picking up and dropping objects to watch for irregularities described in section 4.5. We must address the challenge of getting the latest and most accurate information without requiring an inordinate number of visits to medical facilities. Automatic tracking of results of the physical tests conducted frequently at home could provide more up to date and accurate data. Following the example of the neuropenia test, patients at home could pick up and put down sensor-equipped objects. Readings from these sensors could be communicated to the medical staff who would likely recommend an office visit and more intensive testing in the event of irregular results. Similarly, we have begun examining both gait analysis and sleep tracking as a means for assessing the long-term effects of some treatments and cancers.

Finally, automatically sensed physiological information, although extremely valuable to individuals, can be even more valuable to the population as a whole. When brought together, data from pre-cancer diagnoses and patients in various stages of the disease and phases of their journeys build a more complete picture. One design concept we created included the mapping of these data onto geographical, chemical, and environmental readings to understand more readily the impacts of these varied contexts. These concepts resonated with both public health officials and patients struggling with finding the links between cancer incidence and potential environmental factors. The development of appropriate sensing and data mining technologies, however, remains a significant challenge for pervasive computing researchers.

5.2 Capture and Access

Our findings also suggest opportunities for applications that ease "the capture of live experiences and provide flexible and universal access to those experiences later on" [2]. As with sensing and context-aware applications, capture and access applications can support activities across phases of the journey and thus should evolve with the patients, survivors, and care networks over time.

Augmenting Patient and Caregiver Memories
To combat the chaos of the time just after a diagnosis, patients and their families need support for documenting and understanding their data. Use of simple audio-recorders were nearly never employed by the patients in this study for multiple reasons, two of which were most common: (1) lack of time or energy to go back and review the recordings or (2) desire to share any information received with someone else combined with confusion about how to share audio recordings[6]. This approach could reduce the overhead of both recording and finding the relevant parts of the conversation later, but applications to support the creation and sharing of these personal medical health records remains an open research problem.

These findings also indicate that new technologies could support the stressful process of meeting with multiple new medical professionals. Although this phenomenon exists in many medical situations, chronic cancer care is of particular interest in this respect for multiple reasons. First, the word "cancer" carries with it the stigma of death for every patient with whom we interacted. Thus, once the diagnosis is uttered, the stress levels are likely to increase immensely. Second, cancer carries with it an enormous number of specialties and subspecialties (e.g., radiologists, chemotherapists, radiology oncologists, and so on). Thus, during this time, patients often repeat information about their symptoms with each new meeting and share records from other physicians. Many technologists within hospitals, including one we interviewed for this study specifically, argue that electronic medical records are the solution to these issues. That solution, however, only takes us part of the way. Pervasive computing has the chance to take us the rest of the way by allowing patients and physicians to capture in rich detail the physiological and individually reported data associated with a new diagnosis.

Monitoring Patient Health Data Over Time
Patients are often asked to keep diaries about or otherwise recount details from particular incidents and demonstrations of symptoms. Sensing platforms and mobile recording applications could support gathering physiological, mental, and emotional data *in situ* at the time of particular patient experiences. These data could support problem-solving and therapeutic interventions as well as augment the memory of stressed patients and their loved ones. For example, physicians sometimes adapt medical technologies used for other conditions in an *ad hoc* way to support cancer care. One such technology is mobile electrocardiographs used in diagnosing and monitoring heart diseases. Likewise, physicians often ask patients to document on paper the readings from "smart scales" that detect bone density, body mass index, and so on. These technologies, while helpful in

---

[6] All of the participants who noted this issue reported considering analog tape recorders and not being either willing or able to send those physical audio tapes to someone else. Use of digital recording might change this attitude, but the overhead of listening to the sound would remain.

tracking patient care over time, must be coordinated with other diagnostic, monitoring, and sensing tools to support the complexity of cancer and the potential side effects of its treatment. As things are currently, there is no way for physicians or patients to get a holistic and immediate view of patient progress and needs. To address these issues directly, we investigated incorporation of such data (e.g., from a Bluetooth enabled scale and from Bluetooth enabled wearable heart rate sensors) into a single data model through the Personal Care Connect system [5]. The next steps for this type of work then are to understand how, when, and who to alert when particular thresholds or anomalies are detected.

Attempting to quantify and to track trends for symptom management is both medically valuable and very difficult. Pervasive computing applications such as home healthcare aids and electronic diaries could support gathering this information on a much more regular basis *in situ*. Mamykina *et al.* found that taking sensor readings, in their case blood glucometers, and reflecting those back to participants through such an electronic diary improved patients' abilities to understand and to manage their own diseases [25]. When managing cancer treatments, similar applications should be developed with cancer-relevant sensing and visualizations. Specifically, some of the most common data element discussed surrounding cancer are blood cell counts and the presence of so-called "cancer markers." These types of data are unique to cancer as a whole but are common across all types of cancer. Thus, they make for appealing data to track over time alongside other data, such as heart rates, weight, bone density, and so on.

Using Captured Data to Support Communication

Recent trends in mobile and photo blogging present interesting opportunities for chronic disease patients and their care networks. With simple phone-based applications, patients could easily share pictures of themselves during or after treatment, quick images of reports (low resolution now, but gaining in resolution as mobile camera-phone technology improves), text or audio-based commentary and more. Given that patients often feel the worst from chemotherapy and other treatments hours after receiving the treatment itself, they may actually be most likely to feel well enough to update interested people on their status during or immediately after a treatment. Therefore, providing mobile support for capturing this type of data and the appropriate healthcare portals for caregivers and patients can be an important goal for supporting quality of life and encouragement to the caregiver network.

Another opportunity for the capture, sharing, and access of patient information centers on diagnostic and monitoring data from physician visits. Many patients reported being uncomfortable or unable to document medical information during medical visits. This discomfort may stem from power differentials between patient and physician, social mores for patients to exhibit trust in their physician and so on. Also, documenting this information while it is being delivered was reported to be extremely difficult due to the added load of both listening and internalizing the information while trying to document it. Thus, providing methods for patients to capture this information immediately after such encounters and relay it to interested parties, while the information is fresh, is an important potential application of mobile technologies.

Another issue prevalent in our findings is the tendency for friends and family to check in too frequently when there is little news or no time to deliver it. Bridging the opportunities for context-aware computing and capture and access applications, people could also take advantage of context-aware availability information such as suggested by Nagel *et al.* [21] and Fogarty *et al.* [15] to stay up to date without further burdening the patients with queries about status at inappropriate times. We cannot simply take the results of those studies and apply them to the cancer domain, because caregiver and patient motivations are quite a bit stronger than in homes and offices of healthy individuals. They do, however, point to the possibility that such availability information could be tailored to the individual stakeholders while being augmented by the extra data collected that are cancer-specific, such as test results and calendars of medical appointments. It may also be important to note at this point that the security of the data becomes an even more important issue when considering cancer care, because so much of it is legally protected private health information. Thus, an open and important research question for others moving forward includes development of models and methods for securely communicating health data on mobile platforms as patients conduct the business of having cancer (e.g., going to the hospital or treatment centers).

Long-term Data-based Reflection

Many survivors commented about forgetting the details of their diagnosis and treatment processes due to temporary memory impairment brought on by stress and by the treatment protocols. By capturing large amounts of data throughout the diagnosis and treatment time periods, these survivors would be able to reflect on that time later. The combination of manually recorded journal entries with automatically recorded sensor data could offer a rich record of the treatment experience. These records offer two distinct advantages. First, there can be substantial therapeutic benefit to survivors to recount their experiences and deal with the trauma of the diagnosis and treatment in a structured manner. Second, these records offer the chance to share NED stories in rich detail to patients currently undergoing treatments. Many patients reported that hearing from people who had "been there" was extremely comforting when they first began their own journeys.

5.3 Remaining Challenges

The depth and breadth of this inquiry has resulted in the development of results that indicate numerous challenges for pervasive computing. We have presented in this section, some of the potential applications and technologies that could be developed in response to these challenges. We hope, however, that this work will inspire others to consider technologies that have not yet been envisioned and are not yet included here, using these recommendations as merely a starting point for exploring the diverse and significant potential for pervasive computing in this domain.

6 Conclusions and Discussion

Cancer is now considered a *chronic* condition, growing both in incidence rates and in number of years that people live past diagnosis. The journey through diagnosis, treatment, and life after cancer is marked by significant changes in lifestyle. Often these changes are informed or accompanied by new uses of technologies. One major contribution of this paper is to position research for pervasive computing technologies for cancer as specifically supporting a chronic condition. With this perspective on cancer, the uppermost needs for technology is supporting the continuous and changing process from the day to day point of view as well as the long-term view of planning, hoping, considering risks, and *living* with cancer.

The opportunities for impact in this field are vast. Since this initial study, we have continued this work, investing in unobtrusive but medically relevant sensing technologies, designing data visualizations to support tracking trends at individual and meta-levels, and creating mobile tools that can be used by cancer patients and their care teams. These designs have had to consider the potentially deteriorated needs of patients physically and mentally and thus borrow heavily from assistive technology. They also must render medically significant data, and thus borrow heavily from medical informatics. However, examination of cancer as a chronic condition means bringing the screening, diagnosis, testing, treatment, and monitoring out of the offices and hospitals and into the homes, schools, and hospice cares of the patients in need. When a disease becomes chronic, quality of life and continuing to live become paramount.

Pervasive computing presents one important avenue to enabling that transition, and importantly. Thus, as researchers, designers, and technologists, the pervasive computing community can empower people anywhere on the cancer journey from pre-cancer to no disease at all to chronic illness to play active roles in their medical treatments. The empirical data presented in this paper offer a starting point for the community to continue this important work. We have suggested design opportunities for both sensing and context-aware computing as well as capture and access applications. We hope that these design opportunities serve as a stimulus to the rest of the community to focus on this important problem that brings with it not only the potential for great human impact but also significant pervasive computing research challenges. With advances in sensing, data analytics, communication and more, people may be able to detect cancer earlier, treat it with greater success and live with it with less concern and greater awareness.

Acknowledgements

We thank the participants and the treatment and support centers who gave time and space to this work. Khai Truong and Aaron Quigley imparted valuable advice on editing of this manuscript. Bree Hayes provided important insights as both survivor and psychologist.

References

1. Unites States Cancer Statistics, 2002 Incidence and Mortality, U.S. Department of Health and Human Services, Editor. Centers for Disease Control and Prevention (2005)
2. Abowd, G.D., Mynatt, E.D.: Charting Past, Present and Future Research in Ubiquitous Computing. ACM Transactions on Computer-Human Interaction 7(1), 29–58 (2000)
3. Abowd, G.D., et al.: Challenges and Opportunities for Collaboration Technologies for Chronic Care Management. In: HCIC 2006 (2006)
4. Association, A.T.: ATA's Federal Policy Recommendations for Home Telehealth and Remote Monitoring, in ATA Public Policy White Papers (2006)

5. Bardram, J.: The Personal Medical Unit – A Ubiquitous Computing Infrastructure for Personal Pervasive Healthcare. In: UbiHealth 2004 (2004)
6. Batra, V., et al.: Remote Healthcare Monitoring using Personal Care Connect. IBM Systems Journal (2006)
7. Consolvo, S., et al.: Computer-Supported Coordinated Care. In: UbiHealth 2003 (2003)
8. Consolvo, S., et al.: The CareNet Display: Lessons Learned from an In Home Evaluation of an Ambient Display. In: Davies, N., Mynatt, E.D., Siio, I. (eds.) UbiComp 2004. LNCS, vol. 3205, pp. 1–17. Springer, Heidelberg (2004)
9. Corbin, J.M.: The Corbin and Strauss Chronic Illness Trajectory model: an update. Sch. Inq. Nurs. Pract. 12(1), 33–41 (1998)
10. Dawe, M.: Desperately seeking simplicity: how young adults with cognitive disabilities and their families adopt assistive technologies. In: Proc. CHI 2006, pp. 1143–1152. ACM Press, New York (2006)
11. Dey, A.K.: Understanding and Using Context. PUC 5(1), 4–7 (2001)
12. Eng, T.R.: Emerging Technologies for Cancer Prevention and Other Population Health Challenges. Journal of Medical Internet Research 7(3), e30 (2006)
13. Eysenbach, G.: The Impact of the Internet on Cancer Outcomes. CA: A Cancer Journal for Clinicians 53, 356–371 (2006)
14. Eysenbach, G., et al.: Shopping around the internet today and tomorrow: towards the millennium of cybermedicine. British Medical Journal 319(7220) (1999)
15. Fogarty, J., Hudson, S.E., Atkeson, C.G., Avrahami, D., Forlizzi, J., Kiesler, S., Lee, J.C., Yang, J.: Predicting Human Interruptibility with Sensors. ACM Transactions on Computer-Human Interaction (TOCHI) 12(1), 119–146 (2005)
16. Holtzblatt, K., Jones, S.: Contextual Inquiry: A Participatory Technique for System Design. In: Namioka, A., Schuler, D. (eds.) Participatory Design: Principles and Practice. Erlbaum, Hillsdale (1993)
17. IMPAC Medical Systems, The West Clinic Interfaces IMPAC with the SOS Patient Care Monitor (2006), http://biz.yahoo.com/prnews/060724/sfm052.html?.v=59
18. Mamykina, L., et al.: Investigating health management practices of individuals with diabetes. In: Proc. CHI 2006, pp. 927–936. ACM Press, New York (2006)
19. McEwen, B.S.: Protective and Damaging Effects of Stress Mediators. The New England Journal of Medicine 338, 171–179 (1998)
20. Morris, M., Intille, S.S., Beaudin, J.: Embedded Assessment: Overcoming Barriers to Early Detection with Pervasive Computing. In: Gellersen, H.-W., Want, R., Schmidt, A. (eds.) PERVASIVE 2005. LNCS, vol. 3468, pp. 333–346. Springer, Heidelberg (2005)
21. Nagel, K.S., Hudson, J.M., Abowd, G.D.: Predictors of availability in home life context-mediated communication. In: Proceedings of CSCW 2004, ACM Press, New York (2004)
22. Rowan, J., Mynatt, E.D.: Digital Family Portrait Field Trial: Support for Aging in Place. In: Proc. CHI 2005, ACM Press, New York (2005)
23. Spradley, J.: The Ethnographic Interview. Holt, Rinehart and Winston, New York (1979)
24. Strauss, A.L., Corbin, J.M.: Basics of qualitative research: grounded theory procedures and techniques. Sage Publications, Newbury Park (1998)

AnonySense: Opportunistic and Privacy-Preserving Context Collection

Apu Kapadia[1], Nikos Triandopoulos[2], Cory Cornelius[1], Daniel Peebles[1], and David Kotz[1]

[1] Institute for Security Technology Studies, Dartmouth College, Hanover, NH 03755, USA
[2] Department of Computer Science, University of Aarhus, 8200 Aarhus N, Denmark

Abstract. Opportunistic sensing allows applications to "task" mobile devices to measure context in a target region. For example, one could leverage sensor-equipped vehicles to measure traffic or pollution levels on a particular street, or users' mobile phones to locate (Bluetooth-enabled) objects in their neighborhood. In most proposed applications, context reports include the time and location of the event, putting the privacy of users at increased risk—even if a report has been anonymized, the accompanying time and location can reveal sufficient information to deanonymize the user whose device sent the report.

We propose AnonySense, a general-purpose architecture for leveraging users' mobile devices for measuring context, while maintaining the privacy of the users. AnonySense features multiple layers of privacy protection—a framework for nodes to receive tasks anonymously, a novel blurring mechanism based on tessellation and clustering to protect users' privacy against the system while reporting context, and k-anonymous report aggregation to improve the users' privacy against applications receiving the context. We outline the architecture and security properties of AnonySense, and focus on evaluating our tessellation and clustering algorithm against real mobility traces.

1 Introduction

Opportunistic sensing has been gaining popularity, with several systems and applications being proposed to leverage users' mobile devices to measure environmental context. In these systems, applications can *task* mobile nodes (such as a user's sensor-equipped mobile phone or vehicle) in a target region to report context information from their vicinity. With opportunistic sensing, applications need not rely on a static sensor deployment, and can instead glean context from any region that mobile nodes visit. Applications of opportunistic sensing include collecting traffic reports or pollution readings from a particular street [19], locating Bluetooth-enabled objects with the help of users' mobile devices [11], and even inferring coffee-shop space availability [35]. Examples of opportunistic-sensing systems include *CarTel* [19], *Mobiscopes* [1], *Urbanet* [32], *Urban Sensing* [6], *SenseWeb* [33] and our own *MetroSense* [5] at Dartmouth College. These systems predominantly rely on mobile nodes whose carriers are humans (or their personal vehicles) in an urban environment, thus putting the privacy of users at risk. For example, location and time, which are often included in context reports, reveal movement patterns of the reporting users.

J. Indulska et al. (Eds.): Pervasive 2008, LNCS 5013, pp. 280–297, 2008.

In many opportunistic-sensing applications, knowing the identities of the devices is unnecessary. Indeed, to protect users' privacy, Tang et al. [35] take the approach of suppressing the node's identity from reports, and Calandriello et al. [3] support pseudonymous or anonymous reports. Unfortunately, knowing users' movement patterns is often enough to deanonymize their reports [26]. Furthermore, a report taken inside Alice's office, for example, allows one to infer that Alice was likely in her office, even if her name was suppressed from the report. We assume that *both* the system and applications may attempt to deanonymize users using information contained in reports, and have developed a system called AnonySense to protect users against these privacy threats. Specifically, no entity should be able to link a report to a particular user.

We Leverage k-Anonymity. To improve users' privacy, *k-anonymity* [34] requires that at least k reports are combined together before being revealed, adding enough "confusion" in the data to make it difficult to pinpoint exact times and locations (and sensor data) for the individuals reporting the data. Even if an adversary knows that a user Alice has reported data, the attacker is unable to distinguish Alice's report from $k-1$ other reports. Existing server-based techniques apply location and time blurring (known as *spatial* and *temporal cloaking*) for combining reports to provide k-anonymity [17,15,12,23,29]. The main challenge with this approach, however, is that users must reveal their private information to a trusted server, resulting in a single point of failure with complete knowledge of users' sensitive information. Approaches that aim to improve the privacy against the system suggest the use of a peer-to-peer (p2p) mechanism for users to aggregate data locally before presenting the data to the server [8,13]. Unfortunately, the p2p approach requires $k-1$ other users to be online (i.e., present) in the user's vicinity. Ideally users should achieve k-anonymity even if the other $k-1$ users visit the same area at a later point within a particular time window (in this regard, a server-based approach can combine reports from users who may have visited a particular location at different times). Another problem is that the $k-1$ users may be located beyond the range of p2p communication (e.g., if Bluetooth is used). Mokbel and Chow outline several challenges [28] in this space and suggest a multi-hop approach to reach such nodes [8]. Their approach, however, assumes that nodes trust other nodes with their location information. Ideally, the p2p protocol should require the nodes to anonymously exchange and combine reports while preserving privacy. Secure multi-party computation [14] provides such solutions, but they are computationally expensive and require the k parties to be online simultaneously, neither of which may be acceptable for mobile, pervasive devices. Last, but not least, the k reports may come from within Alice's office (e.g., during a meeting), making it obvious that Alice is at her office, exposing her location privacy. Spatiotemporal cloaking must therefore take into account that some spatial regions can leak information about users even if k-anonymity is obtained.

Local Location Blurring to Improve k-Anonymity. Location blurring by users' devices [20,10] can indeed improve the privacy of users. In this approach, the granularity of the user's reported location is altered *before* sending the report to the system, thereby adding uncertainty to the user's location and hence protecting their identity. The level of blurring, however, may not be sufficient to prevent deanonymization by the system. For example, blurring Alice's location to a region larger than her office might be insufficient at 2am, when she is the only person usually present in that region at that time. While existing solutions allow users to specify the amount of location blurring [30,18], we believe this approach is unrealistic for opportunistic sensing, which is a secondary application with no direct benefit to the user. Therefore, *an automatic mechanism is needed to blur the user's location without their intervention.*

AnonySense—Anonymous Tasking and Reporting. We present AnonySense, a general-purpose framework for anonymous tasking that is designed to provide users with privacy from the ground up. Using AnonySense, applications can deliver tasks to anonymous nodes, and eventually collect reports from anonymous nodes. Furthermore, nodes accepting tasks cannot be linked with nodes submitting reports. Since cryptographic anonymity cannot prevent inference-based attacks on privacy, we provide a multi-layered approach to improve the user's privacy. We present a novel solution based on *tessellation*, which partitions the geographical area into *tiles* large enough to preserve the users' privacy. Users report locations at the granularity of these tiles. At a high level, a tile represents a region (centered on a public space) that k users normally visit during a typical interval (e.g., 5 minutes), thereby ensuring that users cannot be identified within a set of k users (with a high probability) if their report is indexed by tile and time interval. Such an approach provides users with what we call "statistical k-anonymity" *before* any report aggregation is performed, and therefore protects users' privacy against the system itself at a lower (first) layer. Our approach, therefore, provides users with location privacy without requiring any user intervention, and is efficient because the amount of blurring is determined locally without the need to communicate with other peers. In this paper, we focus on blurring the location and time of a device's reports, and assume that environmental sensing itself does not leak (too much) information about the reporting user to the system. To further protect the users' privacy against applications, however, reports are aggregated at a higher (second) layer to ensure that several, namely ℓ, reports are combined before sending context information to applications, thereby implementing ℓ-anonymity at the sensed-context level and providing better privacy against applications. AnonySense thus ensures privacy throughout the tasking lifecycle without requiring any user intervention.

Our Contributions

- We present AnonySense, a *general-purpose* framework for anonymous opportunistic tasking, that allows any authorized application to leverage sensors on mobile devices while preserving the privacy of users.
- We develop a new *automatic local blurring* technique where users report locations based on a tessellation large enough to provide statistical k-anonymity against the system. Additional report aggregation is performed to provide ℓ-anonymity against applications.
- We evaluate our tessellation technique based on real mobility traces representing 6,553 active users over 77 days and show that a reasonable tradeoff can be achieved between users' privacy and spatiotemporal granularity.

Paper Outline. We present AnonySense's architecture and formalize the notion of privacy in Section 2, then describe our tessellation-based technique in Section 3. We present our trust assumptions and protocol for anonymous tasking in Section 4, followed by an evaluation of the privacy provided by tessellation in Section 5. We discuss several related issues Section 6, and conclude in Section 7. Focused on anonymity, this paper omits some design and implementation details of our system due to lack of space.

2   Architecture

In what follows, we describe the architecture of our context tasking and reporting system, as well as the threat model and desired security properties.

2.1   System Overview

AnonySense is a general-purpose system that allows applications to collect and process (e.g., view, store, monitor and fuse) large volumes of sensed data from urban areas, inspired by the MetroSense [5] vision of opportunistic sensing. Applications can specify tasks using an expressive language, annotated with appropriate spatial and temporal semantics. Applications can use collected data to learn, infer or analyze contextual information related to everyday human-behavior patterns, natural phenomena and sporadic social or environmental events. Following the new sensor-networking paradigm that leverages humans or mobile objects in the sensing infrastructure, AnonySense implements context collection though *opportunistic sensing*, where mobile (mainly) sensing devices voluntarily participate in the system's data-sensing capabilities. Overall, AnonySense offers the following core functionality: applications submit specifications called *tasks* for collecting context through sensing, which are answered by the system through a *privacy-preserving* opportunistic context-collection technique that employs a mobile set of heterogeneous sensing entities.[1]

We identify three parties in our model: the *application*, the *system* and the *users*. An application connects to the system through an interface to request collection of context data from the users' devices. Given a context request, the system employs a *static networking infrastructure* that it owns and controls and a *mobile sensing infrastructure* that the users implement collectively. The static networking infrastructure consists of servers that are responsible for anonymously contacting mobile sensor devices to request sensor data, anonymously collecting sensor data back from the devices, and aggregating the data into context information. The mobile sensing infrastructure consists of individual users carrying sensor devices that dynamically participate in the data collection process. AnonySense's architecture is presented in Figure 1.

The primary goal for AnonySense is to protect users' anonymity with respect to their sensing activity; privacy is desirable not only in its own right, but also as a key factor in encouraging voluntary participation [22]. Indeed, any opportunistic human-centered sensing system should be protecting privacy of its members to support its own existence

---

[1] This is a necessity rather an assumption: indeed, participants in an opportunistic context collection system have different sensing profiles as they carry devices with different sensing capabilities and they are not like-minded with respect to participation patterns and privacy concerns.

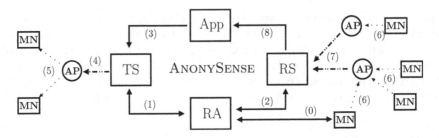

Fig. 1. The AnonySense architecture. A collection of sensor-equipped mobile nodes (MNs), owned by participating *users*, register (0) in the system through the registration authority (RA); RA also certifies the authenticity of the *system*'s components: (1) the task server (TS) and (2) report server (RS). *Applications* (App) submit (3) tasks to the TS; the MNs occasionally download (4,5) new tasks from the TS using the Internet and any available wireless access point (AP). The task specifies when the MN should sense information, and under what conditions to submit reports. MNs report (6) sensed data via APs and their reports eventually arrive (7) at the RS. At its convenience, the App fetches (8) the data from the RS.

and ensure proper context collection. AnonySense maintains anonymity at two levels: protecting the user's anonymity against the system (through anonymous protocols and a tessellation-based technique for k-anonymous location blurring) and protecting the user's anonymity against the applications (through ℓ-anonymous report aggregation). Before describing these properties, we define the system's components.

The mobile sensing infrastructure consists of individual *mobile nodes* (MNs), which are devices with sensing, computation, memory, and wireless communication capabilities. These mobile nodes may be *motes* or, we anticipate, cellphone-class devices. Mobile nodes are carried by people, or are attached to moving objects, such as vehicles.[2] The *carrier* of a node is the person carrying the node, or the owner of the vehicle.

Applications specify the desired context as *tasks*, which specify when and what sensor readings to collect, and when to report these readings back to the system. After accepting a task, an MN produces a series of *reports*, each of which is a tuple of the form (taskID, location, time, data...). We defined a simple and expressive Lisp-like language called *AnonyTL* for applications to specify what reports to produce, over what region of space-time, and under what conditions (either periodic or value threshold).

The static networking infrastructure consists of several components, each of which may be distributed or replicated:

- A *Task Server (TS)* that accepts tasks from Apps, and distributes tasks to MNs.
- A *Report Server (RS)* that receives and aggregates sensor reports.
- A *Registration Authority (RA)* that registers participating users and their mobile nodes, installing the AnonyTL interpreter and the cryptographic certificates necessary to later validate the authenticity of the MN to the system, and certificates for the MN to validate the authenticity of the TS and RS.

---

[2] For simplicity we explicitly assume only mobile nodes. In general, our system can also include static nodes, attached to stationary objects (e.g., buildings), controlled by the system or administered by individual members of the system.

– A set of *access points (APs)* that are wired to the Internet. As described in Section 4, we rely on APs to collect anonymous statistics about user associations for the generation of tessellation maps.

2.2 Threat Model and Desired Properties

Users participate in the system on a voluntary basis by enabling their mobile nodes to respond to tasks distributed by the system and contribute reports. This opportunistic sensing functionality, however, is implemented by nodes reporting sensed data while their carriers are performing everyday activities, and thus tied to many aspects of users' professional, personal and social lives. Consequently, data reports designed for context collection carry explicit or implicit sensitive information about the carriers of the nodes. This information is primarily related to a spatiotemporal component describing a user's activity, since any report annotated with a (time, location) pair clearly reveals the exact time the carrier was at a certain location, and secondarily to a data-related component of the report, i.e., the actual sensed data. On the surface, these reports are anonymous, that is, they are not tagged by the node's identifier. De-identified reports, however, may not provide sufficient anonymity. By associating pairs of time and location with *observed* or *predictable* activity patterns of individuals, sensitive information about carriers can be revealed or inferred. Using recent terminology [24], the *digital footprints left by users implementing opportunistic sensing are easily obtainable* and are a rich source of information for inference about users' location and activity. And even if such inferred information cannot possibly form an undeniable attestation about a user's behavior,[3] it can easily provide statistical inferences about a user's behavior that correspond to reasonably high confidence levels or that can hold with almost certainty.

This threat is directly addressed by AnonySense. The adversary in our anonymity model is an entity that, we must assume, has unlimited access to the users' activities and social, professional or personal every-day life patterns over an unlimited time window extended both in the past and in the future *but not in the present*. That is, the adversary is knowledgeable but not omniscient. In particular, we instantiate this entity to two concrete cases: (1) the system itself, that is, the AnonySense software and hardware and their owners, and (2) the applications and their users. We assume that these two adversaries can observe, collect and learn any information related to the activities of any number of individual users of the system, and the adversary's goal is to deanonymize reports obtained through AnonySense for the time period when a particular user is not under direct observation by the adversary.

In this setting, our goal is to apply privacy-protection techniques in a trade-off between anonymity and context accuracy. We apply the principles of k-anonymity [34] to design mechanisms that allow opportunistic sensing in our model, such that the following two properties are satisfied:

Privacy against the system. To protect users against the system, we provide statistical k-anonymity to any participating user. Thus, even though the system may observe

---

[3] Indeed, since reports carry no identification labels (at least from a computational point of view through the use of "unbreakable" cryptography), a user can always deny that a certain report came from his or her device (e.g., if brought to court or been accused for a certain behavior).

all reports, it is statistically difficult to link any report to a specific user within a set of k users based on the location or timestamp within the report. Furthermore, nodes also remain (statistically) k-anonymous during the process of receiving tasks and sending reports. Here, k is a known, system parameter controlling the users' anonymity against the system.

Privacy against applications. To protect users against the applications, we provide ℓ-anonymity to any participating user. That is, at least ℓ reports are combined together before the aggregate is revealed to the application. Here, ℓ is an anonymity parameter enforced by the system. We impose no assumption on the relation of k and ℓ. In practice k might be equal to ℓ.

Our techniques ensure that when a node is tasked, neither the TS nor any AP will learn the identity of the node or its carrier. Similarly, when the node later sends a report, neither the RS nor AP will be able to identify the node or its carrier. We also ensure that the system cannot link the tasking event to the reporting events, or link the multiple reports that a single node may submit.

In the next section, we present mechanisms that achieve the above goals.

3   Tessellation

To protect the user's privacy against the system, an MN needs to blur the location in its reports. We aim for a statistical form of k-anonymity, reporting a region rather than a point. The challenge is to divide a geographical area into an appropriate set of regions, such that each region is large enough to provide k-anonymity (usually), but small enough to retain a reasonable level of location accuracy. Our method "tessellates" the area into tiles, according to historical patterns of user locations.

Tessellation Map Generation. We assume that AnonySense has access to anonymous user-presence data for the geographical area covered by the organization's pervasive environment. In our evaluation we show how such datasets are easily obtained from Wi-Fi AP association counts from within the organization. Given recent historical data, AnonySense generates a tessellation of the area such that each tile represents a region that k users typically visit within a time interval t (e.g., 5 minutes). In reports sent to the system, MNs include the tile ID (obtained from the tessellation map) and time interval ID (time is partitioned into periods of length t). Users are, therefore, able to perform local spatiotemporal cloaking.

We begin the tessellation by constructing a Voronoi diagram at the granularity of the dataset. For example, if the data represents "location" symbolically by AP name, then we first map the AP locations as points on a plane and then construct a Voronoi diagram. For each resulting region (or polygon) we calculate the number of association counts across all time periods, and compute the threshold number of association counts that represent the p-th percentile of all the counts. For example, with $p = 95\%$, a polygon may have threshold value 12, indicating that 95% of the time periods have at least 12 associated users. In effect, we expect high values of p to be better predictors of k-anonymity, as is verified in Section 5. Next, we cluster the resulting polygons into *tiles* such that the sum of the threshold values for each polygon exceeds k. We use this value of k as the predicted statistical k-anonymity provided by each tile.

In Section 5 we describe our approach as applied to a specific dataset, and study how much a user's actual k-anonymity deviates from the predicted k-anonymity.

4 Protocol

Before we describe our privacy-preserving protocol for anonymous tasking and reporting, we detail the trust assumptions between the various entities in AnonySense.

4.1 Trust Assumptions

Mobile Nodes. We assume that all MNs communicate with the TS and RS using Wi-Fi APs. MNs do not trust the APs to maintain their location privacy. For now we assume that APs are owned by a single organization, and may collude with the TS and RS. MNs trust the RA to certify the identities of TS and RS. The MN, therefore, can establish secure connections (e.g., SSL) to the correct TS and RS. Likewise, the RA certifies each MN, which can then prove to the TS and RS that it is a valid node in the system. As we explain below, MNs can prove their validity anonymously.

Applications. Like MNs, applications also trust the RA to certify the TS and RS. Apps must trust the TS and RS to deploy tasks and collect reports as demanded and, additionally, to collect reports only from valid MNs. For now Apps are not certified. In the future we may either require Apps to authenticate, or require the *querier* (user of the App) to authenticate.

Task Server and Report Server. The TS and RS trust the RA to certify valid MNs in the system. The RA is responsible for issuing calibration certificates to MNs, attesting to the fact that the MNs' sensors are properly calibrated, as well as authentication certificates. For simplicity, we assume an authentication scheme such as Direct Anonymous Attestation (DAA) [2], but it may also be possible to use other proposed anonymous authentication schemes [3]. If MNs include trusted hardware such as the Trusted Platform Module (TPM) [36],[4] DAA can also allow the TS to verify the integrity of the MN. For example, the TPM can assert that the MN has not been tampered with, and is running unmodified and authorized software. We leave such TPM-based "remote attestation" to future work.

4.2 Tasking Protocol

We first consider the protocol for anonymously assigning tasks to MNs.

Task Generation. The App generates a task using the tasking language and sends the task to the TS using a server-authenticated SSL channel. This way, the TS accepts tasks from applications and can avoid tampering by third parties. As part of the task, the

---

[4] TPMs are now installed on most new laptops, and we expect mobile devices to include TPMs in the near future [27].

application specifies an expiration date, after which the task is deleted by the TS and MNs. The TS generates a unique task ID for the task, and sends the application an acknowledgment that contains this task ID along with a TS-signed certificate for the task ID. The application later uses this certificate to access reports for the task.

Tasking Language. The AnonyTL tasking language allows an application to specify a task's behavior by providing a set of acceptance conditions, report statements, and termination conditions. The acceptance conditions are evaluated by the MN after retrieving tasks from the TS; for example, these conditions indicate that the MN must have certain sensors. Report statements periodically check a set of report conditions against polled sensor values, and if the conditions are met, report application-specified fields to the RS. These periodic evaluations continue until a termination condition is satisfied, at which point the task is removed from the MN's task pool. We note that tasks are *not executable code*; tasks specify sensor readings desired at a particular granularity, and under what conditions an MN should report data. As a simple example, the following task collects temperature measurements from sensing devices in the Sudikoff building every one minute, and reports temperature values that do not belong to ComfLevel, a predefined range of comfortable temperatures, after being annotated with the corresponding time and location of the reading.

```
(Task 20534)(Expires 1896000453)
(Accept (In location 'sudikoff'))
(Report (temp senseTime location)
        (Every 1 Min) (Not (In temp ComfLevel)))
```

Tasking Nodes. When MNs have Internet access, they periodically poll the TS for tasks over a server-authenticated SSL channel. For each connection, the MN uses DAA to prove to the TS that it is a valid MN in the system, without revealing its identity. The TS delivers all outstanding tasks to the MN. (In future work, MNs may download a random subset of tasks, or the MN may also reveal certain attributes thereby reducing the number of tasks downloaded at the expense of some privacy.)

Since the MNs do not trust APs with their location privacy, an MN contacts the TS only when it is associated with a popular AP, that is, the AP's polygon alone meets the k-anonymity test.

The MN ignores any tasks it has considered in an earlier download, and considers the acceptance conditions of new tasks. During DAA, an MN proves to the TS that it is a valid node, and if TPM-enabled, can prove that it is operating in a secure configuration. The task is deactivated on the TS when it reaches its expiration date.

Reporting. The MN processes the task using the AnonyTL interpreter, reading sensors when required and generating reports as necessary. The MN stores reports in an outgoing queue; when the network is available, and there are queued reports, the MN contacts the RS over a server-authenticated and encrypted channel. As with the tasking protocol, MNs submit reports only when connected to popular (k-anonymous) APs. The MN uses DAA to prove its validity to the RS without exposing its identity. To prevent the RS from linking multiple reports within or across tasks, the MN must make a separate connection to the RS for each report.[5] Most importantly, the time and location values in the report are specified using the granularity from the tessellation map. Location is reported at the granularity of tiles, and time is reported at the granularity of time periods used for generating those tiles. As a result, users are given statistical k-anonymity based on the historical implication that the number of users visiting this tile in this interval is likely to be greater than k.

Data Fusion. The RS aggregates reports from a task before delivering the aggregated results to the application. Reports are combined using standard k-anonymity techniques with parameter ℓ, according to which individual fields of the reports are either generalized (i.e., values become less specific) or suppressed (i.e., values are not released). This ℓ-anonymity provides the second layer of privacy protection to the mobile user. The specific aggregation method depends on many factors such as the type of data sensed (such as a picture, an audio file, or temperature reading) and the needs of the App. A detailed discussion of aggregation methods is beyond the scope of this paper.

Report Collection. The App polls the RS for available context using a server-authenticated and encrypted channel. The application presents the TS-issued certificate with the task ID, proving that it is authorized to access the reports for that task. Encryption prevents eavesdroppers from learning potentially sensitive context data.

MAC Address Recycling. Using DAA for anonymous authentication is useless if an MN can be tracked using its static MAC address, because MNs assume the APs may collude with other components of the system. We assume the MN changes its MAC and IP addresses using one of the standard mechanisms [16,21] so that an MN's report and task actions may not be linked, but leave its implementation to future work. Addresses should be recycled for *each* report for maximum privacy, thereby ensuring reports are unlinkable. Recently, Pang et al. have shown how users' privacy can be reduced through 802.11 fingerprinting [31], so it may be necessary to seek other methods beyond MAC-address rotation to maintain privacy against especially snoopy APs.

5   Evaluation

Due to the ready availability of wireless traces from CRAWDAD.org, we did not perform a live simulation of AnonySense on real devices. Instead, we used historical movement traces to run simulations for different system parameters.

We generated a tessellation of the Dartmouth College campus based on the data set publicly available from CRAWDAD [25]. This data set represents the locations of (anonymized) wireless-network users: each entry represents a user's device associating, reassociating, or disassociating from an AP on campus. Before constructing the Voronoi diagram, as described in Section 3, we flattened the AP locations to two dimensions by ignoring the "floor number" provided for each AP. (We leave three-dimensional tessellation for future work.) This planarization step causes some locations to have tight clusters of APs that result when a tall building has an AP at the same location on every

---

[5] For performance reasons we plan to explore batch reporting, at some trade-off to privacy.

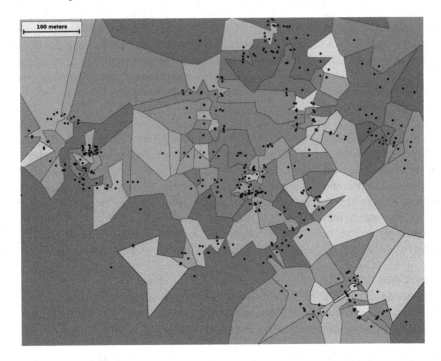

Fig. 2. We generated a Voronoi diagram using the set of APs (represented as black dots). We then combined neighboring polygons to form tiles, the colored tiles in the figure, such that $k \geq 10$ for each tile between the hours of 12pm–6pm from 9/24/2003–10/31/2003. In general, the area of a tile is roughly inversely proportional to the number of AP associations in that area.

floor; thus, we group APs that are within a certain Euclidean distance of each other into a single AP. Given this set of points on the plane, we generated a Voronoi diagram to produce a polygon for each AP, and applied our clustering algorithm to generate a tessellation of the geographical region. We generated tessellation maps for 6-hour time periods in the day (due to varying mobility patterns throughout the day), and focused only on the time period 12noon–6pm in our experiments.

Figure 2 shows a tessellation for $k = 10$, with a time granularity of 10 minutes. The points within the tiles indicate the locations of APs that were clustered together for that tile. There are 90 tiles in Figure 2, the smallest and largest being 82 m^2 and 2,694,063 m^2, with a median area of 1629 m^2. We note that the tiles near the edges of the Dartmouth campus tend to have a large area because we do not crop the tiles to the general campus area.

Although the tessellation map was generated using historic AP visitation data, we expect a user's k-anonymity to be similar to the historically observed values. To evaluate this claim, we measured the deviation of a user's anonymity from the expected k-anonymity using the same 2003 Dartmouth dataset. We generated the tessellation map for data from the 24 September–31 October range, first half of their Fall term, and then evaluated AnonySense with the visits from the 1 November–10 December range. This was done by calculating the effective anonymity for each tile using the same counting

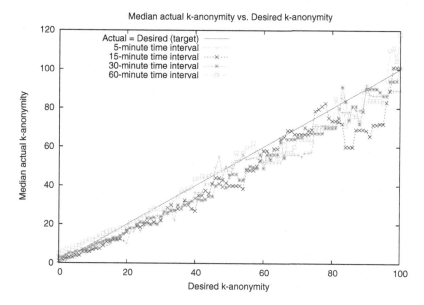

Fig. 3. This graph plots the median of the actual k-anonymity attained across all tiles against the desired k-anonymity. We can see that the expected minimum k-anonymity closely matches the desired k-anonymity regardless of the time interval used.

heuristic used in its generation, at the 95th percentile (i.e., 95% of the time, what value was the tile's effective k-anonymity greater than?) Figure 3 illustrates the performance of our technique for various time blurring intervals. The objective is to achieve a simulated k-anonymity equal to the desired k-anonymity parameter (95% of the time) used to generate the tiling, and the figure demonstrates that this level of k-anonymity is closely matched with the expected value. It also shows that the accuracy of our tiling method is mostly independent of the time interval used to generate the tiling. This is important, as it means that it is possible to select a time interval without sacrificing anonymity (although, of course, spatial accuracy will be sacrificed, as we show in Figure 4.)

We then evaluated the trade-off between temporal and spatial accuracy, for different levels of k-anonymity. Figure 4 shows this trade-off, with a roughly inverse relationship between the two. This result, along with the fact that the quality (with respect to k-anonymity) of our tessellations is independent of the time interval chosen, means that statistical k-anonymity can be maintained regardless of an application's desired spatial accuracy, at the cost of temporal accuracy.

Finally, we evaluated the distribution of actual k-anonymity for specific instances of our tessellation. Figure 5 shows one such distribution for $k = 10$ and $t = 10$. The histogram shows that our algorithm not only gives anonymity to a majority of users, but actually gives most users significantly greater anonymity than the tessellation parameters require.

We note that the clustering algorithms used to generate the tessellation are not necessarily ideal. As can be seen in Figure 2, some of the tiles have elongated and irregular shapes, which would not necessarily translate to "useful" locality readings from

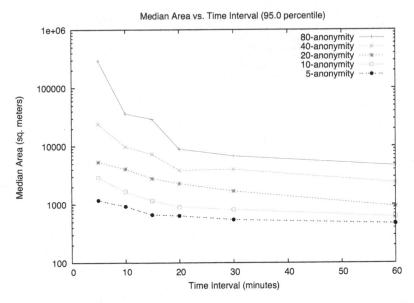

Fig. 4. This graph plots the median spatial granularity against the chosen time granularity for various values of desired k-anonymity. We see that for a given k, time granularity can be traded off for spatial granularity. Increasing the amount of k anonymity requires larger tiles, and thus reduces the spatial granularity. Note the log scale.

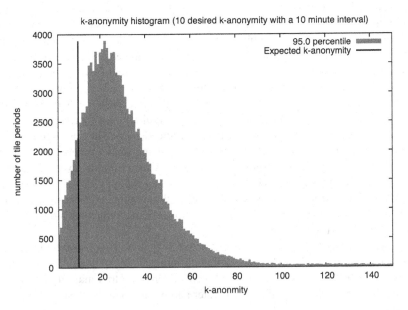

Fig. 5. This histogram shows the distribution of actual k-anonymity achieved during each tile-time-period combination for desired $k \geq 10$ and $t = 10$ minutes

a human point of view. Although the shapes of the tiles do not affect AnonySense's privacy properties (assuming the basic tile generation rules are met), more sophisticated clustering algorithms that favor compact tiles might give better results, while still maintaining similar values for k.

6 Discussion

There are many issues raised by this approach, and several challenges remain.

Real-Time Information. Due to the opportunistic nature of its sensing model, Anony-Sense is inherently not a real-time context collection system. Not only is there an inevitable system delay arising from intermittent MN connectivity and task acceptance conditions, but AnonySense intentionally maintains the time-location trade-off for a given level of k-anonymity. Thus, an application needing timely information would likely sacrifice significant location accuracy at all but the busiest of sensing locations.

Varying the Degree of k-Anonymity. One natural suggestion would be to allow users to specify their desired degree of k-anonymity, and pick the right tile to match the specified k. We caution against this approach, because the user's preferred degree of anonymity can itself leak information about the user. Consider the example where a known paranoid user prefers k-anonymity with $k = 200$. Receiving a report with a large blurred range can be linked to that user. Users' privacy is therefore maximized when all users use the same value of k.

Privacy. AnonySense takes a conservative approach at providing users with privacy, by blurring all dimensions of a report. Specifically, ℓ reports are combined so that time, location, and sensor readings are aggregated according to standard techniques used in the literature. We plan to explore other forms of privacy, where the fidelity of some dimensions of reports are preserved. For example, location blurring may be sufficient to provide users with privacy even if their identities are known. Indeed, much of the work on location privacy related to sharing location with contacts assumes that the identity of the person is known, and the location is blurred enough to provide users with privacy. AnonySense, however, aims to provide stronger privacy. For example, Alice may select a campus-level location granularity, but still leaks the exact time she arrives on campus.

Security Metrics. Quantifying the privacy of users is a hard problem. We assume a strong attack model, where adversaries can build histories of users, and then try to deanonymize reports obtained from the tasking service. We further assume that the system itself may misuse the information about the time and location of sensor reports, by blurring the location and time, but we trust the system to properly anonymize (aggregate) the sensor data. Blurring the sensor data *at the nodes* may be possible, using a similar tessellation map built from historical sensor data. We do not evaluate such an approach because of lack of data. Furthermore, we believe that the blurring of environmental sensor data (such as room temperature or pollution levels) will provide diminishing returns to a user's privacy in addition to what is already provided by time and location blurring.

Collecting User-Presence Data. For simplicity we assume that users trust an entity called the *Map Server (MS)* to collect AP-association traces and generate the tessellation map accurately. There are several avenues for future work for MNs to maintain anonymous associations with the APs, but allow the APs to accurately count MNs, and allow the MNs to verify the accuracy of the resulting map. We hint at two such approaches based on standard cryptographic techniques. (1) Users authenticate with APs using a variant of anonymous authentication that allows only one authentication per time period [4]. Users obtain a token from the APs certifying that some anonymous user successfully associated with that AP. The user posts this token onto a public bulletin board. These AP-association "logs" can be then used for generating tessellation maps. Using the publicly posted information, users can verify that their associations have been used in generating the tessellation map. Note that the bulletin board is *not* trusted storage. If the bulletin board cheats by throwing away some data, it can be observed by users with high probability. Such techniques are common to e-voting protocols [7]. (2) Alternatively, users can maintain a vector of location visits during a day (e.g., using GPS traces or by counting their AP associations) and upload their vectors to the bulletin board at the end of the day. Such techniques are standard to the "homomorphic encryption" family of e-voting protocols [9].

Location Data, and Tessellation. We describe our tessellation approach using data about the location history of wireless-network users, which is provided as a sequence of associations with Wi-Fi APs. The movements are discrete, hopping from one location to another, and the locations are discrete points on the plane. In other settings, such as locations obtained from GPS, the locations are continuous (any coordinate on the earth) and the movements may be less discrete (a path connecting waypoints). We believe that our tessellation approach can be adapted to other location models, such as heat maps showing continuous mobility distribution, although the details remain future work.

7   Conclusions

We present AnonySense, a comprehensive system aimed at preserving the privacy of users in opportunistic-sensing environments. AnonySense uses a protocol for anonymous tasking and reporting, and performs report aggregation to provide k-anonymity against applications. We show how users can proactively improve their privacy against the system by using a novel technique based on *tessellation*. Using our technique, users' devices can automatically blur time and location information in reports to provide users with statistical k-anonymity. Automatic blurring is achieved by reporting locations at the granularity of *tiles*, where the tiles are generated based on historical data. We evaluated our approach using real AP-association traces from the CRAWDAD dataset representing 6,553 active users over 77 days and show that a reasonable tradeoff can be achieved between users' privacy and spatiotemporal granularity.

Acknowledgments

This research program is a part of the Institute for Security Technology Studies, supported by Grants 2005-DD-BX-1091 awarded by the Bureau of Justice Assistance,

60NANB6D6130 awarded by the U.S. Department of Commerce, and by the Institute for Information Infrastructure Protection (I3P) under an award from the Science and Technology Directorate at the U.S. Department of Homeland Security. The second author was additionally supported by the Center for Algorithmic Game Theory at the University of Aarhus under an award from the Carlsberg Foundation. Computations were performed on cluster machines supported under NSF grant EIA-98-02068. The views or opinions in this paper do not necessarily reflect the views of the sponsors. We thank the MetroSense team at Dartmouth College and Vijay Bhuse for their helpful comments.

References

1. Abdelzaher, T., Anokwa, Y., Boda, P., Burke, J., Estrin, D., Guibas, L., Kansal, A., Madden, S., Reich, J.: Mobiscopes for human spaces. IEEE Pervasive Computing 6(2), 20–29 (2007)
2. Brickell, E., Camenisch, J., Chen, L.: Direct anonymous attestation. In: CCS 2004: Proceedings of the 11th ACM Conference on Computer and Communications Security, pp. 132–145. ACM Press, New York (2004)
3. Calandriello, G., Papadimitratos, P., Hubaux, J.-P., Lioy, A.: Efficient and robust pseudonymous authentication in VANET. In: VANET 2007: Proceedings of the Fourth ACM International Workshop on Vehicular Ad Hoc Networks, pp. 19–28. ACM Press, New York (2007)
4. Camenisch, J., Hohenberger, S., Kohlweiss, M., Lysyanskaya, A., Meyerovich, M.: How to win the clonewars: efficient periodic n-times anonymous authentication. In: Proceedings of the 13th ACM Conference on Computer and Communications Security (CCS 2006), pp. 201–210. ACM Press, New York (2006)
5. Campbell, A., Eisenman, S., Lane, N., Miluzzo, E., Peterson, R.: People-centric urban sensing. In: The Second Annual International Wireless Internet Conference (WICON), pp. 2–5. IEEE Computer Society Press, Los Alamitos (2006)
6. CENS Urban Sensing project (2007), http://research.cens.ucla.edu/projects/2006/Systems/UrbanSensing/
7. Chaum, D., Ryan, P.Y.A., Schneider, S.A.: A practical voter-verifiable election scheme. In: de Capitani di Vimercati, S., Syverson, P.F., Gollmann, D. (eds.) ESORICS 2005. LNCS, vol. 3679, pp. 118–139. Springer, Heidelberg (2005)
8. Chow, C.-Y., Mokbel, M.F., Liu, X.: A peer-to-peer spatial cloaking algorithm for anonymous location-based service. In: GIS 2006: Proceedings of the 14th Annual ACM International Symposium on Advances in Geographic Information Systems, pp. 171–178. ACM Press, New York (2006)
9. Cramer, R., Gennaro, R., Schoenmakers, B.: A secure and optimally efficient multiauthority election scheme. In: Fumy, W. (ed.) EUROCRYPT 1997. LNCS, vol. 1233, pp. 103–118. Springer, Heidelberg (1997)
10. Duckham, M., Kulik, L.: A Formal Model of Obfuscation and Negotiation for Location Privacy. In: Gellersen, H.-W., Want, R., Schmidt, A. (eds.) PERVASIVE 2005. LNCS, vol. 3468, Springer, Heidelberg (2005)
11. Frank, C., Bolliger, P., Roduner, C., Kellerer, W.: Objects calling home: Locating objects using mobile phones. In: LaMarca, A., Langheinrich, M., Truong, K.N. (eds.) Pervasive 2007. LNCS, vol. 4480, Springer, Heidelberg (2007)
12. Gedik, B., Liu, L.: Location privacy in mobile systems: A personalized anonymization model. In: ICDCS 2005: Proceedings of the 25th IEEE International Conference on Distributed Computing Systems, pp. 620–629. IEEE Computer Society Press, Los Alamitos (2005)

13. Ghinita, G., Kalnis, P., Skiadopoulos, S.: Prive: anonymous location-based queries in distributed mobile systems. In: WWW 2007: Proceedings of the 16th International Conference on World Wide Web, pp. 371–380. ACM Press, New York (2007)

14. Goldreich, O., Micali, S., Wigderson, A.: How to play any mental game or a completeness theorem for protocols with honest majority. In: ACM Symposium on Theory of Computing, pp. 218–229 (1987)

15. Gruteser, M., Grunwald, D.: Anonymous usage of location-based services through spatial and temporal cloaking. In: MobiSys 2003: Proceedings of the 1st International Conference on Mobile Systems, Applications and Services, pp. 31–42. ACM Press, New York (2003)

16. Gruteser, M., Grunwald, D.: Enhancing location privacy in wireless LAN through disposable interface identifiers: a quantitative analysis. Mobile Networks and Applications 10(3), 315–325 (2005)

17. Hoh, B., Gruteser, M.: Protecting location privacy through path confusion. In: SECURECOMM 2005: Proceedings of the First International Conference on Security and Privacy for Emerging Areas in Communications Networks, pp. 194–205. IEEE Computer Society Press, Los Alamitos (2005)

18. Hong, J.I., Landay, J.A.: An architecture for privacy-sensitive ubiquitous computing. In: Proceedings of MobiSys 2004, Boston, MA, USA, June 2004, pp. 177–189 (2004)

19. Hull, B., Bychkovsky, V., Zhang, Y., Chen, K., Goraczko, M., Miu, A.K., Shih, E., Balakrishnan, H., Madden, S.: CarTel: A Distributed Mobile Sensor Computing System. In: 4th ACM Conference on Embedded Networked Sensor Systems (SenSys) (November 2006)

20. Iachello, G., Smith, I., Consolvo, S., Chen, M., Abowd, G.D.: Developing privacy guidelines for social location disclosure applications and services. In: Proceedings of the 2005 Symposium on Usable Privacy and Security (July 2005)

21. Jiang, T., Wang, H.J., Hu, Y.-C.: Preserving location privacy in wireless LANs. In: MobiSys 2007: Proceedings of the 5th International Conference on Mobile Systems, Applications and Services, pp. 246–257. ACM Press, New York (2007)

22. Johnson, P., Kapadia, A., Kotz, D., Triandopoulos, N.: People-Centric Urban Sensing: Security Challenges for the New Paradigm. Technical Report TR2007-586, Dartmouth College, Computer Science, Hanover, NH (February 2007)

23. Kalnis, P., Ghinita, G., Mouratidis, K., Papadias, D.: Preserving anonymity in location based services. Technical Report TRB/06, National University of Singapore, Department of Computer Science (2006)

24. Kapadia, A., Henderson, T., Fielding, J.J., Kotz, D.: Virtual walls: Protecting digital privacy in pervasive environments. In: LaMarca, A., Langheinrich, M., Truong, K.N. (eds.) Pervasive 2007. LNCS, vol. 4480, pp. 162–179. Springer, Heidelberg (2007)

25. Kotz, D., Henderson, T., Abyzov, I.: CRAWDAD trace dartmouth/campus/movement/aplocations (v. 2004-11-09) (November 2004), Downloaded from http://crawdad.cs.dartmouth.edu/dartmouth/campus/movement/aplocations

26. Krumm, J.: Inference attacks on location tracks. In: LaMarca, A., Langheinrich, M., Truong, K.N. (eds.) Pervasive 2007. LNCS, vol. 4480, pp. 127–143. Springer, Heidelberg (2007)

27. Mobile Phone Work Group, Trusted Computing Group, www.trustedcomputinggroup.org/groups/mobile

28. Mokbel, M.F., Chow, C.-Y.: Challenges in preserving location privacy in peer-to-peer environments. In: Seventh International Conference on Web-Age Information Management Workshops, p. 1 (2006)

29. Mokbel, M.F., Chow, C.-Y., Aref, W.G.: The new Casper: query processing for location services without compromising privacy. In: VLDB 2006: Proceedings of the 32nd International Conference on Very Large Data Bases, pp. 763–774. VLDB Endowment (2006)

30. Myles, G., Friday, A., Davies, N.: Preserving privacy in environments with location-based applications. IEEE Pervasive Computing 2(1), 56–64 (2003)

31. Pang, J., Greenstein, B., Gummadi, R., Seshan, S., Wetherall, D.: 802.11 user fingerprinting. In: MobiCom 2007: Proceedings of the 13th Annual ACM International Conference on Mobile Computing and Networking, pp. 99–110. ACM Press, New York (2007)
32. Riva, O., Borcea, C.: The Urbanet revolution: Sensor power to the people! IEEE Pervasive Computing 6(2), 41–49 (2007)
33. Microsoft Research SenseWeb project (2007),
    http://research.microsoft.com/nec/senseweb/
34. Sweeney, L.: k-anonymity: A model for protecting privacy. International Journal of Uncertainty, Fuzziness, and Knowledge-Based Systems (2002)
35. Tang, K.P., Fogarty, J., Keyani, P., Hong, J.I.: Putting people in their place: An anonymous and privacy-sensitive approach to collecting sensed data in location-based applications. In: Proceedings of the SIGCHI Conference on Human Factors in Computing Systems (CHI), pp. 93–102 (2006)
36. Trusted Computing Group (TCG) (May 2005),
    https://www.trustedcomputinggroup.org/home

Privacy Protection for RFID with Hidden Subset Identifiers*

Jacek Cichoń, Marek Klonowski, and Mirosław Kutyłowski

Institute of Mathematics and Computer Science,
Wrocław University of Technology, Poland
ul. Wybrzeże Wyspiańskiego 50-370 Wrocław
{Jacek.Cichon,Marek.Klonowski,Miroslaw.Kutylowski}@pwr.wroc.pl

Abstract. We propose very simple and cheap but nevertheless effective protection against privacy threats for RFID-tags. For the *hidden subset* RFID-tags proposed in this paper, the ID string presented by an RFID-tag evolves rapidly. It is is not the bit value that enables one to recognize a tag. Instead, a reader detects some invariant properties that are hard to be recognized by a curious illegitimate reader.

The solution is not based on any cryptographic primitive, it relies only on properties of random sets and on linear mappings between vector spaces. The solution proposed is well suited for low-end devices, since all mechanisms can be easily implemented by circuits of a small size.

1 Introduction

RFID Technology and Privacy. RFID-tags, which are tiny devices with very limited memory and low computational power, can influence a big number of application areas. Their primary functionality is identification of objects which they are attached to. The major point is that reading identifiers contained in an RFID-tag is possible in a wireless way, and so without any manual manipulation. Therefore RFID-tags can be considered as successors of widely used bar-codes. However, they offer features that go far beyond elimination of manual manipulation of objects in order to read a tag. So there are many potential applications of RFID-tags in diverse areas (as a starting point of discussion on these issues see e.g. [9]).

There is a vast and sometimes overoptimistic literature on RFID-tags with interesting and important application proposals. However, the number of systems deployed is much lower than one could expect. This is not a coincidence alone for the reason that some basic security problems have not been solved yet. One of the major problem is preventing leaking sensitive information due to the fact

* This work was partially supported by EU within the 7th Framework Programme under contract 215270 (FRONTS). It was initiated within the 6th Framework Programme under contract 001907 (DELIS). Marek Klonowski was beneficiary of domestic grant for young scientists awarded by The Foundation for Polish Science in the years 2006-2007.

J. Indulska et al. (Eds.): Pervasive 2008, LNCS 5013, pp. 298–314, 2008.
© Springer-Verlag Berlin Heidelberg 2008

that an RFID-tag is typically a passive device and the readers are not authorized by the tag.

The main problem considered in this paper is that readers can collect information on all RFID's in their proximity. This information may be gathered on a large scale, analyzed, and then misused. Most people generally underestimate possibilities of data mining in such data sets. Surprisingly, many important data can be obtained with such methods, even if certain information are missing or anonymized. A good example of this type, quite convincing for the general public is determining identity of a holder of a prepaid SIM card, which can be performed by analyzing the graph of phone connections.

Particularly vulnerable are systems based on RFID-tags with unique static binary ID's written at the moment of tag's creation. If the ID remains unchanged during the tag's life-cycle and there is no authorization of the readers accessing the RFID's, then some valuable data on RFID holders are available explicitly. In this case, there is even no need to gather data or cover a substantial area by the malicious readers - some key locations might suffice for certain purposes.

In particular, people may be traced by tracing RFID-tags that they are holding. Moreover, the RFID holder might be unaware of the RFID readers talking to her or his tag and therefore be unaware where and when he has been traced. So RFID's is a perfect technology not only for good purposes, but also may become a cheap and effective "Big Brother" network. It concerns not only violations of personal privacy, but also industrial espionage, and organized crime. Privacy threats caused by RFID-tags were recognized almost immediately after deploying the first RFID-based systems and stopped their wide-spread development (recall for instance the case of METRO company in Germany and severe discussions regarding personal data protection there). Actually, the problem was recognized already in 2001 while designing Auto-ID Center protocols.

Except users' privacy violation via tracing there are other major threats for RFID-systems. One of them is *cloning*. In this attack, the tag's ID is simply copied into the memory of another tag (clone). This is a crucial problem for many application areas where tags are used for access control, movement control, billing purposes, and so on. If a tag allows an RFID reader to overwrite its memory, then it can be exploited by malicious readers performing many attacks. For instance, the reader may destroy a tag by writing junk contents. In this way one could easily attack the systems deployed by competitors.

It should be underlined that all data concerning RFID-tags observed must be protected with particular care (and cost) from unauthorized use of their data. Indeed, they may be regarded as personal data and underlie the very strict rules of personal data protection acts in many countries. Non-obeying these rules is often a criminal act with respectively harsh penalties.

Design Goals. In this paper we are interested in passive RFID-tags with very small memory and severely limited computational power that does not allow a tag to perform any non-trivial cryptographic operation. Even computing values of commonly used hash functions can be regarded as too expensive. Therefore we cannot use any classical cryptographic authentication protocol in order to satisfy privacy protection and security demands. Basically, we cannot use any purely cryptographic method.

In this paper look for a solution which solves the basic privacy problem for RFID-systems:

1. an RFID-tag shows its ID in order to fulfill its basic identification goal;
2. an RFID-tag prevents any unauthorized reader to understand its answer.

We focus on techniques that can provide a fair level of security, but at the same time are so rudimentary that a hardware implementation is very easy and cheap.

While examining simplicity and efficiency of a solution might be a simple task (easily backed by empirical data), this does not apply to security guarantees. In this case it is insufficient to show that there is no (obvious) way to break the scheme, or that all previously used methods fail. We need some evidence that there is no attack or it is more expensive than the value of the system or data attacked. Clearly, no experiment may confirm that such an attack does not exist. Let us remark that if a security mechanism implemented in hardware turns out to be faulty, then there in no way to install a patch which would solve the problem, as it is the case for software components. Therefore, we may face necessity of replacement of devices on a very large scale with severe economic consequences. For this reason we have to pay a lot of attention to formal security guarantees when designing hardware systems.

Previous Privacy Protection Methods. So far a few methods have been designed to protect the RFID-systems from the threats discussed above. This topic has been covered by survey papers (see [6,7,11,12]).

The simplest method it is to switch off a tag permanently, or *kill* a tag [8], when a particular triggering event occurs. Of course, even for retail stores this solution has certain disadvantages - one cannot use the tags as a proof of product origin, when there is a dispute with a consumer. Temporary blocking tags might be a better solution. For instance solution form [8] prevents recognition of any tag in a particular location, if *tree walking algorithm* is used. A method based on unblocking with passwords ([14]) is much more flexible. However, this requires implementing hash functions, which is relatively expensive for the RFID tags. One can also partially disable a tags antenna [10] - through reducing the tag's communication range no uncontrolled read operations are possible, the tag must be placed in just a few centimeters from the reader.

There is a separate design line of privacy protection for RFID-systems based on dynamic changes of tag's content. Changes are carried out in such a way that only a legitimate user is able to link them. Golle et al. [4] (see also [1]) introduce idea of *universal re-encryption*. Their encryption scheme allows anyone to re-encrypt a ciphertext *without knowing the public key* corresponding to the ciphertext. Moreover, only the owner of the private key is able to say if two given ciphertexts correspond to the same plaintext. Golle et al. proposed that this scheme can be applied for RFID-tags: the tag's ID is encrypted by its creator/issuer. If the tag is in the proximity of a computationally strong reader, then the ciphertext is re-encrypted and the reader overwrites the old ciphertext. A serious disadvantage of this method is that it requires deploying trusted readers and relatively large size of RFID's memory.

In [3], we propose spontaneous random changes of single ID-bits at random positions. After getting a bit string from a tag, the reader seeks a tag in the database with the closest ID - the corresponding entry should correspond to the tag observed. The idea is that a tag ID evolves all the time and if an adversary does not see the tag for some time, the link between the old and new values is lost. The main disadvantage is that the adversary may cause spontaneous changes and the tag cannot be recognized by legitimate readers as well.

Paper Contribution. In this paper we present a construction that provides a high security level against unauthorized readers: only the readers that share secret information with a tag can recognize it. At the same time the tag does not use any cryptographic mechanism; the solution is based on complexity of combinatorial problems and hidden linear equations. For this reason, its hardware implementation is extremely simple.

The main disadvantage of the scheme is that it requires quite fair amount of computation on the reader side, when a new unrecognized tag appears at some location. The other disadvantage is that a reader or a background system must have access to secrets shared with the tag. However, this seems to be inevitable for any design that is not based on asymmetric cryptography and each tag has different secret material.

The solution presented in this paper is probably not the ultimate solution. It is meant rather as opening a new line of research, and independent security evaluation focused on practical situations and demands should follow.

Organization of the Paper. Sec. 2 presents the basic construction. In Sec. 3 we discuss random choice of characteristic sets and the consequences of the construction. In Sec. 4 we concern linkability of a tag to previous values given by the tags, as well as false recognition of a tag. In Sec. 5 we describe the danger of cloning a tag and present two countermeasures.

In Appendix (Section 6) we present auxiliary mathematical results on vectors and matrices of random bits which are used in this paper. For completeness, we also provide proofs of these facts.

2   Hidden Subsets RFID-Tags

Outline of the Algorithm. We describe here a simplified version of our construction, the ultimate construction reaching high security standards will be described in Sec. 5.1. and 5.2.

We consider memory of an RFID-tag as a list of single-bit registers. We shall talk about (n, k)-tags, where the memory is divided into parts of sizes, respectively, n and k (see Fig. 1). The first, longer part is called the *random* part. The second part of k registers (generally k is small, even $k = 1$ is possible) is called the *dependent* part.

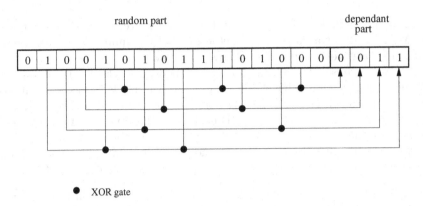

Fig. 1. Design idea of a hidden subset RFID tag. Example of a $(16, 4)$-tag.

For each bit of the dependent part, a distinct *characteristic set* is chosen. A characteristic set is a non-empty subset of $\{1, \ldots, n\}$ and determines registers from the random part that determine one bit from the dependent part. The characteristic sets of a tag are known only for the tags' creator.

The simplest approach to choose a characteristic set is to toss an (asymmetric) coin for each $i \leq n$ and to put i into the characteristic set if tails are obtained. We shall later discuss the process of production of a tag in more detail.

The main point is that it is not the contents of the random part that identifies a tag: for identifying a tag we use relations between the random and the dependent part. Every time when a tag is read, all its bits from the random part are randomly and independently overwritten. Then each single bit b from the dependent part is re-computed as an XOR of values in positions indicated by the characteristic set of b in the random part of the tag.

A legitimate user that knows the characteristic sets can easily recognize the tag. It simply recomputes the values that should appear in the dependent part according to the characteristic sets of the tag. At the same time, without knowing characteristic sets one cannot check the relations that in fact define a tag.

It is crucial for our design that the bits in the random part are changing at random spontaneously. For this reason it is impossible to trace a tag based on the contents of the random part.

Formal Description. Let $|A|$ denote the number of elements of set A. Let $x \in_R A$ mean that the element x is chosen from the finite set A uniformly at random. Let $[n]$ stand for $\{1, \ldots, n\}$. Symbol $\oplus_A \xi$ denotes XOR of those bits of a bit string ξ that are taken from positions i such that $i \in A$. The ith bit of bit string Z is denoted by $Z(i)$. If $C \subseteq [n]$ then $\overrightarrow{C}$ denotes the characteristic function of the set C, i.e. $\overrightarrow{C}(i) = 1$ if $i \in C$ and $\overrightarrow{C}(i) = 0$ if $i \in [n] \setminus C$. We say that a collection $\{C_1, \ldots, C_k\}$ of subsets of $[n]$ is linearly independent, if the collection $\{\overrightarrow{C}_1, \ldots, \overrightarrow{C}_k\}$ of vectors from $\{0, 1\}^n$ is linearly independent over the binary field $\mathbb{Z}_2$.

Let X_T, Y_T and C_T^i $(C_T^i \subseteq [n])$ denote the random part, the dependent part and the ith characteristic set of tag T, respectively. An RFID tag with $|X_T| = n$ and $|Y_T| = k$ is called an (n, k)-tag. Notice that each (n, k)-tag T defines a function $T : \{0, 1\}^n \to \{0, 1\}^k$ by the formula

$$T(\xi) = (\bigoplus_{C_T^1} \xi, \ldots, \bigoplus_{C_T^k} \xi).$$

It is worth to remark, for purposes of formal analysis of properties of investigated tags that T is a linear mapping between $\{0, 1\}^n$ and $\{0, 1\}^k$, treated as linear spaces over field $\mathbb{Z}_2$.

Tag Reading and Update Operation. The following procedure is carried out automatically during each read operation, as well as during initialization of tag T. It is performed by the tag and only triggered by the reader:

```
procedure Update(T)
begin
    X_T ∈_R {0, 1}^n;
    for i = 1 to k
        Y_T(i) := ⊕_{C_T^i} X_T;
end;
```

In this algorithm fresh, random bits are placed in the random part of the tag and then k consecutive bits of the dependent part are computed. Let us remark that if a tag does not succeed to finalize these operations, then the tag fails to fulfill the required relationship between the random and dependent parts. However, this is not an issue, since performing the next update (correctly executed) recovers the relationship of the bit values.

On the other hand, after getting an answer X, Y the reader tries to match the answer with answers that would be given by each candidate tag. Namely, for each candidate tag S the following equations are checked for $i = 1, \ldots, k$:

$$Y(i) = \bigoplus_{C_S^i} X$$

till the first moment when the equality does not hold. Then candidate S gets excluded. If all equalities hold, then the tag examined is regarded to be S. Let us remark that the search need not to be performed by the reader itself – the answer X, Y can be forwarded to a center that holds secret information. This may be advantageous due to ease of holding secret information.

3   Random Choice of Characteristic Sets

Details of Constructing a Tag. *Random choice* of characteristic sets might mean many different processes, so let us fix some details. This is quite important when we concern cryptanalysis – these details may have considerable influence on the system properties.

We assume the following process of creating (n, k)-tags. First a parameter $p \in (0, 1)$ has to be fixed. Then during the personalization process of an RFID-tag the sets $C_T^1, \ldots, C_T^k \subseteq [n]$ are generated using $n \cdot k$ independent coin tosses with the probability of success (i.e. of choosing 1 as a value of the characteristic function at a given input) equal to p. We call this scenario an (n, k, p)-*production schema*.

In Sec. 6 we discuss influence of each parameter of the production schema on the effectiveness and security of hidden subset RFID systems. At this point let us remark that on one hand small p results in a small number of connections (and a small hardware layout), while on the other hand a small p reduces the number of possible characteristic sets and makes brute force attack less difficult.

The most important issue considered here is linear independence of the characteristic sets created in this way. Note that linear dependence is a highly unwelcome property - this implies linear dependence between the bits in the dependent part. Since the number of dependent bits is relatively small, such a linear dependence is easy to detect through a small number of read operations and analysis of the answers. Then the discovered dependencies in the dependent part may serve as a *fingerprint* of the tag concerned. In other words, in this case it is not necessary to look for characteristic sets that yield to specific dependent bits - which is the main problem from combinatorial point of view.

Theorem 6 from Appendix states that $C_T^1, \ldots, C_T^k$ are linearly independent with probability at least $1 - \mathrm{Upd}(n, k, p)$ where

$$\mathrm{Upd}(n, m, p) = \frac{1}{2^n} \sum_{a=1}^{m} \binom{m}{a} \left(1 + (1 - 2p)^a\right)^n . \tag{1}$$

Below we discuss the values given by this estimation.

For production schema of the form $(n, 30, 0.5)$, the probability that the collection $C_T^1, \ldots, C_T^k$ is linearly dependent is bounded from above by 2^{30-n}. So for $n \in \{128, \ldots, 1024\}$ we get pretty good guarantee that characteristic sets are linearly independent.

Table 1 contains upper bounds on probabilities of production of dependent tags in schema $(n, 30, 30/n)$ for various n. Notice that the expected number of elements in a characteristic set for (n, k, p)-production schema is $p \cdot n$. So in the case considered the size of independent sets oscillates around 30, so the characteristic sets are quite sparse. Nevertheless, we see that again probability of getting linearly dependent characteristic sets is acceptably low. In this case one can simply check dependence of characteristic sets by standard methods of linear algebra and reject linearly dependent characteristic sets.

Table 1. Upper bounds on probability of getting linearly dependent characteristic sets for schema $(n, 30, 30/n)$

n:	128	256	512	1024
p:	$4.28 \cdot 10^{-14}$	$4.16 \cdot 10^{-13}$	$1.12 \cdot 10^{-12}$	$1.79 \cdot 10^{-12}$

Details of Recognizing a Tag. Let us fix an (n, k, p)-production schema and let us assume that all tags considered in this subsection have been generated according to this schema.

Assume that a reader has to check, if a tag T in its proximity is a tag T_0. The procedure depends on the size of the dependent part. If $k = 1$, then the reader scans the tag t times. Each time it gets X_T and Y_T, it checks whether

$$Y_T(1) = \bigoplus_{C_{T_0}^1} X_T. \tag{2}$$

Note that for each read operation an Update is performed, so different scans are in some sense independent. If the observed tag was really T_0, then (2) always holds. Otherwise, if $C_{T_0} \neq C_T$, then equality (2) does not hold with probability $\frac{1}{2}$. So $T \neq T_0$ remains undetected with probability 2^{-t}. The main problem with this approach is that the reader must be sure that it is talking with the same tag. A single malicious message obtained by the reader may be misinterpreted as one of the t answers mentioned and the tag may become rejected.

We claim that if k is sufficiently large, say $k = 30$, then a single scan fully suffices. equals 2^{-k}. However, the argument is incorrect, since the tests corresponding to different characteristic sets are not completely independent: namely they may concern overlapping sets of bits. Let us consider a tag T; in this case the reader checks for each $j \leq k$ whether

$$Y_T(j) = \bigoplus_{C_{T_0}^j} X_T, \tag{3}$$

which is equivalent to

$$\bigoplus_{C_{T_0}^j} X_T = \bigoplus_{C_T^j} X_T \quad \text{for } j = 1, \ldots, k.$$

The last equation can be written in the following way

$$\bigoplus_{C_{T_0}^j \oplus C_{T_0}^j} X_T = 0 \quad \text{for } j = 1, \ldots, k.$$

By Theorems 5 and 6 from Appendix we deduce that the family

$$\mathcal{S} = \{C_{T_0}^1 \oplus C_T^1, \ldots, C_{T_0}^k \oplus C_T^k\}$$

is linearly independent with probability at least $1 - \mathrm{Upd}(n, k, 2p(1-p))$, where expression $\mathrm{Upd}(n, k, p)$ is given by equation (1). Furthermore, if family $\mathcal{S}$ is linearly independent, then using Theorem 7 from Appendix, we deduce that

$$\Pr\left[\bigwedge_{j=1}^k (\bigoplus_{C_{T_0}^j \oplus C_{T_0}^j} X_T = 0)\right] = \frac{1}{2^k}.$$

From the inequality $\Pr[A] \leq \Pr[A|B] + \Pr[B^c]$ we finally get

$$\Pr\left[\bigwedge_{j=1}^k (\bigoplus_{C_{T_0}^j} X_T = \bigoplus_{C_T^j} X_T)\right] \leq \frac{1}{2^k} + \mathrm{Upd}(n, k, 2p(1-p)).$$

Concluding, we have obtained the following result:

Theorem 1. *Let T_0 and T be random tags created according to (n, k, p) production schema. Then the probability that an answer of T will be accepted as an answer of T_0 is bounded by*

$$\frac{1}{2^k} + Upd(n, k, 2p(1 - p)),$$

where $Upd()$ is an expression defined by equality (1) and probability concerns choice of T and T_0 and the choice of the values for the random part.

In particular, if $p = \frac{1}{2}$, then the tag $T \neq T_0$ can be recognized as T_0 (a false positive recognition) with probability not higher than $2^{-k} + 2^{-n+k}$. Therefore, if tags were created with $(n, 30, 0.5)$-production schema, then probability of a false positive recognition is not higher than $2^{-30} + 2^{-n+30}$.

Let us consider the $(n, 30, 30/n)$-production schema. It can be numerically checked that for all $n \geq 128$ we have $Upd(n, 30, 2 \cdot \frac{30}{n}(1 - \frac{30}{n})) < 5.82 \cdot 10^{-24}$, so we see that in this case the probability of a false positive recognition is less than $2^{-30} + 2^{-77}$. So we see that for both production schemes considered in this paper our estimates are very close to 2^{-30}, which is more than satisfactory from a practical point of view.

4   Sets of Tags

In this section we consider issues that arise when we have got not a single tag, but a batch of tags and an observer tracing communication between the tags and a reader.

Unlinkability. Let us formally define *unlinkability*. Intuitively, in the context of our protocol, unlinkability means that an adversary is unable to recognize a RFID-tag within a set of other tags after performing update procedure. More formally, we can express unlinkability in the following way which is a kind of a standard approach in provable security area:

Definition 1 (Linking Game). *Let us assume that there are L RFID-tags in a system. An adversary scans all these tags t times. Then the challenger chooses at random one out of L tags, performs the update operation on it and presents the result to the adversary. The adversary has to say which tag has been chosen by the challenger.*

Any pair $(\xi, \eta) \in \{0, 1\}^n \times \{0, 1\}^k$ is called an observation of an (n, k)-tag. We say that an (n, k)-tag T is *consistent* with a sequence $\{(\xi_i, \eta_i)\}_{i=1,\ldots,t}$ of observations if

$$T(\xi_i) = \eta_i \quad \text{for } i = 1, \ldots, t,$$

where $T(\xi)$ means the contents of the dependent part of T, if the random part contains ξ. We say that the set of observations $\{(\xi_1, \eta_1), \ldots, (\xi_t, \eta_t)\} \cup \{(\xi, \eta)\}$ is *consistent*, if there is a tag T that is consistent with these observations. The following lemma is a basic fact from linear algebra:

Lemma 1. *A set observations* $\{(\xi_1, \eta_1), \ldots, (\xi_t, \eta_t\} \cup \{(\xi, \eta)\}$ *is consistent, if the vectors* $\xi_1, \ldots, \xi_t, \xi$ *are linearly independent.*

Notice that an adversary tends to loose in the Linking Game, if there are a lot of tags in the system which are consistent with the last and all previous observations.

Let $T_1, \ldots, T_L$ be a family of tags in the system. Let $(\xi_{i,j}, \eta_{i,j})$ (for $i \in [L]$ and $j \in [t]$) be the result of observing the ith tag during the jth scan. Let (ξ, η) be the result of the last observation presented to the adversary.

Let us fix $a \in [L]$. Let p_a denote the probability that the set of vectors $\{\xi_{a,1}, \ldots, \xi_{a,t}\} \cup \{\xi\}$ is linearly independent. From Theorem 6 from Appendix we get $p_a \geq 1 - \mathrm{Upd}(n, t+1, p)$. So, by Lemma 1, we get the following result:

Corollary 1. *Consider the Linking Game with t trials for a family of L tags created according to (n, k, p)-schema. Then the probability that at least one tag is inconsistent with the last observation is at most*

$$L \cdot \mathrm{Upd}(n, t+1, p). \tag{4}$$

The expression (4) gives an upper bound on the probability that an adversary has any advantage after t scans of the whole system. Notice that the estimation (4) does not depend on the parameter k. Moreover, if $p = \frac{1}{2}$, then the upper estimate is simply $L \cdot \frac{2^{t+1}}{2^n}$. Next, it can be checked numerically that if $n \in [128, 1024]$ and $t \leq n - 40$, then $\mathrm{Upd}(n, t+1, \frac{30}{n}) < 2.3 \cdot 10^{-10}$. From this we easily deduce the following result:

Corollary 2. *Consider the Linking Game with t trials for a family of L tags from (n, k, p)-schema. Suppose that $n \in [128, 1024]$, $p = \frac{1}{2}$ or $p = 30/n$ and $t < n - 40$. Then for all $L < 2^{n-t-32}$ the probability that the adversary has any advantage (meaning that at least one tag can be excluded) is less than 2^{-30}.*

Remark: we get similar but more precise estimates for $p = \frac{1}{2}$, if we use Theorem 3 from Appendix instead of Theorem 6.

Finding a Tag in a Batch of Tags. Let us consider the case that a legitimate user would like to know if TAG_0 is in the range of his reader. We assume that the characteristic sets of TAG_0 are known to the user. Moreover, we assume that in the proximity of the reader there are L tags. The reader sends sequentially the queries to the tags and the tags reply with their current identifiers. Obviously, for each query the TAG_0 gives a response coherent with its characteristic sets with probability 1. Let us assume that a tag different from TAG_0 will give an answer coherent with TAG_0 with probability $q < 1$, independently from the answers of the other tags (this is an approximation of the real situation since with a small probability there are some linear dependencies which increase the probability of coherence compared to the case when the characteristic sets are linearly independent). Recall that some estimations of q have been given by Theorem 1.

Search Procedure. The legitimate user queries t times the batch of RFID-tags. If response of any tag is not coherent with TAG_0, then it is excluded from the batch and does not answer the subsequent queries from the reader in this session. If after t steps no tag is left, we say that TAG_0 was not in the batch. Otherwise we assume that it is present.

Theorem 2. *Assume there is a batch of L tags without TAG_0. Assume also that a tag different from TAG_0 yields an answer coherent with TAG_0 with probability q independently of all other tags. Then after t queries the system concludes (erroneously) that TAG_0 is in the batch with probability $1 - (1 - q^t)^L$.*

Proof. Let A_t denote the event that at least one of L tags different from TAG_0 responds coherently with TAG_0 to t consecutive queries. Similarly, let A_t^i denote the event that the ith tag responds coherently with TAG_0 to t consecutive queries. Of course, $A_t = \bigcup_{i=1}^{L} A_t^i$. Let A^c denote the complement of event A. So, we have

$$\Pr[A_t] = \Pr[\bigcup_{i=1}^{L} A_t^i] = 1 - \Pr[\bigcap_{i=1}^{L} (A_t^i)^c]$$

$$1 - \prod_{i=1}^{L} \Pr[(A_t^i)^c] = 1 - \prod_{i=1}^{L}(1 - \Pr[(A_t^i)]) = 1 - (1 - q^t)^L. \qquad \square$$

In Sec. 3 we observed that the probability of false positive recognition of a tag in all cases considered there is less than 2^{-30}. Hence we may use Theorem 2 with $q2^{-30}$ and since $1 - x \approx e^{-x}$ for $x \approx 0$, we get

$$1 - (1 - q^t)^L \approx 1 - \exp(-\frac{L}{2^{30 \cdot t}}) \approx \frac{L}{2^{30 \cdot t}}.$$

Numerical experiments show that this is a very precise upper estimate. Hence for practical considerations we may assume that the probability of a false positive recognition of a tag in a batch of L tags after t scans is bounded by $\frac{L}{2^{30 \cdot t}}$. So even if a batch is large, say $L = 2^{30}$, then after two scans the probability of a mistake is bounded by 2^{-30}.

5   Cloning Tags and Countermeasures

Cloning a Tag. Suppose that an adversary observed n times an (n, k)-tag and let $(\xi_1, \eta_1), \ldots, (\xi_n, \eta_n)$ be the sequence of his observations. Using Lemma 2 from Appendix we deduce that the set of vectors $\{\xi_1, \ldots, \xi_n\}$ is linearly independent with probability ≈ 0.289. Therefore, with high probability for each $i \in [k]$ an adversary can solve the following system

$$\begin{cases} \langle X, \xi_1 \rangle = \eta_1(i) \\ \quad \cdots \\ \langle X, \xi_n \rangle = \eta_n(i) \end{cases}$$

of linear equations, where $\langle X, \xi \rangle$ denotes the scalar product of vectors X and ξ. Then, obviously, a solution for X is a solution for the characteristic function the ith hidden subset of the observed tag. So, after n observations an adversary is able, with relatively high probability, to produce a fully functional copy (a clone) of the observed tag. However, no number $m < n$ of observations is sufficient to clone the observed tag: after m observations there are at least 2^{n-m} possibilities for each characteristic set, so the total number of tags consistent with this observations is at least $2^{k(n-m)}$.

We see that the scheme presented, despite nice properties, would be of little use - n read operations on a tag would lead to disclosure of characteristic sets and full traceability of the tag.

We have proved in Sec. 3 that a legitimate user can correctly recognize a tag with probability close to $1 - 2^{-k}$ during a single scan. On the other hand, we have proved that an adversary needs about n scans to be able to clone or trace the tag. It is acceptable, if we assume that the adversary is unable to read a tag too frequently. Some discussion about necessary *timeouts* can be found in [5].

However, we may prevent the mentioned attack without complicated hardware mechanism such as timeouts. In the subsections below, we show that simple change of tag's design alleviates cloning attack.

5.1 Double Answers

We may adapt a more effective strategy related to a solution from [13]:

> Each time a tag is scanned, it gives two answers. One of the answers is the contents of the tag's memory. The second answer is a random string of the same length. Moreover, the two answers are given in a random order.

Of course, it is still possible to recognize a tag by a legitimate reader: both answers are analyzed, but we expect that only one of them passes the test (3). (Note that in this case we cannot use the scheme with $k = 1$.)

Now, the adversary has to solve the following problem, which seems to be computationally infeasible for sufficiently large n:

> Consider a system of m linear equations Q with n unknowns having a unique solution $\boldsymbol{w}$. The coefficients in Q have been chosen at random. The system Q is embedded in a system R of $2m$ linear equations, where the equations $2j - 1$ and $2j$ are: the jth equation of Q and a random equation given in a random order. The problem is to compute $\boldsymbol{w}$ when the system R is given.

We can remark that a brute force approach to solve this problem is inefficient, since probability of getting a system of inconsistent linear equations is low when the number of equations considered is much lower than n (see Theorem 3).

5.2 Permuting the Answers

One of the most obvious tricks is to mix the random part with the dependent part at random in each tag (so, the adversary does not know anymore if a bit from the suffix is really used for the equalities defining a tag). However, much more promising design direction is to shuffle answer bits of a tag using iterated permutation σ^L of some permutation σ with a large order, which is known only to the owner of a tag, and the number L is a positive natural number sent to the tag by the reader.

Let us explain the idea with a few more details. Consider an (n, k)-tag and suppose that σ is a permutation of the set $\{1, \ldots, n + k\}$. We assume that the permutation σ is known only to the owner of a tag. Suppose that the reader sends a number L to the tag. Then the tag computes, as before, the "ID" $(\xi, \eta) = (d_1, \ldots, d_{n+k})$. Next, the tag iterates L times the permutation σ to transform the answer, where $\sigma(d_1, \ldots, d_{n+k}) = (d_{\sigma(1)}, \ldots, d_{\sigma(n+k)})$. Hence, finally, after the Lth iteration it obtains the sequence $(d_{\sigma^L(1)}, \ldots, d_{\sigma^L(n+k)})$ and this is the answer which is sent back to the reader.

An adversary, whose goal is to clone a tag, has to recover not only the linear mapping from the space $\{0, 1\}^n$ into $\{0, 1\}^k$, but also the permutation σ. This extension of the (n, k)-tags makes also the trivial replay attack impossible, since the answers generated by such tags depend on the information sent by the reader. Finally let us note there are a lot of permutations of the set $\{1, \ldots, 158\}$ of large order – the maximal order of permutation of this set is approximately $1.9 \cdot 10^{12}$.

6   Final Remarks

Security as well as efficiency of the system as a whole depends on several parameters. The choice of the parameters (n, k, d) of the production schema have the following consequences for system properties:

- parameter n has influence on the number of steps an adversary must trace to recover the tag's all hidden characteristic sets; growing n increases the number of necessary steps,
- parameter k has influence on the probability of a correct recognition of a tag by an legitimate user; growing k decreases the probability of a false-positive;
- parameter p has influence on the production costs and on unlinkability properties; from the point of view of chip size a small size is advantageous, while from the point of view of the Linking Game the probability $p = \frac{1}{2}$ is optimal.

It should be also emphasized that hidden subset RFID-tags do not require any sophisticated circuit design. Indeed, a tag from (n, k, p) production schema requires, on average, only $k \cdot n \cdot p$ XOR gates.

It may occur that an answer of a tag does not identify a unique tag. Namely, the answer might be consistent with characteristic sets of at least two different tags known to the reader. This *ambiguity* problem is the main drawback of the solution based on dynamic ID's presented in the paper [3]. Note that this is not a serious issue for the scheme presented in this paper: it suffices to read the tag a few times in order to eliminate false ID's concerned during the first read operation.

Still, the scheme requires fine tuning and detailed analysis concerning security for the architectures presented in Sec. 5.1 and 5.2.

References

1. Ateniese, G., Camenisch, J., de Medeiros, B.: Untracable RFID Tags via Insubvertible Encryption. In: 12th ACM CCS 2005, pp. 92–101. ACM Press, New York (2005)
2. Blömer, J., Karp, R., Welzl, E.: The Rank of Sparse Random Matrices over Finite Fields. Random Structures and Algorithms 10(4), 407–419 (1997)
3. Cichoń, J., Klonowski, M., Kutyłowski, M.: Privacy Protection in Dynamic Systems Based on RFID Tags. In: 4th IEEE International Workshop on Pervasive Computing and Communication Security, Proceedings of PERCOM 2007 Workshops, pp. 235–240. IEEE Computer Society, Los Alamitos (2007)
4. Golle, P., Jakobsson, M., Juels, A., Syverson, P.F.: Universal Re-encryption for Mixnets. In: Okamoto, T. (ed.) CT-RSA 2004. LNCS, vol. 2964, pp. 163–178. Springer, Heidelberg (2004)
5. Juels, A.: Yoking-Proofs for RFID Tags. In: Proceedings of the Second IEEE Annual Conference on Pervasive Computing and Communications Workshops, p. 138. IEEE Computer Society Press, Los Alamitos (2004)
6. Juels, A.: RFID privacy: A Technical Primer for the Non-Technical Reader. In: Privacy and Technologies of Identity: A Cross-Disciplinary Conversation, Springer, Heidelberg (2005), available from: http://www.rsasecurity.com/rsalabs/staff/bios/ ajuels/publications/rfid_privacy/DePaul23Feb05Draft.pdf
7. Juels, A., Pappu, R.: RFID Privacy: An Overview of Problems and Proposed Solutions. IEEE Security and Privacy 3(3), 34–43 (2005)
8. Juels, A., Rivest, R.L., Szydlo, M.: The Blocker Tag: Selective Blocking of RFID Tags for Consumer Privacy. In: 10th ACM CCS 2003, pp. 103–111. ACM Press, New York (2003)
9. Molnar, D., Wagner, D.: Privacy and Security in Library RFID Issues, Practices and Architectures. In: 11th ACM CCS 2004, pp. 210–219. ACM Press, New York (2004)
10. Moskowitz, P.A., Lauris, A., Morris, S.S.: A Privacy Enhancing Radio Frequency Identification Tag: Implementation of the Clipped Tag. In: PerTec 2007, Proceedings of PERCOM 2007 Workshops, pp. 348–351. IEEE Computer Society Press, Los Alamitos (2007)
11. Langheinrich, M.: A Survey of RFID Privacy Approaches. In: Workshop on Ubicomp Privacy - Technologies, Users, Policy. Workshop at Ubicomp 2007 (2007), available from: www.vs.inf.ethz.ch/publ/papers/langhein2007-ubipriv.pdf
12. Langheinrich, M.: RFID and Privacy. In: Security, Privacy, and Trust in Modern Data Management, Springer, Heidelberg (2007)
13. Rivest, R.L.: Chaffing and Winnowing: Confidentiality without Encryption, https://people.csail.mit.edu/rivest/chaffing.txt
14. Weis, S.A., Sarma, S.E., Rivest, R.L., Engels, D.W.: Security and Privacy Aspects of Low-Cost Radio Frequency Identification Systems. In: Hutter, D., Müller, G., Stephan, W., Ullmann, M. (eds.) Security in Pervasive Computing. LNCS, vol. 2802, pp. 201–212. Springer, Heidelberg (2004)

Appendix A: Mathematical Facts

In this section we prove some fact about random $0-1$ matrices, which we use for analysis of properties of (n, k)-tags. All presented proofs are elementary - they use only elementary combinatorics and basic probability and a bit of linear algebra.

Lemma 2 (see e.g. [2]). *Let $(\xi_i^j)_{i,j\in[n]}$ be a sequence of stochastically independent 0-1 random variables such that $\Pr[\xi_i^j = 1] = \frac{1}{2}$ for each i and j. Let $x^{(j)} = (\xi_1^j, \ldots, \xi_n^j)$ for $j \in [n]$. For $0 \le k \le n$, let $p_{n,k}$ be the probability of the event that vectors $x^{(1)}, \ldots, x^{(n-k)}$ are linearly independent over the field $\mathbb{Z}_2$. Then*

$$p_{n,k} = \prod_{a=k+1}^{n} \left(1 - \frac{1}{2^a}\right).$$

Proof. Let N_k be the number of sequences of length k of vectors from the vector space $\mathbb{Z}_2^n$ which are linearly independent. It is easy to see that $N_1 = 2^n - 1$ and $N_{k+1} = N_k(2^n - 2^k)$. Using this recurrence formula we get $N_k = \prod_{l=0}^{k-1}(2^n - 2^l)$. The total number of all sequences of length k of vectors from $(\mathbb{Z}_2)^n$ is $(2^n)^k$. So

$$p_{n,k} = \frac{N_k}{(2^n)^k} = \prod_{l=0}^{k-1} \left(1 - \frac{1}{2^{n-l}}\right) = \prod_{a=k+1}^{n} \left(1 - \frac{1}{2^a}\right). \qquad \square$$

Notice that $p_{n,0} = \prod_{a=0}^{n-1}(1 - 1/2^a)$. It can be checked that $\lim_n p_{n,0} = 0.2887\ldots$ and that the convergence of this sequence is very fast. For example, we have $p_{5,0} = 0.298004$ and $p_{10,0} = 0.28907$. Therefore, a collection of n random 0-1-vectors of length n is linearly independent with probability about 0.289.

Theorem 3. *Let $(\xi_i^j)_{i,j\in[n]}$ be a sequence of stochastically independent 0-1 random variables such that $\Pr[\xi_i^j = 1] = \frac{1}{2}$ for each i and j. Let $x^{(j)} = (\xi_1^j, \ldots, \xi_n^j)$ for $j \in [n]$. For $0 \le k \le n$, let $p_{n,k}$ be the probability of the event that vectors $x^{(1)}, \ldots, x^{(n-k)}$ are linearly independent over the field $\mathbb{Z}_2$. Then*

$$1 - 2^{-k} < p_{n,k} < 1 - 2^{-(k+1)}.$$

Proof. If vectors $x^{(1)}, \ldots, x^{(n-k)}$ are linearly dependent over $\mathbb{Z}_2$, then there exists a nonempty subset A of $[n-k]$ such that $\sum_{a\in A} x^{(a)} = 0$. By the stochastic independence assumption we get

$$\Pr\left[\bigoplus_{a\in A} \xi_j^{(a)} = 0\right] = \frac{1}{2},$$

for any fixed subset A. Moreover, these events are stochastically independent for $j \in [n]$. So

$$\Pr\left[\sum_{a\in A} x^{(a)} = 0\right] = \left(\frac{1}{2}\right)^n.$$

Since there are $2^{n-k} - 1$ possible choices of an nonempty set A, so

$$\Pr\left[x^{(1)}, \ldots, x^{(n-k)} \text{ are dependent }\right] < \frac{2^{n-k}}{2^n} = \frac{1}{2^k}.$$

Hence $p_{n,k} > 1 - \frac{1}{2^k}$.

The upper bound follows directly from Lemma 2, namely, we have

$$p_{n,k} = \prod_{a=k+1}^{n} \left(1 - \frac{1}{2^a}\right) \leq 1 - \frac{1}{2^{k+1}}.$$ □

Let us emphasize that the approximation in Theorem 3 does not depend on parameter n.

Theorem 4. *Let* $\xi_1, \ldots, \xi_m$ *be a sequence of stochastically independent 0-1 random variables such that* $\Pr[\xi_i = 1] = p$. *Then*

$$\Pr\left[\bigoplus_{i=1}^{m} \xi_i = 0\right] = \tfrac{1}{2}(1 + (1 - 2p)^m).$$

Proof. Obviously, it is enough to find the probability that we have an even number of successes during m stochastically independent trials, if each trial succeeds with probability p. Let P_{even} denote probability of this event and let P_{odd} denote probability that the total number of successes is an odd number. Let $q = 1 - p$. Then $P_{even} + P_{odd} = 1$ and

$$P_{even} - P_{odd} = \sum_{2|k} \binom{m}{k} p^k q^{m-k} - \sum_{\neg(2|k)} \binom{m}{k} p^k q^{m-k} = \sum_{k} \binom{m}{k} (-1)^k p^k q^{m-k},$$

so $P_{even} - P_{odd} = (-p+q)^m = (1-2p)^m$. Therefore $2 \cdot P_{even} = 1 + (1-2p)^m$. □

Theorem 5. *Let* $X_1, \ldots, X_n, Y_1, \ldots, Y_n$ *be a sequence of independent* $0-1$ *random variables such that* $\Pr[X_i = 1] = \Pr[Y_i = 1] = p$ *for each* i. *Let* $Z_i = X_i \oplus Y_i$. *Then* $Z_1, \ldots, Z_n$ *is a sequence of independent 0-1-random variables such that* $\Pr[Z_i = 1] = 2p(1-p)$.

Proof. The independence of the set $Z_1, \ldots, Z_n$ of random variables is clear. The rest follows from the following equalities: $\Pr[Z_i = 1] = \Pr[X_i = 1 \wedge Y_i = 0] + \Pr[X_i = 0 \wedge Y_i = 1] = 2p(1-p)$. □

Recall that

$$\mathrm{Upd}(n, m, p) = \frac{1}{2^n} \sum_{a=1}^{m} \binom{m}{a} (1 + (1 - 2p)^a))^n.$$

Theorem 6. *Let* $(\xi_i^j)_{i,j \in [n]}$ *be a sequence of independent 0-1 random variables such that* $\Pr[\xi_{i,j} = 1] = p$. *Let* $a_i = (\xi_i^1, \ldots, \xi_i^n)$. *Then for* $0 < m \leq n$ *the set of vectors* $\{a_1, \ldots, a_m\}$ *is linearly dependent with probability at most* $\mathrm{Upd}(n, m, p)$.

The proof of Theorem 6 is almost the same as the proof of lower bound of Theorem 3. There is only one important difference: since the values $0, 1$ of random variables ξ_i^j are not equally probable, we have to apply Theorem 4.

Theorem 7. *Let* $\alpha^{(1)}, \ldots, \alpha^{(s)}$ *be a sequence of linearly independent 0-1 strings of length* n, *and* $(\omega_1, \ldots, \omega_s) \in \{0, 1\}^s$. *Let* $(\xi_i)_{i \in [n]}$ *be a sequence of stochastically* *independent random* 0-1 *variables such that* $\Pr\left[\xi_i = 0\right] = \frac{1}{2}$ *for each* $i \in [n]$. *Then*

$$\Pr\left[\bigwedge_{j=1}^{s}\left(\bigoplus_{\alpha_i^{(j)}=1} \xi_i = \omega_j\right)\right] = \frac{1}{2^s}. \tag{5}$$

Proof. Let us consider a function $F : \{0,1\}^n \to \{0,1\}^s$ defined by the formula

$$F(x_1,\ldots,x_n) = \left(\bigoplus_{\alpha_i^{(1)}=1} x_i, \ldots, \bigoplus_{\alpha_i^{(s)}=1} x_i\right).$$

Then F is a linear mapping from $\{0,1\}^n$ to $\{0,1\}^s$ treated as linear spaces over $\mathbb{Z}_2$. Moreover, from the algebraic independence of $\alpha^{(1)},\ldots,\alpha^{(s)}$ we deduce that the rank of the mapping F is s, i.e. $\mathrm{img}(F) = \{0,1\}^s$. Since $\dim(\ker(F)) + \dim(\mathrm{img}(F)) = \dim(\{0,1\}^n)$, we deduce that $\dim(\ker(F)) = n - s$. Therefore the solutions of the equation $F(x) = (\omega_1,\ldots,\omega_s)$ form an affine subspace of $\{0,1\}^n$ of dimension $n - s$. Therefore

$$|\{x \in \{0,1\}^n : F(x) = (\omega_1,\ldots,\omega_k)\}| = 2^{n-s}.$$

Finally, observe that each vector $x \in \{0,1\}^n$ is a realization of random variables $(\xi_1,\ldots,\xi_n)$ with probability $1/2^n$, so $\Pr\left(F(\xi_1,\ldots,\xi_n) = (\omega_1,\ldots,\omega_s)\right) = \frac{1}{2^n} \cdot 2^{n-s} = \frac{1}{2^s}$. $\qquad\square$

Let us note that the assumption of linear independence in Theorem 7 is necessary. Indeed, if an $\alpha^{(u)}$ can be expressed as a sum of certain other strings $\alpha^{(j)}$, then ω_u must be obtained in a similar way from the corresponding bits ω_j. So, in particular, for certain $(\omega_1,\ldots,\omega_k)$ the value of ω_u is wrong and the probability from Equality (5) is 0.

Author Index

Lecture Notes in Computer Science

Sublibrary 3: Information Systems and Application, incl. Internet/Web and HCI

For information about Vols. 1– 4564
please contact your bookseller or Springer

Vol. 4803: R. Meersman, Z. Tari (Eds.), On the Move to Meaningful Internet Systems 2007: CoopIS, DOA, ODBASE, GADA, and IS, Part I. XXIX, 1173 pages. 2007.

Vol. 4802: J.-L. Hainaut, E.A. Rundensteiner, M. Kirchberg, M. Bertolotto, M. Brochhausen, Y.-P.P. Chen, S.S.-S. Cherfi, M. Doerr, H. Han, S. Hartmann, J. Parsons, G. Poels, C. Rolland, J. Trujillo, E. Yu, E. Zimányie (Eds.), Advances in Conceptual Modeling – Foundations and Applications. XIX, 420 pages. 2007.

Vol. 4801: C. Parent, K.-D. Schewe, V.C. Storey, B. Thalheim (Eds.), Conceptual Modeling - ER 2007. XVI, 616 pages. 2007.

Vol. 4797: M. Arenas, M.I. Schwartzbach (Eds.), Database Programming Languages. VIII, 261 pages. 2007.

Vol. 4796: M. Lew, N. Sebe, T.S. Huang, E.M. Bakker (Eds.), Human–Computer Interaction. X, 157 pages. 2007.

Vol. 4794: B. Schiele, A.K. Dey, H. Gellersen, B. de Ruyter, M. Tscheligi, R. Wichert, E. Aarts, A. Buchmann (Eds.), Ambient Intelligence. XV, 375 pages. 2007.

Vol. 4777: S. Bhalla (Ed.), Databases in Networked Information Systems. X, 329 pages. 2007.

Vol. 4761: R. Obermaisser, Y. Nah, P. Puschner, F.J. Rammig (Eds.), Software Technologies for Embedded and Ubiquitous Systems. XIV, 563 pages. 2007.

Vol. 4747: S. Džeroski, J. Struyf (Eds.), Knowledge Discovery in Inductive Databases. X, 301 pages. 2007.

Vol. 4744: Y. de Kort, W. IJsselsteijn, C. Midden, B. Eggen, B.J. Fogg (Eds.), Persuasive Technology. XIV, 316 pages. 2007.

Vol. 4740: L. Ma, M. Rauterberg, R. Nakatsu (Eds.), Entertainment Computing – ICEC 2007. XXX, 480 pages. 2007.

Vol. 4730: C. Peters, P. Clough, F.C. Gey, J. Karlgren, B. Magnini, D.W. Oard, M. de Rijke, M. Stempfhuber (Eds.), Evaluation of Multilingual and Multi-modal Information Retrieval. XXIV, 998 pages. 2007.

Vol. 4723: M. R. Berthold, J. Shawe-Taylor, N. Lavrač (Eds.), Advances in Intelligent Data Analysis VII. XIV, 380 pages. 2007.

Vol. 4721: W. Jonker, M. Petković (Eds.), Secure Data Management. X, 213 pages. 2007.

Vol. 4718: J. Hightower, B. Schiele, T. Strang (Eds.), Location- and Context-Awareness. X, 297 pages. 2007.

Vol. 4717: J. Krumm, G.D. Abowd, A. Seneviratne, T. Strang (Eds.), UbiComp 2007: Ubiquitous Computing. XIX, 520 pages. 2007.

Vol. 4715: J.M. Haake, S.F. Ochoa, A. Cechich (Eds.), Groupware: Design, Implementation, and Use. XIII, 355 pages. 2007.

Vol. 4714: G. Alonso, P. Dadam, M. Rosemann (Eds.), Business Process Management. XIII, 418 pages. 2007.

Vol. 4704: D. Barbosa, A. Bonifati, Z. Bellahsène, E. Hunt, R. Unland (Eds.), Database and XML Technologies. X, 141 pages. 2007.

Vol. 4690: Y. Ioannidis, B. Novikov, B. Rachev (Eds.), Advances in Databases and Information Systems. XIII, 377 pages. 2007.

Vol. 4675: L. Kovács, N. Fuhr, C. Meghini (Eds.), Research and Advanced Technology for Digital Libraries. XVII, 585 pages. 2007.

Vol. 4674: Y. Luo (Ed.), Cooperative Design, Visualization, and Engineering. XIII, 431 pages. 2007.

Vol. 4663: C. Baranauskas, P. Palanque, J. Abascal, S.D.J. Barbosa (Eds.), Human-Computer Interaction – INTERACT 2007, Part II. XXXIII, 735 pages. 2007.

Vol. 4662: C. Baranauskas, P. Palanque, J. Abascal, S.D.J. Barbosa (Eds.), Human-Computer Interaction – INTERACT 2007, Part I. XXXIII, 637 pages. 2007.

Vol. 4658: T. Enokido, L. Barolli, M. Takizawa (Eds.), Network-Based Information Systems. XIII, 544 pages. 2007.

Vol. 4656: M.A. Wimmer, J. Scholl, Å. Grönlund (Eds.), Electronic Government. XIV, 450 pages. 2007.

Vol. 4655: G. Psaila, R. Wagner (Eds.), E-Commerce and Web Technologies. VII, 229 pages. 2007.

Vol. 4654: I.-Y. Song, J. Eder, T.M. Nguyen (Eds.), Data Warehousing and Knowledge Discovery. XVI, 482 pages. 2007.

Vol. 4653: R. Wagner, N. Revell, G. Pernul (Eds.), Database and Expert Systems Applications. XXII, 907 pages. 2007.

Vol. 4636: G. Antoniou, U. Aßmann, C. Baroglio, S. Decker, N. Henze, P.-L. Patranjan, R. Tolksdorf (Eds.), Reasoning Web. IX, 345 pages. 2007.

Vol. 4611: J. Indulska, J. Ma, L.T. Yang, T. Ungerer, J. Cao (Eds.), Ubiquitous Intelligence and Computing. XXIII, 1257 pages. 2007.

Vol. 4607: L. Baresi, P. Fraternali, G.-J. Houben (Eds.), Web Engineering. XVI, 576 pages. 2007.

Vol. 4606: A. Pras, M. van Sinderen (Eds.), Dependable and Adaptable Networks and Services. XIV, 149 pages. 2007.

Vol. 4605: D. Papadias, D. Zhang, G. Kollios (Eds.), Advances in Spatial and Temporal Databases. X, 479 pages. 2007.

Vol. 4602: S. Barker, G.-J. Ahn (Eds.), Data and Applications Security XXI. X, 291 pages. 2007.

Vol. 4601: S. Spaccapietra, P. Atzeni, F. Fages, M.-S. Hacid, M. Kifer, J. Mylopoulos, B. Pernici, P. Shvaiko, J. Trujillo, I. Zaihrayeu (Eds.), Journal on Data Semantics IX. XV, 197 pages. 2007.

Vol. 4592: Z. Kedad, N. Lammari, E. Métais, F. Meziane, Y. Rezgui (Eds.), Natural Language Processing and Information Systems. XIV, 442 pages. 2007.

Vol. 4587: R. Cooper, J. Kennedy (Eds.), Data Management. XIII, 259 pages. 2007.

Vol. 4577: N. Sebe, Y. Liu, Y.-t. Zhuang, T.S. Huang (Eds.), Multimedia Content Analysis and Mining. XIII, 513 pages. 2007.

Vol. 4568: T. Ishida, S. R. Fussell, P. T. J. M. Vossen (Eds.), Intercultural Collaboration. XIII, 395 pages. 2007.

Vol. 4566: M.J. Dainoff (Ed.), Ergonomics and Health Aspects of Work with Computers. XVIII, 390 pages. 2007.